D1266285

A CERTAIN EVENTUALITY...

A CERTAIN EVENTUALITY...

BRITAIN AND THE FALL OF FRANCE

P.M.H. BELL

D
750
B44

08202

SAXON HOUSE

MENDOCINO COLLEGE LIBRARY

© P. M. H. Bell, 1974

All rights reserved. No part of this publication may be reproduced, stored in a retrieval system, or transmitted in any form or by any means, electronic, mechanical, photocopying, recording or otherwise without the prior permission of D. C. Heath Limited.

ISBN: 0 347 00010 X

Library of Congress Catalog Card Number: 74-473

Printed in Scotland by Robert MacLehose Ltd.

LIST OF CONTENTS

Brt (NBC)
11.95
6/76

PART 2

SALVAGE OPERATIONS

PREFACE

The fall of France in June 1940, an event of startling suddenness and crucial importance for the British government and people, destroyed the alliance on which Britain's entire approach to the war against Germany had been based. Both policy and strategy were affected: the nature of the war was transformed, and British ideas had to be drastically revised.

The first part of this book describes how the British government and people reacted to the fall of France; the second part examines the attempts to save something from the wreckage of the alliance by dealing with the French fleet and empire, and establishing relations with de Gaulle and the Vichy government. This story forms part of one of the greatest and most memorable crises in British history, and the events discussed had far-reaching consequences for relations between Britain and France in the years following 1940.

It is a great pleasure to have an opportunity to thank those who have helped in the writing of this book. Professor John C. Cairns and Dr Geoffrey Warner kindly read parts of the manuscript and made valuable comments. Sir Robert Parr and Lord Rennell of Rodd were most generous with their time and knowledge in discussing with me the events of 1940, in which they played a part. My wife and father worked hard to shorten and improve a lengthy draft, and Professor David Quinn provided valuable advice at various points in the book's preparation. I am also glad to thank the University of Liverpool for several research grants; and the Librarian and staff of Birkenhead Central Library for allowing me the privilege of reading microfilms in their library over an extended period. Transcripts of

Preface

Crown-copyright records in the Public Record Office appear by permission of the Controller of H.M. Stationery Office, which is gratefully acknowledged. Finally, it is a particular pleasure to record my thanks to Mr. F. W. D. Deakin, who first guided me in research on this subject many years ago when I was a graduate student at St. Antony's College, Oxford.

All those mentioned have contributed to such merits as this book may possess. Its defects and errors remain my own responsibility.

P. M. H. BELL.

School of History,
University of Liverpool.
December 1973

A CERTAIN EVENTUALITY...

PART 1
THE BREAKDOWN OF THE ALLIANCE

Chapter 1

THE ALLIANCE

On 3 September 1939 the British and French governments declared war on Germany, though they did not contrive to do so at the same time. The British declaration was at 11 a.m., and the French at 5 p.m., so that for six hours the British were at war while the French were not. In practice this was of little importance, because neither country followed up its declaration of war with positive military action to assist the hard-pressed Poles, who had been attacked by Germany two days earlier. Britain and France were allies, but they had difficulty in co-ordinating their policies, and found rapid military action either impossible or undesirable. After all the problems and conflicts of Anglo-French relations during the previous twenty years, this was not surprising, and on the central question of policy towards Germany, the two countries had been more often in dispute than in agreement. Conflicts of interest during the peace conference of 1919 had been followed by differences on reparations and German rearmament. The British held the view that the Versailles settlement was both unjust and unworkable, and should be revised in Germany's favour, while the French believed that it was both right and necessary to enforce the treaty, though after 1923 in fact they ceased to do so. For twenty years the British played the role of mediators between France and Germany, to Germany's advantage. It was only after a series of concessions, culminating at Munich in 1938, that Britain decided that she must take a stand against Germany. Even then, while the British would stand, it was the French who would have to fight, because the British contribution to the Allied armies in France at the beginning of the war was only four divisions. There were more to come, but a large army would take a long time to create.

The Germans destroyed Poland in September 1939, and then delayed any move in the west, so that there ensued the period of inactivity on the land front between France and Germany which came to be known as the 'phoney war'. During this period, which extended for some eight months, the British and French had ample time to think about their strategy, their war aims and their relations with one another.[1]

The main feature of Franco-British strategy was planning for a long phase of defensive warfare, with the emphasis on economic measures and the power of blockade. Much trust was placed in the view that in a long war the Allies were bound to win, because their own resources and those of their empires were so great, and sea power gave them access also to the immense potential of the United States. During this defensive phase, there were certain pressing strategic problems, of which that posed by Holland and Belgium was particularly important. Both these countries wished to remain neutral and to avoid the risk of provoking the Germans by consultations with the British and French. On the other hand, as soon as they were attacked, they would expect the British and French to go to their aid, which would create the military problem of an advance from a prepared position on the Franco-Belgian frontier into Belgium and Holland, to fight an encounter battle with the advancing German army. This was a daunting prospect, but the alternative — to stand fast on their defence lines and watch the Dutch and Belgians be overrun — was politically impossible. Plans were therefore formulated, one of which involved an advance into Belgium to the river Dyle, with the Allied left wing pushing also into southern Holland. This was the scheme put into operation on 10 May 1940, when the Germans invaded the Low Countries, and it ended in the evacuation from Dunkirk.

The French and British also spent much time on plans and speculation about possible operations outside the main theatre in western Europe. Ideas were canvassed for a Balkan front; for bombing the Soviet oil-fields in the Caucasus; and for cutting off the supply of iron ore from Sweden to Germany — this last possibly to be combined (during the Soviet-Finnish Winter War) with helping the Finns against the USSR. The recital of these ideas conjures up a strange vision of men who were apparently prepared to risk war with Germany and the USSR at the same time, even though conscious that they were not yet strong enough to fight the Germans alone. It was true that after the Nazi-Soviet pact of August 1939 the two countries were working together, and that their economic co-operation meant a serious leak in the Anglo-French blockade of Germany, but it was surely fortunate that little arose from all this speculation. The Balkan front did not materialise, neither was the Caucasus bombed, but there was a Scandinavian campaign (or strictly the Norwegian campaign of April-June 1940) which involved a significant diversion of forces from France, and, more important, brought down Chamberlain's government in Britain.

The period of the 'phoney war' produced little military action, but much discussion concerning war aims. Both Britain and France went to war reluctantly, with none of the enthusiasm of 1914. The British were largely united in their determination to fight — the Ministry of Information estimated that only some ten per cent of the population were opposed to the war.[2] However, there was little fire or sense of involvement, partly because of the strange silence of the phoney war, partly because the membership of the government was little different from that of peacetime, still headed by Chamberlain, who rightly described himself as a man of peace. The French were much less united, and there was a substantial group of politicians (including Bonnet, Flandin, and Laval, all previous Foreign Ministers) whose aim remained an accommodation with Germany. There was a large Communist party, which although weakened and confused by the Nazi-Soviet pact and harassed by the government, still used its discipline and influence to oppose the 'imperialist war'. On the Right there were other groups which still believed that Hitler was preferable to Blum, the socialist Premier of the Popular Front government in 1936. Behind all this, among the mass of the French people who accepted the war, lay the weariness left over from 1914-18 and the troubled inter-war years.

The knowledge of this situation caused both British and French governments to dwell on war aims more than was entirely suitable in a war which they had still to fight. They felt they had to produce convincing reasons as to why they were at war, and some vision of the future which could conjure up enthusiasm in place of mere acceptance, or unity in place of division. Much of this discussion was abandoned when fighting started in earnest, but some issues were of continuing importance. Notably there was the question of

5

whether the fight was against Germany as a power and the Germans as a people, or against Nazism as a system and Hitler as a tyrant. Moreover, if victory alone (whether over Germany or Nazism) was not sufficient as a war aim, and it was desirable to offer some new and better society when the war was over, how should that society be ordered? There developed the idea that one vision which might be offered was that of an Anglo-French federation or union, perhaps to be the nucleus of a European or 'western' union.

Such an idea was encouraged by the convincing outward appearance of Anglo-French co-operation in the winter of 1939-40. The two countries had learned the lessons of the 1914-18 war, and immediately recreated the Supreme War Council at which the two Prime Ministers, with other senior ministers and advisers, met to discuss policy and strategy. There was an Anglo-French Purchasing Board to co-ordinate the procuring of armaments in the USA, and later a Joint Economic Planning Committee. There were permanent military representatives who were intended to work as a joint staff, though responsible to their own military chiefs at home.

On 28 March 1940 the two governments put a suitable façade on this imposing structure by publishing a joint declaration. Its gestation had been lengthy, largely because the British went through the laborious procedure of consulting the Dominions, only to find that South Africa insisted on not being associated with the declaration. Rather than give a public impression of disunity in the Commonwealth, it was eventually decided to leave the Dominions out.[3] When complete, the document declared that neither Britain nor France would negotiate an armistice or peace treaty except by mutual agreement; that they would not discuss peace terms before reaching agreement on the conditions necessary for their long-term security; and that they would maintain their community of action after peace was made.[4] At the time, the main purpose of this declaration was to give an assurance that, after victory, the conflicts of policy which had plagued Britain and France between the wars would not recur. The undertaking not to negotiate separately for an armistice or peace was treated as a formality; Paul Reynaud, who became Prime Minister of France in place of Daladier on 22 March 1940, told the Chamber of Deputies that this was a matter of honour — 'in reality, the question does not arise'.[5]

In Britain, there was little discussion of the joint declaration, and rather more attention was given to a broadcast by Churchill (then

First Lord of the Admiralty) in which he used the phrase 'joined in indissoluble union',[6] when speaking of the two countries. In order to arouse public interest it was agreed by the British Cabinet, on the day the Anglo-French declaration was published, that future meetings of the Supreme War Council should be more frequent and regular, and that the question of creating a permanent Allied secretariat should be examined. Sir Orme Sargent, a senior Foreign Office official, argued that if such meetings were held regularly, British public opinion would come to accept them as part of the normal machinery of government, and they would become a nucleus for other forms of Anglo-French co-operation after the war.[7] Sargent's motives for urging this course had been set out in a memorandum of 28 February. He believed that after the war, the French would demand a permanent occupation of Germany in order to achieve their own security, but that Britain would not wish to undertake such an occupation; instead, France must be offered a system which would 'for all international purposes make of the two countries a single unit in post-war Europe', an effective counter-weight to eighty million Germans. He thought it would be necessary to educate the British public to accept such an idea, and that their education should start at once. Halifax, the Foreign Secretary, supported these views, and Chamberlain requested the Ministry of Information to promote the idea.[8]

Numerous articles propounding the idea of Anglo-French union subsequently appeared in the British and French press, some directly government-inspired. The Royal Institute of International Affairs was called upon, and Sir Alfred Zimmern wrote a paper on Anglo-French relations accompanied by a draft 'Act of Perpetual Association' between the two countries. Lord Hankey, former Secretary to the Cabinet, then Minister without Portfolio in Chamberlain's government, was appointed chairman of a committee on post-war Anglo-French collaboration which met for the first time on 30 April and discussed Zimmern's paper. It met for the second and last time on 21 May. The committee was sceptical concerning the detailed working out of a scheme of association,[9] and there was also uneasiness elsewhere. Within the Labour party, for example, there was anxiety about the mere idea of community of action mentioned in the declaration of 28 March, because Labour MPs were afraid of the French right wing, and did not wish to be committed to co-operation with any French government, whatever its principles.[10] On the whole, it is doubtful whether the campaign to educate the British people on the advantages of union with France had much success.

There were misgivings even in the official circles where the idea of Anglo-French unity was being pressed. How reliable were the French? Georges Mandel, formerly Clemenceau's *chef de cabinet* and profoundly anti-German, urged the British Ambassador in Paris, Sir Ronald Campbell, to press on with the declaration about no separate peace because, while Daladier (then Prime Minister) was sound on this issue, Mandel would not vouch for the soundness of some other government.[11] Passing on this advice on 23 February 1940, Campbell added that there was no question at that time of Daladier being overthrown, but inside a month he was gone. He was replaced by Paul Reynaud, who on 22 March secured a majority of only one vote over his opponents and those abstaining. Campbell did not care to prophesy a long life for Reynaud's government.[12] In the Foreign Office, one official thought that Reynaud's reception by the Chamber showed the strength of 'certain treacherous elements mainly on the right, whose activities we may well fear'.[13] In Paris, Oliver Harvey (Minister at the British Embassy) wrote in his diary that 'the bad men' — Laval, Flandin, Bonnet — were raising their heads, and would become a danger if a prolonged government crisis were to be coupled with a German peace offensive.[14]

There were also doubts about Reynaud himself, though not about his courage and energy, which he had shown at the Ministry of Finance, nor about his determination to prosecute the war. His sympathy with Britain was well known, as was his personal friendship with Churchill whom he admired greatly. He was highly intelligent, and an excellent debater, but, granting him all these qualities, Campbell still expressed reservations in the portrait he sent to London when Reynaud became Prime Minister. Some observers thought he was clever but superficial — he had the nickname of 'Mickey Mouse', which Campbell considered apt. He was very much a Parisian, with no following in the country as a whole; also, he was 'despised by the average politician for the way in which he frequents, and apes the manners of, a class to which he does not belong'.[15] This was a reference to the salon of Reynaud's mistress, Hélène de Portes, whose influence on him was widely known. Later, during the Norwegian campaign, Campbell found Reynaud impulsive and over-loquacious on strategic matters — 'I am afraid Reynaud's pocket Napoleon proclivities may give us some trouble', he wrote to Halifax. Halifax replied that he thought Reynaud was a light-weight, too much inclined 'to say something that will turn an immediate corner without always enough regard for what will follow'. Even more serious than such diagnoses of Reynaud's character was the political fact of his feud with Daladier, which not only hamstrung his government but was considered by Campbell to be irreparable.[16]

There thus emerged a less than satisfactory picture of the government with which Britain was to seek closer ties, though naturally none of this appeared in public. Outward appearances were well maintained, and the press and radio of the two countries exchanged compliments. André Maurois, whose archetypal British officer of the 1914-18 war, Colonel Bramble, was well known on both sides of the Channel, was recalled to write his usual delightful pieces about the BEF in France.[17] Somerset Maugham visited France, and on his return broadcast on the intensity of the French war effort and the determination of the French people.[18] *The Times* gave a glowing account of French industry — 'transformed into a gigantic war machine . . . in full blast for victory . . . the output of arms surpasses the highest hopes'.[19]

There was little criticism in this roseate picture of Allied harmony, and of France at war, which was presented to the public, though it is not possible to know how much of it was believed by either the people or the government. There was, however, one exchange of views within the Foreign Office which showed that well-informed officials were at any rate disinclined to believe bad reports when they heard them. On 25 January 1940 Lord Dunglass (now Sir Alec Douglas-Home) reported to the Foreign Office a conversation he had had with Kenneth de Courcy, editor of a private news-letter. De Courcy had just returned from France, and said that French morale, especially in the army, was becoming extremely low; that Daladier knew this but was afraid to tell Chamberlain; and that Laval and Bonnet also knew it and hoped to profit from it. Moreover, there existed an understanding between these last two and Marshal Pétain, then ambassador in Madrid. One Foreign Office official minuted that this was only what he would expect from de Courcy, and that all reports showed that French morale was well maintained, though there was a group of politicians anxious to turn Daladier out. The story about Pétain was new and might be worth investigating, but he could hardly believe it. Another official wrote: 'Mr. de Courcy is a calamitous man'. Sir Alexander Cadogan, the Permanent Under-Secretary, wrote to Campbell to say that the Foreign Office did not attach any importance to de Courcy's views, but thought Campbell should know what he had been saying, especially about Pétain. Five months later, on 22nd June 1940, another official took up the file and added a melancholy minute: 'Mr. de Courcy's prophecy reads remarkably today'.[20]

A shrewd observer noted later that after the French collapse many English people remembered hints during the phoney war that the French did not have their hearts in the conflict, and that there was some danger of exaggerating these in retrospect as much as they had been minimised at the time.[21] While this remains a fair warning, the exchanges just described are at least indicative that the Foreign Office view of France, though more sombre than the dazzling purity of the propaganda view, was still over-optimistic. This was understandable: in war, optimism is almost a duty, and a pessimist may well be called a defeatist.

The end of the phoney war coincided with an unexpected event in British politics. The difficulties and defeats of the Norwegian campaign forced a House of Commons debate on Chamberlain's government, and this became an inquisition on the conduct of the war and the leadership of the Prime Minister. At the end of the debate, on 8 May, the Labour party forced a division, in which the government majority fell so drastically that Chamberlain resigned. Churchill was appointed Prime Minister on 10 May 1940. These events were of crucial importance for both the political unity of the country and the character of its leadership. Political unity, impossible under Chamberlain, was achieved under Churchill through a coalition of the three main parties, and this sustained the country during the great crisis caused by the fall of France. The character of British leadership was transformed by Churchill's energy, determination and zest for battle. The whole manner of Britain's response to the collapse of France was affected by Churchill's personality, not least by his affection for France and his friendships with many Frenchmen. The new Prime Minister, in marked contrast to his predecessor, was more pro-French than most of his ministers or the British people as a whole, and this was sometimes to have important effects on British policy.

NOTES

1. There is a valuable discussion of Anglo-French relations during the 'phoney war' in D. W. J. Johnson, 'Britain and France in 1940', *Transactions of the Royal Historical Society,* fifth series, vol. 22. See also J. M. D'Hoop, 'Les projets d'intervention des Alliés en Méditerranée orientale, 1939-40', *La Guerre en Méditerranée, 1939-45,* Comité d'Histoire de la 2e Guerre Mondiale (Paris 1971), 237-56.

2. INF 1/264, report of 18 May 1940 on the background situation to civilian morale, dealing with the period September 1939-May 1940.

3. See the minute by Makins, 26 March 1940, describing the development of the declaration, FO 371/24298, C4623/9/17. For the extensive correspondence with the Dominions, see generally FO 371/24297-8.

4. The text is in Hansard, *Parliamentary Debates,* Commons, series 5, vol. CCCLIX, cols. 40-41. (To be cited as *H.C. Deb.*) Minutes of the Supreme War Council in CAB 99/3, SWC(39/40) 6th Meeting (28 March 1940).

5. *Journal Officiel de la République Française,* numéro spécial, 7 April 1948, printing the debate of the Chamber of Deputies in secret session (19 April 1940), 101.

6. See e.g. *Spectator* (5 April 1940).

7. CAB 65/7, WM(40)77 (28 March 1940), FO 371/24298, C5079/9/17, minute by Sargent (29 March 1940).

8. FO 371/24298, C4444/9/17, minutes by Sargent, 28 February 1940, Halifax, 29 February, Chamberlain, 1 March, C4442/9/17, Perth to Sargent, 19 March 1940.

9. FO 371/24299, C5162/9/17, minute by Leeper, 26 March 1940, enclosing Zimmern's paper; C5818/9/17, Hankey to Halifax, 9 April 1940; C6307/9/17, minutes of the first meeting of the committee; FO 371/24298, C4442/9/17, Sargent to Perth, 22 June 1940.

10. J. Harvey (ed.), *The Diplomatic Diaries of Oliver Harvey, 1937-1940* (London 1970), 31 March 1940, 344.

11. FO 371/24297, C2986/9/17, Campbell to Cadogan, 23 February 1940.

12. FO 371/24309, C4383/65/17, Campbell to Halifax, 22 March 1940.

13. *Ibid.,* minute by Makins.
14. *Harvey Diaries,* 25 March 1940, 341.
15. FO 371/24309, C4658/65/17, Campbell to Halifax, 27 March 1940.
16. FO 800/312, H/XIV/422, 424, 425, Campbell to Halifax, 29 April and 1 May 1940; Halifax to Campbell, 30 April 1940.
17. André Maurois, *The Battle of France* (London 1940).
18. W. Somerset Maugham, *France at War* (London 1940).
19. *The Times,* 3 April 1940.
20. FO 371/24308, C1420/65/17, minute by Makins on conversation with Dunglass, 25 January 1940; minute by Kirkpatrick, same date; minute by Cadogan, 26 January 1940; Cadogan to Campbell, 29 January 1940; minute by Ward, 22 June 1940.
21. R. B. McCallum, *England and France, 1939-1943* (London 1944), 42.

Chapter 2

THE STRAINS OF BATTLE

At 5.30 a.m. on 10 May 1940 the Germans began their offensive in the west. At 12.30 a.m. on 17 June France asked for an armistice. The intervening thirty-eight days saw a crushing and spectacular German victory, the rapidity of which surprised both sides. In the earlier stages of this brief campaign, between 10 May and 10 June, the alliance between Britain and France was subject to the strains of battle, and in the final stage it dissolved. Such problems were peculiar neither to this alliance nor to the events of 1940. No wartime alliance works smoothly, and history has recorded difficulties and recriminations between allies since the Spartans failed to hasten to the aid of the Athenians at Marathon. However, the situation was unduly aggravated by an unusually intricate system of command and communication in the Allied armies in France, fashioned on the assumption that warfare would be slow-moving, as it had been on the western front in 1914-18. In the event, the German assault moved with bewildering speed, reducing the French and British command to confusion.

The battle fell into two phases. In the first, between 10 May and 4 June, the Germans struck through the Ardennes to the Channel, cut off the Allied armies in Flanders, and eliminated them from the campaign. In the second, from 5 June onwards, they developed an offensive along the Somme and Aisne which finally destroyed the remaining French resistance.

(i) 10 May-4 June
The Germans opened their offensive by invading Holland and

Belgium in the early hours of 10 May, which drew the French and British, according to their prepared plan, into the Low Countries; they swung forward like a door on its hinges, the hinge being the forest of the Ardennes. Then on 12, 13 and 14 May, the German armoured divisions struck at the hinge, and on 13 May Guderian's corps crossed the river Meuse at Sedan. By 20 May the French Ninth Army and the northern wing of the Second Army were shattered. On the same day the German armoured forces reached Abbeville, near the mouth of the Somme, having headed westwards from the Meuse at Sedan and Dinant. To the north of this thrust, the French First Army Group, the BEF and the Belgian army were cut off. The Dutch army had already surrendered.[1]

The significance of these events slowly became clear through the fog of war and chaotic communications. At first, the French High Command thought that the Germans would head for Paris after their break-through. When instead they reached the Channel and cut off the northern armies, the first action to be considered was the mounting of a counter-offensive, from both north and south, to cut through the narrow corridor of the German advance. This plan was sketched, but not put into effect, by the French Commander-in-Chief, General Gamelin, on 19 May. On the same day, Reynaud dismissed Gamelin, and replaced him by General Weygand, once Foch's chief of staff, who had retired from the service and been recalled at the outbreak of war to command the French forces in Syria. Despite his age (he was seventy-three), he retained great energy, and had a high military reputation. He assumed command on 20 May, and by the 22nd produced a plan (commonly called the Weygand plan) which closely resembled Gamelin's original idea — an offensive from north and south. When this proved impracticable, it was briefly succeeded by a scheme to hold a perimeter round Dunkirk as a permanent bridgehead, supplied by sea. Then this was succeeded by a plan to evacuate as many men as possible from Flanders, and bring them back to France. In fact the Flanders campaign ended with the evacuation of a large part of the British and French armies from Dunkirk and the nearby beaches.

Such an account gives events an appearance of order which at the time was totally lacking. Neither Weygand in Paris nor the British Chief of the Imperial General Staff in London, General Ironside, knew what was happening on the battlefield. The concepts of counter-offensive, saving a bridgehead, and evacuation succeeded one another, not neatly and in order, but raggedly and pell-mell, amid a confusion confounded by the surrender of the Belgian army at midnight on 27/28 May, leaving gaps which had to be hastily plugged.[2] It is not surprising that this morass of ignorance, chaos and disaster caused difficulties between the British and French. There emerged three main centres of conflict: the Arras operations of 21-23 May; the evacuation from Dunkirk; and the question of British air support in the battle of Flanders.

The Arras operations were of limited importance in themselves, but they led to a serious Franco-British dispute arising from discrepancies between decisions taken in Paris and actions on the field of battle. On 22 May, at a meeting in Paris, Weygand expounded to Reynaud and Churchill his plan for a counter-offensive from north and south against the German corridor across Flanders to the sea. Both Prime Ministers endorsed the plan, and it was agreed that the BEF, under Lord Gort, and the French First Army, commanded by General Blanchard, should attack south-westwards the next day, the 23rd.[3] On the battlefield, however, the situation looked very different. A small British force under General Franklyn had made a successful local counter-attack near Arras on 21 May, but by the 23rd this was in imminent danger of being surrounded by the Germans. That evening Franklyn secured from Gort an order to retreat[4] — the very day after the two Prime Ministers and Weygand had agreed on an offensive. Weygand was extremely angry, claiming that the orders for the retreat must have come from London, and that it was impossible to command an army which remained dependent on another capital. Reynaud sent telegrams of complaint to London, emphasising that Churchill had agreed to Weygand's plan, and that unity of command was vital.[5]

In fact, no orders for a retreat had been issued from London, where the Cabinet were unaware of the events during 23 May. After the news had reached him, Churchill told the Cabinet that he was sure that Gort's action had been necessary, but that the French had grounds for complaint about the lack of communication.[6] The episode appeared to end satisfactorily on 25 May, when Weygand apologised for his hasty conclusions to Sir Edward Spears, who arrived in Paris that day as Churchill's personal liaison officer with Reynaud.[7] (Spears was an old friend of Churchill's and had a distinguished record as a liaison officer with the French army in the 1914-18 war.) However, it subsequently appeared that this was not the end of the matter; Weygand harked back to it on 6 June, when he received news of another British retreat — this time by the 51st Highland Division — which he said was a repetition of what had happened at Arras.[8] More important, after the French armistice the British retreat from Arras figured prominently in the French argument that the British had let them down during the battle of Flanders.

The evacuation from Dunkirk was an altogether more serious matter than the Arras affair, and a crucial episode in the breakdown of the Anglo-French alliance. On 19 May, Gort told the British government that it might be necessary for him to retreat to Dunkirk and evacuate the BEF from there. General Ironside immediately maintained that this was not acceptable, but on 20 May plans began to be made in case the unacceptable came to pass.[9] On 25 May, Gort realised the full danger of his position and the impossibility of mounting an attack southwards. On his own responsibility, he abandoned the idea of an offensive to the south, moved two divisions to plug a gap between the BEF and the Belgian army, and began his retreat to Dunkirk.[10] After this crucial decision had been taken, it received the full support of the British government, which turned with an almost tangible sense of relief to the task of bringing home the BEF — even though its accomplishment seemed at that time almost impossible.

On 26 May the order was given for operation DYNAMO (the code name for the evacuation) to begin. Reynaud (in London that day) was informed, and asked Weygand to issue corresponding orders to the French forces in Flanders, but it was not until the 29th that these were sent. This delay was not the responsibility of the British, but nonetheless there was an air of ruthlessness about the way the British government dealt with the French after DYNAMO had been ordered. On 27 May Churchill told the Cabinet: 'It was clear that we could not allow the security of our Army to be compromised in order to save the First French Army'.[11] In order to avoid reproaches, he sent out a minute on the 29th urging the necessity for the French to share in the evacuation, and not be dependent on their own shipping. Yet on the same day he told the Cabinet that 'British troops should on no account delay their withdrawal to conform with the French, otherwise there would be a danger of getting no troops off. Any French troops that arrived at the coast should, of course, be embarked with our own'.[12] On 31

May, at a meeting with Reynaud in Paris, Churchill said emphatically that the evacuation should proceed on equal terms — 'bras dessus, bras dessous', he said. He also insisted at one point that the British should form the rearguard in the evacuation, though finally this was reduced to an agreement that they should do so for as long as possible.[13] In fact the last British forces were taken off on 2 June, and the last French forces on the 4th. Between 30,000 and 40,000 French soldiers were left behind to surrender, having covered the retreat of those who escaped.

The numbers of British and French troops evacuated at different stages in the operation, and the great disproportion between those numbers in the early days, emerge clearly from the following table:

Numbers of troops from Dunkirk landed in England[14]

Date	Total withdrawn	British*	Allied †
0600 hrs 27 May	3,373		
Midnight 28/29 May	17,321		
Midnight 29/30 May	55,603		
Midnight 30/31 May	134,809		
Midnight 31 May/1 June	194,241	172,241	22,000
Midnight 1/2 June	256,038	203,107	52,931
Midnight 2/3 June	292,380	222,568	69,812
Midnight 3/4 June	310,216	224,301	85,905
1415 hrs 4 June	335,490	224,301	111,172

* In addition to these figures, 27,936 British were brought over before the main evacuation started — see Roskill, p. 216.
† Nearly all French, but including some Belgians.

It was of course important that the overwhelmingly British rescue ships continued their dangerous work between 2 and 4 June to bring off French troops; but the fact remained that the British went first, and the French last — indeed, many of the French did not go at all. The compelling reasons for the British actions are clear, yet there still stands out the contrast between Churchill's genuine sympathy with the French and the determination of the Cabinet (including Churchill) to give priority to the BEF.

The psychological significance of Dunkirk was profoundly

different for the British and French peoples: the British troops were going home, but the French to a foreign land. For the British, Dunkirk was a great national achievement. The part played by the passenger ships and small civilian craft gave the operation a particular aura in the public mind, well expressed by J. B. Priestley in a broadcast about the pleasure-steamers like the *Brighton Belle* and the *Gracie Fields,* which left 'that innocent foolish world of theirs to sail into the inferno . . .'.[15] None of this could make any appeal to the French. Above all, Dunkirk was for the British a tremendous relief, the first collective lifting of the heart felt in the war. For the French, it was a disaster on the road to further disasters.

The third cause of discord between Britain and France was the use of British air power, especially fighter aircraft, in the battle of Flanders. On 10 May there were six British fighter squadrons in France, and four more were sent by 12 May.[16] On the 14th Reynaud telephoned Churchill and asked for ten more fighter squadrons to be sent at once — the first appeal of many, growing increasingly desperate in tone and often supported by the British commanders in France. These requests forced a series of profoundly difficult decisions on the British Cabinet.

The question of fighter reinforcements for France had been discussed in the Cabinet on 13 May, before any French request was received, and both Churchill and Air Chief Marshal Newall (Chief of the Air Staff) had stressed the danger of denuding Britain of its fighter defence.[17] On the 15th, this stand was maintained, and the Cabinet agreed to refuse Reynaud's appeal for ten more squadrons,[18] but the following morning the question was re-opened. Newall, impressed by reports of the strain and fatigue being suffered by the pilots serving in France, recommended sending the equivalent of four squadrons as reinforcements. Churchill urged the need 'to do something to bolster up the French', and suggested increasing the number to six, but did not press this against Newall's opposition.[19] After this meeting in the morning of 16 May, Churchill flew to Paris to confer with Reynaud and other French leaders. This visit impressed upon him for the first time the gravity of the situation, and the despondency and confusion of the French government. He telegraphed his impressions to the Cabinet that evening, and asked that six more fighter squadrons should be sent (over and above the four agreed on that morning) to give French morale a chance to rally. When the Cabinet met at 11 p.m. on the 16th to consider Churchill's request, Newall explained that there were only six complete Hurricane squadrons in the United Kingdom, and proposed a compromise by which they should operate over France from bases in Kent, three before noon and three after noon each day. The Cabinet agreed, and Churchill (though it was not what he had asked for) made the best of it, rousing Reynaud from his bed to tell him the news.[20]

Thus the British Cabinet departed from its apparently firm resolve of 15 May that no more fighter squadrons should be sent to France, and this caused Dowding, Commander-in-Chief of Fighter Command, grave anxiety. On 16 May (before the late-night decision concerning the six squadrons) he wrote a formal letter to the Air Minister, pointing out that the most recent estimate of the minimum fighter strength needed for the defence of the United Kingdom was fifty-two squadrons, and his force had already been reduced to the equivalent of thirty-six. He asked, as a matter of paramount urgency, that the Air Ministry should decide what in fact *was* the minimum strength necessary for the defence of the country, and then adhere to it, sending no more fighters to France however insistent the appeals. Dowding concluded solemnly that if an adequate fighter force was kept in Britain, and the fleet remained in being, the country could carry on the war single-handed. However, if the fighter force was drained away in France, defeat there would also involve the final defeat of Britain. Thus, at a very early date, this letter placed the question of fighter squadrons for France in its wider, and indeed rightful context of the possible withdrawal of France from the war.

Dowding's arguments were referred to the Chiefs of Staff, who reported to the Cabinet on 18 May. They endorsed his serious view of the situation, and emphasised that reserves of fighters were quite inadequate to meet the rate of losses being suffered in France. If France fell and Britain had to face the German air force deployed on bases from Norway to Brittany, the future situation would be worse still. They asserted therefore that: 'we have reached the absolute limit of the air assistance that we can afford to France, if we are to have any chance of protecting the United Kingdom, the Fleet, our sea-borne trade, our aircraft industry, and all the vital centres throughout the country on which we must depend for our ability to continue the war'. They did not believe that 'to throw in a few more

19

squadrons, whose loss might vitally weaken the fighter line at home, would make the difference between victory and defeat in France'. In Cabinet, Churchill argued for a time that more might still be done to help the French, but finally concurred in the opinion of the Chiefs of Staff, as did the other ministers.[21]

During the next few days, all except three of the RAF fighter squadrons in France were moved to England, as the area held by the Allies in Flanders rapidly dwindled. However, during the evacuation from Dunkirk every available squadron of Fighter Command was in fact engaged in the battle, and the British committed all their fighters to save the BEF, though they had earlier refused to do so in order to save the land battle.[22] The reasons for this were partly practical — Dunkirk was close to England, and fighters could fly over it without the further risks of being based in France — but the main reason was simply national self-interest. Although the British did not accept French arguments that the battle in France would be crucial to both Allies, they did see very clearly the importance of saving the BEF, both for emotional reasons and for the future defence of Britain.

Arras, Dunkirk, and the British fighter squadrons were the main bones of contention between the British and French in the early stages of the battle in France, inevitably accompanied by a good deal of personal friction. There was a running fire of harsh criticism of the British from the French side, notably from Weygand and General Vuillemin, the commander of the French Air Force. These comments were often addressed to Spears, who rarely failed to give as good as he got, and who commanded a remarkably vivid and cutting turn of phrase. There was also much unfriendly British comment on the French. Cadogan wrote in his diary on 17 May: 'Gather French haven't fought at all — simply shattered by air-tank attack. Troops and guns hardly used'. On 19 May he wrote: 'French army not fighting . . . Gamelin (thank heaven) sacked . . .'[23] Hugh Dalton, the Minister of Economic Warfare, recorded in his diary on 20 May: 'A.V.A. (A. V. Alexander, First Lord of the Admiralty) says the French are being perfectly useless. Their First Army is no good'.[24] When Gort returned from Dunkirk, he told the Cabinet on 1 June that the French General Blanchard was 'of the professorial type . . . no initiative, no drive and no determination'. General

Billotte had looked impressive, but 'he was in fact completely flabby'. Gort had praise for only one French general, de la Laurencie, who had at one stage grown disgusted with his own commanders and asked to come under Gort; he later left Blanchard and the First Army, and brought his corps into the perimeter at Dunkirk. Gort strongly urged the Cabinet that de la Laurencie and his men should be brought to England — he is not recorded as saying anything about the others.[25]

However, there were occasional exceptions to these strictures on the French army. Ironside, who on one occasion took the French side on the question of the fighter squadrons, reproved a Labour member of the War Cabinet on 17 May: 'I found that Greenwood was inclined to say "these bloody gallant Allies". I told him that we had depended upon the French Army. That we had made no Army and that therefore it was not right to say "these bloody Allies", It was for them to say that of us'.[26] Given the general record of the inter-war years, and especially British military policy, this view may in retrospect command much sympathy, but at the time it seems to have found little echo.

It would be a mistake to attach too much importance to expressions of hostility towards the French. If the bond of common interest between Britain and France had endured, such comments would now be either passed over or treated as the superficial utterances of men under strain — which in part they doubtless were. On the other hand, they cannot be ignored, and as the bond of common interest weakened, they assumed increasing importance.

(ii) 5-14 June.

By the night of 4/5 June, the French army was attempting to consolidate a line along the rivers Somme and Aisne to meet the end of the Maginot Line at Longuyon. The whole front was longer than at the beginning of the battle, and yet the Belgian army, the greater part of the BEF, and the French northern armies had been lost. Weygand had at his disposal only sixty-two French and two British divisions, and some of these existed more on paper than in reality. The Germans had 140 divisions, including the highly successful and self-confident Panzer divisions.

The German offensive was resumed on 5 June, sustaining the remarkable momentum of their attack. They attacked first on the Somme, and then on 9 June along the Aisne. Weygand's defensive plan rested on holding a series of strong-points which were to be defended to the last, because he did not believe that, with their weak numbers and lack of reserves, the French armies could achieve an orderly retreat. For Weygand, it was the Somme-Aisne line or defeat, as he explained in writing to Reynaud on 29 May.[27] The French fought hard, and with some initial success, but the odds were too heavy, and the German tactics of infiltration and rapid movement were more effective than the French static defence. By 9 June the Germans were well past the Somme; by the 10th their armour had also successfully crossed the Aisne. The battle on the Somme-Aisne line had been lost. It was also on 10 June, for full measure, that Mussolini — hastening to the help of the victor — declared war on France and Britain.

This phase of the battle was so one-sided and so short that there was little practical opportunity for British intervention. British forces had suffered heavily in Flanders, and were in no state for immediate fighting. Although the Dunkirk evacuation had saved large numbers of men, very little of their equipment had been salvaged. Moreover, they were tired and disorganised, and it would take time to re-form them into an effective fighting force. The fighter squadrons of the RAF, too, had suffered heavily; and in any case all the arguments against committing them to the battle in France had already been debated at least twice. In these circumstances, it is a striking fact that the provision of further British help to France was seriously discussed, occupying a great deal of time and energy on the part of the Cabinet and Chiefs of Staff. One British division and parts of the 1st Canadian Division were actually sent to France — and had to be brought back in haste. This came about partly because French requests for aid were insistent and desperate; partly because hope persisted for some time that the French line would hold; but above all because Churchill was adamant that the question of sending help to France must be taken seriously and pressed to the very limits of what was possible.

On 29 May two documents, one French and one British, set out the terms in which each government had to consider the problem. Weygand presented Reynaud with a note, stating that the French army had been ordered to fight to the end on its present positions, but that the superiority of the enemy was such that the front might be breached, in which case France would be unable to continue the co-ordinated defence of her territory. He asked that the British government should be informed of this situation, and should send two or three divisions, tank, anti-tank and anti-aircraft units, and the support of the RAF.[28] On the same day in Britain, the Chiefs of Staff reported to the Cabinet on the prospect of a German invasion of the United Kingdom. They pointed out that in the near future the Germans might either concentrate their main effort on destroying the French army and knocking France out of the war, or merely hold the line in France and launch a major attack on Britain. They thought it highly probable that Germany was already preparing such an attack, and it could not be assumed that she would move slowly. This was a warning which the Cabinet could not ignore; invasion had to be treated as a serious possibility, whether or not France remained in the war.

French requests for British support came in an unremitting stream from 29 May onwards. Every British reply, whether an explanation of the difficulties, a promise to review the situation, or a firm proposal and time-table of movements, was challenged in sharp and often acrimonious terms. In the British Cabinet, Churchill insisted on doing whatever was possible to help the French, to the disquiet of some of his colleagues. Cadogan wrote on 2 June: 'Cabinet 6.30. French howling for assistance on the Somme. Perhaps we should give them a token, but it's so much down the drain. It won't do any good — It won't prevent the French reviling us . . . Decision postponed for report of Chiefs of Staff. Labour members, Neville [Chamberlain], H. [Halifax], and, I think, A. Sinclair, think with me. Sentimental Winston rather doubtful'. Then on 4 June: 'Cabinet 11.30. Discussed reply to French appeal. W.S.C. [Churchill] trying hard to send out fighters to help them. But they're *no use*. If I could see any sign of the French fighting I should take a risk. But they don't . . . But I'm afraid W.S.C. will have his way'.[29]

Cabinet minutes recorded the story in less emotional terms. On 2 June, the Prime Minister laid before the Cabinet telegrams from Reynaud, Weygand and Vuillemin, asking for three fresh British divisions to be sent to France at once, followed as soon as possible by units made up of troops evacuated from Dunkirk. They also wanted the maximum British air strength to be based in France, and Vuillemin asked for twenty fighter squadrons. Members of the Cabinet emphasised the difficulty of re-equipping the BEF, and the danger of denuding the country of fighters. Churchill, however, also spoke of the danger of a French collapse if help were refused:

France might make a separate peace, and Britain be faced eventually with a French government not merely out of the war but positively hostile. He wished to tell the French that Britain would send three divisions in five to six weeks, the 1st Canadian Division leading; reconstitute the Air Component of the BEF; and allow the existing air forces in France to continue to operate from there. Fighter support would be confined to these forces, but British bombers would be used against targets indicated by the French Commander-in-Chief. These suggestions were referred to the Chiefs of Staff.[30]

The Chiefs of Staff reported next day, 3 June. They acknowledged the importance of keeping large German forces engaged in France; the shock which the collapse of France would be to the British people; and the danger of a pro-German government in France joining Britain's enemies. Against this, they thought that the French leaders had lost hope of victory; that it was extremely improbable that the weakened French army could hold its elongated line; that it was doubtful whether British forces could affect the outcome of the imminent battle; and that there was a serious danger of invasion at home. They also believed that any forces sent to France would virtually have to be 'written off'. Their conclusion from these well-balanced arguments was that the grave military consequences of a collapse of French resistance drove them to recommend the acceptance of further risks by taking the following measures. The BEF headquarters should be re-established in France at once, and two divisions sent over, the first leaving in about a week. (They opposed sending the Canadian Division, because although it was ready to go overseas, it was also the most effective mobile reserve for home defence.) The despatch of further divisions should, they felt, be governed by circumstances. As to the air, they recommended that the six bomber and three fighter squadrons in France should be brought up to strength, and that the bomber force in Britain should give support as necessary.[31]

It was plain from the wording of the report that the Chiefs of Staff had gone as far as they could, and rather further than they wished, to help the French. But Churchill wanted to go further still, and in Cabinet suggested sending three divisions rather than two, provided that the French could supply artillery for the third. (He agreed that it would be unwise to send the Canadian Division at once.) On air forces, he pointed out that if the recommendations were followed, there would be fewer British aircraft in France than at the start of the battle. This statement, with its implication that more might be sent, drew heavy fire from Newall and Dowding, who were present for this discussion. Newall emphasised that fighter losses were much heavier in France than over Britain; during the fighting in May, between half and three-quarters of a squadron had been lost every day. Dowding produced a graph, showing the wastage of Hurricanes in operations in France from 8 to 18 May, averaging twenty-five per day, against four per day coming off the production line. If this had continued throughout May, there would have been no Hurricanes left by the end of the month. The loss of trained pilots was even more serious than that of aircraft, and Dowding said that if the Germans mounted a heavy air attack against Britain at that moment, he could not guarantee air superiority for more than forty-eight hours.

Summing up, Churchill pointed out that to the French it looked as if, while they were making a supreme effort on land, the British had 500 fighters which they were withholding from the air battle. However, he agreed with the Chiefs of Staff that Britain could only afford to bring up to strength the squadrons already in France. The Cabinet agreed on the lines of a telegram to Reynaud which conformed closely to the recommendations made by the Chiefs of Staff, though the possibility of sending a third division was also included. The message was to explain that the heavy losses of the past three weeks made it impossible to send any further fighter squadrons to France at present, though this might be reconsidered later.[32]

Even after all this discussion, Churchill insisted on holding back the telegram to Reynaud so that the Cabinet could review it again on 4 June. He reverted to his view that the British could not refuse to maintain the same number of squadrons as were in France when the battle commenced. (On 10 May there were six fighter squadrons in France; on 4 June there were three.) He had received figures from Lord Beaverbrook, the Minister of Aircraft Production, showing that there were now more aircraft available in the country than before 10 May. 'We could never keep all that we wanted for our own defence while the French were fighting for their lives'. However, after a long and arduous debate, the main terms of the message to Reynaud remained unchanged.[33] The significance of the episode lay in Churchill's insistence on further discussion over what might reasonably have been considered a foregone conclusion.

25

This did not mean that the Prime Minister dealt gently with the French. He pushed the Cabinet and Chiefs of Staff as far as he could, but he was also stern in his messages to Reynaud, and when the French Premier protested on 5 June that British help would come too late, Churchill replied sharply: 'Permit me to observe that your divisions picked out of Dunkirk are not to enter the line for a month. We are trying to send one of our seasoned divisions in a fortnight'. He also remarked that Vuillemin's demand for twenty squadrons had been altogether unreasonable, and had made a very bad impression in London.[34]

However, in the event the British again went beyond the Cabinet's decision. On 6 June the RAF had 144 fighters operating over France, mainly from English bases, but using advanced landing grounds in France. This was equivalent to twelve squadrons, because the Hurricane squadrons were down to twelve aircraft at this time.[35] Moreover, two extra fighter squadrons went to France on 8 June. On land, the 52nd Division disembarked, as did leading elements of the Canadian Division, the latter being finally ordered to France despite all opposing arguments.[36] So Churchill got at least part of what he wanted, and more help was sent than had been originally agreed. In the air, this meant further losses; on land, it put General Brooke, (commanding the new BEF) in a very dangerous position. Arriving at Cherbourg on 13 June to find the French defence in dissolution, on the 14th — with Weygand and Georges — he signed a note agreeing to take part in holding a 'redoubt' in Brittany. None of the three generals believed this could be done, and Brooke at once told London that the whole situation was impossible. Churchill was still hard to convince, and it was only after Brooke spoke to him directly on the telephone that he was persuaded that there was no further point in going on. Brooke was freed from French command, and told to withdraw his forces to England.[37] Fortunately, the prediction of the Chiefs of Staff that any divisions sent to France would have to be written off was proved false; the troops were evacuated, though without most of their equipment.

The French were convinced throughout that the British contribution to the battle's final stage was wholly inadequate. When the German offensive opened on 5 June, Weygand had handed Reynaud a note saying that appeals to Britain had been in vain, and that the French were bearing the weight of the attack without the benefit of any further British help.[38] Later, Weygand was indignant that Brooke first signed the paper about the Breton redoubt, and then immediately secured his release from French command. Such complaints were natural, although Weygand could hardly expect the British to commit all their resources to a battle which — at least from 12 June — he himself knew to be lost. From the British viewpoint, it must appear in retrospect that Churchill's determination to help the French took him too far. The greatest risk, that of fatally weakening the air defence of Great Britain, was avoided, even though more fighters were committed than Dowding had wished, but Brooke and his forces were exposed to grave dangers in a useless cause.

NOTES

1. For excellent accounts of the campaign, see L. F. Ellis, *The War in France and Flanders, 1939-40* (London 1953); G. Chapman, *Why France Collapsed* (London 1968), and A. Horne, *To lose a Battle* (London 1969).

2. See John C. Cairns, 'Great Britain and the Fall of France', *Journal of Modern History,* vol. XXVII (December 1955), for an excellent account of the confusion prevailing both on the battlefield and in the Allied command.

3. CAB 99/3, SWC(39/40)12th Meeting, 22 May 1940; CAB 65/13, WM(40) 134th Conclusions, Confidential Annex, 22 May 1940; Ellis, 112-13.

4. Chapman, 192-4; Ellis, 131-2.

5. P. Reynaud, *La France a sauvé l'Europe,* vol. II (Paris 1947), 153-7; M. Weygand, *Rappelé au Service* (Paris 1950), 116-17; Weygand's testimony in *Rapport fait au nom de la Commission chargée d'enquêter sur les événements survenus en France de 1933 à 1945,* Paris n.d., *Témoignages,* vol. III, 366 (this will be cited as *Événements, Rapport,* or *Événements, Témoignages;* P. Baudouin, *Neuf Mois au Gouvernement* (Paris, 1948), 71-2; W. S. Churchill, *The Second World War,* vol. II, *Their Finest Hour* (London 1949), 62-3.

6. CAB 65/7, WM(40)135, 136, 138; CAB 65/13, WM(40)136th Conclusions, Confidential Annex.

7. *Ibid.,* WM(40)139th Conclusions, Confidential Annex; E. L. Spears, *Assignment to Catastrophe* (London 1954), vol. I, *Prelude to Dunkirk,* 186-7.

8. Spears, *Assignment to Catastrophe,* vol. II, *The Fall of France,* 74-5; Baudouin, 128-9.

9. For accounts of the Dunkirk operation, see Ellis, 171-248; S. W. Roskill, *The War at Sea,* vol. 1, *The Defensive* (London 1954), 212-28; J. Mordal (H. Cras), *La Bataille de Dunkerque* (Paris, 1948), and the same author's *Dunkerque* (Paris 1960).

10. Ellis, 148-9; J. R. Colville, *Man of Valour: The Life of Field Marshal the Viscount Gort* (London 1972), 215-17.

11. CAB 65/13, WM(40)141st Conclusions, Confidential Annex.

12. *Ibid.,* WM(40)146th Conclusions, Confidential Annex; Churchill, 94.

13. CAB 99/3, SWC(39/40)13th Meeting, 31 May 1940; Spears, vol. I, 308-9, 315.

14. Table slightly adapted from CAB 66/8, WP(40)195, 7 June 1940.

15. J. B. Priestley, 'Excursion to Hell', *Listener,* 13 June 1940.

16. Ellis, 3, 7, 372-4.

17. CAB 65/13, WM(40)120th Conclusions, Confidential Annex.

18. *Ibid.,* WM(40)123rd Conclusions, Confidential Annex.

19. *Ibid.,* WM(40)124th Conclusions, Confidential Annex.

20. CAB 99/3, SWC(39/40)11th Meeting, 16 May 1940; CAB 65/7, WM(40)125; Churchill, 40-46; Reynaud, vol. II, 96-100.

21. CAB 67/7, WP(40)159, 18 May 1940, with Dowding's letter attached; CAB 65/13 WM(40)131st Conclusions, Confidential Annex; Basil Collier, *Leader of the Few* (London 1957), 192-4.

22. Ellis, 312.

23. David Dilks (ed.), *The Diaries of Sir Alexander Cadogan, 1938-1945* (London 1971), 17, 19 May 1940, 285-6.

24. Dalton Diary, 20 May 1940.

25. CAB 65/7, WM(40)151; cf. Chapman, 215, 222-3, 227 on de la Laurencie.

26. R. Macleod and D. Kelly (ed.), *The Ironside Diaries, 1937-1940* (London 1962), 313.

27. See below, 22-3.

28. Weygand, 149-51; Reynaud, vol. II, 183-4.

29. *Cadogan Diaries,* 293-4.

30. CAB 65/13, WM(40)152nd Conclusions, Confidential Annex.

31. CAB 66/8, WP(40)189, 3 June 1940, which was largely based on CAB 80/12, COS(40)418(JP), 1 June 1940.

32. CAB 65/13, WM(40)153rd Conclusions, Confidential Annex.

33. CAB 65/13, WM(40)154th Conclusions, Confidential Annex.
34. CAB 65/13, WM(40)156th Conclusions, Confidential Annex; cf Spears, vol. II, 50-61.
35. CAB 65/13, WM(40)157th Conclusions, Confidential Annex, 7 June 1940.
36. CAB 65/13, WM(40)156th Conclusions, Confidential Annex, 6 June 1940; Ellis, 296, 367.
37. Ellis, 296-300; Chapman, 304-5; Churchill, 169-71; Sir Arthur Bryant (ed.), *The Turn of the Tide,* Alanbrooke Diaries, vol. I (London 1957), 165-81. For the story of the so-called Breton redoubt, see Cairns, 384-6.
38. Reynaud, vol. II, 271.

Chapter 3

"BRITISH STRATEGY IN A CERTAIN EVENTUALITY"

The minutes of the British Cabinet for 27 May 1940 include the following brief and somewhat technical entry: 'The War Cabinet had before them two Reports by the Chiefs of Staff (WP(40) 168 and 169) and a Note by the Minister without Portfolio (WP(40) 171). A record of the discussion is contained in the Secretary's Standard File of War Cabinet Conclusions'.[1] This cryptic minute concealed consideration of one of the gravest questions ever faced by a British government: whether the country could continue the war alone if France fell. The key document was a report by the Chiefs of Staff entitled 'British Strategy in a Certain Eventuality', a euphemistic wording regularly used in such papers in place of a direct reference to a French collapse.[2] How did the British government look on such a possibility? First, when was it realised that France was going to be defeated? Next, assuming such a defeat, what courses were considered? The main choice was simple but awesome: to make peace, or continue the war. If the war went on, there were two broad questions to be answered: what strategy should be adopted to replace that based on the French alliance; and what specific steps should be taken to salvage something from the wreck of France?

The realisation that France *might* collapse came remarkably early in the course of the battle; the certainty that she *would* do so came equally remarkably late. For a long time it seemed possible that the French army would yet hold on; and even when that chance had gone the British government clung to the hope that there would be no armistice or separate peace, and that the French government

31

would continue the war from outside France. This was, after all, what the Polish, Norwegian, Dutch and Belgian governments had already done. There was an ebb and flow of fear and hope as the British government watched events in France, and tried to gauge their meaning.

In the very early stages of the battle, it was by no means clear in London what was happening. On 13 May, when Guderian's armour crossed the Meuse and quite possibly decided the issue of the campaign, Churchill told the Cabinet that he was 'by no means sure that the great battle was developing'. This was backed up by the CIGS, Ironside, who said that the Germans had only used mechanised forces so far, and these would inevitably be compelled to retire unless the main German army moved forward. They would know within the next forty-eight hours.[3] Much indeed happened in that time, and on 14 May it was known that the Germans were across the Meuse near Sedan.[4] That evening, Reynaud telephoned Churchill and told him that the situation was very serious: the Germans were attempting a fatal blow towards Paris, and the line was pierced south of Sedan. At 7.30 the next morning Reynaud rang again, telling Churchill in English: 'We are beaten; we have lost the battle'. Churchill did not believe him. He remembered March 1918, and was sure the German advance would slow down in a few days. He told the Cabinet that there had been 'an alarmist message' from Reynaud.[5]

This impression persisted during the morning of 16 May, when the Cabinet was informed that the French had ordered substantial withdrawals on the northern front, involving the BEF. Churchill thought that withdrawal was not justified by 'the penetration of the French line by a force of some 120 German armoured vehicles'. Cadogan put it more vividly in his diary, writing that Churchill: 'Sprang up and said he would go to France — it was ridiculous to think that France could be conquered by 120 tanks . . . '. Cadogan added his own thought: 'But it may be!'[6] Churchill wrote in his memoirs, some years later: '. . . I did not comprehend the violence of the revolution effected since the last war by the incursion of a mass of fast-moving heavy armour. I knew about it, but it had not altered my inward convictions as it should have done'.[7]

Churchill's visit to Paris on 16 May quickly changed his attitude. When he returned to London on the 17th, his account was not completely gloomy — he thought there was a reasonable hope that with four or five days' respite from air attack, the French would be able to rally — but despite this, the general impression he conveyed was one of disaster. Cadogan noted in his diary: 'Cabinet at 10 (17 May). W.S.C. gave an account of his trip. French evidently cracking, and situation awful. Nothing much to be done and no decision taken'.[8] Churchill's views were best indicated by his actions. On the day of his return, he asked Chamberlain to form a small committee to examine the consequences of the French government's possible abandonment of Paris, and the withdrawal of the BEF from France. The committee met that evening, and Cadogan noted that Halifax was attending, 'to consider how we proceed when France has capitulated and we are left alone. Just as well to prepare for that'. The committee reported to the Cabinet the very next day, 18 May, on 'the situation in which we might find ourselves obliged to continue our resistance single-handed in this country . . . '.[9] The measures recommended will be described later,[10] but at this early stage there was no doubt as to the issue: the Cabinet was making ready for the possible fall of France. The Chiefs of Staff were set to work on the same problem, and on 19 May considered a draft report by the Joint Planning Sub-Committee on 'British strategy in a certain eventuality'.[11] Churchill's visit to France on 16/17 May had transformed his view of the situation, and the machinery of government was at work on the new problems which would arise if France fell. All this was within ten days of the start of the battle.

Nevertheless, it was still only the *possible* fall of France. There was no certainty that the battle would be lost, and indeed no certainty even about its progress. For example, on 22 May it was only known from an intercepted German message that a British force had counter-attacked near Arras on the 21st.[12] There was a natural tendency to look for hopeful signs, and Colonel Redman, a liaison officer with the War Cabinet secretariat in France, wrote on 18 May that the tanks could not go on for ever, and perhaps the corner had been turned. On 21 May Churchill told the Cabinet that the situation was more favourable than the obvious symptoms might indicate; the Germans had probably only left small forces in the towns through which they had passed.[13] Churchill was further encouraged by his meeting with Weygand in Paris on 22 May,[14] and always sustained by his own natural belligerence and optimism. However, another natural optimist, Dalton, was moved at this time to look into the depths of what might lie ahead. During a late-night talk with Hugh Gaitskell, then serving in the Ministry of Economic Warfare, he wondered: 'If we lose the war, and have Hitler as Emperor of Europe and King of England, would it be bearable to go on living, especially with Himmler and all that? . . . But we are an immense distance from such large catastrophes as yet'.[15] This doubtless reflected the mood of the small hours, but it also showed the true dimensions of what was at stake — it was not only the fall of France which loomed ahead as the German tanks reached the Channel.

By 26 May the depths were indeed opening: on that day even Churchill's hopes of Weygand's counter-offensive ended, and Gort was directed to withdraw the BEF to Dunkirk, though with no hope of evacuating more than a quarter of its men. Reynaud also came to London on the 26th, and Churchill told the Cabinet before he arrived that they must be prepared for him to say that the French could not carry on the fight.[16] While Reynaud did not say that in so many words — though in fact on 25 May the French *Comité de Guerre* had formally considered the possibility of defeat and a separate peace[17] — there was no doubt as to his meaning. Cadogan noted: 'Cabinet at 2. W.S.C. gave us account of his conversation with Reynaud at lunch. R. doesn't *say* that France will capitulate, but all his conversation goes to show that he sees no alternative . . . '.[18] Reynaud had reported that, apart from the troops in the Maginot Line, there were only fifty French divisions facing 150 German divisions from Montmédy to the sea. Weygand did not think his army could resist a German onslaught for long. Sea power would not help, because if Germany commanded the resources of the land mass from Brest to Vladivostock, blockade could not win the war. The USA offered little hope, because its munitions industry was as yet feeble. Where then could France look for salvation? The only idea Reynaud offered was an approach to prevent Italy from entering the war, and thus release French forces from the Italian frontier. Reynaud hinted that he himself would not sign peace terms, but that he might be forced to resign.[19]

The question of an approach to Italy raised a very important discussion in the British Cabinet, which will be examined later. Meanwhile, the French Premier had left the British government in no doubt as to the position, and on 28 May Churchill held a meeting of ministers who were of Cabinet rank but not members of the War Cabinet, telling them that 'No countenance should be given publicly to the view that France might soon collapse, but we must not allow ourselves to be taken by surprise by any events'.[20]

Reports from the British Embassy in Paris confirmed Reynaud's picture of the situation. Campbell wrote to Halifax on 27 May that Reynaud had spoken to him of France fighting on for the sake of honour — she would do so as long as he was in control, but he might be replaced. Apart from Reynaud, Campbell thought the only strong man was Mandel. 'It is the sort of fatalistic mood that is prevalent which is so distressing. I had hoped that after the first stupefaction there would be a violent reaction. People are still not getting as angry as I would like to see'.[21] Spears wrote to Ismay on the same day that there was no furious reaction to the German invasion as there had been in 1914. He had seen Pétain (whom Reynaud had brought into his government on 18 May): 'I would not say his morale is shaken, because that is impossible, but he regards the situation as catastrophic and he does not see a way out'.[22] On 30 May Campbell wrote again: 'The fact is that there is practically no single Frenchman among those who know the full gravity of the situation that does not feel — even if he does not admit it — that France is beaten'. Pétain was very feeble, and seemed to have lost hope; Weygand was tired but clear-headed — and also seemed to have lost hope.[23]

On 4 June Campbell reviewed the situation at length. After eight months of comparative inactivity, during which German propaganda had done much to undermine French fighting spirit, the French had been stunned by the German breakthrough. Government and officials had been paralysed, and the whole nation gripped by 'a sort of mass fear engendered by the German technique and spread by hordes of terror-stricken refugees'. There had later been some recovery, stimulated by anger at the surrender of the Belgian army and what was seen as the treachery of King Leopold. Weygand had decided to defend the Somme-Aisne line at all costs; but because this was made the supreme test, there was a danger that a German breakthrough there might bring a fresh wave of despair. There was a distinct possibility, even probability, that the Germans would overcome French resistance on the Somme-Aisne line, then without much difficulty occupy the Paris region, which contained three-quarters of what remained of French industry. Weygand had warned the government that if this happened, the defence of France could not be continued in any organised manner.

This raised the question of what the French government would do if and when it became clear that further resistance in France was hopeless. The plan was for the government to go to Bordeaux if Paris were endangered, and Campbell thought there would be no weakening until that stage was reached, but thereafter, he found it difficult to say what would happen. Reynaud and Mandel insisted that France would never make terms, even if the government had to go to French North Africa, but Reynaud often qualified such statements by observing that they held good so long as he was in control. Campbell wrote that he could never decide whether Reynaud was sincere in his protestations of inflexible resolve, or whether at some moment he would allow himself to be set aside in favour of a government which would make a separate peace. Even if he were sincere, the forces in favour of peace might be too strong for him, for these certainly existed, both inside and outside the government. Inside, Campbell named de Monzie, and expressed doubts about Daladier; outside, Laval and Flandin were the most dangerous. If the Germans captured Paris and then offered a separate peace, Campbell would not lay long odds on the government going to North Africa rather than taking up such an offer. He did not think that Italian action would materially affect the issue, though a declaration of war might depress the undecided still further.

Campbell concluded by saying that it was his duty to set all this down, though he had not lost hope that the situation might be restored, and he never allowed such pessimistic thoughts to pass his lips when talking to the French.[24] This was indeed a remarkably accurate and prescient despatch. When it was received in London on 6 June, its importance was recognised and it was circulated to the Cabinet and the King. Campbell himself reinforced his despatch with a hand-written letter to Cadogan on 5 June, saying much the same things in less formal language: 'I don't want to be pessimistic, but I frankly haven't much faith in the ability of the French to hold these advancing hordes . . . When once the Germans have got Paris, the French resistance will be as good as broken, I am afraid. And if the Government get to Bordeaux, without being nabbed on the way, it seems unlikely they will be able to hang on very long. This may sound rather highly coloured, but I don't believe it is, with this new kind of warfare'.[25]

At this stage, Campbell had by no means lost sympathy with the

French, and he wrote to Halifax on 7 June that one must make allowances for the fact that 'France is faced with the prospect of early extinction'. He pointed out that Weygand had had no idea of the disastrous state of affairs when he took over, and was under tremendous strain for a man of seventy-three. Nevertheless, sympathy did not cloud his judgement, and the letter continued: 'At the present moment I believe Reynaud and Mandel to be the only ones (not excluding Weygand) who would stand for refusing an armistice at any price. Nor would I absolutely guarantee Reynaud when it came to the point. In any case he could hardly play a lone hand if Pétain and possibly Weygand abandoned him'.[26] This was another accurate piece of analysis.

Even at this late date there were flashes of optimism about the French situation, though perhaps more out of desperation than conviction. Redman wrote to Ismay on 7 June that the French were pleased with their defensive tactics, which seemed to be having some success, and he thought French morale was rising. On 10 June he still thought they were fighting well, though he was concerned at the extent of the German advance.[27] Campbell himself telegraphed on 8 June that he found Reynaud in better heart, and anxious to send General de Gaulle to London for consultations.[28] De Gaulle, only very recently promoted to general, had been appointed as Under-Secretary for War in a government re-shuffle on 5 June. He visited London and saw Churchill on 9 June, conveying a better impression of French morale and determination than he had recently received.[29] Harvey too at this time found Reynaud 'in fairly good fettle — less complaining'.[30]

Such views offered some justification for hope, but they weighed little against the facts of the German advance and the considered views of the British Ambassador in Paris. (From the evening of 10 June, he was no longer in Paris, but in retreat to the Loire and then Bordeaux — further convincing evidence of the situation in France.) On 11 June Churchill went to France to confer with Reynaud and other French leaders. When he returned on the 12th, he told the Cabinet that 'it was clear that France was near the end of organised resistance', and that 'a chapter in the war was now closing'.[31] Hope had been prolonged for a surprising and perhaps unreasonable length of time after Churchill returned from Paris on 17 May, with the first realisation of the likelihood of French defeat in his mind. There was no longer any room for doubt.

37

Resistance in France was coming to an end, and the best the British could hope for was that the French government would go abroad — as others had done — and continue the war from there. Even then, the German army and air force which had been engaged in France would be free to turn against Britain, which would certainly involve air attacks, and quite possibly invasion. Moreover, the German navy, and especially the U-boats, would have bases along the French Channel and Atlantic coasts, from which they could operate against British sea-routes in the Atlantic. Britain depended on these routes for her war effort and her very life: imports of food, raw materials, arms and equipment; communications with the Dominions, the Empire, and the USA. In such adverse circumstances, there was serious doubt as to whether Britain could continue the war against Germany, or would have to make peace.

The question of at least making tentative enquiries about peace terms was discussed by the British War Cabinet early in the crisis, on 26, 27 and 28 May. The discussions arose out of Reynaud's visit to London on 26 May, and his proposal to approach Italy in the hope of persuading Mussolini to stay out of the war. Consideration of the proposal led, obliquely, to consideration of the possibility of making peace, since it seemed logical that an approach to Italy might lead to such further developments as Italian mediation between the Allies and Germany, and even the discussion of a general peace settlement. This appears to have been the nearest approach made by the British Cabinet to considering negotiations with Germany at the time of the fall of France.

Italy was allied to Germany by the so-called Pact of Steel, but had not entered the war in 1939. She declared herself to be, not neutral, but non-belligerent, which was an open hint of Mussolini's intention to come into the war at some convenient point. During the phoney war, both British and French had taken some trouble to avoid offence or provocation to Italy. In the course of the battle in France, the French government grew increasingly anxious to make an attempt to buy continued Italian non-belligerence by offering concessions in the Mediterranean area. The French might be able to offer territorial concessions, or joint control in Tunisia; but when Mussolini talked about being a prisoner in his own sea, it was the British bases at Gibraltar, Malta, and Suez to which he mainly referred. For the French to make an effective approach to Italy, therefore, it was necessary to persuade Britain to join them, and to offer Mussolini something substantial from the British Mediterranean possessions. This was unlikely to be welcome to Churchill, who was averse to yielding up any British territory. On 16 May Churchill had already appealed to Mussolini, in very general terms and with no hint of concessions, to abstain from entering the war; the reply had been uncompromising, and Churchill was unwilling to go any further,[32] but in their desperate plight the French pressed for further approaches to be made. One such was made through President Roosevelt of the USA, who agreed to tell Mussolini that the Allies would welcome his participation in the final peace conference, and to ask him to set out Italian claims in the Mediterranean; these terms would be the *quid pro quo* for an Italian undertaking to stay out of the war. The President put this proposition to Mussolini on 26 May, but it was turned down on the 27th.[33] Meanwhile, the French also wished to make a direct approach to Italy, and at the *Comité de Guerre* on 25 May there was general agreement that Reynaud should ask the British what sacrifices they were willing to make to keep Italy out of the war.[34]

This was the position when Reynaud came to London on 26 May. The British Cabinet met before his arrival, when Churchill emphasised to his colleagues the likelihood of a French withdrawal from the war, and it was against this dark background that Halifax introduced the matter of Italy. In the war as a whole, he said that the question was now not so much one of imposing a complete defeat on Germany, but of safeguarding the independence of the British Empire, and if possible that of France. At an interview the previous evening, 25 May, the Italian Ambassador (Bastianini) had made tentative enquiries as to whether the British government would agree to a conference — which by inference would have included Germany and France as well as Britain and Italy. He had maintained that Mussolini's chief wish was to secure peace in Europe, and Halifax replied that peace and security in Europe were also Britain's main object, and the government would consider any proposals which might lead to this, provided British liberty and independence were assured. France had been informed of this approach. Churchill commented that 'peace and security might be achieved under a German domination of Europe. That we could never accept'. He was opposed to any negotiations which might lead to a derogation of British rights and power. Chamberlain enquired as to whether it

39

would be possible to ask the French if Italy could be bought off, which might keep matters going for a time. Churchill agreed that this was worth bearing in mind.[35]

There the matter rested until the Prime Minister reported to the Cabinet at 2 p.m. on 26 May, after his first conversation with Reynaud. Reynaud had made a strong case for an approach to Italy as the only move open, and had said Italy would probably ask for the neutralising of Gibraltar and the Suez Canal, the demilitarising of Malta, and a change in the status of Tunisia. The offer of such terms might keep Italy out of the war. Churchill had told the French Premier that Britain would not give in on any account, and had generally tried to stiffen his resolution. In discussion, Halifax declared himself in favour of approaching Italy, on the assumption that Mussolini would not want Germany to dominate Europe, and would wish to persuade Hitler to take a reasonable attitude. While doubting whether anything would come of such a move, Churchill agreed that the War Cabinet would have to consider the matter.[36]

After this, Halifax went to see Reynaud, who again put forward his ideas for an approach to Italy, which Halifax summarised in a memorandum for the Cabinet. First, Reynaud proposed that Britain and France should explain to Mussolini the danger of his position if Germany dominated Europe. Second, they should state that they would fight to the end for their independence, with the ultimate help of the USA. Third, if Mussolini would co-operate in obtaining a settlement of all European questions which would safeguard the independence and security of Britain and France and form a basis for a just and durable peace in Europe, the Allies would discuss with him the matters in which he was primarily interested, and try to find solutions. Finally, they should ask Mussolini to state secretly the Mediterranean questions which he would like to see settled. The most far-reaching of these suggestions was the third, since a general European settlement would clearly involve Germany.[37]

After Reynaud left London, an informal meeting of the five members of the War Cabinet was held.[38] Churchill said that Britain was in a different position from France, because she still had powers of resistance and attack, and also because Germany would offer better terms to France than to Britain. 'If France could not defend herself, it was better that she should get out of the war rather than that she should drag us into a settlement which involved intolerable terms. There was no limit to the terms which Germany would impose upon us if she had her way'. He hoped the French would hold on, but at the same time the British must avoid being forced into a weak position by going to Mussolini and requesting him to ask Hitler to treat Britain nicely. Halifax said he did not disagree with this, but attached more importance than Churchill to letting the French (as he put it) try out the possibilities of the European equilibrium. He could see no harm in an approach on the lines that Britain would not for a moment consider terms which affected her independence, but that if Mussolini was alarmed at Hitler's power and willing to think in terms of the European balance, she might consider Italian terms.

Chamberlain was opposed to the idea of offering Mussolini a deal on specific places in return for staying out of the war, but would accept a general approach: 'If Signor Mussolini was prepared to collaborate with us in getting tolerable terms, then we would be prepared to discuss Italian terms with him'. At this point Churchill stated that it would be best to decide nothing until they saw how much of the BEF could be saved from France. Halifax explained to his colleagues how far the government had already gone towards Italy, and expounded the approach which had been made through Roosevelt, giving an account of a meeting which he himself had had with Bastianini earlier in the afternoon of 26 May. He had told the Italian Ambassador that if Britain could propose a discussion of outstanding problems with Italy without fear of a rebuff, she would be willing to take the matter further. Moreover, Halifax had said that the British 'would never be unwilling to consider any proposal made with authority that gave promise of a secure and peaceful Europe'. Churchill commented that the suggested approach to Mussolini implied that if Britain were prepared to return Germany's colonies and make concessions in the Mediterranean, she could get out of her difficulties. He thought no such option was open: or instance, the terms offered would certainly prevent Britain from completing rearmament. Halifax replied that in this case they would be refused.

Churchill considered that Hitler now thought he had the whip hand, and that the only thing to do was to show him that he could not conquer Britain. If France could not continue the war, then Britain must part company with her. Still, he said finally, he would not object to some approach to Mussolini. Greenwood thought that Mussolini would ask for Malta, Gibraltar, and Suez; he was sure the negotiations would break down, but that Hitler would know of them, and British prestige would consequently be damaged. Halifax's final contribution was that 'if we got to the point of discussing the terms of a general settlement and found that we could obtain terms which did not postulate the destruction of our independence, we should be foolish if we did not accept them'. The ministers agreed to consider the matter again next day, when Sinclair, leader of the Liberal party, should be invited.[39]

This discussion raised broad issues, and it was clearly possible that an approach to Mussolini might lead beyond the simple purchase of continued Italian non-belligerence to consideration of a general settlement with Germany. The next day the five members of the War Cabinet, together with Sinclair, continued the talks. Chamberlain argued that while an approach to Mussolini would be ineffective, the French were already blaming the British for the defeat in Flanders, and it would be unfortunate if they were also able to claim that we had denied them even the chance of negotiating with Italy. Sinclair was sure that an approach to Italy would be futile, for Britain was in a tight corner, and any sign of weakness would encourage the Germans and Italians and also undermine morale at home. Attlee too held that 'the suggested approach would be of no practical effect and would be very damaging to us. In effect, the approach suggested would inevitably lead to our asking Signor Mussolini to intercede to obtain peace terms for us'. Even if we persuaded Mussolini to stay out of the war, this would make little material difference to the French position. He was supported by Greenwood: 'If it got out that we had sued for terms at the cost of ceding British territory, the consequences would be terrible'. Churchill spoke in the same vein. He said he was increasingly oppressed by the futility of the suggested approach, which Mussolini would treat with contempt, and which would 'ruin the integrity of our fighting position in this country'. He doubted whether the French were as ready to give in as Reynaud had said, and 'Anyway, let us not be dragged down with the French'. The best way to help Reynaud was to show him that, whatever happened to France, Britain would fight it out to the end. Even if Britain were beaten, she would be no worse off than if she now abandoned the struggle. 'Let us therefore avoid being dragged down the slippery slope with France. The whole of this manoeuvre was intended to get us so deeply involved in negotiations that we should be unable to turn back'.

Chamberlain agreed that the proposed approach would serve no useful purpose, but he still wished to avoid offending the French by turning the suggestion down outright. He suggested using delaying tactics by referring to Roosevelt's initiative, which should not be interfered with at this stage. There was general agreement that a reply should be sent to Reynaud on these lines, but Halifax again launched the discussion into deeper waters. There were, he said 'certain rather profound differences of points of view which he would like to make clear'. First, he thought it would be valuable to persuade the French to say that they would fight to the end for their independence (a phrase included in Reynaud's suggestions for approaching Italy). Second, he 'could not recognise any resemblance between the action which he proposed, and the suggestion that we were suing for terms and following a line which would lead us to disaster'. His own view was that he would be willing to fight to the finish if British independence was at stake, 'but if it was not at stake he would think it right to accept an offer which would save the country from avoidable disaster'. Churchill replied that the issue before them was difficult enough in itself, without their getting involved in 'an issue which was quite unreal and was most unlikely to arise. If Herr Hitler was prepared to make peace on the terms of the restoration of German colonies and the overlordship of Central Europe, that was one thing. But it was quite unlikely that he would make any such offer'. Halifax pursued his course: suppose, he said, that the French army collapsed, and Hitler offered peace terms, to which the French replied that they could not treat alone, but only with their allies; and suppose that Hitler then offered terms to both France and Britain, would Churchill be prepared to discuss them? The Prime Minister replied that: 'he would not join France in asking for terms; but if he were told what the terms offered were, he would be prepared to consider them'. Chamberlain thought that Hitler's tactics would be different: he was likely to make a definite offer to France, and then when the French said that they had allies, he would say: 'I am here, let them send a delegate to Paris'. It was the recorded opinion of the War Cabinet that 'the answer to such an offer could only be "No"'.

After this, Greenwood brought the Cabinet back to the question more immediately before them, which was whether the proposed approach to Mussolini would stave off a French capitulation.

Halifax said he thought it would not have any material effect, but he did not wish to send the French a flat refusal. This led to a decision to send a temporising reply, on the lines earlier suggested by Chamberlain, referring to Roosevelt's current approach to Mussolini.[40]

In his diary Halifax wrote a note on this meeting which made the difference between Churchill and himself appear even sharper. 'At the 4.30 Cabinet we had a long and rather confused discussion about, nominally, the approach to Italy, but also largely about general policy in the event of things going really badly in France. I thought Winston talked the most frightful rot, also Greenwood, and after bearing it for some time I said exactly what I thought of them, adding that if that was really their view, and if it came to the point, our ways must separate. Winston, surprised and mellowed, and when I repeated the same thing in the garden, was full of apologies and affection. But it does drive me to despair when he works himself up into a passion of emotion when he ought to make his brain think and reason'.[41] Halifax told Cadogan that same afternoon: 'I can't work with Winston any longer', to which Cadogan replied: 'Nonsense: his rhodomontades probably bore you as much as they do me, but don't do anything silly under the stress of that'.[42] Halifax thus momentarily saw the difference of attitude as a matter for resignation.

The whole Cabinet discussion was indeed crucial, and there were three separate points at issue. First, there was the question of whether the direct approach to Mussolini proposed by the French, with or without the mention of specific territorial concessions, would be worthwhile in itself. There was general agreement that it would not — that not even an offer of named places would keep Mussolini out of the war, and that in any case Italian intervention would make little difference to the battle in France. Second, there was the question whether such an approach, even if not worthwhile in itself, was yet worth pursuing in order to placate the French. Here too there was general agreement: the Cabinet did not wish to go far in this direction, but they did prefer to avoid presenting a blank refusal to the French proposal. There was a general welcome for Chamberlain's suggestion for a temporising manoeuvre. Third, there was the question of whether an approach to Mussolini should be considered, not on the narrow grounds of keeping Italy out of the war or pleasing the French, but on the wider grounds that there was a chance of Italian mediation and an opportunity to find out whether Germany would offer acceptable peace terms. To this, Churchill, Attlee, Greenwood and Sinclair were all opposed, arguing that such a course was too dangerous to embark upon and would be destructive of British morale. Halifax, on the other hand, was in favour of pursuing this enquiry in order to find out what the situation was, even though he recognised that German terms would almost certainly affect British independence, and therefore be unacceptable. The divergence of views between Halifax and Churchill on this issue was exacerbated by what Halifax considered to be Churchill's emotional approach to a question demanding the use of reason. However, the arguments put by Churchill (and Halifax's other opponents) do not, at least in the Cabinet record, appear unduly emotional; it was a rational argument to say that one could not embark on a negotiation, or even an enquiry, and then simply withdraw at will and return to a position of defiance. It is also questionable whether Halifax was right in thinking an emotional approach out of place. An interesting commentary may be found in Cadogan's diary, where on 27 May he wrote disparagingly about Churchill's rhodomontades, yet on 2 June he was himself misquoting Shakespeare: 'I'd really sooner cut loose [from France] and concentrate on defence of these islands — come the four quarters of the world in arms!'. On 15 June he was back again with *King John*: Everything *awful,* but "Come the three corners of the world and we will shock them" '.[43] Was this rhodomontade? Or perhaps the truth was that the situation was dramatic, and called forth dramatic language; and that emotion may have been as good a guide as reason.

The long Cabinet discussion on 27 May opened up all these matters, but closed none of them. In the afternoon of 28 May the whole ground was covered again, because a further message had been received from the French government asking the Cabinet to re-examine the question of an approach to Italy. By this time it was known that Mussolini had completely rejected the approach made by Roosevelt. The same six ministers were present, and the discussion closely followed the lines of the two previous days. Halifax reported that Sir Robert Vansittart (formerly Permanent Under-Secretary at the Foreign Office, now acting in the ill-defined capacity of diplomatic adviser to the government) had discovered that the Italian Embassy had it in mind that Britain 'should give a clear indication that we should like to see mediation by Italy'. Churchill said it was clear that the French purpose was to see Mussolini acting as mediator between the British and Hitler: 'He [Churchill] was determined not to get into this position'. He reverted to this more than once, emphasising his belief that 'M. Reynaud's aim was to end the war'. Chamberlain stated that mediation at this stage could only be most unfortunate, and that if Britain held out she would later be able to 'obtain terms which did not affect our independence'. Attlee repeated the view that if the French proposal was followed, it might be impossible to rally the morale of the British people, and Greenwood said that 'so far as the industrial centres of the country were concerned, they would regard anything like weakening on the part of the government as a disaster'.

Halifax continued to maintain that if Mussolini wished to act as mediator, and could produce terms which did not affect British independence, the Cabinet ought to consider them. He agreed this was most unlikely; but added that 'we might get better terms before France went out of the war and our aircraft factories were bombed, than we might get in three months' time'. He still did not see what Churchill found so wrong in the French suggestion of trying out the possibilities of mediation; and in reply to a remark by Greenwood, he said that nothing he had proposed 'could even remotely be described as ultimate capitulation'.

The meeting adjourned at 6.15 p.m., and reassembled at 7 p.m. to consider a final draft of the reply to Reynaud. In the intervening three-quarters of an hour, Churchill had a meeting with all ministers who were of Cabinet rank but not members of the War Cabinet. In his memoirs, he wrote that at this meeting he said, 'quite casually, and not treating it as a point of special significance: "Of course, whatever happens at Dunkirk, we shall fight on" '. He received a marked demonstration of support. Dalton, who was present, wrote in his diary that Churchill had told them that 'It was idle to think that, if we tried to make peace now, we should get better terms from Germany than if we went on and fought it out . . . We should become a slave state, though a British Government which would be Hitler's puppet would be set up — under Mosley or some such person'. Britain would fight it out. Dalton recorded: 'Not much more was said. No-one expressed even the faintest flicker of dissent'.[44]

Is it too much to construe Churchill's remark about the futility of thinking that Britain would get better terms by immediate negotiations as a counter to Halifax's statement in the War Cabinet that she *might* get better terms? Or to think that the Prime Minister's remarks were in no way casual, but were designed for a specific purpose — to make sure of his support outside the War Cabinet? At any rate, when Churchill went back to the resumed meeting of the War Cabinet at 7 p.m., he told his colleagues that the ministers. outside the War Cabinet 'had expressed the greatest satisfaction when he had told them that there was no chance of our giving up the struggle. He did not remember having ever before heard a gathering of persons occupying high places in political life express themselves so emphatically'. However, there was at this point no further discussion. Halifax and Chamberlain had completed a draft reply to Reynaud with which Churchill was entirely satisfied, and which was indeed based on his own earlier draft. This reply pointed out that since Reynaud's visit to London on 26 May the situation had worsened through the capitulation of the Belgian army, which made it more unlikely than before that Germany would offer acceptable terms; that offers once made to Mussolini could not be withdrawn, and his reply to Roosevelt's approach had been wholly negative; and that therefore, 'without excluding the possibility of an approach to Signor Mussolini at some time, we cannot feel that this would be the right moment . . .' It added that the effect on British morale, now resolute, would be extremely dangerous. The situation could only be improved by showing that 'we still have stout hearts and confidence in ourselves . . . if we both stand out we may yet save ourselves from the fate of Denmark or Poland . . .'[45]

When Harvey, at the Embassy in Paris, read this telegram to Reynaud, he agreed that it was best to turn down the appeal for a further approach to Mussolini, but added in his diary: 'I am slightly worried however by text of telegram which seems to envisage possibility of Musso mediating at a later date. It looks as if Halifax may have evolved some scheme for mediation by Italy on an offer of terms to Italy. Incredible though it sounds, I cannot put it past him. It would be fatal'. On 2 June he heard from a Foreign Office official visiting Paris that 'Halifax, as I suspected, had been anxiously exploring possibility of peace proposals *à la* Lansdowne, but P.M. had flatly turned them down'.[46] Nothing could show more clearly the significance of what had transpired in the War Cabinet. If

47

Harvey could read between the lines of a strongly-worded telegram and divine what had lain behind it, it is easy to see where an actual decision to approach Mussolini would have led.

In the event, nothing came of all this. After receiving the British reply, the French government decided to go ahead alone with an approach to Mussolini, though without making any precise offers. They did so on 31 May, only to have their overtures summarily rejected on 2 June. The British were informed of this attempt, and did not try to prevent it, but declined to be associated with it.[47]

However, although nothing eventually happened, the War Cabinet discussions of 26, 27 and 28 May 1940 marked a decisive point in British history, and by implication in the history of Europe. There can be no doubt that if the War Cabinet had agreed to the French proposal, and approached Mussolini with a view to mediation, they could not have gone back on that decision. Once the possibility of negotiation had been opened, it could not have been closed, and the government could not have continued to lead the country in outright defiance of German power. That the importance of the discussions was understood at the time is shown by the exceptional procedure of confining them to the five members of the War Cabinet itself, with the addition only of Sinclair in his capacity as leader of the Liberal party.

If the British government was not to try for mediation or peace, it had to consider how to continue the war without France. In fact, this consideration was concurrent with the discussions which have just been described. It has already been noted that when Churchill returned from Paris on 17 May he asked Chamberlain and a small committee to examine the situation which would arise if the French government withdrew from Paris. The report of that committee on 18 May envisaged the continuance of the war by Britain single-handed until the USA came to her help. She would have to abandon existing methods, and resort to 'a form of government which would approach the totalitarian'. It would be necessary for the government to assume complete control over property, business and labour; and the broad outline of such a scheme was set out by the committee. It was emphasised that public support would be vital, since it would be impossible to impose such measures in the face of strong opposition. The presentation of the measures to the public would therefore be a matter of crucial importance, and one demanding very fine judgement. On the one hand, the British people would have to be convinced of the necessity for the measures; on the other hand it would be disastrous for the morale of the French if they were to suspect that Britain was preparing for their collapse. In addition to these general considerations, the committee listed a number of specific matters which should be dealt with in the event of a French collapse, including the removal from France of gold, machine tools, arms and equipment; the sailing of warships and merchant ships from French ports; the destruction of ships on the stocks; and the blocking of harbours.[48]

Chamberlain's proposals dealt mainly with the reorganisation of government and resources to meet the crisis of the fall of France, but it was also necessary to re-assess the whole of British strategy, which until May 1940 had been based on the Franco-British alliance. On 25 May the Chiefs of Staff presented to the Cabinet a long paper on 'British strategy in a certain eventuality', which commenced: 'The object of this paper is to investigate the means whereby we could continue to fight single-handed if French resistance were to collapse completely, involving the loss of a substantial proportion of the British Expeditionary Force, and the French Government were to make peace with Germany'. They thus began with one pessimistic assumption which was quickly belied — the men of the BEF, though not their equipment, were saved. Other assumptions of the paper were also pessimistic, and not all fulfilled: that all French territory, including North Africa, would be accessible to the enemy; that Italy would enter the war; that Spain, Portugal, and the Balkans (except Turkey) would fall under enemy control. On the credit side, the Chiefs of Staff assumed that Britain could count on the economic and financial support of the USA, which might be extended to active participation in the war; and also that the Soviet Union (then linked to Germany by the Nazi-Soviet pact) would be alarmed by the rapid growth of German power. They emphasised that American co-operation was essential if the war was to be won, and this became the key to much of British policy and strategy.

Working on these assumptions, the report asked first whether Britain could hold out until help came from the USA, the Dominions and Empire; and secondly whether, having held out, she could defeat Germany. The Chiefs of Staff concluded that it would

49

be possible to hold out, provided air superiority could be maintained, and stated in a summary document presented on 26 May: 'While our Air Force is in being, our Navy and Air Force together should be able to prevent Germany carrying out a serious sea-borne invasion of this country'. If Germany gained complete air superiority, it was felt that the Navy could hold off invasion for a time, but not indefinitely; and if German forces gained a firm footing ashore, British land forces would not be sufficient to repulse them. 'The crux of the matter is air superiority'.[49]

On the second question, as to whether Germany could ultimately be defeated, the Chiefs of Staff envisaged that this might be achieved by a combination of economic pressure, air attack, and subversive action designed to create revolt in occupied countries. They considered that economic pressure would be the vital factor, since even control of western Europe and parts of North Africa would not give the Germans all the resources they needed; they would be short of a number of materials (notably rubber, tin, nickel and cobalt); short of food; and in time, short of oil. In general, this section of the report was inevitably speculative, and somewhat over-optimistic. The immediate problem was how to get through the next few months, with the Germans across the Channel and no effective allies. On this, the Chiefs of Staff offered a reasoned case for hope, and indeed their views were vindicated by events: air superiority was the crux, and air superiority was maintained, though by a narrow margin.[50]

On 27 May the Cabinet gave its general approval to this report by the Chiefs of Staff, although — as on other occasions — Churchill did not give it a wholly easy passage. He thought the estimates of British and German air strength were unduly pessimistic, and also argued that France might not collapse completely, but become neutral, with some northern ports remaining outside German occupation. However, the Cabinet accepted the report. Attlee commented belligerently that there was no reason to regard the German tanks as invincible — any landing force must be counter-attacked and destroyed at once.[51] Coming at the same time as the discussions regarding an approach to Italy (though in a separate meeting), the determined mood of the Cabinet was significant.

It was thus agreed that Britain had a fighting chance of survival if France fell, and there was a vague prospect of ultimate victory, largely depending on the increasingly active co-operation of the United States. The framework of a new British strategy for continuing the war alone was outlined, but there remained the immediate, and often very detailed, problems of what could be saved materially from a French collapse. On this, a good deal of the planning and preparation done was overtaken by the speed of events in France and was therefore unproductive. The process of detailed planning was set in motion by Hankey, who had been a member of Chamberlain's committee, and who wrote to Halifax on 27 May a letter 'too secret to entrust to any typist'. He thought that if the French insisted on making a separate peace, they should only be released from their obligation not to do so on certain conditions including the following: the entire French fleet and merchant marine should go to British ports; any remnant of the French air force which the Chief of the Air Staff could utilise, and any volunteers, should come to Britain; the French should hand over large quantities of weapons, with their ammunition; Britain should also obtain machinery for manufacturing French types of ammunition, together with any machine tools which the Ministry of Supply thought valuable, and skilled workmen to use them; the French should be asked to destroy a large part of their oil stocks, believed to amount to 3,600,000 tons; the British should arrange to inherit French orders for aircraft and other supplies in the USA; and some attempt should be made to secure the French gold reserves. All this, Hankey argued, must be done before the French entered into negotiation with the Germans.[52]

Halifax passed this letter to some of his officials, who noted the difficulties involved in Hankey's programme. Strang doubted whether the French would agree to the transfer of all the assets listed by Hankey, because by doing so they would provoke the Germans into making their terms more severe. Cadogan noted: 'We can't ask the French to do this before the event. It would sap the rest of their morale'.[53] The problem was put to Campbell in Paris on 3 June, in a letter from Cadogan which reached the ambassador just as he was completing his long despatch on the likely course of events in France. Campbell went through the list, not very hopefully. By the time collapse became imminent, the air force would have virtually ceased to exist, and military material would be scarcely recoverable. Eighty per cent of French industry would already be in German hands, with its machine tools and skilled workers unless they were

51

08202

MENDOCINO COLLEGE LIBRARY

evacuated. He could see no difficulty about material ordered from the USA; thought the French must be made to destroy oil stocks as they retreated; and would make enquiries about the gold. The ambassador thought the French fleet was much the most important item in the list. 'It is hardly conceivable', he wrote, 'that any armistice terms would not include its surrender. If the French *were* to let us down, they would presumably go the whole hog'.[54]

In London, there were various meetings between 8 and 12 June on the points raised by Hankey. Admiral Pound, the First Sea Lord, thought the surrender of the French fleet would be so humiliating a demand that any naval commander would do his best to avoid it. The most the British could hope for was that the fleet would be sent to the bottom rather than surrender — once sunk, there would be nothing the Germans could do about it. In the last resort, he thought, 'if the French would not sink their fleet, we could perhaps do it for them'.[55] The other matters were also discussed at length between Hankey and representatives of the ministries concerned — Aircraft Production, Admiralty, Supply, Labour, Economic Warfare, the Home Office.[56] Most of this proved to be in vain, because events in France moved so quickly and became increasingly outside British control. However, there was at least something prepared when, on the morning of 11 June, Churchill asked at short notice for a memorandum on the considerations which would arise if French resistance collapsed. Cadogan and Hankey, using the material already collected, were able to write a paper and give it to the Prime Minister before the morning was out,[57] and Churchill took it with him when he flew to France that afternoon. This visit marked the end of one phase in British relations with France and the beginning of another. Despite all the uncertainty about the future, the Prime Minister could at least travel in the confident knowledge that the British course of action 'in a certain eventuality' had been thoroughly explored.

NOTES

1. CAB 65/7, WM(40)141.
2. CAB 66/7, WP(40)168, 25 May 1940.
3. CAB 65/13, WM(40)120th Conclusions, Confidential Annex.
4. CAB 100/3, Cabinet War Room Interim Report, up to 1800 hrs, 14 May 1940.

5.   CAB 65/7, WM(40)123; Churchill, 36-9; Reynaud, vol. II, 93-4.
6.   CAB 65/7, WM(40)124; *Cadogan Diaries,* 16 May 1940, 284.
7.   Churchill, 39.
8.   CAB 65/7, WM(40)126; *Cadogan Diaries,* 17 May 1940, 285.
9.   CAB 65/13, WM(40)128th Conclusions, Confidential Annex; *Cadogan Diaries,* 17 May 1940, 285; Churchill, 48.
10. See below, 48-9.
11. CAB 79/4, COS Committee minutes, 19 May 1940.
12. CAB 100/3, Cabinet War Room Daily Record, No. 262, 0700 hrs 21 May-0700 hrs 22 May 1940.
13. CAB 21/1183, Redman to Ismay, 18 May 1940; CAB 65/7, WM(40)132.
14. See above, 15.
15. Dalton diary, 21 May 1940.
16. CAB 65/13, WM(40)139th Conclusions, Confidential Annex; this meeting was held at 9 a.m. on 26 May.
17. P. Dhers, 'Le Comité de Guerre dù 25 mai 1940', *Revue d'Histoire de la deuxième Guerre mondiale,* May-July 1953, 129-35.
18. *Cadogan Diaries,* 26 May 1940, 290.
19. CAB 65/13, WM(40)140th Conclusions, Confidential Annex.
20. Dalton diary, 28 May 1940.
21. FO 800/312, H/XIV/437, Campbell to Halifax, 27 May 1940.
22. CAB 21/1282, Spears to Ismay, 27 May 1940.
23. FO 800/312, H/XIV/439, Campbell to Halifax, 30 May 1940.
24. FO 371/24383, C7074/5/18, Campbell to Halifax, 4 June 1940; also C7121/5/18, with important minutes.
25. FO 371/24383, C7074/5/18, Campbell to Cadogan, 5 June 1940. Cadogan showed the letter to Halifax, who discussed it with Churchill.
26. FO 800/312, H/XIV/444, Campbell to Halifax, 7 June 1940.
27. CAB 21/1183, Redman to Ismay, 7 and 10 June 1940.
28. FO 271/24383, C7121/5/18, Campbell to Halifax, 8 June 1940.
29. CAB 65/7, WM(40)159, 9 June 1940.
30. *Harvey Diaries,* 9 June 1940, 383.
31. CAB 65/7, WM(40)163; cf. Churchill, 142. For the events of the meeting, see below, 59-62.
32. Churchill, 107-8.
33. E. L. Woodward, *British Foreign Policy in the Second World War,* vol. I (London 1970), 234-5.

34. Dhers, 129-35; Reynaud, vol. II, 200.
35. CAB 65/13, WM(40)139th Conclusions, Confidential Annex.
36. CAB 65/13, WM(40)140th Conclusions, Confidential Annex.
37. CAB 66/7, WP(40)170.
38. The five ministers who were formally members of the War Cabinet were: Churchill, Attlee, Chamberlain, Greenwood, and Halifax. It was highly unusual for these to meet without the presence of other ministers and senior officers. The Secretary to the Cabinet was present at this informal meeting after the first fifteen minutes.
39. CAB 65/13, WM(40)140th Conclusions, Confidential Annex and attached papers.
40. CAB 65/13, WM(40)142nd Conclusions, Confidential Annex.
41. Lord Birkenhead, *Halifax* (London 1965), 458.
42. *Cadogan Diaries,* 27 May 1940, 291.
43. *Cadogan Diaries,* 2, 15 June 1940, 293, 299.
44. Churchill, 88; Dalton diary, 28 May 1940.
45. CAB 65/13, WM(40)145th Conclusions, Confidential Annex.
46. *Harvey Diaries,* 29 May, 2 June 1940, 372, 377. Lord Lansdowne had advocated a compromise peace with Germany in 1916 and 1917.
47. Woodward, vol. I, 239-40; Cairns, 381-2.
48. CAB 65/13, WM(40)128th Conclusions, Confidential Annex, including the report of Chamberlain's committee, the members of which were: Attlee, Halifax, Anderson (Home Secretary), and Hankey (Chancellor of the Duchy of Lancaster).
49. CAB 66/7, WP(40)169, 26 May 1940; Churchill, 78-9.
50. CAB 66/7, WP(40)168, 25 May 1940; cf. J. R. M. Butler, *Grand Strategy,* vol. II, September 1939-June 1941 (London 1957), 209-17.
51. CAB 65/13, WM(40)141st Conclusions, Confidential Annex.
52. FO 371/24383, C7074/5/18, Hankey to Halifax, 27 May 1940.
53. *Ibid.,* minutes by Strang and Cadogan, 30 May 1940.
54. *Ibid.,* Cadogan to Campbell, 3 June 1940; Campbell to Cadogan, 4 June 1940.
55. *Ibid.,* Cadogan to Campbell, 8 June 1940.
56. *Ibid.,* records of meetings between Hankey and others, 10, 11 and 12 June 1940.
57. *Ibid.,* minutes by Churchill and Cadogan, 11 June 1940.

Chapter 4

PRELUDE TO ARMISTICE

By 11 June, the French attempt to hold the German armies on a line along the rivers Somme and Aisne had failed. On the evening of 12 June, at a meeting of the French Cabinet at the Château de Cangé, near Tours, Weygand told ministers that the co-ordinated defence of the country was at an end; the only way to prevent the break-up of the armies, with consequent demoralisation and civil disorder, was to seek an armistice, which he therefore asked the government to do.[1] In later years, Weygand was sharply criticised by some Frenchmen for defeatism, and for stepping outside his proper province as a soldier in offering political advice. Whatever the judgement on the second of these counts, there can be no doubt that his military assessment was accurate, and the French government was faced with complete military defeat.

They had two possible courses of action before them: to ask for an armistice; or to leave France and continue the war from North Africa. (That they should go to London does not appear to have been seriously considered.) These alternatives had been under discussion for some time. The possibility of an armistice was entered into at the *Comité de Guerre* on 25 May, and it was also the subject of conversations between individual ministers. The idea of continuing the war from North Africa was first mentioned by Reynaud to his staff on 16 May; and on 29 May he wrote of continuing the struggle from Brittany while sending the fleet and air force to North Africa. He also proposed to call up two classes of conscripts and send them to North Africa.[2]

Within the French government, the most important advocates of an armistice were Weygand and Pétain. When Weygand replaced Gamelin, much was made of his high military reputation as Foch's right-hand man; moreover, he had been appointed Commander-in-Chief as recently as 19-20 May. For a Prime Minister to dismiss a Commander-in-Chief is a serious matter at any time, but for Reynaud to dismiss Weygand, whom he had appointed with such a flourish so recently, was virtually impossible. Weygand was therefore in a very strong position, and that of Pétain was even stronger. The latter had been brought into the government by Reynaud on 18 May, in the honorary post of Vice-Premier and Minister of State, to lend the government the prestige of his great name. Moreover, he retained the highest reputation from his record in the 1914-18 war; not only was he the victor of Verdun, and thus the embodiment of French resolution, but also the doctor who had cured the fever which broke out in the French army during the mutinies of 1917, the firm but sympathetic father of his soldiers. In a country where the President of the Republic counted for little, especially in the colourless person of Albert Lebrun (who held the post in 1940), and where ministers came and went, changing and yet always the same, Pétain represented stability. He was soon to achieve the aura of a monarch, or a saviour. In the disaster of 1940, he was to emerge for many as the father of his people, his courage attested by past service, his integrity undoubted, his affection for the soil of France striking a chord in what was still to a large degree a nation of peasants.

Chief among the reasons which led Pétain and Weygand to advocate an armistice was the belief that not only the battle of France but the entire war was lost. Resistance in North Africa was impossible, and to attempt it would only worsen the situation in France itself. It was also thought impossible for Britain to continue the war alone — her fate had been decided on the battlefield of France, and her defeat or (more likely) surrender would not be long delayed. Given this basic assumption, a number of other reasons came into play. First, any hesitation in asking for an armistice meant a useless sacrifice of French lives. Second, it was important to secure an armistice while there were still enough disciplined units to maintain order in France and avert revolution or anarchy. Third, Pétain certainly, and Weygand probably, were convinced that Britain would make peace after only a token resistance, having first sacrificed France: it was therefore both necessary and right that

France should move first and prevent Britain from reaping the benefits of taking the initiative in peace negotiations. Fourth, they were both determined not to leave the soil of France, which in their soldierly code would amount to desertion in the face of the enemy. Finally, there was the wish to rebuild, even recreate France, and to save her from what they saw as the political and spiritual morass of the Third Republic; in this context, defeat could be almost welcomed as the refiner's fire to purify the soul of France.[3]

These views gained the support of an increasing number of ministers as the time went by, but they did not have a clear majority in Reynaud's Cabinet even by 16 June, when Reynaud finally resigned.[4] The most prominent ministers in the other camp, who advocated going to North Africa to continue the war, were Reynaud himself and Mandel, who became Minister of the Interior on 18 May. Of the two, Mandel was the tougher and more ruthless. He was a Jew, which may have intensified his opposition to Nazi Germany, and also rendered his motives and loyalties suspect in some quarters. Reynaud, weakened by his lack of support in the country and in political circles, was tense and nervy, liable to swing from depression to elation and back again. In the last days of his government he was extremely tired, trying to keep a grip on events through a scattered and shifting administration, with ministers who, having lost their departments, had little to do except talk. Nonetheless, Reynaud sustained a running argument against his opponents, refuting their basic premise and holding that the war was not lost, but could be carried on by the French fleet and empire, in alliance with the British who would certainly fight on. He denied that it was possible to come to terms with Nazi Germany as one might have done with the Kaiser, sitting round a table and discussing a treaty. This was an illusion: life was not like that any more — 'Hitler is Ghengis Khan', Reynaud declared. Moreover, it was not in France's own best interests to separate herself from Britain and the USA: 'it is impossible to conceive the future of France without the friendship and support of the Anglo-Saxon world'.[5] Seen from this point of view, resistance was not a useless sacrifice of lives; and even when the army ceased to be capable of resistance, there was an alternative to an armistice in following the example of the Dutch, who had ordered a military capitulation which did not involve the government in negotiation.

It was with a French government thus divided that the British government had to deal in the last days before the French request for an armistice. The background to British relations with France was the bitter and confused debate which went on within the French government; and it was the outcome of this debate, rather than British policy, which determined the course of those relations.

From 10 June onwards, the British Embassy in France worked under acute difficulties. They left Paris about 9 p.m. on 10 June, and made a slow journey along roads thronged with refugees to Tours, where they arrived about 3 a.m. on the 11th. It then took another hour to find the Château de Champs-Chevrier, where the Embassy was to be housed. There followed a strange interlude, with a touch of the idyllic about it amid the havoc of defeat. Harvey described their stay in this 'charming 16th century château with a moat. We are entertained by the Baroness de Champs-Chevrier in person who wears a black dress, and white band round her throat and white tennis shoes . . . Lovely park and woods all around. We are like a little camp with our lorries, our wireless and R.A.F. and R.E. personnel'.[6] Despite the presence of wireless personnel, telegrams were sent and received through the telegraph office at Tours, where Campbell found some three hundred incoming telegrams piled up which the French Foreign Ministry cypher clerks, who had been travelling all night, were too weary to tackle.[7]

When the Embassy moved with the French government to Bordeaux, on 13-14 June, their communications problem was eased, and for some days they were able to telephone London again. But at first they worked from the British Consulate at Bordeaux, squeezed into three rooms, with stairs and passages full of refugees wanting to get out of the country. Hours were spent searching for people they wanted to see: 'Greatest confusion in Bordeaux, nobody knows where anybody is or the way anywhere. We spend hours driving up and down, losing our way and finding nobody to guide us — a nightmare'. (This was Harvey writing in his diary.) Campbell, in his final despatch, confined himself to remarking that the conditions 'constituted a serious handicap to our activities'.[8]

The course of British policy towards France between 11 and 16 June may be divided into three phases. First, between the 11th and 13th, there were Churchill's two visits to France and conferences with Reynaud. Then, between the 13th and 15th, attention was concentrated on appeals being made to Roosevelt, in the hope that he would say something sufficiently definite about American intentions to encourage the French to continue the fight. Third, on 15 and 16 June the French asked for British permission to approach Germany for terms, and the British made varying replies. This third phase came to an end during the evening of 16 June, when Reynaud resigned and Pétain formed a government which without more ado made an approach to Germany. Throughout these three phases, the British tried to persuade France to hold on and continue the war. Their means of persuasion were mostly verbal — appeals and offers for the future — but also diplomatic in the form of approaches to the USA, and to some small degree miliary in the landing of fresh troops in France. Meanwhile, British preparations for the collapse of France and for fighting on alone continued.

Before Churchill went to France on 11 June, there had been a certain reluctance on the part of both the Prime Ministers to meet. On 10 June Churchill told the Cabinet that he had been wondering whether to go to Paris, but that if he did the French would again ask for more fighter squadrons than Britain was willing to send, and he preferred therefore to send Spears (who was on a visit to London) with a personal message for Reynaud. Later that day, Churchill changed his mind, and wished to go to Paris that evening and see Reynaud the next day. Reynaud replied that this would be difficult to arrange, since Weygand was moving his headquarters, and Reynaud himself planned to visit the battle zone the following day. Campbell thought that the visit involved some danger and was unnecessary,[9] but Churchill was now set on the idea, and a meeting was arranged for 6 p.m. on 11 June at Weygand's headquarters at the Château du Muguet, near Briare. Churchill told the Cabinet that it was necessary to concert 'a grand strategic plan' with the French; to discuss the despatch of additional British forces to France; to discourage any movement towards a separate peace; and to emphasise that Britain would hold out whatever happened.[10] This was a somewhat nebulous programme. To formulate a grand strategic plan was in the circumstances quite impossible, and does not seem to have been attempted. The despatch of additional forces to France had been fully discussed in writing, and it was hard to see what could be added except personal unpleasantness. In fact the main content of the meeting proved to be the insistence by the French that their situation was truly desperate, and exhortations to the French by Churchill.

On the subject of British help in the battle, Churchill tried to put the British effort in the best light, saying that the Canadian Division was disembarking that night, and another division would come on about 20 June. If the French could hold on until the spring of 1941, there would be twenty or twenty-five British divisions ready. This can have offered little comfort to Weygand in his appalling difficulties. On fighter aircraft, the French pressed for more squadrons to be based in France. Georges offered the view that heavy air intervention over the river Marne could yet tip the scales there, and Reynaud commented that history would say that the battle of France was lost for want of aircraft. Churchill added lack of tanks, and German numerical superiority. Neither the British nor the French changed their position on this question, though Reynaud returned to the attack when the conference resumed for a short session at 8 a.m. the next morning, 12 June. Churchill confined himself to saying that he would again put the matter to the British Cabinet, which would consider it sympathetically.

The French description of their military situation made a grim impression on Churchill and his companions — Eden, the Minister for War, and General Dill, who had replaced Ironside as CIGS. Weygand emphasised the exhaustion of the French armies, which were fighting on their last line. If this was broken — and it had already been breached in two or three places — he did not believe that co-ordinated defence of the country could be continued. He had no reserves. Churchill asked for Georges to be invited to give his own account, but this only confirmed that of Weygand. After the meeting, Churchill took Georges (an old friend) aside and asked him again if the situation was really so grave. Georges assured him that it was, but Churchill still found it hard to believe in his heart that the French army was on the verge of total defeat. As before, when he visited Paris on 16 May, it took a trip to France and a personal meeting with the French generals to bring home the gravity of the position; if the meeting served no other purpose, this was its justification. The impression made at the meeting was reinforced that evening, when Churchill dined with Reynaud, and over the brandy the French Premier told him that Pétain had made up his mind that peace must be made with the Germans; he had written a paper about this, which he had shown to Reynaud, but had not yet handed to him. Churchill told the Cabinet after he returned that Pétain was a dangerous man at this juncture — he had always been a defeatist, even in the last war, Churchill added.

The Prime Minister's main object in going to France was to exhort and encourage the French, and this he did to the best of his very considerable ability. He opened the main meeting by declaring that whatever happened Britain would fight on to the end. Urging that Paris should be defended, and should swallow up German armies in its rubble, he invoked the days of March 1918, when defeat had seemed imminent but was averted. He also proclaimed that defeat in France was not the end of the war, which would become a war of continents. In the early morning session of 12 June he returned to these efforts, putting precise questions to the French. He asked about the defence of Paris: Weygand said that Paris had already been declared an open city. He asked about counter-attacks across the lower Seine: Weygand did not believe he could hold out long enough to collect the necessary reserves. He asked whether, if co-ordinated defence broke down, the French could fight a 'war of columns' which would enable them to hold on until the USA came into the war: Weygand did not think this feasible.

Describing the visit to the Cabinet, Eden said that Churchill had had a remarkable effect on the French, lifting them from a state of despair to one of hope. It is doubtful, however, if there was much truth in this. Pétain and Weygand both thought that Churchill was willing to sacrifice France — and in particular to cast Paris into the flames — for the sake of Britain, at a time when he was not willing to throw Fighter Command into the same furnace. When Churchill talked to Pétain about 1918, the Marshal observed that in 1918 the British had had sixty divisions in the line; without troops the exhortations carried no weight. The effect on Reynaud was probably different, since there is considerable evidence that he reacted well to the impact of Churchill's personality, and was temporarily stiffened and invigorated; but, like the effect of some stimulant drug, the mood passed quickly, leaving the subject prone to further depression.

At the close of the second session of the conference, in the morning of 12 June, Churchill asked that if any serious deterioration in the situation caused the French to consider taking grave decisions, the British government should be informed at once, and given the opportunity for consultation. He said this twice, with

61

great emphasis. After the meeting, he also spoke briefly to Admiral Darlan, the Commander-in-Chief of the French navy, about the necessity for keeping the fleet out of German hands. Although Darlan assured him that he would never surrender the fleet, and in the last resort would send it to Canada, Churchill reported to the Cabinet on his return that there was always the danger that Darlan would be overruled by politicians.[11]

Churchill and Eden reported to the British Cabinet at 5 p.m. on 12 June, when Churchill emphasised that the end of organised resistance in France was near — though he still did not draw the conclusion that no more forces should be sent to France. There was little that the Cabinet could do. Eden pointed out that Reynaud would shortly face a crucial Cabinet meeting, at which he would be confronted by his opponents, and that his hand might be strengthened by some encouragement from the USA, and by a British assurance that whatever happened Britain would stand by France and do her utmost to recover France's possible losses. It was decided that Churchill should send suitable messages to Roosevelt and Reynaud.[12]

The French Cabinet met at 6.30 p.m. the same evening at the Château de Cangé, when Weygand informed them that co-ordinated resistance was at an end, and asked them to seek an armistice. Reynaud argued against this, and said that in any case the British must be consulted first. He agreed to a suggestion (apparently initiated by Dautry, the Armaments Minister, who was opposed to an armistice) that when Churchill came to France to consult with Reynaud he should be invited to meet the French Cabinet.[13]

That evening, Reynaud telephoned Churchill and asked him to return to France. He did so, and met the French Premier in the prefecture at Tours at 3.30 p.m. on 13 June. Reynaud was accompanied by Paul Baudouin, who on 5 June had been appointed Under-Secretary at the Foreign Ministry in a re-shuffle in which Reynaud became his own Foreign Minister. Churchill was accompanied by Halifax, Beaverbrook, Cadogan, and General Ismay; Campbell and Spears were also present. Reynaud opened the meeting by summarising Weygand's report of the previous evening on the military situation, and his view that it was necessary to ask for an armistice. He said that he intended to send a message to Roosevelt, telling him that the end was near in France and that the fate of the Allies lay in the hands of the USA. His Cabinet had also charged him to ask what the British attitude to a French request for an armistice would be. He was conscious that France had made an agreement not to sue for a separate armistice or peace, but Weygand and others had stressed the sacrifices France had made, and the shock which would be felt if Britain refused to recognise that she was now incapable of going on.

Churchill's first reply was to express sympathy for French suffering, but to hope that France would fight on, if necessary from North Africa. Britain, he said, would fight on whatever happened. Reynaud replied (with, Spears noted, a touch of irritation and irony) that his question did not concern what England would do. His question was this: supposing a French government (the present one or another) were to say that they must come to terms with Germany, would Britain acknowledge that France had given her best and could do no more, and was entitled to make a separate peace while maintaining solidarity with Britain?

While the point was put in the form of a hypothetical question, there was no doubt of the reality and immediacy of the issue. Cadogan wrote in his diary: 'He [Reynaud] said French army bust and asked us to release him from no-separate-peace-agreement'.

Churchill replied that while Britain would waste no time in reproaches or recriminations, this did not mean that she would consent to action contrary to the agreement not to make a separate peace. The first step should be for Reynaud to put the position squarely to Roosevelt, and they should await his reply before considering any alternative. If Britain won the war, France would be restored to her dignity and greatness.

Reynaud said that he was much moved by Churchill's statement. He would telegraph to Roosevelt and point out that the USA was involved in the fate of France and Britain, and that the three should not allow themselves to be destroyed separately. Churchill stated that they could leave this aspect until Roosevelt's reply was received; if it was favourable, and counselled a continuation of the war, this would be a new factor. In any case, there would be questions to be discussed between Britain and France. The British were moving towards a total blockade of the whole of Europe, and the Nazis for their part would seize anything they needed for their own supplies. France could not escape the consequences of these facts, and antagonism between France and Britain might well result. This was his reply to the part of Reynaud's question which had referred to France maintaining solidarity with Britain even though asking for a separate peace. Churchill was delivering a warning that this would not be possible.

Churchill then asked for a short adjournment in order to confer with his British colleagues, and for twenty minutes they walked round the garden of the prefecture — 'a hideous rectangle surrounded by laurel bushes', Spears recalled. All agreed with what Churchill had said, and that there was nothing further to be done at that time. When the meeting resumed, the Prime Minister said that his colleagues concurred with his statements, and it could be assumed that the British Cabinet would also agree. Reynaud said he was personally convinced that Roosevelt would take a step forward, and that France would be able to continue the war alongside Britain.[14]

The meeting, which lasted two hours, was the last session of what was still called the Supreme War Council, and when it was over Churchill and his colleagues flew straight home. For some reason, never satisfactorily explained, Reynaud did not transmit the invitation for Churchill to attend the next meeting of the French Cabinet that evening. This would at least have offered a further opportunity for consultation, and for Churchill to have met Reynaud's colleagues, none of whom were present at the Supreme War Council.[15]

That evening, Churchill reported to the British Cabinet that he had told Reynaud that: 'We were . . . not in a position to release France from her obligation. Whatever happened, we would level no reproaches or recriminations at France; but that was a different matter from consenting to release her from her pledge'. Halifax added that Reynaud had seemed in a more determined mood at the end of the meeting, and that it ought to be possible to get France to follow the example of Holland (where the army had capitulated but the government continued the war). There was discussion of a telegram from Roosevelt to Reynaud, a copy of which had been received in London, and which will be examined shortly.[16] Churchill proposed telegraphing Reynaud to tell him that the President was already being very encouraging. Attlee thought some dramatic message should be sent for publication, to hearten the French people, and it was generally agreed that 'an announcement in dramatic terms of the solidarity of France and Great Britain should be issued. We might say that "France and Great Britain were one" ". This emerged as a decision to issue a statement proclaiming the 'indissoluble union' of the French and British peoples and Empires.[17]

At the meetings at Briare on 11-12 June, and at Tours on the 13th, the British had exhorted the French to fight on, but without much effect. More important, the British had been compelled to face the fact that French resistance was coming rapidly to an end, and that a request for an armistice might shortly be made. This issue had been postponed (or as some hoped, avoided altogether) by the device of an appeal from Reynaud to Roosevelt, supported by Churchill. Exchanges between France, Britain and the USA dominated the forty-eight hours between the evening of 13 June and the evening of the 15th. In retrospect, it is hard to see what was expected from these appeals to Roosevelt, since only Congress could declare war, and in June 1940 this was not even a remote possibility. Moreover, even a declaration of war would have amounted only to a gesture, since the American armed forces were small, and American industry was not yet geared to war production. Roosevelt was already doing what he could to supply the Allies with equipment, especially aircraft, in the face of serious objections from the American armed services which needed the material themselves.[18] Little more was likely to be sent at that moment, whatever appeals were made. The telegrams sent to and fro across the Atlantic have, therefore, a curious air of unreality; and some of the interpretations placed on them verged on make-believe.

On 10 June, Reynaud had sent Roosevelt a message which already contained an element of fantasy, or perhaps bravado. The French armies, he wrote, were fighting against enormous odds. They would fight before Paris, behind Paris, in a province; the struggle would be continued from North Africa, and if necessary from the French colonies in America. Reynaud declared that he was himself about to join the armies to intensify the struggle, and he appealed to Roosevelt to declare publicly that the USA would give the Allies their moral and material help by all means short of sending an expeditionary force.[19] On 13 June Roosevelt agreed to the publication of this message, and sent a full reply to the effect that the USA was doing everything in its power to send material aid to the Allies, and that these efforts were being redoubled. The President declared himself impressed by Reynaud's determination.[20] This telegram was brought into the British Cabinet meeting in the late evening of 13 June, where Churchill described it as a remarkable message which came as near to a declaration of war as the President could without Congress. He even argued that no head of state would send such a message unless he was certain his country would come to the aid of the recipient. There was a general feeling in the Cabinet that the implications of the message might be clearer to Anglo-Saxon minds than to the French, who would be looking from something more definite. It was necessary therefore to point out to the French, who lacked this Anglo-Saxon clairvoyance, that the message contained two points which were tantamount to a declaration of war: first, the promise of all material aid; and second, a call to go on fighting even if the government was driven out of France.[21]

These points were somewhat toned down in the telegram sent by Churchill to Reynaud in the early hours of 14 June, but the essence remained. Churchill wrote that 'If France on this message of President Roosevelt's continues in the field and in the war, we feel that the United States is committed beyond recall to take the only remaining step, namely, becoming a belligerent in form as she already has constituted herself in fact'. He also telegraphed to Roosevelt, thanking him for his 'magnificent message', and asking that it should be published, since he thought it would certainly decide the French against making peace. However, Roosevelt refused to agree to publication of his telegram to Reynaud, and insisted that it was in no sense intended to commit the USA to military participation in the war. This was a necessary douche of cold water.[22]

Meanwhile, before Roosevelt's telegram reached Reynaud, the French Premier drafted the appeal agreed on at the final meeting of the Supreme War Council. He told Roosevelt that France faced a choice: to fight on, with the government leaving the country; or to ask for an armistice. The government could only choose the first path if there was a chance of victory, however distant — if there was a light at the end of the tunnel, which could only come from the intervention of the USA. He appealed to Roosevelt to throw American strength into the scale. Roosevelt's reply to this appeal reached Reynaud during the evening of 15 June. The President expressed his admiration for the French struggle, and told Reynaud again that the US would redouble her own efforts to supply the

Allies with material. The USA would not recognise any infringement of French independence or territory; but, he concluded, these declarations had no military implications, since only Congress could make engagements of that kind.[23] Agonised appeals could not convert the moral and material support of the USA into military intervention, and the French and British would have to work out their own salvation.

Meanwhile the French government, divided and confused, had made its way from the châteaux of the Loire to Bordeaux, along roads crowded with refugees. The journey took most of the day of 14 June, and then the ministers and officials had to find and settle into another new set of makeshift offices in various public buildings and hotels. Bordeaux was to be the scene of the last two days of the Franco-British alliance.

After Churchill and his party left Tours on the evening of 13 June, the British Cabinet continued to explore ways and means of keeping the French in the war, while at the same time preparing for their surrender. First, the French were encouraged to fight on, and after the British Cabinet met late on 13 June Churchill drafted the message designed to hearten the French people, first suggested by Attlee. This paid tribute to the courage of the French armies, and went on: 'We take this opportunity of proclaiming the indissoluble union of our two peoples and of our two Empires'. It also declared that Britain would never 'turn from the conflict until France stands safe and erect in all her grandeur . . .'[24] As a means of heartening the French people, this was probably wasted effort; but the idea of indissoluble union was shortly to be taken further.

The British could also strike a harsher note. In the morning of 14 June a message reached London from Spears, saying that 'extremely pernicious rumours' were abroad that Britain would free France from her engagement not to make a separate peace if the USA did not declare war. Mandel had advised Spears that the British government should scotch these rumours (which came from Baudouin) by stating bluntly that they would not release France from her obligations, and that the declaration of 28 March had been made to meet just such a case as had now arisen.[25] The British reply was firm, though less blunt than Mandel wished. Campbell was asked to draw Reynaud's attention to the rumours, and to ask his help in killing them. Reynaud was reminded that Churchill had said nothing which implied acquiescence in a separate armistice or peace.[26]

Churchill was still grieved by the plight of France, and conscious of the paucity of the British contribution to the battle. At 5 p.m. on 14 June he held another meeting with ministers outside the War Cabinet, telling them that organised resistance in France was at an end and that he hoped the French government would go overseas. He said there was only too much scope for recrimination on both sides, but this would be pointless. 'Very few British divisions have fought in France. At the end, very few indeed. French losses have been out of all proportion to ours, in every sphere'.[27] The same day, the Cabinet was still trying to maintain a balance between withdrawing lines of communication troops and some stores from France, and keeping up the movement of fresh forces to France. Both moves were agreed on, and Churchill refused to hold up the movement of the 52nd and Canadian Divisions to France, which he thought was going too slowly.[28] It was only that evening that General Brooke was finally released from French command.

Meanwhile the British planning for 'a certain eventuality' went on. Most of the attempts to salvage material (such as machine tools, industrial diamonds, and gold) came to nothing because of the chaotic state of affairs in France, though there were occasional successful forays. At this stage the main product of all the planning was a series of papers — albeit important papers. There was a report by the Chiefs of Staff on 11 June, detailing methods of denying French resources to the Germans.[29] There was a draft prepared by the Chiefs of Staff for Lord Lothian, the British Ambassador in Washington, on .13 June, setting out the likely consequences of the fall of France, and the help Britain would need from the USA; this was not actually sent until 18 June.[30] Important instructions were prepared for British representatives in French overseas possessions, to be sent in advance of a French surrender but only acted upon when the word was given.[31] There was also an *aide-mémoire* by the Chiefs of Staff, dated 14 June, on British requirements from the French in various circumstances; this was prepared for use in discussions with the French government which in fact never took place.[32] A further long report by the Chiefs of Staff on 15 June dealt with questions relating to the French Empire.[33] The economic aspects of a French collapse were also examined in great detail, and a short paper by Dalton, the Minister of Economic Warfare, dated 16 June, was accompanied by an immense memorandum by Greenwood dated the 17th. Dalton's paper dealt with means of economic pressure on the French colonies,[34] while Greenwood's reviewed the whole range of economic consequences of the fall of France in terms of gains for Germany, losses for Britain, and possible redeeming features.[35]

These papers mostly influenced British policy after the French asked for an armistice, notably on the issues of the French empire and blockade policy, but in one respect the planning for a French collapse exercised an immediate effect on events. This concerned the French fleet, which was early recognised as the matter most urgently affecting British security. In their report of 11 June, the Chiefs of Staff stated that any German peace terms would certainly include the surrender of the fleet to Germany, and indeed that Germany 'would be most unlikely to agree to an armistice until the French fleet had been surrendered'. If the French government decided to capitulate, it was unlikely that they would allow the fleet to come to Britain. The report argued that since the British could not afford to see the French fleet added to the German and Italian navies, they must either persuade French warships to join the British fleet, or press the French to sink their ships.[36] The Chiefs of Staff stressed on 14 June that it was vital for the French to move the fleet to British ports *before discussing terms with Germany*. Otherwise the Germans will insist on its surrender. In the last resort they must scuttle their Fleet rather than surrender it'.[37] These recommendations weighed heavily in the minds of British ministers when, on 16 June, events in France finally brought their deliberations to a head.

During 15 June, the situation in France was rapidly deteriorating. Campbell telegraphed from Bordeaux during the afternoon that unless Roosevelt's reply to Reynaud's appeal contained an assurance of an early declaration of war, he thought the decision to ask for an armistice might follow very rapidly. 'In that event General Spears and I would do our utmost to obtain scuttling of the fleet. But we have little confidence now in anything'.[38] Campbell next asked for a warship to be sent to Bordeaux to secure the evacuation of the Embassy, the Dominion legations, and the Polish and Belgian governments in exile, because there was no further organised resistance to the German advance, and Bordeaux might be their next objective.[39] He reported that Pétain and Weygand were determined to resign unless an armistice was requested or the USA declared war.[40] The Ambassador then sent news that there was to be a Cabinet meeting at 4 p.m., when Reynaud would hold out for resistance, and if not supported would resign.[41]

When the French Cabinet met, Reynaud argued in favour of the 'Dutch solution' — a military capitulation, with the government going overseas to continue the war. Pétain, under the influence of Weygand, opposed this course as being dishonourable for the army. A suggestion made by Frossard was taken up and elaborated by Chautemps (both ministers of some political standing in the Cabinet), to the effect that the government could not go overseas to carry on the war without the support of French public opinion; the French people would not understand the necessity for such a move unless they were convinced that German terms were unacceptable; and therefore the best course was to obtain British permission to seek terms for an armistice, which could then be shown to be unacceptable. In this way, the government would not only avoid breaking its word to Britain but would also win public understanding in France. A majority of ministers apparently favoured the suggestion, which seemed to patch up the unity of the Cabinet and postpone the crucial decision on an armistice, though in fact it reached that very decision by a back door. Reynaud reluctantly assented and transmitted details to London.[42] He told the British government that the approach for terms would be made through the USA; that the surrender of the French fleet would be unacceptable; and that if the British refused their consent, he would have to resign. While Reynaud was preparing this message, he received Roosevelt's reply of 15 June to his final appeal for American intervention. He therefore added that it had been agreed at Tours that if Roosevelt's reply was negative the question of a French request for an armistice would be reconsidered. This had now happened, and the question must be put afresh.[43] Commenting on this message, Campbell and Spears reported that if Reynaud resigned, he could not guarantee that his successor would regard the surrender of the fleet as an unacceptable condition for an armistice. They also reported that Mandel advised strongly against Britain consenting to any request for an armistice, which he considered would make abject surrender inevitable.[44]

This was the situation which faced the British Cabinet when it met at 10.15 a.m. on Sunday, 16 June. Certain points stood out. First, Reynaud's Cabinet held that the surrender of the fleet would be unacceptable. Second, a successor to Reynaud might not take the same view. Third, if Britain refused to permit the request for an armistice, Reynaud would resign. The conclusion therefore seemed to be that if Britain wished to safeguard the French fleet, it would be best to allow the request for terms to be made. Against this, there was Mandel's advice that to condone any request for terms would be fatal. The choice before the British Cabinet was thus between acceptance of the French proposal, as the best way of safeguarding the French fleet, and its rejection in an attempt to hold the French government firmly to its obligations.

Before the Cabinet opened its discussion, Churchill asked Admiral Pound to report on the dispositions of the French fleet. The Prime Minister then put the main question thus: 'We had now to decide whether we should release them [the French] from their obligations to us not to enter into any discussion of terms. The question of their acceptance or refusal of such terms would arise later when the terms themselves were known'. Chamberlain thought there was no hope that the French would maintain further resistance in France itself; the British objectives must therefore be firstly to save the French fleet, and secondly to ensure that 'a French Government of some sort' remained in being to carry on the war. If the British objected to the French enquiry, Reynaud would resign and his successor could not be relied on to save the fleet. He thought they had no choice but to consent, while insisting that no terms should be accepted without consultation with Britain. Attlee and Halifax agreed with this reasoning. The discussion which followed mainly concerned the wording of British consent, Eden alone at one point drawing attention to Mandel's advice that Britain should expect no less of the French than of the Poles, Norwegians and Dutch — but he too later accepted the general view.

With regard to the phrasing of the British message, Churchill wished to make it an absolute condition that 'the French Fleet should sail forthwith for British ports pending any discussion of armistice terms'. No impression should be given that through the mere resignation of Reynaud the French would be freed from their obligations to Britain, or that Britain herself would have any part in enquiries or negotiations. A telegram was drafted which embodied these points, the most important being: '. . . provided, but only provided, that the French Fleet is sailed forthwith for British harbours pending negotiations, His Majesty's Government give their full consent to an inquiry by the French Government to ascertain the terms of an armistice for France'. This was despatched at 12.35 p.m.[45] Later, at 3.10 p.m., another telegram was sent, emphasising that the British expected to be consulted as soon as armistice terms were received.[46]

It may be that the British Cabinet erred in thus giving its consent to a French request for terms. Mandel had been in favour of an uncompromising reply, and it is possible that Reynaud too would have preferred a straightforward negative, so that he could take a firm stand based on British intransigence. Spears thought that a dangerous door had been opened to the French defeatists. A few days later, on 22 June, Vansittart wrote that it was 'an expensive error . . . It set us on a downward path up which we have never been able to climb again'.[47] However this may be, the British position so far was clear. They consented to the French enquiry, subject to the plain condition that the French fleet set sail forthwith for British harbours. It was not enough for them to be assured (as Reynaud had done) that the surrender of the fleet would be regarded as unacceptable: the British wanted it under their own hand. This position might be criticised, but it could not be misconstrued.

At this point all was thrown into confusion by an offer of union between Britain and France, which added another spectacular element to a dramatic day.[48] This project originated with a group of men, both French and British, including Jean Monnet, chairman of the Franco-British economic co-ordinating committee; René Pleven, one of his associates; Corbin, the French Ambassador; Leo Amery, the Secretary of State for India; Vansittart; and Desmond Morton, a friend of Churchill's who was acting as one of his private secretaries. On 14 June, Amery circulated to a number of ministers a memorandum arguing that it was absolutely vital to Britain that France should remain in the war; that French resources should be saved to continue the struggle outside France; that the USA should enter the war; and that the Germans should be prevented from invading Britain. 'For all these objects, real unity of Great Britain and France, dramatically expressed and fully realised by the two peoples, is the indispensable condition.' Unity would support French morale and appeal to American idealism. To this end, the two governments might make a dramatic declaration of their solidarity of interest, and state that they would act as one through a joint Cabinet; there might be a joint meeting of the two parliaments, or a specially formed parliament composed of delegations from each.[49]

This memorandum was discussed in Cabinet on the morning of 15 June, when Chamberlain said he thought it misleading in places, and that the proposals on a joint Cabinet and parliament did not seem fully thought out. Churchill argued that the real question was what could be done to uphold the French, and if there could be a statement on unity 'in a dramatic form which would make a big appeal to the French, so much the better'. If the French government came to London, it would be easy to hold frequent meetings of the Supreme War Council, which would resemble a joint Cabinet. Attlee thought there would be difficulties in having a joint Cabinet with the French, because of the position of the Dominions, while Sinclair said it might be worth while to make a further declaration if it meant that Britain could secure the French fleet and French aircraft. It was not an enthusiastic discussion.[50]

The following morning, 16 June, de Gaulle (then French Under-Secretary for War, who was in London to discuss military questions) was called in by Corbin and Jean Monnet to help them promote the idea of a declaration of union as an alternative to the British granting consent to a French request for terms. A text was prepared by these three, together with Vansittart and Morton. The matter was raised when Corbin and de Gaulle lunched with Churchill, who was sufficiently impressed to send a telegram *en clair* to Campbell: 'Please ask Monsieur Reynaud to delay action on telegram No. 368 until he has received a further and most important communication from me this evening'.[51] (No. 368 was the telegram agreeing to the French request to ask for terms, on condition that the fleet came to British ports.) This message only reached Campbell and Spears after they had already acted on their earlier instructions, but it showed that before the British Cabinet met that afternoon Churchill was willing to anticipate his colleagues' agreement on the offer of union.

When the British Cabinet met at 3 p.m. on 16 June, Churchill and Halifax gave brief accounts of what had happened since their morning session, and the draft proclamation of union was read out. It was then discussed in some detail, and a number of changes were made.[52] The opening clauses making a declaration of indissoluble union and creating a Franco-British Union went through with only minor amendment, though the flat statement that 'France and Great Britain shall no longer be two nations but one' was changed to: 'France and Britain shall no longer be two nations, but one Franco-British Union'. The proposal for immediate common citizenship was felt to be acceptable, and the pooling of resources to restore war damage was agreed. Proposals to abolish customs duties were another matter, raising problems concerning the Ottawa agreements and other commercial treaties. A common currency was also held to be simply impractical, and these last two proposals were deleted. The clauses on a single War Cabinet, the uniting of the two parliaments, and the writing of a constitution for the Union evoked doubts. The proclamation might declare that there should be a single War Cabinet, but in fact it would be necessary to keep two Cabinets, with a 'super Cabinet' in addition. This would be very similar to existing arrangements, merely using the term 'War Cabinet' instead of 'Supreme War Council'. It was not thought practicable for the two parliaments to legislate together, though there might be some arrangement for occasional joint sessions. A written constitution would not pose an insuperable obstacle, provided that it was kept on very broad lines. On military matters, a phrase declaring that Britain was 'raising at once a new army of several million men' was re-cast in more cautious words: 'The nations of the British Empire are already forming new armies'. A unified command for the forces of the two countries was agreed to be unobjectionable, because in existing circumstances it would mean British predominance.

In general discussion, Sinclair and Greenwood supported the proposal, though the latter stressed that the proclamation should be kept as simple as possible. Lord Caldecote, the Dominions Secretary (formerly Sir Thomas Inskip) said that if the union was intended to continue after the war it raised issues too stupendous to comment on at such short notice — there would be serious constitutional difficulties, and he feared the scheme might provoke grave criticism in the country. However, it would be a different matter if the proposal related only to the period of the war and that immediately following. (It does not appear that the important question of the duration of the union was dealt with any further.) Halifax later assured Hankey, who was appalled by the whole idea, that the offer 'was only designed for the period of the war', but this is by no means obvious from the text.[53] Nevertheless, Halifax thought they must be prepared to take some risks, and that the only aspect of the document which raised really fundamental issues was the phrase that France and Britain should no longer be two nations but one — this was amended in the final draft. Churchill said that his first instinct had been against the idea, but they must not let themselves be accused of lack of imagination. Some dramatic announcement was necessary to keep the French going.

At 3.55 p.m., during the meeting, news was brought in that the French Cabinet was to meet at 5 o'clock, and Reynaud had told de Gaulle on the telephone that if he had a favourable answer from the British on the proposed proclamation by that time, he thought he could hold the position. This dramatic touch ('enter a messenger') emphasises the rushed and urgent nature of the discussion. The draft was hastily amended and approved. A message was to be telephoned to Reynaud before 5 o'clock, and Churchill, Attlee and Sinclair, representing the three main political parties, were to meet the French Premier as soon as possible to discuss the draft and related questions.[54]

After the Cabinet discussion was over, de Gaulle telephoned the text to Reynaud, and Churchill also spoke to him briefly. When de Gaulle's call came through, Reynaud was talking to Campbell and Spears about the earlier telegrams authorising France to ask for terms, and was raising objections. Campbell reported that the fresh news 'acted like a tonic' on Reynaud, who said that 'for a document like that he would fight to the last'. Reynaud left to read the proposal to President Lebrun, and Campbell and Spears sent a messenger after him to say that the earlier telegrams about British consent to a request for terms 'should be considered as cancelled'.[55] This wording was repeated by Campbell in his final despatch, written in London and dated 27 June 1940, where he wrote that he received a message that the earlier communications 'should be regarded as cancelled, and I informed M. Reynaud accordingly'. Similarly, Harvey wrote in his diary that no sooner was the telegram about an armistice and the fleet delivered than instructions came 'to cancel it'.[56] But the telegram actually sent from London at 4.45 p.m. said 'Please suspend action'. A telegram sent at 8 p.m. began: 'Following is reason why you have been asked to suspend action on my telegrams Nos. 368 and 369'.[57] How the transformation from 'suspend' to 'cancel' came about is not clear — Spears thought later

75

that it might have resulted from a hurried attempt to paraphrase the telegram, which was always done for security reasons.[58] For whatever reason, the British government's intention of *suspending* action on the telegrams was lost at Bordeaux, and an unfortunate confusion was created.

In retrospect, away from the tense atmosphere of that hectic time, it is hard to see why the offer of union was taken so seriously. The circumstances were certainly dramatic, but this did not mean that statemanship had become a department of scene-painting. To sketch a few battlements on paper and label them 'Franco-British Union' could make no difference to the realities of the situation, and this was sharply revealed when the French Cabinet met; Reynaud read the draft proclamation, but it was scarcely discussed. Those who wanted an armisitice were already full of resentment against Britain; those who did not want an armistice would fight for France, not for some newly-invented union. The scheme was brushed aside, in order to get to the real question of whether or not to ask for terms. The only consequence of the proposal was that Reynaud did not read out, or even convey the sense of, the earlier British telegrams; on 16 June the French Cabinet did not therefore hear of the British consent to a French request for terms, nor of the condition attached to that consent: that the fleet should be sent to British ports.[59] The earlier, clear-cut British position had been lost, sacrificed to what proved to be the spectacular irrelevance of the offer of union. There had always been some difficulty in the simultaneous pursuit of the two aspects of British policy towards France in the crisis — to try to keep France in the war, yet also to prepare for her collapse. On 16 June, the British Cabinet first tried to take an important precaution against a French collapse by securing the fleet; they next tried a last desperate throw to keep France in the war by the offer of union. The two strands of British policy thus crossed and tangled in dangerous confusion.

The French Cabinet of 5 p.m. on 16 June proved the last straw for Reynaud. During the evening, he resigned, and President Lebrun called on Pétain to form a government, which he did almost at once. The new government made no further ado about consultation with Britain. At 12.30 a.m. on 17 June the new Foreign Minister, Paul Baudouin, asked the Spanish Ambassador to transmit to Germany a request for terms for an armistice and for peace. At 1 a.m. the same morning, he told the British Ambassador what he had done. Already, during the evening of the 16th, Churchill, Attlee and Sinclair had been fetched back from Waterloo station, where they had gone on the first stage of their journey to meet Reynaud. News had reached London that a French ministerial crisis had arisen, and the meeting arranged for 17 June was impossible.[60] A parting of the ways between Britain and France had been reached.

NOTES

1. Reynaud, vol. II, 313-16; Weygand, 211-14; Baudouin, 149-51; Yves Bouthillier, *Le Drame de Vichy,* vol. I, *Face à l'ennemi, face à l'allié* (Paris 1950), 54-9; C. Chautemps, *Cahiers secrets de l'Armistice* (Paris 1963) 118-30.

2. Reynaud, vol. II, 100, 184-5; André Truchet, *L'Armistice de 1940 et l'Afrique du Nord* (Paris 1955), 11-14.

3. This sketch is composed from the large amount of French memoir material and testimony which has accumulated around the events of 1940. For an authoritative discussion, see Henri Michel, *Vichy Année 40* (Paris 1966), 25-40, 52-4.

4. The question of whether there was or was not a majority in favour of an armistice in Reynaud's Cabinet has been much discussed. See H. Amouroux, *Le 18 juin 1940* (Paris 1964), 69, n.1, and A. D. Hytier, *Two Years of French Foreign Policy: Vichy 1940-1942* (Paris and Geneva 1958), 361-2, for analyses of the different accounts.

5. Reynaud used these phrases during the French Cabinet meeting on the evening of 12 June 1940. Reynaud, vol. II, 313-16; Bouthillier, vol. I, 57.

6. *Harvey Diaries,* 10 and 11 June 1940, 384-5.

7. FO 371/24311, C7341/65/17, Campbell to Halifax, 27 June 1940, paras. 10, 12. This was Campbell's final despatch on the last period of his mission in France, composed just after his return to London. It is a long and valuable document, consisting of 132 numbered paragraphs.

8. *Harvey Diaries,* 15 June 1940, 389-90; FO 371/24311, C7341/65/17, Campbell to Halifax, 27 June 1940, para. 2.

9. CAB 65/7, WM(40)160; FO 371/24383, C7182/5/18, Campbell to Halifax, 10 June 1940; *Harvey Diaries,* 10 June 1940, 384.

10. CAB 65/7, WM(40)161, Cabinet meeting at 12.30 p.m., 11 June 1940, before Churchill's departure for France.

11. For Churchill's visit to France on 11-12 June, see: CAB 65/7, WM(40)163; CAB 65/13, WM(40)163rd Conclusions, Confidential Annex; CAB 99/3, SWC(39/40)14th Meeting, 11 June 1940, 15th Meeting, 12 June 1940; Reynaud, vol. II, 297-311; *Événements, Témoignages,* vol. III, 736 (testimony of Georges); Churchill, 136-40; Spears, vol. II, 138-71; Weygand, 200-205.

12. CAB 65/7, WM(40)163; CAB 65/13, WM(40)163rd Conclusions, Confidential Annex.

13. See the references on 77, note 1.

14. CAB 99/3, SWC(39/40)16th Meeting, 13 June 1940; Churchill, 158-61; Spears, vol II, 201-18; *Cadogan Diaries,* 13 June 1940, 297-8; Baudouin, 154-9. Paul Reynaud, *Au Coeur de la Mêlée* (Paris 1951), 770-4, prints the French record kept by Captain de Margerie.

15. For the French Cabinet meeting on the evening of 13 June, see Reynaud, vol. II, 322-5; Baudouin, 160-4; Bouthillier, vol. I, 66-7; Weygand, 215-19; Chautemps, 130-4; Spears, vol. II, 225-6.

16. See below, 65-6.

17. CAB 65/7, WM(40)165; CAB 65/13, WM(40)165th Conclusions, Confidential Annex.

18. See John McVickar Haight, *American Aid to France* (New York 1970).

19. Reynaud, vol. II, 295-6.

20. CAB 65/13, WM(40)165th Conclusions, Confidential Annex; Churchill, 162-3.

21. CAB 65/13, WM(40)165th Conclusions, Confidential Annex.

22. *Ibid.,* Churchill, 163-6.

23. Reynaud, vol. II, 330-31, 347-8.

24. FO 371/24301, C7146/9/17, Halifax to Campbell, 14 June 1940; Churchill, 165.

25. FO 371/24383, C7182/5/18, Campbell to Halifax, 13 June 1940; Spears, vol. II, 218-20.

26. *Ibid.,* Halifax to Campbell, 14 June 1940; CAB 65/7, WM(40)166.

27. Dalton diary, 14 June 1940.

28. CAB 65/13, WM(40)166th Conclusions, Confidential Annex; CAB 80/13, COS (40)462, 14 June 1940, note by Hollis enclosing minute by Churchill.

29. CAB 66/8, WP(40)201, 11 June 1940.

30. *Ibid.,* WP(40)203, 13 June 1940.

31. FO 371/24311, C7278/65/17, Hollis to Strang, 14 June 1940; minute by Strang for Cadogan, 14 June 1940; circular telegram to representatives in French territories, 15 June 1940.

32. CAB 80/13, COS(40)466, 14 June 1940.

33. CAB 66/8, WP(40)207, 15 June 1940.

34. CAB 67/7, WP(G)(40)156, 16 June 1940.

35. *Ibid.,* WP(G)(40)155, 17 June 1940.

36. CAB 66/8, WP(40)201, 11 June 1940.

37. CAB 80/13, COS(40)466, 14 June 1940.

38. FO 371/24310, C7263/65/17, Campbell to Halifax, 15 June 1940, No. 407, despatched 1.30 p.m.

39. *Ibid.,* same to same, 15 June 1940, No. 408, despatched 2.45 p.m.

40. *Ibid.,* same to same, 15 June 1940, No. 409, despatched 4 p.m.

41. *Ibid.,* same to same, 15 June 1940, No. 413, despatched 6.05 p.m.

42. Reynaud, vol. II, 338-42; Baudouin, 168-70; Bouthillier, vol. I, 76-9; Chautemps, 154-7. See also *Événements, Témoignages* vol. IV, 975, 1081 (Lebrun); vol. V, 1426-7 (Monnet); vol. VIII, 2475-81 (Bouthillier). It has been disputed whether there was in fact a majority in favour of the Chautemps proposition. Chautemps himself, 141-2, insists that the proposition was made on 16 June, but this cannot be reconciled with the rest of the evidence.

43. FO 371/24310, C7263/65/17, Campbell to Halifax, 15 June 1940, No. 420, received 1.20 a.m. 16 June.

44. *Ibid.,* same to same, 15 June 1940, No. 422, received 4 a.m. 16 June; cf. Spears, vol. II, 263-73, describing conversations with Reynaud and Mandel.

45. CAB 65/13, WM(40)168th Conclusions, Confidential Annex, including text of telegram to Campbell, No. 368.

46. FO 371/24310, C7263/65/17, Halifax to Campbell, 16 June 1940, No. 369.

47. Spears, vol. II, 282-5; Reynaud, vol. II, 348-9; FO 371/24310, C7263/65/17, minute by Vansittart, 22 June 1940.

48. For accounts of the offer of union, see Léon Noël, 'Le projet d'union franco-britannique de juin 1940', *Revue d'Histoire de la deuxième Guerre mondiale,* No. 21 (January 1956); D. Thomson,

79

'The proposal for Anglo-French Union in 1940', Zaharoff Lecture, 1966; Max Beloff, 'The Anglo-French Union Project of June 1940', in *The Intellectual in Politics* (London 1970), 172-99.

49. FO 371/24301, C7357/9/17, memorandum dated 14 June 1940, unsigned but enclosed in Amery to Halifax, 15 June 1940.

50. CAB 65/13, WM(40)167th Conclusions, Confidential Annex.

51. FO 371/24310, C7263/65/17, Halifax to Campbell, 16 June 1940, No. 370, transmitting message from Prime Minister; sent by telephone, 3.10 p.m. See Spears, vol. II, 291-4, for the sequence of events at Bordeaux.

52. Texts of the first draft and the final version are printed in the Appendix, 303-5.

53. FO 800/312, H/XIV/455, Halifax to Hankey, 23 June 1940.

54. CAB 65/7, WM(40)169.

55. FO 371/24311, C7294/65/17, Campbell to Halifax, 16 June 1940, No. 428, despatched 7 p.m.; cf. Spears, vol. II, 291-3.

56. FO 371/24311, C7341/65/17, Campbell's despatch, 27 June 1940, para. 33; *Harvey Diaries,* 16 June 1940, 391.

57. FO 371/24310, C7263/65/17, Halifax to Campbell, 16 June 1940, No. 371; FO 371/24311, C7294/65/17, same to same, 16 June 1940, No. 374.

58. Spears, vol. II, 294, note.

59. Reynaud, vol. II, 352-6; Baudouin, 174-5; Bouthillier, vol. I, 86-9; *Événements, Témoignages,* vol. IV, 975-6, 1016 (Lebrun): vol. V, 1320, 1427, 1455 (Rio, Monnet, Laurent-Eynac); vol. VII, 2074 (Marin). Louis Marin, 'Contributions à l'histoire des prodromes de l'armistice', *Revue d'histoire de la deuxième Guerre mondiale,* No. 3 (June 1951), especially 20-21. At the trial of Pétain after the war, Reynaud maintained that he summarised the telegrams to the Cabinet, but the evidence is against him.

60. Baudouin, 177-8; F. Charles-Roux, *Cinq Mois Tragiques aux Affaires Étrangères* (Paris 1949), 52-3; FO 371/24311, C7294/65/17, Campbell to Halifax, 17 June 1940, No. 433; Churchill, 186

Chapter 5

ARMISTICE

Eight days after the French request for armistice and peace terms, at 12.35 a.m. on 25 June, two armistices — between France and Germany on the one hand, and between France and Italy on the other — came into force. During these eight days, the dealings between France, Germany and Italy lay at the centre of interest. The British government found itself outside the main-stream of events, compelled to watch as if from the bank of a river, and indeed to try to divine from the bank what *was* the main current of events, and what were only eddies. The British urgently asked to be consulted about the terms being secured by the French, but in vain. Before examining the events of 17-24 June as they appeared to the British at the time, it will be best to outline the main events in France and in the French negotiations with the Axis powers.

The new French government formed by Pétain in the evening of 16 June contained eighteen members of whom eleven had belonged to Reynaud's government. However, this appearance of continuity was deceptive, since the surviving ministers had all either opposed Reynaud on the question of an armistice, or had supported Chautemps' prevaricating proposition. Moreover, the key positions were taken not by parliamentary politicians, but by service officers (of whom there were five in the government) or by non-political experts from the world of commerce and administration. Notably, Marshal Pétain was Premier; General Weygand was Minister of Defence; General Colson, Minister of War; Admiral Darlan, Minister of Marine; and General Pujo, Air Minister.[1]

The most influential members of the new government — Pétain,

Weygand, Darlan and Baudouin — were all anti-British in outlook. All had been alienated by the clashes at Arras and Dunkirk, by the British refusal to commit more fighters to the battle in France, and by what they saw as Britain's willingness to sacrifice France in her own interests. It was true that the politician most distrusted by the British government, Pierre Laval, was not at first a member of Pétain's ministry, but his absence was accidental and only temporary. Pétain offered Laval the Ministry of Justice. Laval held out for the Foreign Ministry, and almost obtained it, but when it was finally refused, he declined to join the government. However, on 23 June both Laval and his ally Marquet took posts as Ministers of State (without departments); on 27 June Laval became Vice-Premier and Marquet Minister of the Interior. Pétain, Weygand, Darlan and Laval all believed that Britain's defeat was imminent; and Laval in particular believed that the military collapse had merely confirmed his long-standing diagnosis that France's only course in foreign policy was to come to an agreement with Germany.[2]

Such was the complexion of the new French government. When its Foreign Minister, Baudouin, met the Spanish Ambassador in the early hours of 17 June, he asked for both armistice and peace terms. Nothing came of the latter — the Germans did not wish to open such a far-reaching question. Nevertheless, Baudouin's wording was symptomatic: the French government was seeking peace, and not just a cessation of hostilities. Laval told a meeting of deputies on 8 July: 'We should have only one aim, to conclude the best possible peace'. Pétain, in a broadcast on 11 July, said that the government must negotiate peace. A peace settlement seemed the only sound course after what was seen as a complete and final German victory, and it also appeared the best basis for the reconstruction and regeneration of the French state.[3]

The French request reached Berlin early on 17 June. On the 18th Hitler met Mussolini at Munich to confer on their course of action and, as it proved, to persuade the Italian dictator to moderate his demands. At 6.30 a.m. the Spanish Ambassador again saw Baudouin, told him that the Germans would receive French plenipotentiaries, and requested their names. These two days of suspense were uneasy ones in Bordeaux. The German advance continued. The French ministers and President Lebrun held frequent discussions as to whether at least a part of the French government should go to North Africa, if only to avoid negotiating under the threat of imminent capture by the Germans. On the evening of 18 June, indeed, it appeared to Chautemps, the Vice-Premier, and to Herriot and Jeanneney, the Presidents of the Chamber and Senate respectively, that a firm decision had been taken to divide the government and send one part, under Chautemps, to Algiers. Preparations for this move continued during 19 June. Plans were made by Herriot and Jeanneney for the evacuation of deputies and senators, and Darlan placed at their disposal a passenger ship, the *Massilia,* to be available the next day, 20 June. She sailed on 21 June, with Mandel, Daladier and other parliamentarians on board, and reached Casablanca on the 24th. However, on 19 June the French government chose its pleni-potentiaries, headed by General Huntzinger. When Baudouin gave their names to the Spanish Ambassador, he also emphasised the importance of establishing a zone in which the French government could function in safety — in other words, to ask the Germans to make it unnecessary for the French to send a part of their government overseas.[4]

On 21 June, at 3.30 p.m., Hitler received the French delegation in the same railway coach in the same place, Rethondes, where on 11 November 1918 the Germans had themselves been compelled to sign an armistice. Huntziger telephoned the terms to Weygand in Bordeaux that evening, and gave his opinion that they were harsh but not dishonourable.[5] The French Cabinet met to consider the terms at 1 a.m. on 22 June, by which time there was no longer any question of ministers going to North Africa, Pétain having ruled this out during the 21st. At 8 a.m. on the 22nd, the French Cabinet met again, and agreed to ask for various changes in the terms. One of these (concerning the demilitarisation of aircraft) was accepted, but the others were refused. The French government then asked that their requests and the German replies should be attached to the armistice as a protocol; but at 6.30 p.m. on 22 June General Keitel, controlling the negotiations on the German side, told the French delegation that they must sign within an hour or the negotiations would be broken off. Huntziger was authorised to sign, which he did at 6.50 p.m. on the 22nd.[6]

On 23 June the French delegation flew to Rome to receive the Italian terms. They found these more moderate than they had feared, and certain French requests for amendments were accepted.

The Italian armistice was signed at 7.15 p.m. on 24 June. The implementation of the German armistice had been made dependent on the agreement of terms with Italy, and so both armistices came into force at 12.35 a.m. on 25 June.[7]

In all this, it was plain that the most important members of the French government were determined to secure an armistice; and Pétain and Weygand insisted that they would never leave the soil of France. They also maintained that they would not accept dishonourable terms, but it is doubtful whether they left any other course open for themselves but acceptance of whatever terms were presented. Certain of their actions made the continuation of resistance in any form virtually impossible. In a broadcast on 17 June Pétain told the French people (including, of course, any soldiers within reach of a wireless set): '. . . I tell you today that we must end the fighting'. For the press, this was changed to 'we must try to end the fighting', but it was too late. The effect of this broadcast was demoralising, even when countermanding orders were sent out — men were naturally reluctant to risk death or capture when the war was either over or so clearly about to end.[8] Moreover, on 18 June Weygand issued an order that all towns of over 20,000 inhabitants were to be considered as open towns, and not defended. Georges protested twice, on 19 and 22 June, that this made defence impossible and played into the hands of the enemy, but Weygand refused to revoke the order.[9] By these two actions, Pétain and Weygand made the already frightful task of holding together the remnants of the French armies even more difficult, and virtually ruled out continued resistance.

It is true that as late as 21 and 22 June Weygand was going through the motions of exploring the possibilities of continued resistance in North Africa. On 22 June he asked General Noguès, the Commander-in-Chief in North Africa, for an urgent report on the possibility of fighting on, assuming that it would be impossible to reinforce him from France. Noguès sent a generally optimistic report, which was ignored — or rather, attention was focused only on the difficulties and shortages of material which he indicated.[10] It may be that the very fact of Weygand's request to Noguès indicated some continuing indecision in the French government, but it is more likely that it was designed only to show that the North African alternative was in fact out of the question.

The main sequence of events thus ran: 17 June, the French

request for an armistice and peace terms; 19 June, the news that the Germans were ready to receive plenipotentiaries; 20 June, the departure of the French delegation; 21 June, the meeting at Rethondes and the receipt of the German terms at Bordeaux; 22 June, the French requests for changes and the signature of the German armistice; 23 June, the receipt of the Italian terms; and 24 June, the signature of the Italian armistice. Up to 21 June, the departure of a part of the French government for North Africa was being actively discussed, and was sometimes treated, however misleadingly, as a firm decision.

From the British point of view, this short but crowded period may be divided into two phases: the days of uncertainty about French intentions, from 17 to 21 June; and the conclusion of the armistices on 22-24 June. Within these phases, it will be best to deal in sequence, first with events in and reports from Bordeaux, and second with the view from London and the actions of the British government.

(i) *The days of uncertainty, 17-21 June*

As British Ambassador to the new French government, Campbell found himself demoted from the position of a confidant to that of an outsider. His former ready access to the French Premier was curtailed, and he found it increasingly difficult to secure information. Campbell felt these difficulties keenly. He worked long hours in chaotic conditions, and there was an air of desperation about some of his telegrams as he tried to keep his government informed of events.

In the early hours of 17 June, Campbell reported that Baudouin, the new Foreign Minister, had seen him at 1 a.m. that morning (that is, immediately after seeing the Spanish Ambassador). Baudouin said that with the defeat of the French armies, coupled with Weygand's warnings that the men might turn on their officers, and the appalling sufferings of the civilian population, no government could leave France and appear to abandon its people to their fate. The new government was thus compelled to ask, through Spain, for the cessation of hostilities, and for the terms on which an armistice would be granted. If the terms were dishonourable, they would be refused, but the French people would then know that there was no way out of their sufferings. The most dishonourable condition would be the surrender of the fleet, which would in no

85

circumstances be accepted. Darlan's appointment as Minister of Marine was an additional guarantee of this. Baudouin added that the generous words used by Churchill at Tours encouraged the French government to hope that, though the British government would not approve of their action, they would at least understand it.

He repeated his assurance about the fleet several times, and Campbell took formal note of it. Campbell expressed great regret that the French government should have gone back on its agreement, but otherwise refrained from recrimination on the grounds that he did not wish to give the impression that Britain intended to wash her hands of France, and so give a pretext for the French to say they were released from their assurances about the fleet.[11]

During the day of 17 June, Campbell tried both to make the British position about the fleet clear to the new French government, and to ascertain what French intentions were. He had a short interview with Pétain, and told him that while he had received gladly the assurance that in no circumstances would the fleet be handed over, it was absolutely essential that when the Germans asked for it, it should already be in British control. Pétain's own view was that the fleet should be scuttled. When Campbell then asked whether, if the German conditions proved to be unacceptable, the government would go to North Africa, Pétain replied that he personally would stay in France, but he supposed a small government might go overseas. Campbell reported that the Marshal was preoccupied with the sufferings of the people, and he found conversation with him fruitless, but would persevere with other ministers.[12]

He telegraphed later that in all his conversations 'I revert in the terms contained in your telegrams Nos. 368 and 369 to the question of the fleet being placed in British control but I never get any satisfaction beyond the reiterated assurance that surrender [to] Germany will in no circumstances be contemplated. I will not cease to urge sailing for a British port'.[13] Campbell saw Baudouin in the late afternoon of 17 June, and insisted that the British government must be consulted before any terms were accepted; but he was very doubtful whether the French would in fact do so. The French government, he telegraphed, had already broken its word by violating the agreement of 28 March, and they were likely to do so again on the question of consultation.[14]

From London on 17 June, the Foreign Office instructed Campbell to inform the new French government of the condition laid down on the 16th for British consent to a request for an armistice. It appeared that the request had already been made, but the fleet had not sailed and so the condition had not been met. If the French persisted in seeking an armistice, Campbell was to insist on the fleet setting sail for British ports at once. Campbell replied that, in order to make certain that the French government was in no doubt as to the British attitude, he had asked Charles-Roux, the Secretary-General at the French Foreign Ministry, to bring the contents of the British telegrams of 16 June to the notice of the government in writing.[15]

By the end of 17 June, then, Campbell had informed his government of the French request for an armistice; told Pétain that it was essential that when the Germans demanded the surrender of the French fleet it should already be in British hands; and asked Charles-Roux to bring the telegrams of 16 June concerning the fleet to the attention of the French government. On 18 June he received further instructions from London. Churchill sent a personal message to Pétain and Weygand, declaring his conviction that they would not injure their ally by handing over the fleet to the enemy, but stressing that they might in fact achieve that result by frittering away the time in which it could be sailed to safety in British or American ports.[16] A later telegram was sent on Churchill's personal instruction, based on a minute by Pound; the latter thought the French were assuming that if, when they received the German terms, there was a clause demanding surrender of the fleet, they could refuse the conditions and still keep control of the fleet's movements. Pound believed that the Germans would so arrange matters as to make it impossible for the French to send the fleet away after the terms were delivered, so the only hope was for them to send it to safety *before* this happened. Campbell was instructed to press these considerations on the French with all possible force, and also to point out that there was no question of the French fleet becoming part of the Royal Navy, only of their free co-operation.[17]

Campbell received these messages during the morning of 18 June, and replied at once that he thought a satisfactory decision about the fleet would be made by the French Cabinet that same morning.[18] He personally delivered Churchill's message to Pétain, who said that the Ambassador need have no misgivings whatever about the fleet. However, Campbell told him this was not good

87

enough, and that within the next few hours the French fleet must be placed outside French control. They were then joined by Baudouin, who said that this decision had been taken, and only remained to be confirmed by the Cabinet that morning. 'He was absolutely categorical', Campbell reported — but added that he would not be entirely happy until he knew that the order had been given and was being carried out.[19] Later that day he telegraphed that the decision had *not* been confirmed by the French Cabinet, but replaced by a unanimous decision to refuse any terms which included the surrender of the fleet.[20] He explained that French ministers had taken the view that France must receive the armistice terms with her armies and fleet still fighting. Demands for the surrender of the fleet would be rejected, and in that case France would go on fighting as long as she could. Before she capitulated on land, the fleet would join with the British navy, or in the last resort scuttle itself. Orders for this were already made out. Campbell deeply regretted that the earlier decision had not been ratified, but reported to London: 'I do believe however that the French are playing straight with us. Marshal Pétain, General Weygand and Admiral Darlan are all men of honour'. He thought the change of mind was partly due to a rather stiffer attitude in the government as a whole, and to this extent it was a healthy sign.[21]

In fact, the French Admiralty were already giving orders to commanders to sail for North African ports rather than Britain. They were absolutely forbidden to allow their ships to fall into enemy hands. On 18 June the unfinished battleship *Richelieu* sailed from Brest for Dakar; and the *Jean Bart,* in an even more unready state, sailed from St Nazaire for Casablanca on the 19th.[22] The French were ensuring that their warships were kept safe from the advancing Germans, but directed to French ports overseas. They intended to keep control of their own fleet for their own purposes.

The impression reported by Campbell that the French government was stiffening its attitude towards Germany was reinforced after the arrival in Bordeaux in the afternoon of 18 June of the First Lord of the Admiralty (Alexander) and the First Sea Lord (Pound). These two men met Darlan that evening, and sent back an optimistic report, having found the situation completely different from that which they expected. Fighting was continuing. The French navy, which was in good heart, had engaged in successful operations against Italy, and would continue to fight until

The British War Cabinet in Chamberlain's Government. Chamberlain resigned in May 1940 after heavy criticism from the Labour Party and many Conservatives over his handling of the Norwegian Campaign. Back row: Kingsley-Wood, Churchill, Hore-Belisha, Hankey. Front row: Halifax, Simon, Chamberlain, Hoare.

(Associated Press)

The Allies capture and destroy the iron ore port at Bjervik, north of Narvik, before evacuating Norway in June 1940. French troops, involved in these operations, landed in Britain and provided some recruits for the Free French.

(Associated Press)

OFFICERS' QUARTERS.

MEDICINE SUPPLIES.

CLERKS.

FOOD.

← TO SLEEPING QUARTERS.

SURFACE of EARTH.

SOLDIERS' QUARTERS.

SOLDIERS' QUARTERS.

AMMUNITION STORES.

SUBTERRANEAN R.R. CONNECTION.

HOSPITAL.

TELEPHONE BUREAU.

AMMUNITION.

DIESEL MOTORS for AIR and LIGHT.

← 325 Feet →

A cross-section of part of the Maginot Line, begun in 1930. This massive fortification embodied the French conception of defensive warfare, and the French defeat was often blamed on the 'Maginot Mentality'. (Keystone Press)

Lord Gort, pictured in France, decorating a French sergeant-major for bravery. This was a conventional exercise in public relations, to demonstrate Anglo-French comradeship to the world.

(Imperial War Museum)

Troops at Dunkirk, wading out to a British rescue ship. Many others were evacuated in smaller pleasure craft, ill-equipped to deal with the heavy German attack which greeted them.

(Keystone Press)

German bombardment of a Dunkirk oil refinery during the evacuation. Other French oil stocks were captured intact by the Germans.

(Keystone Press)

At the same time, the French fronts were under heavy attack. Artillery in action in the early morning behind the lines of the Western Front.

(Keystone Press)

terms were known; if these included the surrender of the fleet, they would be rejected. Before capitulation in France, the fleet would be sailed to friendly ports or in the last resort destroyed. They reported that they had found Darlan 'very friendly and determined'.[23]

The same evening, Campbell tried to sum up what he described as an extremely confused situation. The French government still refused to give him any clear idea of their intentions, especially on a move to the colonies — he wondered whether they themselves knew what they intended to do. However, they were asserting with increasing determination that dishonourable terms would be rejected, and then the government would leave. Campbell's total impression remained one of uncertainty. He felt that he could not believe anyone implicitly, with the exception of Pétain, but the latter would only talk in generalities — 'mostly about the sufferings of the people'.[24]

During the next day, 19 June, these doubts were to some extent removed, and the impression of a tougher attitude among the French leaders grew stronger. That day, Pound returned to London while Alexander remained in Bordeaux as the representative of the British Cabinet. In the morning Alexander and Campbell saw Pétain and Baudouin, who told them that the Germans were to receive a French delegation. They also said that the French Cabinet had decided that on the approach of German forces to Bordeaux, the President of the Republic, the Presidents of the Chamber and Senate and three or four ministers would go overseas, probably to Algiers, to carry on the government. Weygand would probably go too, to co-ordinate further French war efforts.[25] Campbell reported to London his satisfaction at this decision, which he and Alexander had welcomed. The conversation had left a good impression on them, and if words meant anything there was no French weakening on the determination to reject dishonourable terms.[26] (In fact there was never any question of Weygand leaving France. Campbell was misled on this point, though at this stage he did not realise it.)

On the same day, 19 June, Lord Lloyd (the Colonial Secretary, who had many contacts in France and was a friend of Weygand) arrived in Bordeaux on a special mission to the French government. He was to take advantage of what seemed to be the more favourable French attitude to revive the Alliance, and he brought specific proposals. The British government offered to provide transport for the French to move as many men and as much equipment as possible to North Africa, in defence of which the British fleet and air force in the Mediterranean would co-operate with French forces. French pilots should be flown there, and would be provided with aircraft from the USA or Britain. Finally, the proposal made to the previous French government to transform the alliance into a total union was confirmed.[27] This was in fact a further effort to persuade France to change course and carry on the war, but it had a dangerous air of unreality about it. How would the French regard the proposal to reinforce North Africa with British aircraft, when they had been told so often that there were no planes to spare for the battle in France? Or the proposal to provide American aircraft, when they knew how few had so far arrived? To revive the offer of union at this stage was complete fantasy, and showed that the British government had no conception of how it had been brushed aside on 16 June. Campbell, in fact, hard pressed to report even day-to-day events, had scarcely mentioned the offer of union since the time of Reynaud's resignation.

The message carried by Lloyd was a flight of over-optimism by the British government, but it is significant that such optimism was still possible at this date (his instructions were drafted on 18 June, and he travelled on the 19th), and that this view in London coincided with the hopeful impressions shared by Campbell, Alexander and Pound in Bordeaux. When Lloyd reached Bordeaux, he went with Alexander and Campbell to see Lebrun. They delivered the British message, suitably presented to fit in with the reported decision that the President and part of the government were to go overseas. Lebrun expressed gratification, but Campbell reported that 'he was in a pitiable condition and nothing definite emerged from the conversation'. The British representatives then saw Pétain and Baudouin, and Lloyd again delivered his message. No specific comment on the actual proposals was recorded by Campbell. Pétain again gave categorical assurances that the French fleet would never be handed over to Germany, though it might have to be scuttled. He was indefinite on the question of the government's going overseas. Baudouin, when pressed, said that departure had been decided in principle, and would be finally settled, with the time of leaving, the following morning. Lloyd, in a private letter written on 22 June, wrote that he had found Pétain 'vain, *ramolli,* and dangerously gaga', but that firm undertakings had been received on the move to Africa and on the fleet. Lloyd and Alexander flew home the next

90

morning, 20 June, having heard that the French government was to leave that afternoon for Perpignan *en route* for North Africa.[28]

On 20 June, Campbell reported to London that the French delegation was to meet the Germans that night to receive terms, and the French government was to move to Perpignan during the day, in order to be able to consider the terms in safety. (Bordeaux had been bombed on the night of 19/20 June.) Lebrun and members of the government would then go on to North Africa.[29] This move seemed sufficiently certain for Campbell to telegraph for transport to North Africa for himself and his staff, and the Admiralty ordered two destroyers to Port Vendres for the early morning of 22 June.[30] But at this stage, what had seemed a definite decision was suddenly arrested. In the evening of 20 June, Campbell reported: 'Last minute change of plan. Germans having offered to reinstate telephone line between Tours and Bordeaux, Government have now decided to remain here to receive terms, which they expect to do tonight'. Campbell still expected to be leaving with the overseas party of the government, but did not know whether they would go from Bordeaux or Port Vendres.[31]

During the night of 20/21 June, Campbell grew increasingly anxious. In the middle of the night he tried in vain to find Baudouin or Pétain, and at 6 a.m. on the 21st he sent the military attaché with a note to Baudouin, formally reminding him that the British government expected to be consulted as soon as terms were received. Baudouin replied that it had always been the intention of his government to do so.[32] Campbell's telegrams to London on 21 June, as he waited for news of the German terms, were short and depressed in tone. He had little solid information, but his impressions were discouraging. Baudouin assured him that the government's intentions remained unchanged, and the move to North Africa was still on — but, Campbell commented, 'even if that is true at the moment, evil influences are at work'.[33] (By that time, in fact, it was no longer true: the move to North Africa was off.) Campbell saw Chautemps, who conveyed an impression of confused intrigues and a kaleidoscopic situation, which was true enough but not helpful. Chautemps also told him of Weygand's belief that France, having made mistakes, deserved to suffer.[34] About midnight that night, 21/22 June, Baudouin telephoned Campbell to say that the terms had been received. With this news, events entered a new phase.

Such was the British view as reported from Bordeaux during the period between the French request for terms and their receipt. It was a confused and shifting view, but the belief on 18, 19 and 20 June that the situation was improving can be plainly discerned. Darlan gave a distinctly hopeful impression about the fleet, and Alexander and Pound were cheered, at least at the time of their meeting with him. The decision to send a part of the government to North Africa seemed to have been firmly taken, but Campbell frequently doubted whether he could believe what he was told, and indeed on the subject of North Africa he was misled. The interlude of optimism rested on shaky foundations. It is time to turn to the view from London during these same days.

In London, one crucial question was, could the new French government be trusted? On 17 June Vansittart told Halifax that he was sure Pétain himself could be trusted — 'I do not believe Pétain to be anything but a man of honour'. He therefore proposed that a message be sent to him, in French, expressing confidence that the victor of Verdun would do nothing contrary to honour; urging resistance by the fleet and in North Africa; and confirming the offer of union. Churchill did not follow this up at once, preferring to consider a message from the King to President Lebrun.[35] Sargent took a different view from Vansittart: 'We cannot trust the new French government. They will be tempted to sell the fleet to the Germans in order in return to obtain better terms'. He passed on the opinion of Roger Cambon, Minister at the French Embassy, that the new government 'would behave worse than King Leopold and that we should not put too much trust in Ad. Darlan'.[36] On 18 June, Sargent again wrote of 'the complete unreliability of the present French Govt.', and suggested sending a Cabinet minister to Bordeaux to help Campbell in dealing with them.[37] A telegram to Lothian, the ambassador in Washington, on 17 June expressed much the same view, that Pétain had disregarded the British stipulation about the fleet, and 'we can have no confidence in further action that he may take' unless he acted on that stipulation.[38] These were the early reactions to the news that Pétain's government had asked for an armistice, in breach both of the agreement of 28 March and of the British conditions of 16 June, whose confused fate was not known in London on 17 June. A crucial influence on the reactions of the British Cabinet was the news of Pétain's broadcast on 17 June, brought in and read out while the Cabinet was in session: 'It is with a broken heart that I tell you today that fighting must cease'. This was accompanied by a report (later found to be false) that French troops had been ordered to cease fire at 12.40 p.m. that day.[39]

In subsequent days, considerable confidence was placed in Darlan. Alexander and Pound repeated their favourable impressions from Bordeaux, and when Pound spoke to the Cabinet on 19 June, after his return from France, he repeated that Darlan was 'very calm and determined', and steadfastly maintained that the fleet would not be surrendered.[40] Throughout the crisis, Pound was to continue to show his trust in the word of his fellow-admiral.

Reports from Bordeaux and advice from London together failed to provide a coherent impression of the character and intentions of the new French government. It was therefore difficult for the British Cabinet to decide on its policy. There were other problems; the Cabinet itself was under intense pressure, with overloaded agendas on which every item was likely to be vital — home defence, internal security, Ireland, manpower and industrial organisation, aircraft production, food control, shipping and relations with the USA and USSR. All had to be dealt with, in addition to the problems of France. It seems that even the superb administrative machine which served the Cabinet was groaning under the weight of work it was expected to do. Cadogan, despite his immense capacity for work, had to write in his diary for 22 June: 'Don't remember what happened (writing on 23). I have had a most scarifying 48 hrs'.[41] He thought, moreover, that too much was going on outside the Cabinet machine, causing confusion and bad decisions. 'No. 10 hall is like behind the scenes at the circus and every crank in the world is getting hold of P.M. and getting half-baked decisions. I won't go on unless this is stopped'.[42]

This outburst, on 19 June, was occasioned by a broadcast by de Gaulle on the previous evening — later to become so famous that de Gaulle was called 'the man of 18 June'. At the time, it was a striking illustration of the uncertainty and indecision in the British government. At a Cabinet meeting at 12.30 p.m. on 18 June, Duff Cooper (Minister of Information) reported that de Gaulle had given him the text of a broadcast he wished to make. De Gaulle had made a marked impression on Churchill and Spears as a man of vigour and courage, willing to stand out against an armistice; but since

Reynaud's resignation he held no ministerial position, and it was by no means obvious that he should be allowed to use the BBC to broadcast to France. Indeed, the Cabinet agreed that 'while there was no objection to the substance of the broadcast, it was undesirable that General de Gaulle, as *persona non grata* to the present French Government, should broadcast at the present time, so long as it was still possible that the French Government would act in a way conformable to the interests of the Alliance'. Then, after the meeting, the members of the War Cabinet were consulted again individually, and agreed that de Gaulle should after all be allowed to broadcast, which he did that same evening.[43] His short speech consisted of a declaration and an appeal. The declaration was that while German tanks, planes and tactics had inflicted a defeat on France, this was not final and hope must not be lost: '. . . nothing is lost for France. The same means which have defeated us can one day bring victory'. France was not alone, but had behind her the French empire, the British empire and its sea power, and the vast industries of the USA. The war was not settled by the battle of France, but was a world war. The appeal was for French soldiers already in Britain, or who might come there, and for specialist engineers and armament workers, to get in touch with him. 'Whatever happens, the flame of French resistance must not and will not be put out'.[44]

Apart from this phrase about resistance, there was no clear indication as to why such men should get in touch with de Gaulle, or what would happen if they did. Nonetheless, the broadcast disturbed Cadogan so much that he demanded to see the draft of de Gaulle's next speech before it was made; and when he read the draft, he had it stopped. De Gaulle intended to declare that the French government had capitulated and was in the power of the enemy. Since it no longer represented the French nation, a new government had been formed in London to take over the destiny of the country.[45] In Cabinet on 19 June, Halifax argued that the British must take care not to offend 'the better French elements' at Bordeaux. British approaches to persuade French colonial authorities to fight on had already drawn a protest from Charles-Roux to Campbell, deploring such moves when French forces were still in the field and when it had been decided to continue the war if German terms were excessive.[46] It was clearly rash to try to subvert the French empire from its allegiance, if it was still thought likely that the Bordeaux government would continue the war. To challenge the validity and authority of that government itself, and to countenance the proclamation of a rival government, would be even more provocative and dangerous. So de Gaulle was muffled. He was allowed to broadcast on the evening of 19 June, but only in general terms — though he still declared that, faced with the collapse of a government in bondage to the enemy, 'I General de Gaulle, French soldier and leader, am conscious that I speak for France'.[47] On 20 and 21 June he did not broadcast at all. On the 20th he went to see Cadogan, who pointed out to him that Weygand might yet go to North Africa to continue the war; de Gaulle said that if this happened he would be the first to offer his services. A small committee under Vansittart, watching over French affairs, agreed on 21 June that public indications of lack of confidence in the French government should be avoided.[48]

The trouble was that the British government were in two minds. They wanted to encourage French resistance to Germany, if need be against the wishes of the Bordeaux government. Yet at the same time they still had some hope that the Bordeaux government itself would go to North Africa and continue the war, and therefore they were afraid to do anything which appeared too subversive and likely to destroy these hopes. The result was a series of hesitant and sometimes conflicting actions.

(ii) The conclusion of the armistices, 22-24 June

The German armistice terms were telephoned to Bordeaux during the evening of 21 June. At midnight, Baudouin telephoned Campbell and told him that the terms had been received; the French Cabinet would consider them at 1 a.m. on the 22nd, after which Baudouin would see the Ambassador.

The German terms provided for the ending of hostilities, and for German occupation of an area comprising rather more than half of France, including the whole of the Channel and Atlantic coasts and the city of Paris. In the occupied zone, Germany was to have all the rights of an occupying power, and the French government and administration were to give it all support and assistance. The French government was to be free to choose its seat in the unoccupied zone, and to transfer to Paris if it wished. The French armed forces (except those necessary to maintain order) were to be demobilised and hand over their equipment to the Germans. All fortifications in the occupied zone were to be handed over in good condition. Article 8 laid down that the French navy (except a part set aside for the protection of the French colonies) was to be demobilised and disarmed under German and Italian supervision, in the ports which were the peace-time stations of the warships concerned. The German government made a solemn declaration that they would not use these ships for their own purposes (except for watching the coast and minesweeping), and that they would make no claim on the French fleet at the conclusion of peace.

The French government was to take no further hostile action against Germany, and was to prevent any members of its armed forces from going abroad. French nationals were forbidden to fight against Germany in the service of states still at war, and any who did so would be treated as *francs-tireurs*. French merchant ships were forbidden to leave port until further orders; ships overseas were to be recalled to France or sent to neutral ports; all aircraft were forbidden to take off. All ports, factories, shipyards, and means of communication in the occupied zone were to be handed over in their existing state. The cost of the German occupation forces in France was to be met by the French government. All German prisoners of war in French hands were to be returned, and the French government was to hand over on demand any German national in French territory — a provision aimed at refugees who had left Germany before the war. French prisoners of war, on the other hand, were to remain prisoners until the conclusion of peace. A German Armistice Commission, to which the French were to attach a delegation, was to control the execution of the armistice conditions, and the armistice would come into force when France agreed on terms with Italy; it could be denounced at any moment, and would cease immediately if the French did not carry out their obligations under its provisions.[49]

These conditions were severe. In particular, the retention of the French prisoners of war gave the Germans a human hold over the French government, while the unspecified occupation costs gave them an economic hold. The occupied zone included the major part of French agricultural and industrial resources, and the Germans held a powerful weapon in their ability to close, completely and at any moment, the demarcation line between the two zones. However, the terms were not so harsh as those imposed on other countries defeated by Germany, and gave France a markedly better status than, for example, that of Poland. Notably, there existed an unoccupied zone and a French government; the surrender of the fleet was not required; and there were no demands on the empire. These limitations had been imposed by Hitler, who did not wish to risk seeing the French fleet (especially its destroyers) join Britain, or having the French resume the war from the empire.

Amendments to the terms which were requested by the French government on 22 June included an alteration to article 8, on the fleet, which would allow French warships — after demobilisation and the landing of ammunition under German and Italian supervision — to sail to North African ports with half their peace-time complements. All the requests were rejected, with the exception of a minor concession on the surrender of military aircraft. On article 8, the Germans declined to make any alteration to the text, but pointed out that the execution of the terms regarding the fleet would be a matter for the Armistice Commission. The final convention was thus almost identical with the original terms.[50]

Campbell received the gist of the German terms from Charles-Roux while the French Cabinet was meeting to discuss them in the small hours of 22 June. When Campbell learned of the condition about the fleet, he at once wrote a note arguing that its character was insidious, and that it would be folly to place any reliance on Germany's word. This note was sent into the meeting, but although Baudouin read it out to his colleagues, Campbell had serious difficulty in getting further information from him at the end of the meeting. Baudouin said that he had to draft a reply to the Germans, and did not have time to talk. When Campbell insisted, Baudouin outlined the clause on the fleet, and said his government were making a counter-proposal that the fleet should be sent to North Africa to be dismantled. Campbell said that North Africa was not sufficiently far away. Reluctantly, and after saying at first that he did not have a copy, Baudouin handed over a text of the terms; and again reluctantly, he took Campbell into the Cabinet room where they could talk more privately. Campbell insisted that he should be received again before the draft reply to the German terms went before the French Cabinet. The Ambassador was angered by this episode, and telegraphed: 'The French have completely lost their (?heads) as witnessed by the shameful scene above described, and are totally unmanageable.'[51]

Before sending his account of this meeting, Campbell telegraphed a translation of article 8, on the fleet, which was received in London during the afternoon of the same day, 22 June, unfortunately with a corrupt passage which obscured the ports where the ships were to be disarmed. He followed this by a summary of the other main terms, and the comment that: 'Diabolically clever German (?terms) have evidently destroyed the last remnants of French courage'. Then he telegraphed the text of articles 1 to 7, and article 9.[52]

At 7.45 a.m. on 22 June, Campbell went to see Pétain and Baudouin before the French Cabinet met to consider its reply to the German terms. He appealed to Pétain not to allow the fleet to fall into German hands, and said that recalling it to French ports to be disarmed under German control was equivalent to surrender. Pétain assured him that the British government need have no qualms — the French hoped to get the fleet away to African ports such as Dakar or Madagascar. Campbell reported that the ministers who were standing round them during this interview, waiting to go into the Cabinet meeting, were distraught.[53] His telegrams that day seem to show that Campbell's own nerves were also on edge. While he was speaking to Pétain, the naval attaché met Admiral Auphan, the Chief of Naval Staff, who assured him that the French government hoped to arrange the internment of the fleet away from home ports — perhaps at Dakar, the French Congo, or Madagascar. No French warship would be handed over to the Germans: the ships would remain under the French flag, with orders that if the Germans or Italians tried to interfere with them, the crews were to sink them at once.[54] Telegrams describing these meetings were despatched, and received in London late that afternoon.

The same afternoon, in Bordeaux, Campbell obtained a copy of the French reply to the German terms from Charles-Roux. He telegraphed that he had obtained the text only with the utmost difficulty, and commented on the change requested about the fleet: 'This is wholly unsatisfactory and is indeed little if any better than German version'. Campbell then forced his way into Baudouin's office and demanded to be received at once, when he told Baudouin that once the ships were in German hands for purposes of control they would never be allowed to leave. Baudouin replied that the Germans would be invited to send control commissioners to ships away from their base ports, and for other ships the scuttling order would be carried out if there were any attempt to interfere with the French crews. Campbell said this was totally unsatisfactory, whereupon Baudouin offered to get Darlan to explain to him exactly how the scuttling order would work.

After this meeting, Campbell reported that he was faced with 'deliberate bad faith on the part of politicians . . . There is an organised conspiracy to keep me from ascertaining the facts'. He found great hostility to Britain among ministers, and had to deal with 'a crook who is now the leading spirit in the government and an old dotard whose word of honour nevertheless remains our only hope'. (The crook was Baudouin, the dotard Pétain.) Campbell's only optimistic thought was that most French warships were in fact away from home ports, and might take the law into their own hands, either with or without orders from Darlan.[55] This telegram was an extreme statement of Campbell's position. For example, it was by no means necessarily the case that he was being deliberately deprived of information. Baudouin was under extreme pressure, working against time — though he had probably also ceased to care very much about the British. Campbell was in fact kept as fully informed as possible by Charles-Roux, and was able to telegraph to his government a full summary of the amendments to the German terms requested by the French, together with the German replies. On the question of the fleet, he reported: 'The proposed modification is not accepted for insertion in the Convention. Germans do not refuse (group indecipherable) acceptance of proposal made but they consider it is a measure of (?allocation) falling within the power of Armistice Commission'.[56] When Charles-Roux handed Campbell the texts of the French and German documents, about 6 p.m. on 22 June, he said that he was instructed to state that Darlan's dispositions were such that 'no ship would be utilisable were an attempt to use it to be made'. Charles-Roux said that this should give the British government complete satisfaction, but Campbell disagreed: 'I naturally repudiated this with contumely and said that this lamentable clause might well make just the difference to us between victory and defeat, and therefore jeopardise also all hope of a future for France'.[57]

At this point, in the evening of 22 June, Campbell decided that he and his staff should leave Bordeaux for England. The Canadian and South African ministers went with him. This step had the effect of ending British diplomatic representation with the French government, though the French continued for some time to have representatives in London, and it did not involve a formal breaking-off of diplomatic relations. Campbell took this step on his own initiative, telling the Foreign Office that the Germans might occupy Bordeaux within the next few hours, and that after burning his cyphers there would be no further purpose in his remaining. He did not wish to become an embarrassment to his government (presumably by being captured), nor to endanger the cruiser *Galatea* which was standing by for him.[58]

Shortly before this, Campbell had learned of and reported the signature of the Franco-German armistice.[59] Harvey noted in his diary for 22 June: 'Armistice signed at 6 p.m. The French Government did not even bother to tell us. H.E. [His Excellency — i.e. Campbell] only learned of it when he called on Weygand tonight'.[60] When Weygand told Campbell that the armistice had been signed, the Ambassador said at once that he intended to leave. He had expressed this intention to Charles-Roux in a conversation at 6 p.m. on the 22nd. He stated that he had been accredited to 'a free and allied government'; his own government would not wish him to stay with a French administration which within a few hours would be under enemy control. It was in any case his duty to go home and consult his government.[61] It thus appears that Campbell had made up his mind to treat the signature of the armistice as the signal for his departure.

Given the information he had, and the acute distrust of the French government which he had developed, it would be difficult to argue that Campbell himself should have stayed in Bordeaux. One British ambassador (Oliphant, Ambassador to Belgium) had already fallen into German hands that summer. It is more arguable that he might have left behind some member of the diplomatic staff, both as a channel of information and as a service to British subjects. The Foreign Office had to telegraph to Washington on 23 June, explaining that Campbell's withdrawal from Bordeaux made it impossible to obtain details of the Italian armistice terms and asking whether the State Department would provide them.[62] As for British subjects, there must have been others who shared the exasperation of two Britons who had been serving with the French army, and who reached Bordeaux only to find that the official representatives of their government had left before them. Fortunately for them, a British warship was still there and took them off.[63]

Campbell's departure caused surprise and dismay in the French government; and later it was to give the French the opportunity to claim that Britain had taken the initiative towards breaking off diplomatic relations.[64] However, none of this weighed with Campbell at the time. Shortly after his return to London, he advanced two explanations of the French surprise at his departure. First, he thought they might have deluded themselves into believing that the French government would be allowed to function freely, so that a British ambassador could be of real service; alternatively, they may have wished to detain him so as to give the impression that the British government condoned their actions. Campbell was sure that the Foreign Secretary would not wish any such impression to be given. He argued that the French government 'had violated the no-separate-peace engagement; they had broken their word, recently renewed in writing, to consult His Majesty's Government on receipt of the German terms; they were meeting my representations with evasions and were treating me personally with discourtesy; and they were on the point of falling under enemy control. In these circumstances it was clear I could render no further service'.[65] There Campbell rested his case. With his departure, there ended the constant flow of information and interpretation which had so far been available to the British government concerning the situation in France.

The Embassy party did not have an easy passage. Leaving Bordeaux for Arcachon at 11 p.m. on 22 June, they embarked in an open sardine boat early in the morning of the 23rd, but when they left the Arcachon lagoon for the open sea the cruiser *Galatea,* which was to pick them up, was nowhere to be seen. Meanwhile the boat rolled in a rough sea, and it was raining heavily. Eventually the naval attaché made contact with the *Galatea* on his portable wireless set, and after a further wait the Canadian destroyer *Fraser* appeared. The party transferred from their sardine boat — no easy task for some elderly landsmen — and were taken to the *Galatea* at St. Jean de Luz. They finally sailed for home about midnight on the 23rd/24th, Harvey's last entry in his diary on leaving France being: 'Very rough. Too tired to be ill'.[66]

In London, the Cabinet met at 10 a.m. on 22 June, with Chamberlain in the chair. Halifax was able to report that the German terms had been received by the French government, but he did not know what they were. The Cabinet confined itself to deciding on a message to France, pressing Britain's right to be consulted, and repeating that she had not released France from her obligations. This telegram also expressed sympathy with the French government, and repeated that Britain would give every assistance if the French continued the struggle.[67] Campbell was also instructed to try to secure an immediate move of a nucleus government overseas.[68] During the day, the King telegraphed to President Lebrun on the question of the fleet.[69]

These were the last gestures of a Cabinet still uncertain of the position. When it next met, at 9.30 p.m. on the 22nd, ministers had before them Campbell's telegrams describing his activities of the night of 21/22 June and up to 8 a.m. on the 22nd, his difficulties in getting information from Baudouin, and the principal German terms.[70] They also knew of a German report that the armistice had been signed, confirmed by a message from Campbell received at the very end of the meeting. The final armistice terms were still unknown. On this information, the Cabinet assumed that the issue was now settled: the French government was accepting conditions which would be broadly those demanded by the Germans. They did not wait to see the final terms before taking a series of decisions designed to keep the French fleet out of German hands and to incite resistance in the French empire.[71] They also decided on broadcasts to be made by Churchill and de Gaulle.[72]

Churchill, in his broadcast on 23 June, said that his government had heard 'with grief and amazement' that the French government had accepted the terms dictated by the Germans. They could not believe that such terms could be accepted by any government possessing 'freedom, independence and constitutional authority'. They would place France and her empire in the power of the enemy, and the whole of French resources, including the navy, would speedily pass into enemy hands. Churchill asserted Britain's continuing confidence of ultimate victory, in which, despite the action of the Bordeaux government, she would cherish the cause of the French people. The British government called on all Frenchmen outside the power of the enemy to assist them in their task; and on all Frenchmen, wherever they were, to aid the forces of liberation.[73] There was here, as well as denunciation of the armistice, an implication that the existing French government did *not* possess freedom, independence and constitutional authority. In this lay the significance of the further decision to allow de Gaulle to broadcast again. Alexander had some misgivings about this, fearing that de Gaulle might alienate many Frenchmen and make it more difficult to safeguard the fleet, but his view did not prevail, and the broadcast was made on the evening of 22 June in terms approved by the Cabinet. De Gaulle denounced the armistice as being not merely capitulation but enslavement, and proclaimed that honour, commonsense and the interests of France commanded that every free Frenchman should continue the fight. He announced the formation of a French fighting force, and appealed for volunteers.[74]

These were strong words, but went little further than what had previously been said. On the morning of the next day, 23 June, the British Cabinet took an important step beyond this point when they considered a proposal put by de Gaulle to Churchill to form a French National Committee — or as Churchill called it, a Council of Liberation. Churchill commented that de Gaulle was a good fighting soldier with a strong personality, but before approving or recognising such a Council, it would be best to find out what other Frenchmen were available to serve on it. Despite this reservation, the Cabinet agreed in principle to recognise a Council of Liberation. Churchill, Halifax and Cadogan saw de Gaulle, who hoped that Reynaud might be head of a provisional government which it would be the National Committee's task to form. After this, de Gaulle broadcast again in the evening of 23 June, announcing the formation of a French National Committee which would account for its acts either to a legal French government, 'as soon as one exists', or to the representatives of the French people when they could meet freely. It would take under its jurisdiction all French citizens in British territory, and assume the direction of all military and administrative bodies in Britain. This broadcast was followed by two statements made on the authority of the British government. The first announced that the armistice terms just signed were considered by the British government to place the Bordeaux government in a state of complete subjection to the enemy, so that it could not be considered the government of an independent country. The second took note of the plan to form a French National Committee, fully representative of independent French elements determined to carry on the war, and declared that the British government would recognise such a Committee, and deal with it on all matters relating to the pursuit of the war.[75] This was not the creation of a new French government, a rival to that headed by

103

Pétain, but it was a step in that direction, and potentially of great importance.

The days of uncertainty were at an end, and the Bordeaux government was now regarded as potentially hostile. Churchill told the Cabinet on 24 June: 'Our relations [with the French government] might well approach very closely to those of two nations at war with each other'.[76] All this preceded the conclusion of the Italian armistice, news of which only reached the British Cabinet during its 6 p.m. meeting on 24 June. Its terms were not known until the 25th, and then only from radio reports.

The main terms of the Italian armistice followed those of the German instrument, though with two major exceptions: Italy was not granted the rights of an occupying power; and France did not have to pay the costs of occupation. Indeed, the Italian zone of occupation was limited to the area so far captured by the Italian army, which was very small. There was to be a demilitarised zone fifty kilometres deep on the Franco-Italian frontier, and other demilitarised zones on the borders between Libya, Tunisia and Algeria. The fortifications and naval bases at Toulon, Ajaccio, Bizerta and Oran were to be demilitarised under Italian supervision. French forces, as in the German terms, were to be demobilised and disarmed, except for those necessary for the maintenance of order. The naval clause simply repeated that in the German armistice.[77] The fact that the Italian terms did not include the occupation of large areas in France or French North Africa was a great relief to the French government, and was very important in inducing the authorities in North Africa to accept the conditions. Otherwise, the main significance of the Italian armistice was that following its conclusion the German armistice would come into force.

The conclusion of the two armistices marked not only the end of hostilities between France and the Axis powers, but also the breakdown of the Franco-British Alliance. From the British point of view, it remained to be seen whether anything could be salvaged from the wreck. The fate of the French fleet was the most urgent question, but it was also possible that the French empire, or parts of it, might be induced to continue the war. There was also the question of the future of de Gaulle and his proposed French National Committee, and whether a new Anglo-French alliance could be forged out of this fragmentary remnant of the old. In all this, the French government under Pétain could not be ignored: there was much to be feared, and perhaps still something to be hoped for from them. The development of these matters in the latter part of 1940 will be the subject of the second part of this book.

NOTES

1. See the analysis in Michel, *Vichy Année 40,* 36-7.
2. Geoffrey Warner, *Pierre Laval and the Eclipse of France* (London 1968), 177, 189, 190-2; Michel, *Vichy Année 40,* 38-40, 52-4.
3. *Ibid.,* 40-42; the quotation is from a number given by M. Michel, See also E. Jäckel, *La France dans l'Europe d'Hitler* (Paris 1968), 53 and note 7.
4. Warner, 178-9; Michel, *Vichy Année 40,* 48.
5. The terms are summarised below, 95-6.
6. Warner, 179-86; Michel, *Vichy Année 40,* 44, 48-51; Jäckel, 59-66.
7. Warner, 188-90; Michel, *Vichy Année 40,* 51-2; Jäckel, 66-7.
8. Michel, *Vichy Année 40,* 42; *Événements, Rapport,* 385-6; BBC *Daily Digest of Foreign Broadcasts,* No. 335, 18 June 1940, Part II, 2A, i; *Le Temps,* composite number for 19, 20, 21 June 1940; Baudouin, 179.
9. *Événements, Rapport,* 388-91; Michel, *Vichy Année 40,* 43.
10. Warner, 187-8; Truchet, 94-5.
11. FO 371/24311, C7294/65/17, Campbell to Halifax, 17 June 1940, No. 433.
12. FO 371/24311, C7301/65/17, Campbell to Halifax, 17 June 1940, No. 437.
13. *Ibid.,* Campbell to Halifax, 17 June 1940, No. 440.
14. *Ibid.,* Campbell to Halifax, 17 June 1940, No. 441.
15. FO 371/24311, C7294/65/17, Halifax to Campbell, 17 June 1940, Nos. 379, 380; C7301/65/17, Campbell to Halifax, 17 June 1940, No. 444.
16. *Ibid.,* Halifax to Campbell, 17 June 1940, No. 397, transmitting message from Churchill; despatched 1.15 a.m., 18 June 1940.

17. *Ibid.,* minutes by Pound and Churchill, 17 June 1940; Halifax to Campbell, 18 June 1940, No. 398.
18. *Ibid.,* Campbell to Halifax, 18 June 1940, No. 447.
19. *Ibid.,* Campbell to Halifax, 18 June 1940, No. 449.
20. *Ibid.,* Campbell to Halifax, 18 June 1940, No. 450.
21. *Ibid.,* Campbell to Halifax, 18 June 1940, No. 453.
22. French Admiralty signals, 0235 hrs, 1912 hrs, 2027 hrs, 2240 hrs, 18 June 1940, *Événements, Rapport,* 443-6.
23. FO 371/24311, C7301/65/17, Campbell to Halifax, 18 June 1940, No. 459, transmitting message from Alexander to Churchill.
24. *Ibid.,* Campbell to Halifax, 18 June 1940, No. 460.
25. *Ibid.,* Campbell to Halifax, 19 June 1940, No. 467.
26. FO 371/24311, C7352/65/17, Campbell to Halifax, 19 June 1940, No. 468. This arrived very corrupt, and was delayed for repetition, which reached the Foreign Office on 21 June.
27. CAB 65/7, WM(40)172, 18 June 1940, Annex.
28. CAB 65/7, WM(40)173, for Alexander's account to the Cabinet on 20 June; FO 371/24311, C7301/65/17, Campbell to Halifax, 19 June 1940, No. 474; C. F. Adam, *Life of Lord Lloyd,* (London 1948), 299-300, including letter from Lloyd to his son David, 22 June 1940.
29. FO 371/24311, C7352/65/17, Campbell to Halifax, 20 June 1940, Nos. 477, 480.
30. *Ibid.,* Campbell to Halifax, 20 June 1940, No. 483; Halifax to Campbell, 21 June 1940, No. 450.
31. *Ibid.,* Campbell to Halifax, 20 June 1940, No. 485, despatched 2.20 a.m. 21 June 1940.
32. FO 371/24348, C7362/7362/17, Campbell to Baudouin, 20 June 1940, Baudouin to Campbell, 21 June 1940; FO 371/24311, C7352/65/17, Campbell to Halifax, 21 June 1940, No. 496; *Harvey Diaries,* 20 June 1940, 397-8.
33. FO 371/24311, C7352/65/17, Campbell to Halifax, 21 June 1940, No. 503.
34. *Ibid.,* Campbell to Halifax, 21 June 1940, No. 505.
35. FO 371/24311, C7301/65/17, minutes by Vansittart and Churchill, 17 June 1940.
36. *Ibid.,* minute by Sargent, 17 June 1940.
37. *Ibid.,* minute by Sargent, 18 June 1940.
38. *Ibid.,* Halifax to Lothian, 17 June 1940.

39. CAB 65/7, WM(40)170, 17 June 1940, 11 a.m.

40. CAB 65/7, WM(40)172, 19 June 1940, 12.30 p.m.

41. *Cadogan Diaries,* 22 June 1940, 305.

42. *Ibid.,* 19 June 1940, 304.

43. CAB 65/7, WM(40)171, and footnote to minute No. 11.

44. Charles de Gaulle, *Mémoires de Guerre,* vol. I, *l'Appel, 1940-1942* (Paris 1954), 267-8; BBC Written Archives, French Scripts, 1940.

45. *Cadogan Diaries,* 19 June 1940, 304-5; Woodward, vol. I, 321-2; FO 371/24349, C7389/7389/17, minute by Cadogan, 20 June 1940.

46. CAB 65/7, WM(40)172.

47. De Gaulle, vol. I, 268-9.

48. *Cadogan Diaries,* 20 June 1940, 305; Woodward, vol. I, 322-3; CAB 21/1454, Committee on French Resistance, 1st Meeting, 21 June 1940.

49. An English translation of the French version of the terms was circulated to the British Cabinet, CAB 66/9, WP(40)224, 27 June 1940. See also *Documents on German Foreign Policy,* series D, vol. IX (London 1956), No. 523; *La Délégation française auprès de la Commission allemande d'Armistice,* vol. I (Paris 1947), 1-8.

50. A summary of the French requests and German replies was circulated to the British Cabinet on 23 June 1940, CAB 66/9, WP(40)217. See *DGFP,* series D, vol. IX, Nos. 522, 524; Warner, 185-6; Michel, *Vichy Année 40,* 49-51.

51. FO 371/24348, C7375/7362/17, Campbell to Halifax, 22 June 1940, No. 514, received 12.45 p.m.; FO 371/24311, C7341/65/17, Campbell's despatch, 27 June 1940, paras. 85, 86. Baudouin, 197-8, does not differ in substance, though he does not mention any unwillingness to give Campbell a copy of the terms.

52. FO 371/24348, C7375/7362/17, Campbell to Halifax, Nos. 511, 512, 513, 515, 516, all of 22 June 1940. The last was received at 5.50 p.m.

53. *Ibid.,* Campbell to Halifax, 22 June 1940, No. 517; cf. FO 371/24311, C7341/65/17, Campbell's despatch, 27 June 1940, paras. 89-93.

54. FO 371/24348, C7375/7362/17, Campbell to Halifax, 22 June 1940, No. 518; cf. FO 371/24311, C7341/65/17, Campbell's despatch, 27 June 1940, para. 95.

55.   FO 371/24348, C7375/7362/17, Campbell to Halifax, 22 June 1940, No. 519, received 3.15 a.m., 23 June 1940.

56.   *Ibid.,* Campbell to Halifax, 22 June 1940, Nos. 522, 526, 527.

57.   *Ibid.,* Campbell to Halifax, 22 June 1940, No. 529, received 2.30 a.m., 23 June.

58.   *Ibid.,* Campbell to Halifax, 22 June 1940, No. 531, received 11.40 a.m., 22 June.

59.   *Ibid.,* Campbell to Halifax, 22 June 1940, No. 530, received 12.35 p.m., 23 June.

60.   *Harvey Diaries,* 22 June 1940, 400.

61.   FO 371/24311, C7341/65/17, Campbell's despatch, 27 June 1940, paras. 104-5.

62.   FO 371/24348, C7411/7362/17, Halifax to Lothian, 23 June 1940.

63.   C. D. Freeman and D. Cooper, *The Road to Bordeaux* (London 1940), 372-3, 383.

64.   See Charles-Roux, 91; by no means a hostile witness.

65.   FO 371/24311, C7341/65/17, Campbell's despatch, 27 June 1940, para. 108.

66.   *Ibid.,* para. 109; *Harvey Diaries,* 22, 23 June 1940, 400-401.

67.   CAB 65/7, WM(40)175; FO 371/24348, C7375/7362/17, Halifax to Campbell, 22 June 1940, No. 458.

68.   *Ibid.,* Halifax to Campbell, 22 June 1940, 400-1.

69.   FO 371/24301, C7146/9/17, Halifax to Campbell, 22 June 1940, No. 464, transmitting message from the King to Lebrun.

70.   See above, 97-8.

71.   See chapters 7 and 8, below.

72.   CAB 65/7, WM(40)176.

73.   Text of broadcast in Woodward, vol. I, 313-14.

74.   CAB 65/7, WM(40)176; text of de Gaulle's broadcast in BBC Written Archives, French Scripts, 1940, and *Discours et messages du Général de Gaulle, 18 juin 1940-31 décembre 1941* (London 1942), 2-4.

75.   CAB 65/7, WM(40)177; Woodward, vol. I, 324-5; FO 371/24349, C7389/7389/17; de Gaulle, vol. I, 79-80, 270.

76.   CAB 65/7, WM(40)178.

77.   The terms of the Italian armistice were circulated to the British Cabinet on 27 June; CAB 66/9, WP(40)224. The text was taken from an official German broadcast. Cf. Michel, *Vichy Année 40,* 51-2, 75.

Chapter 6

BRITISH OPINION AND THE FALL OF FRANCE

From the outbreak of the war until May 1940, not only was the whole of British strategy based on the existence of the French alliance, but British propaganda also proclaimed its importance and solidarity. The natural expectation of the British people was that, as in 1914-18, the alliance would continue at least until the end of the war. How then was the unexpected, rapid and total collapse of French power presented to the British public? What interpretations were placed on that collapse by the organs of public opinion? And what were the reactions of the British people themselves? These questions were closely connected with the political and military matters which have so far been dealt with, for propaganda was a weapon of war, and the morale of the British people was of vital political and strategic importance.

Before attempting to answer these questions, some examination of government censorship and control of news is necessary. These matters were dealt with by the Ministry of Information, which was in 1940 a much criticised department. Its head in Churchill's administration, Duff Cooper, came under heavy attack in the press, one example being the furore over a scheme by the Ministry to survey public opinion by means of sample polls on particular questions. The surveyors were at once nicknamed 'Cooper's snoopers', and there was a highly critical debate in the House of Commons. The *Spectator,* not at the time a radical or anti-government paper, declared: 'The opinions held by the people of Great Britain are not the concern of the Ministry of Information. It is no part of its official function to bolster up their morale'.[1] Much of the criticism levelled at the Ministry may have been unfair — and certainly the British people have now grown accustomed to having their opinions on all manner of questions investigated by surveys and polls — but it is significant that the press in general adopted such an attitude. The necessity for censorship on matters of fact which might help the enemy was generally recognised even if often thought to be mistakenly applied, but anything savouring of government control or censorship of opinion was resented and opposed.

The system of censorship actually applied by the government was, at least in theory, very flexible. In one sense it was true to say that there was *no* censorship, in that the authorities had no power to prohibit publication, even on matters involving information. However, the censor did have power to *authorise* publication, and with such authority a publisher was protected from prosecution under the Defence Regulations. This was often called 'voluntary censorship', because it was not in itself an offence in law to publish material which had not been submitted to the censor, or even to ignore the recommendations of the censor on material submitted. Even so, the deterrent effect of being open to prosecution if one did not submit material to the censor and then accept his ruling was considerable. On military matters, of course, the Service departments exercised their own censorship on the information which they released for publication. On opinion, as distinct from information, there was no censorship. The Ministry of Information often provided guidance on opinions which it thought suitable to express, and could state that it was undesirable to publish other views; in rare cases this could be put so strongly as to say that publication of certain views was not in the public interest. However, it held no legal veto on expression of opinion. In 1940 it was not even an offence to try to influence public opinion against the war, though it became an offence if false statements were made for this purpose.[2]

In one sense this system looked milder than it was, because the reserve powers of the government under the Defence Regulations were sweeping. For instance, they provided the means to suppress a newspaper, as was done at a later stage with the *Daily Worker*. Yet it was also true that to mount a prosecution, even under the Defence Regulations, required serious consideration, and presented some difficulty. Ministers and officials disliked much of the material which was published, whether informative or expressing opinions. Ministry of Information officials frequently pointed out to complainants from the Foreign Office that they did not have legal powers of censorship to prevent the publication of some item which attracted disapproval. There was, however, sometimes a screen of self-censorship by editors which is hard for an outsider to detect. This arose either through fear of prosecution, genuine patriotism, or concern for some element of public opinion. George Orwell, for example, was to encounter the latter in 1944 when he sought a publisher for *Animal Farm,* only to find that, while it was easy to publish criticism of Churchill, it was much harder to publish criticism of Stalin.[3]

Government intervention affected the publication of both information and opinion about the fall of France. During the last week of May the War Office was extremely reluctant to give out any information at all on the position of the BEF. *Communiqués* were rare, and said very little; to mention names of units was entirely forbidden.[4] Again, on 2 June, when the evacuation of British troops from Dunkirk was approaching completion but that of the French had made little progress, the BBC and the press were warned against publishing either total figures of those evacuated or separate figures for the different nationalities. The same measures were applied to a broadcast by Eden on the evening of 2 June.[5]

With regard to opinion, there are examples of strong guidance being given to press and radio on various questions. At the end of May 1940, much thought was given to the presentation to the British, and also the American, public of the operations in Flanders and the situation of the BEF. Vincent Massey, the Canadian High Commissioner, was particularly anxious to counteract German propaganda in the USA, and to avoid any appearance of Anglo-French dissension. Meetings were held between Ministry of Information and Foreign Office officials to consider the problem, and the Ministry undertook to provide guidelines for counter-propaganda to prevent a belief in German invincibility from growing up. It was necessary to emphasise that the Germans had failed to break the Allied defences; that they had committed all their mechanised forces; and that if this assault could be held, they would never again be able to strike such a blow. The contrast should be pointed between the potential power of the British and Allied empires and 'the small endurance of the German nation', to show that the Germans needed to win outright that summer while the Allies only had to hold on in order to secure ultimate victory.[6] This general line of argument, especially that the Germans had to win quickly, was indeed often followed by the press, although it was being used before these suggestions were made; it was also adopted in private, even by shrewd and well-informed observers. Attlee, in Cabinet on 26 May, declared that Hitler must win by the end of the year. Harvey, in Paris, wrote in his diary on 23 May: 'I am certain that if we can repel the present attack we shall win. The Germans are putting their all in because they cannot wait'.[7] So it would be unwise in this case to attribute much influence to an attempt to guide opinion: it appears rather that the required opinion already existed.

Another example of guidance occurred at the beginning of June, when Lord Perth (a senior official at the Ministry of Information and formerly Ambassador at Rome) agreed with Halifax that it was desirable to do everything possible to maintain French morale and to soothe what Perth called their perhaps over-tender susceptibilities'. Halifax raised in Cabinet the importance of ministers making suitable references to French achievements in their broadcasts and other speeches, and Churchill agreed to recommend decorations for General Blanchard and Admiral Abrial after the Dunkirk operation.[8] Similarly, Admiral Godfrey, the Director of Naval Intelligence, urged on the Foreign Office on 1 June the need to counter German propaganda about the separation of the Allies. Cadogan agreed, and proposed a message from the King to President Lebrun, which was duly sent on 4 June.[9] These suggestions were followed by a spate of articles in the press praising French achievements and courage, though it is not clear how far these were directly government-inspired.

Again, at the time of the Franco-Italian armistice, the Foreign Office prepared a 'suggested line for publicity', arguing that the apparent moderation of the terms was deceptive, and that the real Italian demands would emerge at the peace treaty, when Italy would seize all the territory she coveted. By accepting the armistice terms, and especially demobilisation and demilitarisation, the French were making themselves defenceless for the future.[10] The press in general followed this line closely.

Bearing in mind that military censorship largely controlled the news of the battle in France, and that expressions of opinion could be guided in varying degrees by government influence, how was the collapse of France reported and explained to the British public? And how did people react to these remarkable events?

In reporting the battle, it was normal for newspapers to print or summarise the British, French and German official *communiqués* — on occasion the German *communiqué* was placed first. Naturally these *communiqués* were not intended to be very informative, but they often mentioned place-names so that it was possible to identify on the map the area where fighting was taking place. There were also despatches from war correspondents in France, usually giving background information or impressionistic accounts of conditions at the front, but occasionally going beyond such limits. On matters of interpretation, there were regular contributions from military commentators, reflecting on the meaning of the news and speculating about the future.

In the first phase of the battle of Flanders, when the Germans broke through on the Meuse, drove to the sea at the mouth of the Somme, and cut off the BEF and large French forces in the north, the tale was told inexorably by place-names. The German *communiqué* of 19 May claimed the capture of St Quentin and Le Cateau. The French reported that Le Cateau had been recaptured — which meant at least that it had been taken in the first place. The reports of both sides on 21 May showed the Germans at Amiens and Arras; they claimed also to be at Abbeville.[11] On 23 May Churchill told the House of Commons that there was heavy fighting in and around Boulogne: the Germans were at the Channel ports, which they never reached in 1914-18.[12] There was thus no possibility of disguising the rapid and startling German advance. In commentary, the general attitude adopted was that the situation was serious but not disastrous. A firm lead in this was given by Churchill in his first broadcast as Prime Minister on 19 May, when he declared that the Germans, 'by a remarkable combination of air bombing and heavily armoured tanks', had made deep penetrations and spread alarm and confusion. 'It would be foolish . . . to disguise the gravity of the hour. It would be still more foolish to lose heart and courage or to suppose that well-trained, well-equipped armies numbering three or four millions of men can be overcome in the space of a few weeks, or even months, by a scoop or raid of mechanised vehicles, however formidable'. He spoke with confidence of the stabilisation of the front in France,[13] and examples of a similar line of thought abounded in the press, of which two must suffice. On 20 May, an article by Liddell Hart, well known as an exponent of mobile warfare and then military correspondent of the *News Chronicle,* described the situation as 'serious but not grave'. Even with 'a steel-shod thrust', the point might be less sharp the second time. The law of diminishing returns should operate — unless there was a lack of anti-tank weapons or a widespread break in morale. Hart wrote that if the immediate danger was checked the outlook should improve, and that even the extent of the existing bulge was not acutely dangerous to the French front as a whole, and did not compare with the German offensives of 1914 and 1918. General Gwynne, writing in the *Daily Telegraph* of the same day, argued that mobile forces alone could not hold a position, and doubted whether the Germans could consolidate their success.

The argument that the Germans desperately needed a quick victory was also much in evidence. For example, the *Daily Herald's* leading article of 18 May warned that readers who were afraid of the truth should cancel the *Herald* and go to some newspaper which would coat the news in pink sugar. This was not the *Herald's* way, and because its readers had been told the truth in the past, they were ready for the present grave developments — 'you are not shocked, not even apprehensive'. However, even after thus preparing the ground, the article went on to say that Hitler had delivered a great blow, but it was only the first punch in a fifteen-round fight; the enemy was over-trained, and worried about his stamina — he needed a quick decision. *The Times* on 27 May chose its analogy from bridge instead of boxing, but the gist was the same: the enemy was playing all his trumps, and if he did not win he would be left with a barren hand.

Given the necessary limits on information, and remembering the hopes and uncertainties of the supposedly well-informed ministers and generals, this presentation by the press was not unreasonable. What was missing, inevitably, was the note of preparation for the collapse of France which was already being foreseen by the British Cabinet. There was on the contrary sometimes a note of excessive optimism. The *New Statesman's* London Diary of 25 May quoted a series of headlines from the London evening papers between 17 and 21 May, all referring to German attacks being repulsed, repelled, or beaten off; such presentation of news was ultimately destructive of good morale, and in marked contrast to sober statements by the Prime Minister, and the diarist wondered whether the Minister of Information could do something about it.

During the brief but intense crisis of the evacuation from Dunkirk, news was, on the British side, kept as far as possible out of the press and off the radio. Comment on the situation varied considerably, and two extreme examples may be cited. The main item on the front page of the *News Chronicle* on 29 May was by William Forrest, correspondent with the BEF, now returned to England. 'It is time to face up to facts, to admit the worst. With the surrender of the Belgian Army, the BEF would seem to be cut off. Escape by sea is the slenderest of hopes. A break-through to the south is a possibility equally remote'. Within the German ring there were as many men as British lost at the Somme in 1916, and as much war material as was lost in the German offensive of March 1918. These analogies were ominous indeed, but knowing the expectations with which the evacuation was begun this was a fair assessment, and it is striking to see it in print at that time. The *Daily Telegraph* on 31 May, on the other hand, published a despatch from its Paris correspondent reporting a belief there that the Germans could be held in Flanders until the Allied troops were withdrawn — which proved very largely true. Other reports fell between these two extremes, and the BBC news — largely taken directly from the Service departments — was vague and anodyne.[14]

When the evacuation was seen to be a success, there was a burst of relief, even exaltation. The *Daily Telegraph* somehow jumped the gun, declaring in its leading article on 1 June: 'It has happened' — the miracle by which alone the BEF could be saved from annihilation. Its main news item on the front page claimed that 75 per cent of the BEF had been brought off, which was roughly correct. *The Times* on 4 June had a ring of pride and triumph in its first leader — which was headed 'Anabasis' in the confident assumption that all its readers knew their Xenophon and his march to the sea. The article declared that: 'no British army is encircled if a way to the sea is open or can be forced'. The Royal Navy, coupled with native resource, had produced a great achievement. On 5 June the *Daily Mirror* followed Churchill in his speech of the 4th, and emphasised that Dunkirk was a miracle of deliverance but not a victory. 'We have escaped what might have been one of the biggest military defeats in our history. That is all'.

The relief, however expressed, could only be temporary, and other dangers immediately sprang into prominence. Invasion appeared imminent. 'Strategicus', in the *Spectator* of 31 May, wrote that Hitler was certain to have plans ready, and mentioned in particular the possibility of the Germans using specially constructed motor boats, each carrying 200 men and capable of crossing the Channel in half an hour — an idea which the Chiefs of Staff had discussed and thought practicable.[15] The *Economist* mentioned the same idea, and pointed out that it was possible that the Germans would succeed in landing some thousands of raiders, though the question of holding the ground thus seized would be a different matter.[16] Invasion did not come; instead, the German offensive in France was resumed more quickly than had been thought possible. In an article in the *Daily Telegraph* on 3 June, Gwynne argued that the Germans would have to pause to reorganise before they could strike again, and thought it might be three weeks before the attack could be resumed. Only three days later, he was having to comment on the Somme offensive of 5 June, and to admit that it had come sooner than he expected. The Paris correspondent of the *Economist,* in a despatch dated 1 June, wrote that the supreme test in France might be only a very few months, or even a very few weeks, away — the word 'only' seems incongruous in retrospect.[17]

In the new battle, the press looked at first for signs of hope. *The Times* referred prominently to estimates that German casualties in the battle of Flanders had already been between 400,000 and 500,000 killed, wounded and missing, so they were bound to be seriously weakened for fresh fighting. Gwynne wrote optimistically about the efficacy of Weygand's system of defence in depth.[18] It was 10 June before the newspapers began to present a seriously gloomy view of the military situation. That day, the military correspondent of *The Times* (Cyril Falls) noted that probably as long ago as 7 June, German tanks were reported to have reached Forges-les-Eaux, twenty-seven miles south-east of Dieppe. 'It is with something of a shock that one realises that the attack here has passed deeply into Normandy'. A careful reader could note that a report in the same issue from the correspondent with the French armies, claiming that nowhere had the French retreated more than fifteen miles from their first positions, was presumably untrue. On 11 June the BBC news bulletins contained the ominous news that the French government had left Paris.

By 12 June the note of dismay was clearer, though still muted by hopeful comments. A hasty visit by André Maurois to London on 11 June, during which he spoke at a press conference and later on the wireless, made a wide impression. The burden of his message was that the French armies needed help in days, not months. The *News Chronicle,* in a leading article about his visit, emphasised that the French army was heroic but outnumbered and overwhelmed by German machines.[19] *The Times* military correspondent stressed the same point on 13 June, and noted that there was no sign of the predicted slackening in the progress of the German offensive. This hope was still present — even Liddell Hart pointed out in the *News Chronicle* of 12 June that it was in the nature of all offensives to decline in momentum. Historically, this was doubtless true — but in 1940 the German offensive became the exception to the rule.

On 14 June the *News Chronicle* carried a despatch by David Scott, correspondent with the French army, saying that no-one now concealed the extreme gravity of the military situation. The French army was very tired, there had been no reliefs, and in some sectors the troops were hardly capable of further resistance. On the same day the *Daily Telegraph* commented, though more obscurely, on the dangers of the position, emphasising that Paris had been declared an open city despite much French talk of defending it to the death. In these circumstances the prominently displayed reports and photographs in all the press on 15 June, describing the despatch of 'a new BEF' to France, with magnificent new equipment and new artillery, struck a distinctly forced and false note.

It is necessary to make allowances for the conditions under which correspondents and commentators worked. The newspapers were always behind the radio in presenting news, and were often even further behind events. For instance, a despatch from a *Times* correspondent in France, dated 16 June, appeared on the 17th. Its contents were gloomy; '. . . for the first time in modern history, the civilised western powers are in imminent danger of being overrun'. The battle was 'entering into a state of extreme confusion'. Even by 16 June such estimates were overtaken by events; by the 17th, Pétain's government had already asked for an armistice, and this news was broadcast during that day. More important than the speed of events in influencing the presentation of news was the need to avoid discouraging the French. Cyril Falls wrote in *The Times* on 18 June: 'The catastrophe which has overtaken the French armies has for some little time appeared to be imminent, yet it was impossible to say anything which might have discouraged or embarrassed Allies striving to ward off complete disaster'.

The same constraints operating upon the reporting and commentaries on the battle worked even more powerfully on public discussion of the French political situation, French morale, and British aid to France. Every effort was made to put the best front on events, and to say only that which was encouraging and hopeful. For example, Hannen Swaffer, a journalist with an individual outlook and a considerable public following, wrote in the *Daily Herald* of 17 May: ' "The French are confident". That is the best news that comes from Paris. Those who know the French Army, its great competence, and its chivalrous courage, will take heart from these words'. This could be matched from many different sources. Even General Spears, before going to France as Churchill's liaison officer, wrote an article for the *Spectator* in praise of Weygand and Pétain — 'the combination of a general who knows when to strike and a general who knows when to hold on to the death'.[20]

Alexander Werth, one of the most knowledgeable and respected journalists writing about France, wrote in the *New Statesman* a notable article which combined sentiments of this kind with an uncomfortable feeling of foreboding, and an evocation of what he felt was threatened. He likened the German assault to that of the Martians in H. G. Wells' *The War of the Worlds* — an analogy which occurred to more than one observer that summer, catching the feeling both of the German mechanised forces and of the advance of an alien civilisation. Werth wrote: 'The French are going to stop it. They must stop it . . . We in Paris feel that it *cannot* happen; one just cannot imagine Hitler driving through the Champs-Elysées, and laying a filthy wreath on the Unknown Soldier's grave . . . Paris is strangely beautiful these days; when you walk down the Seine . . . you cannot help feeling a fearful pang in your heart, as you look at the familiar beauty of it all — the river and the bridges and the Louvre . . . and the little bistros with the zinc counters — a whole immense, beautiful civilisation and a whole art of living threatened by the army of crawling monsters . . .'[21] This passage still has the power to move any Englishman who knows and loves Paris: in May 1940 it must have been heart-rending. It foreshadowed the disaster which was to come, even while saying that it could not happen.

When the battle of Flanders was ending at Dunkirk, there was a considerable effort in the British press (as the Ministry of Information desired) to soothe French susceptibilities and emphasise the part played by the French army. There was much appreciative comment on the French role at Dunkirk, and Vernon Bartlett wrote a front-page article in the *News Chronicle* on 31 May, saying that a section of the French army 'is still shielding the British withdrawal to the coast, with very little hope indeed that it can itself be saved'. The *Daily Herald* of 3 June wrote: 'We do not forget that French armies helped to cover the retreat . . .' Dunkirk, and the anticipation of a renewed German offensive in France, produced a flood of exhortation for Britain to send more help to France in spite of the danger of invasion. Right across the political spectrum, the press emphasised and repeated this demand with a unanimity which appeared to owe more to feeling than to calculation, and which went well beyond the actual plans of the government to send help to France. To take just two examples, the *Scotsman* declared on 5 June that 'it is in France that the war will be won or lost, and it is there that we must be as strong as possible if we are to hold the enemy's onslaught . . .' The *Daily Mirror* on 14 June stated: 'The French do not need our tributes and our praise. They need aeroplanes, tanks, guns, men.'

The desire of editors to send more British reinforcements to France as late as 14 June may have proceeded from a combination of a sincere sympathy for France with a failure to grasp the reality of the situation there. When Maurois visited London on 11-12 June, he realised that his audiences had not understood the real nature of the war or the defeat — they listened, he wrote, 'as if I were a being from another planet'. A friend who invited him to dinner, in a special effort to show understanding of his difficulties, assured him that there was no need to change into a dinner-jacket.[22] If indeed men's minds had failed to grasp the full disastrous import of events in France, they were presumably enlightened in the next few days. Paris fell on 14 June, and on the 15th there was a great lament in the press over the fate of 'the intellectual capital of Europe' and 'one of the great lamps of civilization'.[23] Two days after mourning the fall of Paris, the press was faced with the new French government formed by Pétain. For a brief moment it was possible to entertain some hope of the new government — the *Scotsman*'s leading article on 17 June remarked that it had a strong military and naval cast, and that Reynaud might have felt this type of government to be best able to judge defence requirements. However, such hope was short-lived. The French request for an armistice was made known to the public by broadcasts on 17 June, and in the press by the 18th. Thus in the space of three or four days the British press passed from urging the despatch of reinforcements to France to commenting on the likelihood of an armistice, and on its significance when it came.

In the evening of 17 June the Prime Minister made a broadcast on the situation following the French request for an armistice. 'The news from France is very bad, and I grieve for the gallant French people who have fallen into this terrible misfortune. Nothing will alter our feelings towards them, or our faith that the genius of France will rise again. What has happened in France makes no difference to British faith and purpose. We have become the sole champions now in arms to defend the world cause. We shall do our best to be worthy of that high honour. We shall defend our island, and, with the British Empire around us, we shall fight on unconquerable until the curse of Hitler is lifted from the brows of men. We are sure that in the end all will be well.'[24] In this brief statement, Churchill made two points which were to be characteristic of British public reaction to the French request for terms. Firstly, there was a general determination in the press not to indulge in any recrimination or blame against the French, possibly influenced by the hope — voiced in the press as it was in the Cabinet — that France might yet fight on overseas; it was certainly modified when the acceptance of the German terms became known. The second point was that whatever France did, Britain would fight on.

The *Daily Herald* wrote on 18 June that France, like Britain, had been unprepared for the pace of the war; France, like Britain, had been led by men dulled by ignorance and complacency. But: 'It was France, not Britain, that had to pay the price of incompetent direction. She has paid it with magnificent bravery. And the payment has only begun'. The *News Chronicle* on the same day said that there would be no disposition in Britain to blame the French. The *Scotsman* wrote nobly: 'we shall not judge her [France] in this

Belgian refugees in flight before the advancing German armies. Scenes like this were later common on the roads of France, blocking the movement of troops and of French ministers when they left Paris for Bordeaux.

(Associated Press)

French map showing the routes taken by the German army during the invasion of France 1940.

(Imperial War Museum)

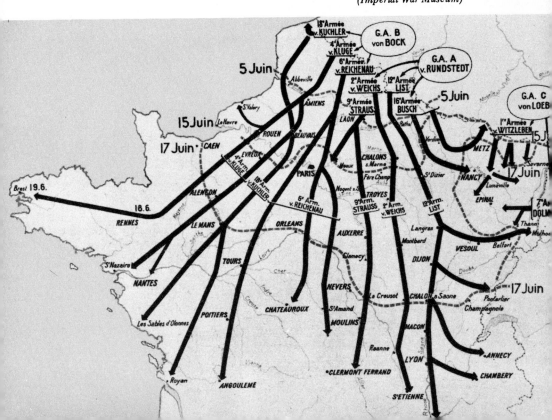

A column of weary German troops arriving at a village on the demarcation line between occupied and unoccupied France.

(Popperfoto)

German troops parading through Paris [?4th July 1940]

(Imperial War Museum)

German soldiers using flame-throwers against a bunker on the Maginot Line. The fortifications were largely intact when the French surrendered.

(Popperfoto)

The campaign in Flanders was a defeat for the BEF as well as for the French army. British prisoners of war, taken by the Germans near Calais, go into a captivity which was to last until 1945.

(Associated Press)

Above: Delegates of the Pétain government sign the armistice in Marshall Foch's railway carriage at Compiègne on 22 June 1940.

(Associated Press)

General de Gaulle leaving no. 10 after the French armistice had been announced. Under the slogan 'Honneur et Patrie' he sought to rally the French against the armistice and against the subsequent Vichy government.

(Radio Times Hulton Picture Library)

hour of anguish'. The *Daily Mirror* struck rather a different note: 'No blame for the true France' — implying that there was a false France which might be blamed. The weekly journals took the same general line as the dailies. The *Spectator* of 21 June stated: 'French troops have fought with incredible gallantry, and no word of accusation against the French for what has happened should be countenanced here. France is still our ally. We associate in a single purpose her restoration and our own preservation'.[25] The *Economist* of 22 June put it even more strongly: 'We lose part of ourselves when France's liberties are trampled underfoot . . . France has borne the brunt of the military struggle. She has received little help from her neighbour and ally . . . There can and must be no recrimination'.[26] The *New Statesman* distinguished between Pétain's government, which was of the ultra-conservative Right, and France as a whole; but in general its sentiments were the same. There should be no bitterness, the French had fought bravely against crushing odds, and had paid for the mistakes of both their own and British leaders. For the future: 'One resolve unites us all, to make of our island fortress the base from which the liberty of the French shall be restored. Our allies of yesterday are our fellow-citizens of tomorrow'.[27]

One of the most striking aspects of the generous comments on the French defeat is the recognition of the paucity of Britain's military effort on land, and the acknowledgement that after Dunkirk the French army had fought virtually alone. There was at the moment of the French defeat a fuller acceptance of the French point of view on these matters than there was to be at later times. Criticism of France in the press was almost non-existent, and the only discordant note detected by a vigilant observer in the Ministry of Information was an assertion in the *Glasgow Herald* on 18 and 19 June that France had not accepted defeat so easily in 1870.[28] The press adopted a harsher note on 24 June, after the German armistice was signed and its terms known. The main news item in *The Times* declared that the terms meant 'the complete capitulation of France. The Pétain Government have agreed to hand over the French fleet, all other armed forces, and all stocks and materials'. The leading article stated that the French government 'can of course be nothing but a puppet of the Nazi regime', and that the terms entailed the conversion of France into a German arsenal for war against Britain. A contrast was drawn between the actions of France and those of other defeated states which had continued the war from outside their own countries. The *Daily Telegraph* asserted that the articles on the French fleet proclaimed the German intention to use the ships against Britain, though arguing that the terms in general were more completely a betrayal of France herself than of this country. The *Scotsman* denounced the terms as 'disastrous and humiliating . . . ignominious capitulation . . . There is no lack of sympathy for the plight of the French people, but this method of ending the struggle is unjustifiable'. The *Daily Herald* asked its readers to compare the terms with Pétain's claim that he would only accept an honourable peace: 'If this be honour, then what is shame?' Such comments were typical: condemnation of the armistice terms, though still with an undercurrent of sympathy with the French people who had been betrayed by their government.

In the torrent of events, the British government's offer of union with France passed without much comment. There was some wish in the Foreign Office to give it more publicity, but the view prevailed that after the French had rejected it, press discussion would merely draw attention to the rift in the alliance, and would be better avoided.[29] Such press discussion as there was tended to be mainly favourable. The *New Statesman* was enthusiastic, proclaiming on 22 June that the offer had 'no parallel in our history for its boldness and imaginative generosity . . . Here at last is the idea which gives to our struggle for European freedom a dynamic meaning. Continental unity must come out of this war. Shall it be on this basis of federal democracy or must it be the hegemony of a German master-race over herds of helots?'[30] Similarly, the *Economist* welcomed the proposal as 'a milestone in the slow journey away from frenzied and stultifying nationalism'.[31] In the *Spectator,* Charles Morgan wrote that Anglo-French union was the only possible nucleus for European federation.[32]

Such comments were characteristic of one type of reaction to the offer of union, but there was another type which was also of some significance. The *Scotsman,* while expressing general support for the proposal, recognised why France would be reluctant to form a union, in that French history had been one of conflict with Britain, and the French might well fear that Britain would be the predominant partner.[33] The *Tablet,* a Roman Catholic weekly, argued that the war had ceased to be for Frenchmen anything but a defence of France: 'The single sovereignty of France is for them the first necessity'. Few Frenchmen, therefore, would have much patience with talk of federal union and internationalism.[34] There was also some doubt as to whether the offer was altogether welcomed in Britain. The *Spectator* in a leading article admitted that the offer of union was a heroic gesture, but doubted whether its implications had been thought out, and concluded that 'it is impossible to regret that in its present form it has lapsed'.[35] Charles Morgan, who was himself in favour of the idea, agreed that many people were glad to think it was dead.

Such views drew attention to the continuing importance of national feeling, while the *New Statesman* and others believed that the war must be fought for something wider than national feeling or interest, and welcomed the offer of union as an earnest pledge that this was to be so. Both views had much support. The war was in part ideological, with Nazism an enemy which nearly everyone could agree to fight, even if they might not have agreed to fight Germany as such. Nevertheless, it is not clear how widespread such an attitude was, compared with patriotism or nationalism. General de Gaulle, for example, successfully based his concept of leadership on the claim that he stood simply for France and French interests — as interpreted by himself. However, it was important that both the internationalist and the patriotic attitudes existed, because this meant that both patriots and those who regarded themselves as being above patriotism could fight with equal determination.

While the offer of union with France brought out the differences between these two approaches to the war, in general the collapse of France brought out their similarities. Churchill, in his brief speech of 17 June, followed his words of grief and sympathy for the French people with the assertion that the fall of France made no difference to British faith and purpose. This sentiment was echoed virtually unanimously in the press. The *Daily Mirror* declared on 18 June that 'Mr. Churchill expresses the soul of Britain'. The *Daily Herald* took the same line: 'We say: *Britain fights on* — to win!' There were frequent evocations of the Napoleonic period, and the *News Chronicle* on 19 June likened the meeting of Hitler and Mussolini at Munich to that of Napoleon and Alexander at Tilsit. *The Times* recalled the crisis after Austerlitz and Jena, and declared that 'Hitlerism will come to its Waterloo'. Among the weekly journals, the *Economist* and *Spectator* argued soberly that Britain must fight on, and had the capacity to do so.[36]

The comments of the *New Statesman* on 22 June were particularly striking and illuminating. The parliamentary correspondent held that the country had received the news of the fall of France with unhysterical bewilderment. 'It was appalled, but also in its insular way it felt that the ring was now clear for the bout everyone had been waiting for, the heavyweight championship of Europe. No doubt many people felt a sense of pride and personal responsibility that at last the future of Europe depended on them'. He felt, however, that in the House of Commons Churchill had not quite risen to his opportunity: 'his response was that of a traditionalist, not of a democratic revolutionary'. There was no attack on 'the old gang' in British politics; the mass of the people were cast only in the role of spectators; there was not enough conscription, requisition, and compulsion. The same line was followed by the editor, Kingsley Martin, according to whom Churchill rightly assumed that the British were a stubborn people, ready to fight to the last ditch. Although he was a natural leader for them at such a time, he underestimated the bitterness felt by the people against those who had allowed the country to be reduced to such a pass, and he failed to understand the social forces at work in Europe. This preamble only threw into bolder relief the conclusion of Martin's article, which was that everyone must stand for that to which he owed the highest allegiance, since everything was threatened by the Nazi regime. 'There comes into my mind today the biblical story of the three men who were told that they would be thrown into a burning, fiery furnace unless they bowed down to false gods. They replied: "Our God whom we serve is able to deliver us from the burning, fiery furnace. But *if not,* be it known unto thee, O King, that we will not serve thy Gods". And we will not'.[37] However much Kingsley Martin differed from one aspect of Churchill's expressed stance, his final attitude of defiance was precisely the same as that of the Prime Minister. It is interesting that in the last resort the language of this defiance was not that of socialism but of the Old Testament.

Kingsley Martin quoted the Book of Daniel, and it is equally striking to see the *Tablet* on 22 June quoting the Puritan John Milton, who wrote that when God had some special work to be performed, 'he called upon his Englishmen to do it'. It was a proud boast, reflected the *Tablet,* and one often lightly made — 'but one we are entitled to carry in our hearts today'. After the disillusionment of the 1920s and 1930s and the consequent reaction against both patriotism and war, the unanimity and determination of the British press in the late June of 1940 were remarkable. The fall of France found the *Daily Mirror, The Times,* the *New Statesman* and the *Tablet* all speaking in the same terms.

In addition to the press one individual voice should be quoted, that of J. B. Priestley, who in the summer of 1940 was one of the most able and popular of all broadcasters. His North-country accent and plain approach gave his talks an air of solidity and frankness. He could not only claim the authority of a political nonconformist, an opponent of appeasement and a one-time advocate of the popular front movement, but he could also quote Nelson at Copenhagen: 'mark you — I would not be elsewhere for thousands'. Priestley commented: 'one reason why I wouldn't be elsewhere for thousands is because of the people here, the ordinary common folk. They are wonderful, and they are better than ever now that we simply have to depend on nobody but ourselves, are at bay in our tight little island'. In another broadcast, he said: 'The issue is plain. We simply can't live with Nazism. Either we destroy it or it destroys us. And I don't believe it can destroy us'.[38] Here Priestley put into words the widespread feeling that the fall of France had clarified the issues at stake, and that the British people were more contented and self-confident when they were left alone to face their enemies.

This was the way in which the fall of France was presented to the British people. How far the presentation was accepted, how closely the opinions of the people coincided with those of the press, it is difficult to assess. On 18 May 1940 the Ministry of Information began a series of daily reports on 'Public opinion in the present crisis', giving a picture of the state of opinion as it appeared to their sources in different parts of the country. (From time to time these sources included surveys by 'Cooper's snoopers'.)[39] Some of these reports illustrated occasions when public opinion apparently followed the lead of government, press, or radio, as, for example those of 21 May which said that morale was noticeably higher, in line with the general tone of the newspapers which had been optimistic about the battle in France.[40] More frequently, however, they indicated popular distrust of both news and government guidance. The Ministry's assessment of the general position on 18

May was that the reporting of the Norwegian campaign had seriously devalued all news sources, though the BBC had suffered less than the press and political leaders.[41] However, the BBC suffered markedly during the period of Dunkirk, when soldiers returned from France objected strongly to the publicity given on the radio to the RAF. The troops said they had seen few fighters over the battle zone, and this cast doubt on all broadcast news, not only about the RAF but also about other subjects.[42] There were other examples of popular scepticism. A reference in a speech by Churchill on 19 May to faith in God was felt in the country to be ominous; while Weygand's 'stand fast' order in the Somme battle was taken to be an SOS.[43] It appears that the British people were often quite capable of reading between the lines, and there must be no assumption that they passively accepted the public version of events.

Certain general points emerged from the flow of daily reports. There was a somewhat illogical combination of confidence in ultimate victory ('we shall win the last battle') with a belief in the power of Hitler and the accuracy of his prophesies ('He's a genius'; 'What's the date for London?').[44] Near the end of May, the reports indicated that opinion was unstable, swinging from day to day between troughs of depression and peaks of hope, and it was noted that such oscillation was beginning to produce bewilderment.[45] At the time of Dunkirk, it was reported that bad news was having a sobering effect, with personal anxieties being overlaid by a deep concern for the BEF. As early as 1 June there was a surge of relief, even elation, at the return of the troops, and the Ministry expressed some anxiety that morale was almost too high, showing a failure to grasp the full significance of the evacuation.[46] The release of tension was followed by signs of depression and detachment, reports of 6 and 7 June stating that although news of the fresh German offensive had brought anxiety, people were jaded and found it difficult to listen to the news. They were weary of perpetual crises.

Reported opinions about France and the French varied considerably. As early as 22 May rumours were current that Churchill had gone to France to prevent the French government from surrendering, and on 24 May there were reports of a marked increase in anti-French feeling ('The French are letting us down'). Then on the 29th it was reported that there were persistent rumours 'seeking to undermine confidence in the *entente cordiale* and in the

French Army'. Immediate action to counter these was held to be necessary. By 31 May, the indications were that such feelings had died down, and this was attributed to the praise which the press had recently given to the French army. On 4 June there were signs of a further decline in anti-French feeling, and of sympathy with Parisians over a recent air-raid on the city; the Ministry believed that this sympathy arose from an identification of Paris with London, and a recognition that the British turn for bombing would soon come. Reports on 7 June indicated feelings of guilt that Britain had done so little in the battle, and the Italian declaration of war ('a stab in the back') produced a further wave of sympathy for France on 11 June. On the 12th there were widespread reports that Maurois' broadcast appealing for help for France had been very effective, and working-class districts were asking why more help was not being sent. Similar views continued to be recorded during the next two days.

The first public reaction to the announcement of the French request for an armistice (made in the 1 p.m. BBC news bulletin on 17 June) was reported to be confusion and shock, but not surprise. Questions which were uppermost concerned the fate of British troops in France, and the future of the French fleet and air force. On 18 June, very little anti-French feeling was recorded, and Churchill's broadcast of words of sympathy and grief were thought to be wholly in line with public opinion. However, on the 19th it was obseved in the Ministry of Information that a latent anti-French feeling existed in the country, and this found indirect expression in the common phrase that 'At last we have no more allies'. On the 20th this feeling was reported to be increasing, and shown in such remarks as 'We're better off without the French', or 'We should have looked after ourselves all along'. On 23 and 24 June, with the conclusion of the Franco-German armistice, there were reports of a widespread feeling that the French had been betrayed by their leaders and politicians, but that indignation was not directed against the French people as such. As early as the 25th it was said that France was taking second place in conversation to the subject of air raids, and by the end of the month — apart from several reports of anxiety about the French fleet — public opinion appears to have turned to other matters.

The question of public reaction to Britain's being left alone to continue the war caused some anxiety in the Ministry of

Information. During the battle in France, the general trend of their reports was that men were more optimistic and less anxious than women, and the lower classes more so than the upper classes. It was believed that prolonged tension had a bad effect on middle-class women, who stayed at home and listened to the news; while many working-class women, who went out to work, were steadier in their morale.[47] On 16-17 June a feeling of gloom and apprehension was reported in the country as a whole, and most obviously among the middle classes and among women. The Ministry's observation on the 17th was that unless there was a strong lead from the Prime Minister defeatism was certain to gain ground, and there would be a serious division between government and people. A public opinion survey on 17 June showed that 75 per cent of the respondents expected the war to continue after the French surrender, while 15 per cent did not; 10 per cent were doubtful. (84 per cent of the men, but only 65 per cent of the women, expected the war to continue.) In reply to another question, 50 per cent of the respondents contemplated Britain's fighting on alone with confidence, and 25 per cent without confidence; 25 per cent were doubtful.[48] This showed a distinct lack of confidence in British chances. Reports of 19 and 20 June spoke of pockets of defeatism amidst a general determination to see it through; among the working and lower middle classes there were some comments that they would be just as well off under Hitler. On 24 June it appeared that reactions against Pétain's government were bringing out doubts about British leaders (if one nation had been betrayed by its leaders, so might another). 'There is no mistaking the tenor of our reports: leadership is in jeopardy'. This mood appeared to pass, and on 28 June the tenor of the reports was that people were calm and confident, though with an undercurrent of distrust of 'appeasement politicians' in the Cabinet. It was generally held that people responded well to firm leadership and clear directions, though not to mere exhortation.

These Ministry of Information reports must be treated with some reserve — to estimate the opinions and morale of a whole people was an almost impossible task. Nonetheless, they offer a valuable comparison with evidence from other sources. One general impression which they convey is of greater anti-French feeling than was shown in the press — but still less than might have been expected in the circumstances. Another is confirmation that the collapse of France was accepted by the country with comparative calm and determination, though with less immediate confidence in the future than was expressed in newspapers and broadcasts.

The general air of calm and confidence in the press did not prevent commentators from examining events in France to try to find the explanation for the collapse, and to extract lessons which might save Britain from a similar fate. Several of their explanations have become a familiar part of any historical discussion on the fall of France, but at the time they had the sharpness and immediate relevance produced by the danger looming on the other side of the Channel. There may have been an unreasoning conviction that 'it can't happen here', but many said that it might, and that it should be prevented by learning from the French disaster.

There were some obvious lessons to be learned. For example, the effect of the flood of refugees in hindering military operations, and in spreading alarm among the civilian population in France, was much emphasised; the general instruction to the British people in case of invasion was to 'stay put'. However the tendency of commentators on the fall of France was invariably to look beyond this kind of explanation to more far-reaching implications. For a military defeat, there were clearly military causes, and it was widely argued that the French had fought the war with the wrong type of strategic thinking and preparation. Their doctrine had placed too much emphasis on defensive strength and in particular on the strength of fortifications. The Maginot Line was treated as the symbol of this — the Maginot folly, the Maginot superstition, the Maginot mentality, were all phrases of the time. In 1940 the Allies had been prepared to meet the German attack of 1914. One obvious lesson from this was that the British must not fall into the same trap in the defence of their island, but must be ready for a war of movement and counter-attack rather than one of static defence.[49]

Nevertheless, military causes only partially explained the French defeat. It was the virtually unanimous view that France had been weakened and rotted from within by internal disunity, by German propaganda, by conspiracy and treachery, and by failure of leadership. Priestley put it in a broadcast: 'They have not been beaten; they have been sold out'. The German blows had been 'delivered against an opponent who had already been weakened *from within*. That is the Nazi technique'.[50] Dalton wrote in his diary after lunching with Spears on 28 June: 'Alas! for that French mansion, for those beautiful French palaces, that the white ants have eaten!'[51]

In this process of internal weakening, much was attributed to German propaganda and the 'fifth column' — treachery organised and financed by Germany — but it was also widely held that the condition of France was ripe for German exploitation. F. G. H. Salusbury, the *Daily Herald*'s war correspondent back from France, wrote in an article of 22 June: 'Essentially there is one reason for the French *débâcle* — France is not a united nation'. Some elements among French politicians and the upper classes preferred fascism to democracy, and were above all afraid of communism; while others, on the Left, regarded a patriotic war as a war merely for the preservation of capitalism. This opinion was shared by many British commentators, though there were differing views of the share of responsibility which might be attributed to Right and Left in French politics. Harold Laski, writing in the *Daily Herald* of 10 July, argued that it was the forces which had brought Napoleon III to power, suppressed the Commune, and victimised Dreyfus which had now sacrificed France to their own vested interests. It followed, therefore, that if the British were to hold firm they must release 'those democratic forces which capitalist democracy has so long held down'. A similar interpretation was offered by William Rust in the *Daily Worker* on 19 June: 'The rottenness exists among the ruling class, the dominant sections of which are pro-Fascist to the core. They fear the power of their own people more than vassaldom at the hand of a foreign imperialism'. He predicted that the capitalists and financiers of Britain, though momentarily frightened of Germany, would in the future 'try to do a Pétain on Britain', but others held that the French Left had its own responsibility for the collapse. A letter in the *New Statesman* pointed out that defeatism and pacifism existed among French socialists as well as among the middle classes.[52] In the same journal, Victor Gollancz argued that movements led by the communists to 'stop the war' had assisted Hitler's victory, and that the French communists had declared that it was imperialist war which was no concern of the working class.[53] There was even an occasional voice claiming that responsibility did not lie only with those in high places, or owners of property, or the politically active. 'It was not only the Communists and the Fascists, the politicians and the generals, and the lovers of property who failed . . . equally guilty were the lovers of beautiful things, and the people who could not bear to see women and children hurt'. This writer considered the lesson to be that the British could only guard against the fate of France by deciding that *nothing* — no loss, no suffering by children or loved ones — would deter them from fighting the Germans.[54]

There was some divergence of opinion over whether similar dangerous divisions, leading to sympathy with the enemy, also existed in Britain. Some on the Left thought they did — Laski and Rust have just been quoted. The *New Statesman* argued that while the new British government under Churchill was a vast improvement on the old, there was still a need to purge the civil service and other high positions of men who had failed in the past, and whose place in society might tempt them to behave as the betrayers of France had done.[55] However, this view does not appear to have been widely shared. A. J. Cummings, in the *News Chronicle* of 22 July, argued that there was no parallel between the French and British situations. In France the fascists, near-fascists and communists had been present in large numbers, and none had had their hearts in the war; but in Britain fascists and communists made up only a tiny fraction of a people determined on war.

The idea of a purge certainly received little official support. Some fascists and fascist sympathisers (including one Member of Parliament) were arrested, and severe measures were taken against enemy aliens in order to prevent fifth column activities. (These measures resulted in numbers of anti-Nazi Germans being taken off to the Isle of Man and elsewhere, and produced a public outcry which tended to show that the dangers of subversion were certainly not overrated in the country.) Attlee made a broadcast early in July in which he said that the overthrow of France had been brought about by the destruction of the unity, confidence and morale of the people. The Nazis had been able to persuade some well-to-do persons that they were the saviours of society from red revolution. But he concluded robustly: 'There is a phrase used a great deal now: "Fifth Columnists". I don't like it. I prefer the old-fashioned word "traitors". I don't think there are many active traitors in this country'.[56] The soundness of this opinion was never put to the acid test of invasion or occupation.

There was one further explanation for the collapse of French morale which was almost universally believed to have an immediate lesson for Britain, and this concerned the role of the censorship in France. There had been occasional grumblings about the working of the French censorship while France was still an ally, and her collapse brought a flood of assertions that the savage censorship of both facts and opinions had made any honest assessment of the situation in the country impossible. As Alexander Werth put it, if one wrote an article setting out the pros and cons of a situation, only the pros remained when it finally appeared — the cons had all been blue-pencilled.[57] It was generally agreed that this had produced a dangerous state of ignorance among the French people, had encouraged rumour and sapped morale. In the British press, there was not only confidence that a similar situation did not prevail in Britain (where, said the *News Chronicle* on 26 June, censorship was liberal and criticism healthy and effective), but also complete determination that it must never do so. The *Daily Herald* on 24 June, for example, proclaimed that parliament and the press defended a democracy from rotting from within — the British owed their new government to the work of constructive criticism in parliament and the newspapers. Hannen Swaffer, in the same paper, reported that some people were talking of censoring opinion, and said that this could not be allowed. What was seen as the dreadful example of France lay behind much of the criticism directed against the Ministry of Information. The *Economist* on 29 June made the same points, and concluded: 'The fact is that the lesson of France has to be learned. There, a main cause of the collapse was the double failure of the men in charge either to face the facts themselves or to permit the French people to know them . . . If the people and rulers of this country are to go "eyes front" to face their greatest peril, they must go with their eyes open'.[58]

NOTES

1. *Spectator,* 9 August 1940, 136-7.
2. INF 1/190, Director-General's Orders A and B, undated in this file copy, but after 31 January 1940; Director's Order No. 32, 22 December 1939, Censorship of Expressions of Opinion.
3. See George Orwell's unpublished preface to *Animal Farm, Times Literary Supplement* (September 1972).
4. CAB 21/1260, memorandum for Ismay, initials illegible, 31 May 1940; *The Times* leading article, 27 May 1940.
5. FO 371/24383, C7149/5/18, minute by Roberts, 2 June 1940.
6. *Ibid.,* note by Caldecote for Churchill, 28 May 1940; memorandum by Whitehead, 28 May 1940; minutes by Balfour, 30 May, and Strang, 31 May 1940.

7. CAB 65/13, WM(40)140th Conclusions, Confidential Annex; *Harvey Diaries,* 23 May 1940, 365, and cf. 369-70.
8. FO 800/312, H/XIV/441, Perth to Halifax, 1 and 6 June 1940, Halifax to Perth, 3 June; CAB 65/7, WM(40)157.
9. FO 371/24301, C7146/9/17, Godfrey to Jebb, 1 June 1940; minute by Cadogan, same date; King George VI to President Lebrun, 4 June 1940.
10. FO 371/24348, C7411/7362/17, minute by Nichols, 26 June 1940, and attached papers.
11. See the *communiqués* printed in *The Times,* 20 and 22 May 1940.
12. *H. C. Deb.,* vol. 361, col. 314.
13. *Listener,* 23 May 1940, 997-8.
14. The texts of the news bulletins are preserved in the BBC Written Archives.
15. *Spectator,* 31 May 1940, 743-4; CAB 66/8, WP(40)178, 29 May 1940.
16. *Economist,* 1 June 1940, 970.
17. *Ibid.,* 8 June 1940, 1007.
18. *The Times,* 5, 6 June 1940; *Daily Telegraph,* 8 June 1940.
19. Maurois, *Battle of France,* 204; *News Chronicle,* 12 June 1940.
20. *Spectator,* 24 May 1940, 712-13.
21. *New Statesman,* 25 May 1940, 660.
22. Maurois, *Battle of France,* 207-8.
23. The quotations are from the *Scotsman* and *The Times,* 15 June 1940.
24. BBC Home News Bulletin, 9 p.m., 17 June 1940; *The Times,* 18 June 1940.
25. *Spectator,* 21 June 1940, 828.
26. *Economist,* 22 June 1940, 1066-7.
27. *New Statesman,* 22 June 1940, 761-2.
28. FO 371/24348, C7678/7362/17, Notes on the Capitulation, 3 July 1940, memorandum by Dorothy Pickles, Part II.
29. FO 371/24311, C7294/65/17, minutes by Millard, 18 June 1940, Ward, 20 June 1940, Speaight, 23 June 1940.
30. *New Statesman,* 22 June 1940, 761.
31. *Economist,* 22 June 1940, 1066.
32. *Spectator,* 28 June 1940, 862.
33. *Scotsman,* 19 June 1940.
34. *Tablet,* 22 June 1940.
35. *Spectator,* 21 June 1940, 828-9.

36. *Economist,* 22 June 1940, 1065; *Spectator,* 21 June 1940, 829.
37. *New Statesman,* 22 June 1940, 764-5.
38. *Listener,* 4 July and 27 June 1940, 16, 1188.
39. INF 1/264. In the early stages, the reports do not indicate specific sources, other than Regional Information Officers and opinion surveys. On 30 September 1940 a new series was begun, a source being given for each item: many were still RIOs, but also, e.g., contact in Marylebone WVS, postal censorship, South Wales.
40. INF 1/264, 21 May 1940. (The following footnotes in this section all refer to this file, and only dates will be given.)
41. Note on the background situation, 18 May 1940.
42. See e.g. reports of 1, 3, 4 June 1940.
43. Reports of 19/20 May, 10 June 1940.
44. Reports of 20, 21, 24 May, 4, 13, 15 June 1940.
45. Reports of 24, 25 May 1940.
46. Reports of 29 May-4 June 1940.
47. Reports of 25 May, 13 June 1940.
48. Report of 18 June 1940.
49. Examples of this argument may be seen in: *Scotsman,* 21 June· 1940; *Daily Telegraph,* 22 June; *The Times,* 24, 25 June; *Daily Herald,* 27, 29 June; *New Statesman,* 29 June, 788-90.
50. *The Listener,* 4 July 1940, 15.
51. Dalton diary, 28 June 1940, note on conversation with Spears.
52. *New Statesman,* 6 July 1940, 13, letter from Odette Kern.
53. *Ibid.,* 13 July 1940, 39.
54. *Spectator,* 5 July 1940, letter from R. A. C. Radcliffe.
55. *New Statesman,* 29 June 1940, 786.
56. *Listener,* 11 July 1940, 39-40.
57. *New Statesman,* 29 June 1940, 788-90.
58. *Economist,* 29 June 1940.

A CERTAIN EVENTUALITY...

PART 2
SALVAGE OPERATIONS

Chapter 7

THE FRENCH FLEET

The conclusion of the French armistices with Germany and Italy destroyed the alliance between France and Britain, and the British government had to consider whether anything could be salvaged from the wreckage. The most pressing question was the future of the French fleet, which had figured so prominently in British dealings with France over the matter of an armistice. In 1940 the French navy was a powerful force, containing a large proportion of modern ships built in the 1920s and 1930s. Its numerical strength was: two battle-cruisers; seven battleships; seven 8-inch gun cruisers; eleven 6-inch gun cruisers; twenty-seven *contre-torpilleurs;* twenty-six destroyers; seventy-seven submarines; one aircraft-carrier and her tender-cum-seaplane carrier; and a large number of smaller craft.[1] Among these warships, the two battle-cruisers (*Dunkerque* and *Strasbourg*) had been completed in 1937 and 1938, armed with eight 13-inch guns, fast and well-armoured. Two of the battleships (*Richelieu* and *Jean Bart*) were also new and would be powerful when work was finished. At the time of the armistice, the *Richelieu* was estimated by the British Admiralty to be 98 per cent complete, and the *Jean Bart* 77 per cent complete, though the latter was still without her main armament of eight 15-inch guns. The other five battleships were old, built during or before the 1914-18 war, though in most cases reconstructed more recently. In comparison, the British possessed more capital ships (eleven battleships and three battle-cruisers), but the newest among them were the *Nelson* and *Rodney,* completed in 1927. The French cruiser force was also modern — the oldest were completed in 1926, which was more recently than many

British cruisers. The *contre-torpilleurs* were a type of warship not used in the Royal Navy, between a destroyer and a light cruiser, armed with 5.5-inch guns and extremely fast.

The strategic importance of the French fleet had to be estimated in the light of two major factors. One was that the German navy had suffered crippling losses in the Norwegian campaign, so that only three cruisers and four destroyers were seaworthy early in June; two battle-cruisers and a pocket battleship were under repair, while the other pocket battleship was refitting. The German surface fleet was thus effectively out of action at the time of the French armistice, which might have led them to abandon all thought of surface action; on the other hand it might have caused them to try to recover their losses by seizing French warships. The second major factor was the entry of Italy into the war. The Italian navy possessed four old but modernised battleships, and two new battleships of the *Littorio* class were due to enter service before the end of 1940; they also had eighteen cruisers, sixty-one destroyers, and over one hundred submarines. So long as the French fleet held the western Mediterranean, and the British the eastern, the Italian navy was held in check. However, with the French fleet neutralised (even if it did not fall into enemy hands), the existing British Mediterranean Fleet would be seriously outnumbered by the Italians. Moreover, the neutralisation or loss of the French naval bases in North Africa — at Mers-el-Kebir and Bizerta — would isolate the British bases at Gibraltar and Malta.

In these circumstances, it seemed likely that at best the Mediterranean would be closed to British shipping and Malta besieged. At worst, on 17 June the Naval Staff raised the question as to whether it would be necessary to abandon the eastern Mediterranean and bring Admiral Cunningham's Mediterranean Fleet to Gibraltar. The Joint Planning Sub-Committee of the Chiefs of Staff argued on 18 June that the political, economic and military reasons for keeping the fleet in the eastern Mediterranean outweighed the naval reasons for its withdrawal. Churchill and Cunningham both opposed the suggestion, which was not taken further; but the fact that it was made illustrates the dismay caused by the likelihood of the French fleet withdrawing from the war.[2] A similar suggestion for abandoning the eastern Mediterranean came from Cadogan on the same day, and was likewise opposed by Churchill, who insisted that naval forces available were sufficient to deal with the Mediterranean as a whole.[3]

Churchill proved to be right, at least in the short run. The Admiralty was able to constitute a new squadron (Force H) under Admiral Somerville, based at Gibraltar; this force, whose principal ships were two battleships, a battle-cruiser and the aircraft-carrier *Ark Royal,* was to operate both in the western Mediterranean and on the Atlantic convoy route from West Africa to Britain. Other gaps, however, could not be repaired. In the event of imminent danger of war with Japan, it had been the Admiralty's intention to leave the Mediterranean to the French navy, and transfer British warships to the Far East, but this was now impossible. Moreover, the armistice had created a major problem of surveillance, since French warships were stationed in many different waters, and if they were to be kept under observation the resources of the Royal Navy would be over-stretched. Such consequences were bound to follow even the withdrawal of the French fleet from the war, and if French warships were to be seized by the Axis powers, greater dangers and difficulties would ensue.

Fears that Germany would seize the French warships were considerable. The lessons of Norway, Holland and Belgium were fresh in men's minds, and it was well known that the Germans moved swiftly, ruthlessly and without regard for agreements. Against this background, the terms of Article 8 of the Franco-German armistice looked sinister in the extreme.[4] Under this article, the French warships were to return to their peace-time stations to be demolished and disarmed under German (or, under the other armistice, Italian) supervision. For about two-thirds of the French navy, this meant returning to Lorient, Brest, Cherbourg and Dunkirk, all in the German-occupied zone.[5] It was not surprising that on 25 June Churchill said in the House of Commons: 'From this text it is clear that the French war vessels under this armistice pass into German and Italian control while fully armed. We note, of course, in the same Article [Article 8] the solemn declaration of the German Government that they have no intention of using them for their own purposes during the war. What is the value of that? Ask half a dozen countries what is the value of such a solemn assurance.'[6] This view was widely shared in the press, the *Spectator* describing the article as 'France's assent to the surrender of the French navy',[7] while the *New Statesman* declared that 'Marshal Pétain has consented to hand over his ships to the enemy . . . .'[8] The *News*

139

Chronicle stated on 1 July that the French government had signed away the fleet, along with its factories and ports. The *Daily Herald,* in a leading article on 26 June cast in the form of a letter to the Prime Minister, held that if French warships obeyed Pétain's orders and sought to return to France, they must be prevented from doing so — 'And in taking action to this end you will have the firmest support of the British people'. On 27 June, the Cabinet while noting that public opinion was insistent that action should be taken against the French fleet, also decided that it would be better if the press did not discuss the matter.[9]

The French Admiralty did not share the British view of the situation, though Darlan thought it likely that the Germans would try to seize the fleet. However, he took all possible precautions to prevent this, and had confidence in his arrangements. Shortly after the armistice was requested, French warships sailed from ports threatened by the advancing Germans. The *Richelieu* sailed from Brest to Dakar, and the *Jean Bart* from St Nazaire to Casablanca, both voyages involving considerable feats of seamanship, because it was the first time either vessel had been to sea.[10] On 20 June Darlan signalled that commanders were to fight to the last unless the regular and independent government of France ordered otherwise; they were not to obey any other government, and no matter what orders they might receive, they were not to hand over an intact warship to the enemy.[11] On 22 June he ordered that a team should be organised on board every ship (capable of being maintained secretly), with the task of sinking the ship or destroying its armament if the enemy tried to use the vessel for his own purposes. The same order was to apply if any foreigner made such an attempt.[12] On 24 June, in the last signal he could send in cypher, Darlan told all his commanders that under the terms of the armistice the demobilised French warships would remain in French hands and in French ports. The order to make secret preparations for sabotage was repeated. Should the Armistice Commission decide that the ships were not to remain in French hands, they were to be sailed to the USA or scuttled without further orders, if no other action was possible to keep them out of enemy hands. In no circumstances were they to pass to the enemy intact.[13]

The reference in these signals to foreigners as well as enemies makes it clear that they were precautions against seizure by the British as much as by the Germans. The French government was determined to keep control of its own fleet, which had immense psychological importance to France as the country's only undefeated force. Moreover, it could be used as a bargaining counter in negotiations with the Axis, and for the defence of the French empire. Darlan reminded his commanders on 25 June that their ships constituted one of the essential elements of France's international position.[14] After the armistices came into force, another powerful consideration entered into French calculations about their fleet: any action in breach of the terms would jeopardise not only the armistice itself but also the whole policy of the French government.[15] This would apply particularly to any real or apparent collusion with the British about the movements of French warships. From the French point of view, all these factors amounted to an overwhelming case for the necessity and practicability of keeping their warships in their own hands.

On 29 June 1940 the British Chiefs of Staff reported that the French fleet was disposed as follows:

(1) In the British Isles: two battleships, four light cruisers, two destroyers, six torpedo boats, and seven submarines, most of which were at Portsmouth and Plymouth.

(2) In western France, at Le Verdon: one destroyer, almost completed.

(3) In southern France: four light cruisers and three destroyers.

(4) In West Africa: at Dakar, one battleship (the *Richelieu*), a destroyer and two submarines; at Casablanca, one battleship (the *Jean Bart*), one light cruiser, six destroyers, one torpedo boat, three sloops, and sixteen submarines.

(5) In North Africa: at Oran and Mers-el-Kebir, two battle-cruisers (the *Dunkerque* and *Strasbourg*), two battleships, seven light cruisers, one torpedo boat, four submarines; at Algiers, six cruisers; at Sfax, four heavy and eight light cruisers, two torpedo boats, three submarines; at other ports, two destroyers and eleven submarines.

(6) In the eastern Mediterranean: at Alexandria, one battleship, four heavy and four light cruisers, one submarine; elsewhere, one destroyer and six submarines.

(7) At Martinique, an aircraft-carrier, a heavy cruiser, and a training cruiser.

(8) At Singapore, a light cruiser.

(9) Convoying and at sea, two cruisers, five destroyers, a torpedo

boat, five submarines, and a seaplane carrier.

Thirty-one submarines were unaccounted for.[16]

From this list, representing the sum of British knowledge at the time, it was clear that very few French warships remained in French metropolitan ports, and only one destroyer remained in a port in the German-occupied zone. The problem for the British, therefore, was primarily one of dealing with vessels which were in either British or French African ports.

Before reaching a conclusion on the problem of the French fleet, the British Cabinet went through a week of indecision, to which many influences contributed. While the armistices were being negotiated, there was the perpetual hope that some form of French resistance would continue, and this was encouraged by the action of Admiral Godfroy's French squadron (Force X) based at Alexandria, which on 21 June took part in a bombardment of Bardia and a sweep along the coast of Cyrenaica to Tobruk. These actions were reported to the Cabinet on 23 June, and seemed to be a very healthy sign.[17] There was also the strong desire of Admiral Pound to trust Darlan; this exasperated Vansittart, who wrote fiercely on 26 June: 'Admiral Darlan has turned crook like the rest. I hope this will be put in its true light to Admiral Pound, who has a deal too much confidence in old friends & sailors of other races'.[18] In addition, there were the practical difficulties involved in any move to allow the French to take some course of action which would effectively prevent the use of their fleet by the Germans, and yet would maintain a threat of force by the British in case of need. If long parleys and time-limits were allowed, French warships in harbour would have time to raise steam, and thus to use their main armament and possibly put to sea. There was also the risk of the loss of British warships to be balanced against the gain of disabling French vessels, if force were actually used.

Various forms of action which would avoid the threat or use of force promised little result. One such possibility, which now appears distinctly odd but was seriously considered at the time, was to attempt to buy the French fleet, or perhaps to persuade the Americans to do so. The idea was put to Churchill by Morton on 17 June, as coming from Lloyd, Alexander and Greenwood, and Churchill passed it on for further comment. A Treasury minute put the cost of building the French navy at £200,000,000, and its current value at £100,000,000. A further minute recommended that the expenditure should be faced if the proposition was otherwise practicable, but — 'Discussion should begin well *below* £100m'. An extraordinary picture is conjured up of the British haggling with the French government over the price of its fleet (which after all consisted of used warships) while the Germans presumably looked on with polite interest. Cadogan was very sceptical, pointing out that if the French wanted to buy off the Germans by handing over the fleet, they would not wish to sell it to the British; equally, if the Germans really wanted the vessels, they would not permit any such transaction.[19] Nonetheless, the idea of persuading the Americans to buy the fleet was brought to the Cabinet by Churchill on 20 June, and referred to the Ambassador in Washington; it then lapsed,[20] having had a surprisingly long life.

The problem presented by the French fleet could not be solved by such methods. Its solution was a puzzle with which the Cabinet grappled inconclusively from 22 June, when news of the signing of the Franco-German armistice reached them, until the 27th when they came to a decision. At a Cabinet meeting at 9.30 p.m. on 22 June, Pound reviewed the position of the French fleet and the movements of the British forces which were being concentrated in the region of Gibraltar. He also reported a signal just received from the Naval Liaison Officer at Bizerta, with the information that a group of four French admirals had been charged by Darlan to take over from him if he lost his freedom of action. They were instructed to carry out his existing orders, that the fleet should fight to the finish and were to accept no instructions from any foreign government. Pound commented that this was in accordance with Darlan's previous assurances, and 'showed that he had taken all possible steps to safeguard our interests'. Churchill took up the point at once, and declared that in a matter so vital to British safety, 'we could not afford to rely on the word of Admiral Darlan'. However good his intentions, Darlan might find himself replaced at any time. The Prime Minister thought that the *Richelieu* and *Jean Bart* were the crucial ships which might alter the course of the war: if they fell into German hands (and the *Bismarck* was also commissioned) Germany would have a force of modern capital ships which Britain could not match. Pound was not hopeful about possible action against them. Dakar, where the *Richelieu* was berthed, had a strongly defended harbour, with 9.4-inch shore batteries as well as the *Richelieu's* own armament. The *Jean Bart* lay at

Casablanca, where the defences were weak, but there was no room to use torpedo-bombers against a vessel in harbour, and bombardment from the sea would be difficult because the battleship would be protected by the mole. Churchill was not impressed. However it was done, perhaps by bombing or mining the harbours, the battleships must be dealt with: 'In no circumstances whatsoever must these ships be allowed to escape'.

Halifax intervened to say that every means of persuasion should be tried before using force, and suggested sending an envoy — 'a naval counterpart of General de Gaulle' — to foster the sympathy for Britain which was believed to exist in the French navy. Churchill agreed — as long as they kept in view the main objective, 'which was that in no circumstances must we run the mortal risk of allowing these ships to fall into the hands of the enemy. Rather than that, we should have to fight and sink them'. Pound argued that whatever approaches the British made, no French captain would act on his own responsibility but would refer to Admiral Estéva at Oran. It was therefore vital to send someone to see Estéva, whom Pound believed to be 'a man of high principles and a determined character who could be trusted'. Duff Cooper was sceptical, holding that Estéva would take his orders from whoever was Minister of Marine in France, and that the British objective should be to foster a revolt against that authority.

Three decisions arose out of all this discussion, the first of which was an agreement to send a further appeal to Darlan through personal messages from Alexander and Pound. (These messages asked for an assurance that, if French warships ceased to fight, the British condition laid down on 16 June should be carried out and the fleet sent to British ports; they had no effect.) Secondly, the Vice-Chief of the Naval Staff, Admiral Phillips, was to fly at once to see Estéva, accompanied by Lloyd who might go on to Tunis and Syria to stiffen French resistance there. (After the meeting, Churchill postponed their departure for twenty-four hours, pending the receipt of further information following the signature of the Franco-German armistice. It was then abandoned.) Thirdly, the Admiralty were to ensure that the *Richelieu* and *Jean Bart* did not leave port.[21] These decisions left the core of the problem untouched, neither did a message from the King to President Lebrun which was sent that evening (22 June) amount to anything significant. This contained one important point: that to have the fleet dismantled even in North African ports would mean leaving it 'where it would be in evident danger of falling into hostile hands'. However, although the message ended by saying that the King relied on the solemn assurances of the French government that they would not accept any conditions involving such danger, in fact the German terms had already been accepted.[22] In any case, if anyone on the French side was going to affect the course of events, it would certainly not be Lebrun.

The next day, 23 June, was spent waiting for information, but on the 24th the Cabinet met three times, at noon, 6 p.m. and 10.30 p.m.; on each occasion, the French fleet was a vital item on the agenda. At noon, Pound again reviewed the position of the various French naval forces. He reported a signal from Admiral Cunningham at Alexandria, that Godfroy's Force X had been ordered to sail to French North African ports but that he would not allow them to put to sea. From Oran, the British Naval Liaison Officer had reported that Darlan's orders to Estéva were that French ships must in no circumstances fall into German or Italian hands, but must remain in French ports; in the last resort, they should be scuttled. The Liaison Officer thought it probable that Estéva would obey any orders issued by the French Admiralty, short of handing ships over to the enemy. Off Casablanca, the destroyer *Watchman* was keeping observation on the *Jean Bart*. At Dakar, the senior British naval officer had reported the comforting news that the *Richelieu* had only anti-aircraft ammunition on board, and that her main armament was incomplete; if necessary, HMS *Dorsetshire* (an 8-inch gun cruiser) would be able to deal with her.

After this review, which was more optimistic than that given two days earlier, no decision was reached. The general view was that everything should be done to get hold of the four new capital ships, or if this was impossible to ensure that they were scuttled. Cunningham's intention to make certain that the French squadron at Alexandria did not escape from British control was approved.[23]

At the Cabinet meeting at 6 p.m., Pound had little more to report. HMS *Watchman* had signalled that the French admiral at Casablanca said he would take orders only from the legal government of France. At home, the Commander-in-Chief, Portsmouth, Admiral James, reported that discipline among the French crews there was deteriorating. Both James and the C-in-C, Plymouth, thought that if the British applied *force majeure* and offered to repatriate all French crews, there would be no resistance. The discussion which followed was long and inconclusive. It was pointed out that the Germans could always find some pretext for seizing French warships when they came into ports under Axis control to be demilitarised; the only safeguard was that they should be scuttled or taken into British possession. However, the part of the French fleet which was already directly under British control, in Alexandria and in harbours in Britain, was of minor importance. The seizure of these ships might cause Darlan and Estéva to feel that they were no longer under any obligation to keep their vessels out of enemy hands. An actual attack on the squadron at Mers-el-Kebir (the *Force de Rade,* including the *Dunkerque* and *Strasbourg*) would be difficult, because the morale of this squadron was high and the harbour defences strong. It was also urged that the use of force against French ships, involving casualties among their crews, should be avoided.

Two alternatives appeared to be available. One was to take action at once, using force if necessary, to ensure that the main units of the French fleet did not fall into enemy hands. The other was to allow French warships to go to the ports laid down in the armistice, watch events closely, and then take action if there was any danger of the ships being seized. No conclusion was reached. It was agreed that Churchill and Halifax should draft an ultimatum to the French government, demanding that warships be scuttled within a specified time; otherwise, the British would take action against them. The Admiralty was asked to prepare an appreciation on the action which would be necessary against French forces not under British control.[24]

When the Cabinet met again at 10.30 p.m., Pound had this appreciation ready. The opening was pessimistic. It was felt that as soon as the British moved to seize or sink French warships, the crews of the remaining ships would become actively hostile, reducing the chances of securing the major part of the fleet. The Germans would also take their own measures to obtain the remaining vessels. The paper then discussed whether, if force was used, it would be better to aim for the French submarines or the capital ships, concluding that the latter were the more important; if they fell into enemy hands, it would be about two months before the Germans could use them efficiently, and three months before the Italians could do so. In a few months, the Italians would have five or six of their own capital ships available, and if two French vessels were added the

British would be unable to keep their fleet in the eastern Mediterranean. If Spain were also to enter the war, the western passage from the Mediterranean could not be controlled. Among the French capital ships, it was most important to eliminate the *Dunkerque* and *Strasbourg,* lying at Mers-el-Kebir. The paper argued that the only chance of success lay in a surprise attack at dawn, without any prior notification; even then, the operation might involve the loss of, or damage to, the two British capital ships available, the *Hood* and *Resolution.* Commenting on this appreciation Pound stated that the probable loss of two British capital ships seemed a heavy price to pay for the elimination, or partial elimination, of the *Force de Rade.* Darlan and the other French admirals had consistently maintained that in no circumstances would the French fleet be surrendered, and Pound's opinion was that the British were more likely to achieve their object by trusting in these assurances than by using force. Therefore, he did not recommend the proposed operation.

The ensuing discussion tended to support Pound's view, emphasising the danger of British losses, the harshness of attacking men who had so recently been allies, and the probability of alienating the French empire by acting against the fleet. Churchill agreed that an operation against the *Force de Rade* would undoubtedly be costly, and might not be successful. The draft ultimatum prepared by Churchill and Halifax was discussed, and re-drafted twice in the course of the meeting. Duff Cooper made the important point that a refusal by Darlan to hand the fleet over intact to the enemy would be tantamount to breaking the armistice: Darlan's dilemma was that this was his only alternative to breaking faith with the British. Churchill insisted that too much weight should not be attached to private messages or the word of individuals. The situation had to be judged in the light of the armistice terms themselves, also bearing in mind the possibility that subsequent peace terms might be more onerous still.

Ultimately, the only decision taken was to detain those French warships which were in British ports. Other action on the French fleet was deferred, as was further consideration of the draft ultimatum to the French government.[25] The discussion had again been inconclusive, and the arguments for and against the use of force seemed evenly balanced, probably tilted against by the weight of Pound's opinion.

On 25 June the situation changed radically, when news came that the *Richelieu* had sailed from Dakar at 2.15 p.m. that day. The Cabinet met at 6 p.m. and authorised the Admiralty to take measures to capture the *Richelieu,* and also the *Jean Bart* if she put to sea. Every effort was to be made to avoid bloodshed, and no more force used than was necessary, but no communication was to be made to the French government until the operation was complete.[26] The Admiralty took immediate action. The cruiser *Dorsetshire* was already sailing south towards Dakar; the *Hood* and *Ark Royal* were ordered to the Canaries; the *Valiant* and two cruisers were sent to patrol off the west coast of Spain. Orders were sent out during the night, and approved by the Cabinet when it met the following morning, 26 June. During the 27th the *Richelieu* was sighted by aircraft from the *Dorsetshire,* and the cruiser herself made contact at 3 p.m. that day. The *Richelieu* at once headed back for Dakar, where she arrived early on 28 June, closely followed by the *Dorsetshire.*[27] This brief northward sortie by the *Richelieu,* with the obvious danger that she was returning to a French port, brought the British Cabinet to a decision. Cadogan noted on 26 June that there had been hesitation about using force, since it was hard to be sure of catching all the ships, and it had been hoped that Darlan could be relied on to scuttle them. 'However, when the *Richelieu* sailed, it was felt that we could no longer trust entirely to Adml. Darlan's pledges, and action has been ordered'.[28]

Two other events may also have contributed to the ending of British hesitation. After the discussion on the *Richelieu* in Cabinet on 26 June, Pound said that in view of the Italian armistice terms there was a grave risk that the *Dunkerque* and *Strasbourg* would sail to a French, or even an Italian, port on the northern shore of the Mediterranean. Two British submarines had been ordered to take station off Oran, and Pound asked whether they should merely report on the movements of the battle-cruisers or take action against them. The Cabinet deferred a decision until the following day, but it was clear that Pound's earlier confidence in the French had been shaken.[29] The other event, ironically, was the receipt on 25 June of a further telegram of reassurance from Darlan. Admiral Odend'hal, the head of the French Naval Liaison Mission in London, told Pound of this signal, which was despatched from Bordeaux on the 24th. It stated that the dispositions under the armistice had been accepted only on the condition that the French fleet remained French, under the French flag, with reduced French crews, which arrangements were not necessarily contrary to British interests. The signal went on to regret the British measures to detain French warships in British ports, which almost amounted to an unfriendly act, and to request their release. Cadogan at once commented that the description of the armistice terms was quite contrary to all other evidence, and that the last part of the message was ominous. It was on this signal that Vansittart minuted that Darlan had 'turned crook like the rest'.[30]

However, these were matters for speculation. The sailing of the *Richelieu* from Dakar was a fact, calculated to cause serious anxiety. When the Cabinet met at noon on 27 June, Pound was able to report that the *Richelieu* was returning to Dakar under watch; but both he and the Cabinet were prepared to adopt a very different view of the French fleet from that which they had taken on the 24th. Pound now told the Cabinet that the real question was what to do about the French ships at Mers-el-Kebir.[31] One course of action would be to sow magnetic mines in the harbour mouth; or, by 3 July, it would be possible to concentrate the *Hood, Nelson, Valiant, Resolution* and *Ark Royal* off the port — a force far stronger than the French squadron. It would then be feasible, Pound continued, to demand that the French ships be demilitarised under British control, that they put to sea and sail to British ports, or that they be sunk within three hours rather than be bombarded. Another possible course of action was to keep two submarines stationed outside the port, with orders to sink any vessels which sailed out. The risks of using force appeared much smaller since the intelligence had been received that the French ships were moored with their sterns to the breakwater, so that the battle-cruisers could not fire out to sea from their moorings. (The *Dunkerque* and *Strasbourg* carried their eight heavy guns in two turrets, both facing forward.)

The discussion which followed was no longer a balancing of the pros and cons of an operation, but a consideration of what specific steps should be taken. It was asserted that public opinion was insistent on some such action as that taken against the Danish fleet at Copenhagen in 1806. Summing up, Churchill said that the Cabinet was agreed in principle that the proposed operation should take place on 3 July. The possibility of offering the French, in addition to the choices outlined by Pound, the further alternative of internment in American ports should be considered. Meanwhile, plans were to be drawn up.[32]

During the next few days, the French government sought on the one hand to get its warships released from British ports, and on the other to persuade the Germans and Italians to make some concession on the armistice terms concerning the fleet. In London, messages were delivered to Pound by Odend'hal, and to the Foreign Office by Roger Cambon, the French *chargé d'affaires*. Odend'hal protested at the British action in detaining French ships at Alexandria and in Britain. Pound told him that the British were by no means satisfied that French warships would be allowed to remain in colonial ports, as the French seemed to think, and he made it clear that if they tried to leave those ports they would be fired on. The only hope for the French empire was that Britain should win the war — 'that was the main thing, and he must not fuss about trifles like this!' A similar reply was sent by the Foreign Office, though as Cadogan remarked, in less nautical terms.[33] The French negotiations with the Axis powers were conducted through the German and Italian Armistice Commissions which had been set up to supervise the terms of the agreements. On 30 June, the French were informed that Germany had agreed that all Mediterranean questions were to be dealt with by Italy, and that in consequence, all French warships actually in the Mediterranean should be disarmed in Mediterranean ports. The exact significance of this is not clear, since the report by Huntziger (head of the French delegation to the German Armistice Commission) spoke only of the exclusion of Dunkirk and Cherbourg from the ports where French warships were to be disarmed; Brest, Lorient, and Rochefort remained. Nonetheless, the French could see some reason for hope in the German-Italian agreement, because the most important part of the fleet was in the Mediterranean, and all the Mediterranean ports were in the unoccupied zone of France.[34]

The French Admiralty tried to convey their hopes to London. On 27 June they signalled to the French Naval Mission there that the terms of the armistice could only be understood in relation to the negotiations with the Armistice Commission, and Odend'hal was to ask the British Admiralty to suspend judgement until these had been concluded. In particular it seemed certain that requests for the immobilisation of warships in unoccupied France would be granted. This signal appears to have been much delayed on its way to London, however, and only in the evening of 1 July was it reported to the British Cabinet that Odend'hal had that morning told Phillips about this appeal to suspend judgement on the terms.[35] A further signal from the French Admiralty on 30 June reported that the Italian government had authorised the stationing of the fleet, with half-strength crews, at Toulon or North Africa; German agreement was awaited. This message seems to have gone rather further than had actually been agreed; in any case it appears to have reached Odend'hal only in a currupt form, and not to have reached the British Cabinet at all.[36]

However, it was too late for such messages to affect the situation. When the French request for the British to reserve judgement on the armistice terms was reported to the Cabinet on 1 July, Churchill commented that 'discussions as to the armistice conditions could not affect the real facts of the situation'.[37] Neither Toulon nor even the North African ports were thought by the British Cabinet to be safe from an Axis *coup,* and, in any case it was felt that time was short. There was no inclination to wait for the result of negotiations in which the British had no faith: even if further undertakings had been given by Germany and Italy these would have commanded no confidence in London. By 1 July the British Cabinet was being asked to reserve a judgement which had already been given.

The Cabinet's decision on 27 June that, if necessary, force should be used against the French fleet was the subject of a cautious and somewhat pessimistic paper by the Joint Planning Sub-Committee on 29 June. Militarily, the committee thought the consequences would be unfavourable. The enemy would probably acquire the French warships in metropolitan ports, together with any which escaped the British attacks, and this might mean an important gain in cruisers and destroyers. There was also some danger of giving the Axis an opportunity to establish forces in North Africa; and there might be difficulties arising from the hostility of French forces in Syria and West Africa. On the positive side, the committee felt that successful action would not bring Spain any nearer to declaring war on Britain, while it would have an advantageous effect on American opinion. So long as Britain kept control of the oceans, even the French colonies would probably be compelled by economic considerations to co-operate with the British. The conclusion was that the committee were unable to gauge French reactions, but at worst these might be extremely serious. 'If, therefore, there is a genuine danger that the action proposed would lead to the active hostility of France and of her colonial possessions, we do not consider that the destruction of these French ships by force would be justified'.[38]

On 30 June the Chiefs of Staff took a different view. Regarding the possibility that the armistice terms might cause the French fleet to fall into German hands, they concluded that they could no longer place any faith in French assurances, nor could they be certain that the French would take any measures to render their ships unserviceable before arriving at metropolitan ports. 'Once the ships have reached French metropolitan ports we are under no illusions as to the certainty that, sooner or later, the Germans will employ them against us'. In particular, if the two French battle-cruisers fell into German hands, the balance of capital ship strength might be seriously tilted against Britain. The main consideration was the need to concentrate the maximum British naval strength in home waters to meet the threat of invasion. 'We are faced with grave issues at home. It is therefore of paramount importance that the uncertainty regarding the French Fleet should be dissipated as soon as possible in order that the ships now shadowing the French Fleet can be released for operations elsewhere'. This meant finishing the matter. The Chiefs of Staff recognised that while action against the French fleet might result in active French hostility, such hostility was in any case only a matter of time if Britain persisted in blockading France. 'In our view, the implications of hastening French hostility are not such as to over-weigh our previous arguments'. They therefore recommended that Operation CATAPULT (the code-name for an operation against the French fleet) should be carried out as soon as possible.[39]

In these circumstances the only question was, how soon? On the evening of 30 June, Churchill told the Cabinet that the date for the operation at Mers-el-Kebir depended on whether or not the *Nelson* was to take part. If they waited for the *Nelson,* the date would have to be 5 July; if they went ahead without her, it could be the 3rd. Churchill favoured the earlier date, and the Cabinet concurred. It was also agreed that there should be simultaneous action against French warships in British ports, Godfroy's squadron at Alexandria, and the cruiser *Emile Bertin* which was berthed at Martinique with a cargo of gold. (This last was abandoned the next day, when Pound reported that the coastal batteries at Martinique made the proposed attack difficult.)[40]

If anything was now likely to halt the proposed operation, it was not news of negotiations between the French and the Axis but rather the objections of the two naval commanders who would have the most difficult parts to play. Cunningham, C-in-C Mediterranean Fleet, would have to deal with Godfroy's Force X at Alexandria; Somerville, commanding the newly-formed Force H, would have to deal with the squadron at Mers-el-Kebir. Both admirals were informed of what was proposed on 30 June, and both objected. Cunningham was particularly forthright: 'I am most strongly opposed to proposal for forcible seizure of ships in Alexandria nor can I see what benefit is to be derived from it'. If the object was to prevent the ships from falling into enemy hands, that had already been achieved by preventing them from leaving Alexandria; alternatively, if it was hoped to obtain them for the British, this was unlikely to be accomplished because Cunningham was sure the French would resist vigorously, probably scuttling their vessels. The attempt would end in unnecessary casualties, 'and a harbour fouled with wrecks'. He also thought the general effect in the Middle East, notably Jibuti and Syria, was likely to be disastrous. On the other hand, if matters were left to take their course at Alexandria, Cunningham thought it probable that lack of pay and shortage of food would cause the French ships to fall into British hands. However, this did not allow for repercussions following the use of force at Mers-el-Kebir, where Cunningham also opposed forcible action although agreeing that he was not in full possession of the facts. He was particularly afraid of alienating those French elements in North Africa which were friendly to Britain.[41] Somerville, after consultation with Captain Holland (formerly naval attaché in Paris), made similar general objections, and pressed Holland's view that offensive action would alienate all Frenchmen. The reply from London was uncompromising: 'It is the firm intention of HMG that if the French will not accept any of the alternatives which are being sent you their ships must be destroyed'.[42]

The British Cabinet took its final decisions at a meeting at 6 p.m. on 1 July, when it considered draft instructions to the commanders involved, and the appreciation made by the Chiefs of Staff on 30 June. Odend'hal's request to suspend judgement on the armistice terms was reported by Pound, but ignored. There was discussion as

F

to whether the immediate demilitarisation of the warships at Mers-el-Kebir should be offered as one of the choices to the French commander there. Against this, it was argued that demilitarisation which could be carried out quickly could probably also be repaired speedily. Pound, however, thought it was the course most likely to appeal to the French, stating that turbines could be destroyed in half an hour, and it would not take much longer to put guns out of action with an oxy-acetylene cutter. The Cabinet decided that demilitarisation should not be offered at this point, but held in reserve, with Somerville authorised to accept it if the other choices were refused. During the discussion of action against the French warships in British ports, it was urged that a party to be given for the French at Plymouth on the evening of 2 July should be cancelled, to avoid giving an appearance of sharp practice. The point was eventually left to the Admiralty, with other details, but there was some incongruity between the Cabinet's ruthless determination on action at Mers-el-Kebir and its straining at the gnat of a party in Plymouth.[43]

The orders to the British commanders involved were sent out on 2 July, for execution on the 3rd. Those to Somerville were that the French squadron at Mers-el-Kebir was to be given four choices:

(1) To sail to British harbours and continue to fight.

(2) To sail with reduced crews to a British port, from which the crews would be repatriated.

(3) To sail with reduced crews to a French port in the West Indies, such as Martinique, where the ships would be demilitarised or perhaps entrusted to the USA.

(4) To sink their ships — the time limit set for this was six hours.

If none of these alternatives was accepted, but instead the French admiral suggested demilitarisation on the spot, Somerville was authorised to agree provided that the measures could be carried out within six hours and would prevent the ships from being used for at least a year. Finally, if the French accepted none of these courses, Somerville was to destroy the vessels at Mers-el-Kebir, particularly the *Dunkerque* and *Strasbourg*. Ships in the neighbouring harbour at Oran were to be destroyed so long as this did not entail any appreciable civilian casualties. A separate operation against Algiers was ruled out.

The choices to be offered to Godfroy at Alexandria were different:

(1) To put his ships at the disposal of the British government.

(2) To put the ships in a condition in which they could not go to sea, keeping skeleton crews on board.

(3) To take the ships to sea and sink them in deep water.

In any case, the squadron was to be out of action before dark. In Britain, French warships were to be seized by armed parties, and a message regretting the necessity for this delivered to captains just before each boarding party arrived. Everything short of bloodshed was to be done to prevent the ships being scuttled.[44]

The events of 3 July need not be related in detail.[45] At Mers-el-Kebir Admiral Gensoul, commanding the *Force de Rade,* refused the proposals put to him by Somerville. A day of exchanges, firstly in writing and later in the course of a long meeting between Gensoul and Captain Holland, failed to find a solution acceptable to both sides. Gensoul pointed out that the first shot fired against him would turn the whole French fleet against Britain, and he affirmed that French warships could not and would not fall into enemy hands and be used against Britain. Holland argued that the British did not believe that Darlan retained freedom of action, and that they wanted to be sure that the fleet was not seized by surprise, whereupon the French admiral assured him that if there was any enemy threat to his position, he would take his ships to Martinique or the USA. The difference here appeared to be one of timing: Somerville's orders required Gensoul to take immediately certain action which the French admiral might be willing to carry out at some future time *if* there was a German threat. To have accepted this latter course would have involved delay and prolonged uncertainty, and since the British government was resolved to finish the matter quickly the divergence of opinion was decisive. It may be that Gensoul made the situation worse by informing the French Admiralty that the British ultimatum was to sink his ships or be fired on; he did not set out the full range of choices offered to him. This strange error undoubtedly heightened feelings in the French government; however, it seems unlikely that it materially affected the issue, since all the courses suggested by the British involved breach of the armistices and were therefore unacceptable to the French government. The fact was that Gensoul had to choose between accepting one of the British proposals, or standing on his existing orders and the terms of the armistice. He chose the latter. Somerville too was bound by his orders, and when Gensoul finally declined to accept any of the British propositions Force H opened fire. In the bombardment, one French battleship, the *Bretagne,* was sunk; the battle-cruiser *Dunkerque* and the battleship *Provence* were badly damaged; but the *Strasbourg* got clear of the harbour and reached Toulon undamaged.

At Alexandria, both sides had a good deal less freedom of action than at Mers-el-Kebir.[46] Godfroy's squadron was in a British-controlled harbour, and unable to put to sea; but on the other hand neither Cunningham nor the British Admiralty wanted to risk a battle in the harbour. Both commanders were thus constrained to negotiate, and their personal relations were friendly enough to facilitate this process. Moreover, at different times both Cunningham and Godfroy ignored orders or suggestions from their respective capitals which would have precipitated a fight. On the evening of 3 July Godfroy broke off negotiations on receiving news of the action at Mers-el-Kebir, but he ignored orders to put to sea and attack the British fleet. Cunningham similarly ignored an order to make sure that the reduction of French crews began before dark on 3 July, also a later suggestion that he should take his ships to sea and then present Godfroy with an ultimatum. In Cabinet on 4 July the Prime Minister was anxious to reach a quick solution, but Eden hoped there would be no hasty decision which might bring on a battle in the harbour. On 4 July, in fact, agreement was reached on a solution, whereby Godfroy consented to the discharge of fuel oil from his ships, and to their being immediately rendered unserviceable for fighting. (This was done by removing the breech-blocks of the heavy guns and depositing them at the French Consulate.) There was later a more detailed convention, in which Cunningham on his part agreed that there would be no attempt to seize the French ships by force.

All French warships in British harbours were seized by boarding parties in the early hours of the morning of 3 July. The only fighting was on board the submarine *Surcouf,* where two men were killed: one French and one British.[47]

There were further operations on 6 and 8 July. On the 6th aircraft from the *Ark Royal* torpedoed the *Dunkerque,* causing severe damage through an explosion on board a ship lying alongside the battle-cruiser. This attack brought the French casualties at Mers-el-Kebir to a total of 1,297 dead. On 8 July an aerial torpedo attack was made on the *Richelieu* in harbour at Dakar. A hit was scored and the battleship damaged, though she could still have put to sea in an emergency.[48]

When all was over, the Chiefs of Staff prepared the following balance sheet on the state of the French fleet:

	Accounted for:		At large:	
	In British ports	Sunk or damaged	Atlantic	W. Mediterranean
Battle-cruisers (2)	—	1	—	1
Battleships (7)	3	3	1	—
8-inch cruisers (7)	3	—	—	4
6-inch cruisers (11)	2	1	3	5
Contre-torpilleurs (27)	3	—	3	21
Destroyers (26)	5	2	7	12
Submarines (77)	9	1	18	49

In most cases, 'western Mediterranean' meant Toulon, where there was a powerful concentration of the *Strasbourg,* several cruisers, *contre-torpilleurs,* destroyers and submarines.[49] This force was later to affect British fortunes, partly by its very existence and partly by its activities, notably at the time of the Dakar expedition in September 1940. On the other hand, of the nine French capital ships, seven had been accounted for in one way or another; while of the remaining two, one (the *Jean Bart*) was unready for action. The existence of the dangerously large squadron at Toulon, and even more important the profound hostility of the French navy, were the price the British had to pay for the advantage gained by dealing with the French capital ships.

The possibility that the French might declare war on Britain in retaliation for the attack on their fleet was seriously considered by the British. A report of 4 July by the Joint Planning Sub-Committee of the Chiefs of Staff assessed the French capacity to take significant military action. The French colonial armies were considered to be too disorganised and weak to be a real threat, except perhaps in West Africa. French fighter planes in France (estimated at about 150 in number) might be used against Britain; and the French air force in Africa (including 250 bombers) might be used against Malta, Gibraltar and British shipping in the Atlantic. French surface ships and submarines outside the Mediterranean might be used as commerce raiders.[50]

The outbreak of hostilities seemed near on 4 July, when Cambon told Halifax that the situation was so grave that it was impossible to foretell what decision the French government might reach. The next morning, Cambon called to announce his resignation, because he was afraid of having to make a communication which — after living twenty-five years in England — would be personally distasteful.[51] In the afternoon of 5 July, a British submarine sank a French cruiser, the *La Galissonière,* without warning. This was in pursuit of orders issued during the operation at Mers-el-Kebir, which should by then have lapsed. Pound was afraid that the French government would think that the British had begun unrestricted attacks on all French warships, and that this might provoke a declaration of war. Late at night and in haste, therefore, the First Lord of the Admiralty authorised a note to Odend'hal to explain that the sinking of the cruiser was a mistake, and to offer apologies. This action was approved in retrospect by the Cabinet at 10 a.m. on 6 June.[52] To apologise for the sinking of a cruiser after the bombardment of a whole squadron may appear somewhat bizarre, but it arose from the Admiralty's urgent desire to avoid a French declaration of war.

Another indication that war might come was the bombing of Gibraltar by French aircraft on 5 July,[53] but this proved to be the limit of French armed retaliation. Darlan's immediate reaction to the events of 3 July had been furious and belligerent. A counter-attack on Somerville's force; the interception of British merchant ships; expeditions against Sierra Leone, Gambia, or possibly the oil-fields of northern Iraq — all were briefly contemplated.[54] However, it appears that Pétain, Baudouin and Laval all opposed military action, and the French government restricted itself to breaking off diplomatic relations with Britain. Meanwhile, on 4 July, the French obtained Germany's agreement to suspension of Article 8 of the armistice, which at least temporarily dispensed with the demilitarisation under Axis control of the remaining French warships.[55] From the British point of view, this was something more to enter in the credit side of the balance. French reactions to the British attack were thus well short of a declaration of war, and the worst British fears were not fulfilled, although a nagging anxiety about potential French hostility continued to plague British policy in later months.

The wider effects of the British operation against the French fleet had also to be taken into account. In Britain, there was no doubt about public reaction. On 4 July the House of Commons received Churchill's statement on the subject with a remarkable demonstration of support, and this was widely echoed in the press. The *Daily Telegraph* held that the action was 'a duty which we had no right to shirk'. The *News Chronicle* had no doubts: 'To be weak is to be destroyed'. The *Daily Herald* claimed that 'Every high and honest motive made our Government's decision inescapable'. Such views were typical. Most papers accompanied their stern approval with regret at fighting a recent ally, and sorrow for the loss of French lives, but the *Daily Mirror* differed in proclaiming: 'Our hard heart does *not* ache over the decision and the action'.[56] Broadly, the attitude of the press was that it would have been suicidal for Britain to allow the French fleet to fall into German hands, which was the only alternative. The Ministry of Information's reports on public opinion showed general approval of the move, which was not only held to be inevitable but also welcomed as a sign of British initiative and aggression. While there were some reports of regret at its necessity, others indicated that the French casualties caused little comment. Anti-French feeling was reported, sometimes directed against the Pétain government and sometimes against France as a whole — it was said that 'we were never *real* friends with the French'.[57]

From the point of view of public approval at home, the British government could be well satisfied. Of foreign opinion, by far the most significant was that in the United States, where both the government and some sections of the public had been watching the French fleet with anxiety. On 1 July, Roosevelt told the British Ambassador that American opinion would support forcible seizure of the French ships. Americans expected them to be seized rather than to fall into German hands, and he himself would do everything in his power to help achieve such a solution. After the event, Lothian reported almost universally favourable comment on the British actions.[58] The chairman of the Senate Foreign Relations Committee said that it had been the fear that such a step would *not* be taken which had shaken some people's confidence in the power of Britain's defence.[59]

Opinion in other neutral countries varied. From Madrid, where it seemed that Spain's entry into the war hung in the balance, the British Ambassador (Sir Samuel Hoare) reported that the British operation had been a great shock to the Spanish public. Spaniards had been hoping that the war was going to end, but the attack on the French ships had 'in a brutal way destroyed all these hopes'. He thought that, provided the action proved to be justified by success, British prestige in Spain would recover.[60] At the other end of the Mediterranean, the ambassador in Turkey reported that the Turkish Foreign Minister was wholly in sympathy with the British move, reflecting the general mood in Turkey.[61] Reports from Stockholm were that Swedish opinion was divided, but the majority of the press was reticent or critical.[62] At a discreet interval after the event, on 16 October, the Soviet naval journal *Krasny Flot* published an article arguing that Germany had intended to use the French fleet against Britain and the British Admiralty had made its practical deductions.[63]

Whatever people thought, the deed was done. On 14 July, Bastille Day, Churchill announced on the radio that 'Our painful task is now complete', and stated that so long as the French warships at Toulon or overseas did not try to move to harbours controlled by Germany or Italy, Britain would not molest them. He made a reference to future relations with the French government in terms which were not wholly bleak, saying that when a friend was struck down, it might be necessary to make sure that his weapon did not pass to the enemy; but one need not bear malice because of his cries of delirium. 'So long as our pathway to victory is not impeded, we are ready to discharge such offices of goodwill towards the French Government as may be possible, and to foster the trade and help the administration of those parts of the great French Empire which are now cut off from captive France, but which maintain their freedom'. There was room for interpretation of this sentence, uncharacteristic in its studied vagueness, but there was nothing vague about the conclusion of Churchill's broadcast: ' . . . there is one bond which unites us all [members of the government] and sustains us in the public regard — namely (as is increasingly becoming known), that we are prepared to proceed to all extremities, to endure them and to enforce them; *that* is our bond of union in His Majesty's Government tonight'.[64] It is fair to see in this a reference to the attack on the French fleet, which to Churchill had been a sad though unavoidable necessity. Once accomplished, he was willing to let it stand as a sign of British will-power, plain to friend and foe alike — 'we are prepared to proceed to all extremities, to endure them and to enforce them'. In all crucial matters, this was true.

NOTES

1. CAB 66/9, WP(40)256, 16 July 1940, Implications of French Hostility, appendix. Cf. *Jane's Fighting Ships, 1942,* 159-200.
2. CAB 79/5, COS Committee Minutes, 17, 18 June 1940; Roskill, vol. I, 296-7; Butler, vol. II, 300-1; Churchill, 390, 392, 563.
3. FO 371/24311, C7301/65/17, minutes by Sargent, Cadogan, and Churchill, 17 June 1940.
4. See above, 95-6.
5. A. Kammerer, *La Passion de la Flotte française: de Mers-el-Kébir à Toulon* (Paris, 1951), 122-3.
6. *H. C. Deb.,* series 5, vol. 362, cols. 304-5.
7. *Spectator,* 28 June 1940, 858, article by *Strategicus.*
8. *New Statesman,* 29 June 1940, 785.
9. CAB 65/13, WM(40)184th Conclusions, Confidential Annex.
10. See the account in P. Varillon, *Mers-el-Kébir* (Paris 1949), 79-80.
11. Signal, 1340 hrs, 20 June 1940, Evénements, *Rapport,* 454.
12. Signal, 1655 hrs, 22 June 1940, *ibid.,* 459; G. Robert, *La France aux Antilles de 1939 à 1943* (Paris 1950), 40-2.
13. Signal, 1243 hrs, 24 June 1940, *Événements, Rapport,* 466.
14. Signal, 1340 hrs, 25 June 1940, *ibid.,* 466; cf. R. E. Godfroy, *L'Aventure de la Force X* (Paris 1953), 45-7.
15. Signal, 1805 hrs, 25 June 1940, *Événements, Rapport,* 469; Kammerer, 119.
16. CAB 80/14, COS(40)505(JP), 29 June 1940, Annex to report of Joint Planning Sub-Committee on implications of action contemplated in respect of certain French ships. In this list, the French *contre-torpilleurs* were classed as light cruisers.
17. CAB 66/9, WP(40)227, 28 June 1940, Weekly résumé of the naval, military and air situation, 20-27 June 1940; CAB 65/7, WM(40)177.

18. FO 371/24348, C7375/7362/17.

19. FO 371/24311, C7352/65/17, minute by Morton, 17 June 1940; Treasury minutes, same date; minute by Cadogan, 19 June.

20. CAB 65/7, WM(40)173; FO 371/24311, C7352/65/17, Halifax to Lothian, 21, 23 June 1940; C7455/65/17, Lothian to Halifax, 24 June 1940.

21. CAB 65/13, WM(40)176th Conclusions, Confidential Annex.

22. FO 371/24301, C7146/9/17, Halifax to Campbell, 22 June 1940, transmitting message from the King to Lebrun.

23. CAB 65/13, WM(40)178th Conclusions, Confidential Annex.

24. *Ibid.,* WM(40)179th Conclusions, Confidential Annex.

25. *Ibid.,* WM(40)180th Conclusions, Confidential Annex.

26. *Ibid.,* WM(40)182nd Conclusions, Confidential Annex.

27. *Ibid.,* WM(40)183rd and 184th Conclusions, Confidential Annexes; FO 371/24231, C7808/839/17, report by Vice-Admiral Lyon, C-in-C South Atlantic, 4 July 1940.

28. FO 371/24328, C7388/7327/17, minute by Cadogan, 26 June 1940.

29. CAB 65/13, WM(40)183rd Conclusions, Confidential Annex.

30. FO 371/24348, C7375/7362/17, minutes by Cadogan, 25 June 1940 and Vansittart, 26 June. Cf. French text of Darlan's signal, *Événements, Rapport,* 466. This text stated that the British action in detaining French warships could only be regarded as an unfriendly act; it seems that Odend'hal toned this down in transmitting the message.

31. Pound actually said Oran, not Mers-el-Kebir, but the *Force de Rade* was stationed at Mers-el-Kebir, a separate naval base some three miles west of the port of Oran, and it seems best to use the proper name, as is done in all French accounts.

32. CAB 65/13, WM(40)184th Conclusions, Confidential Annex.

33. *Ibid.,* WM(40)185th Conclusions, Confidential Annex; FO 371/24321, C7483/839/17, minute by Strang, memorandum by Cambon, minute by Cadogan, all 28 June 1940, draft note by Cadogan, 29 June.

34. *Délégation française,* vol. I, 20-27; Michel, *Vichy Année 40,* 231-3; P. M. H. Bell, 'Prologue de Mers-el-Kébir', *Revue d'Histoire de la deuxième Guerre mondiale,* January 1959, 28-9, 32-3.

35. *Événements, Rapport,* 472; CAB 65/14, WM(40)190th Conclusions, Confidential Annex.

36. *Événements, Rapport,* 473; Kammerer, 134; Butler, vol. II, 220
37. CAB 65/14, WM(40)190th Conclusions, Confidential Annex.
38. CAB 80/14, COS(40)505(JP), 29 June 1940.
39. CAB 80/14, COS(40)510, 30 June 1940, *Aide-mémoire* by Chiefs of Staff Committee.
40. CAB 65/13, WM(40)188th Conclusions, Confidential Annex; CAB 65/14, WM(40)190th Conclusions, Confidential Annex.
41. Cunningham Papers, 52566, Admiralty to Somerville, 0435/29, and to Cunningham, 1531/29, both despatched 30 June 1940; Cunningham to Admiralty, 1105/30, 30 June; Lord Cunningham of Hyndhope, *A Sailor's Odyssey* (London 1951), 243-6.
42. ADM 1/10321, Admiralty to Somerville, 1820/1, 1 July 1940; Churchill, 208.
43. CAB 65/14, WM(40)190th Conclusions, Confidential Annex.
44. CAB 65/8, WM(40)191, annexes; Cunningham, 246-7.
45. The most recent account is Warren Tute, *The Deadly Stroke* (London 1973). See also Roskill, vol. I, 243-4; I.S.O. Playfair, *The Mediterranean and Middle East,* vol. I (London 1954), 132-7; Cunningham, 246-55; Kammerer, 159-74, 224-8, 237-9; Varillon, 95-169. Gensoul's report, dated 9 July 1940, is printed in Kammerer, 506-15; cf. his testimony in *Événements, Témoignages,* vol. VI, 1897-1908.
46. Cunningham, 246-55; Godfroy, 56-76; ADM 1/10321, C-in-C Mediterranean, Diary of events, 3 and 4 July 1940; CAB 65/14, WM(40)193rd and 194th Conclusions, Confidential Annexes.
47. WM(40)192nd Conclusions, Confidential Annex; Kammerer, 237-40.
48. CAB 65/14, WM(40)195th, 196th, 198th Conclusions, Confidential Annexes; Playfair, vol. I, 137: Roskill, vol. I, 245; Kammerer, 176, 243-6; Varillon, 153.
49. CAB 66/9, WP(40)256, 16 July 1940, Implications of French hostility; see especially paras 5-8 and the Appendix.
50. CAB 80/14, COS(40)529(JP), 4 July 1940.
51. CAB 65/8, WM(40)194.
52. CAB 65/14, WM(40)195th Conclusions, Confidential Annex; FO 371/24321, C7483/839/17, memorandum to Castellane, 6 July 1940; Godfrey to Odend'hal, 6 July; Halifax to Consul-General, Algiers, 7 July.
53. CAB 65/14, WM(40)195th Conclusions, Confidential Annex.

54. Michel, *Vichy Année 40,* 236-7; Warner, 196; A. Schérer, 'La Collaboration', in P. Arnoult *et al, La France sous l'occupation* (Paris 1959), 19.

55. *Délégation française,* vol. I, 38-44.

56. See the press on 5 July 1940.

57. INF 1/264, reports of 4, 5, 6, 8 July 1940.

58. FO 371/24321, C7553/839/17, Lothian to Halifax, 1 and 9 July 1940.

59. *The Times,* 6 July 1940.

60. FO 800/323, H/XXXIV/38, Hoare to Halifax, 8 July 1940.

61. FO 371/24321, C7483/839/17, Knatchbull-Hugessen to Halifax, 6 July 1940.

62. *Ibid.,* Mallet to Halifax, 6 July 1940; Carey to Jebb, 10 July 1940, enclosing telegrams from naval attachés.

63. FO 371/24322, C11211/839/17, Cripps to Halifax, 18 October 1940.

64. *Listener,* 18 July 1940, 75-6.

Chapter 8

THE FRENCH EMPIRE

The terms of the armistices compelled the British government to regard the French fleet as an immediate threat to the security of Great Britain and its communications; the action taken to meet this threat was swift, ruthless and to a considerable degree successful. The other element of French power which survived the defeat of June 1940 was the French empire. Here, the problems posed for British policy were different, and the potential danger to British security was much less acute. There were also possible advantages to be gained for Britain, although these were not of immediate importance. Vast areas and distances were involved in any policy regarding the French empire, while the resources available to implement such a policy were totally inadequate. In these circumstances, British action was tentative, in marked contrast to the determination shown in the case of the fleet. Since most of the attention and resources of the country were inevitably devoted to home defence, the result was a series of half-measures and a good deal of speculation, which by the end of July had brought no results of any significance: the French empire remained intact, under the authority of the existing French government, and out of the war.

In 1940, France possessed widespread territories overseas, the most important of which were in Africa. In North Africa lay Algeria, which legally was not a colony but three departments of France itself, though its separateness was acknowledged by the existence of a Governor-General in the capital, Algiers. To the east and west of Algeria lay the protectorates of Tunisia and Morocco, where the governments of the Bey of Tunis and the Sultan of

Morocco maintained a somewhat theoretical existence under the powerful guidance of French Residents-General. Further south was the large federation of colonies comprising French West Africa: Senegal, Mauritania, Guinea, Soudan, the Ivory Coast, Dahomey, the Niger; also Togo, formerly a German colony but now held by France under mandate from the League of Nations. Each of these territories had its own governor, under the supervision of the Governor-General at Dakar. In central Africa, there was a similar federation of colonies constituting French Equatorial Africa: Gabon, the French Congo, Chad, and Ubangi-Shari. The seat of the Governor-General was at Brazzaville in the Congo — situated across the river from Leopoldville, capital of the Belgian Congo. Adjoining French Equatorial Africa, but administratively distinct, was the mandated territory of the Cameroons, again a former German colony.

Together, all these territories formed a continuous block of land stretching from the Mediterranean and North Atlantic to the boundaries of the Belgian Congo and the Anglo-Egyptian Sudan. Also in Africa were the colony of French Somaliland, with its capital at Jibuti (adjoining British Somaliland but otherwise surrounded by Italian territory), and the large island of Madagascar, off the east coast of Africa. In the Middle East, France was the mandatory power for Syria and the Lebanon. In the Far East, she held Indo-China. In the Caribbean, she controlled French Guiana and a number of islands, notably Martinique and Guadeloupe. In the Pacific, there were a number of French islands, notably Tahiti and New Caledonia. Finally, France still retained small possessions in India, and the islands of St Pierre and Miquelon off Newfoundland.

In June 1940 the British government hastily reviewed the strategic and economic importance of the French empire, and tried to decide what action to take if resistance in metropolitan France should collapse. On 14 June the Chiefs of Staff offered the opinion that, provided the French were still determined to resist, there was everything to be said for encouraging them to fight on in North Africa; they even thought that this might make it possible to conquer Tripoli and deter Spain from entry into the war, and therefore recommended that the French government itself should be urged to instruct colonial authorities to continue to co-operate with the British, whatever happened at home.[1]

This was followed on 15 June by a more sombre appreciation.

The Chiefs of Staff now assumed that the French government would cease hostilities and accept terms applicable to the whole empire, including the use of French territory for operations and perhaps the use of colonial economic resources for the benefit of the Axis powers. In such circumstances, the best the British could hope for was to induce the French colonial authorities to continue the war independently of the home government; the worst they could expect was that the authorities would tamely acquiesce in any and every German demand. In either case, the effect on Britain would be crucial. With France out of the war Britain's principal weapon against Germany was economic, largely depending on the ability to control Europe's external supplies at source as distinct from trying to intercept them in transit. The exercise of such control over the products of the French empire in order to prevent them from reaching countries outside the British or American economic orbit, was of great importance. There would equally be advantages in being able to divert at least some of these products to Britain's own use.

A detailed survey of the economic resources of the French empire was made by Greenwood, Minister without Portfolio, on 17 June. The principal exports of the French empire in 1938 were as follows:

FOODSTUFFS (thousands of tons)

	Total	To U.K.
Sugar	26.7	—
Groundnuts	538.1	—
Tea	2.0	0.1
Coffee	67.1	—
Palm oil and kernels	83.0	—
Tapioca products	9.0	—
Maize	636.8	—
Rice	1,059.4	37.4
Wheat	338.4	—
Cocoa	52.2	5.2

RAW MATERIALS (thousands of tons)

	Total	To U.K.
Petroleum	3.8	—
Rubber	57.6	2.6
Iron ore	1,193.2	592.4*
Tin	143.7	0.1
Copper	1.2	—
Zinc	5.8	—
Manganese	47.4	—
Antimony	4.6	—
Graphite	3.2	5.0 (thus in the original: 0.5?)
Phosphates	3,458.2	360.8
Hardwoods	88.7	2.8
Esparto	36.2	2.5

*Excluding exports from Morocco.

These figures were for the last full calendar year of peace, but in June 1940 the situation was somewhat changed by the circumstances of the war. British imports from the French colonies were growing, and plans had been made for further increases. In particular, British imports of iron ore from Sweden had been cut off by the German occupation of Norway, and the mines in Spain were in unfriendly hands. Britain therefore planned to draw extra supplies from French North Africa, and the loss of that source of iron ore would be serious. Phosphates, coming mostly from Morocco, were another item whose importance to Britain had been intensified by the war. The campaign to grow more food in Britain demanded extra supplies of fertilisers, while shipping problems made it desirable that these should be imported from sources as near as possible to the British Isles. Moroccan phosphates therefore meant a good deal to the Ministries of Agriculture, Food and Shipping.

These were economic advantages which Britain was in danger of losing, and if she failed to secure control of the resources of the French empire the iron ore, phosphates, and the small but important supplies of manganese (mostly from Morocco) would go to meet German needs. Of the foodstuffs, the groundnuts and palm-oil were not vitally important to Britain because of the large supplies from her own West African colonies, but would represent for Germany a significant source of margarine, cooking oils and feedstuffs for cattle.[2]

The French empire also provided bases which would help the British to enforce their blockade of Europe, but which in German hands would help to break that blockade and intensify the U-boat warfare against British shipping. In their appreciation of 15 June, the Chiefs of Staff referred particularly to Dakar as a well-equipped base which it was essential to deny to the enemy — they did not think it necessary for the British to use it themselves, because there was already a base available at Freetown, in Sierra Leone. They also felt it was necessary to prevent Madagascar from being used by German commerce raiders. In the Middle East, an Axis occupation of Syria would bring them to the borders of the oil-bearing regions of Iran. Finally, in the Far East the Chiefs of Staff recognised the danger that the collapse of France would open the way to a Japanese advance into Indo-China, with consequent danger to Malaya and Singapore.

The economic and strategic importance of the French empire was unmistakable, but the policy to be adopted by the British was not so clear. The Chiefs of Staff made a rough division of the French territories into those whose sea communications would be under enemy domination, and those where they would be under British control. Without the French fleet, Britain would be unable to dominate sea communications in the western Mediterranean. The Chiefs of Staff therefore concluded that it would not be possible for the British to utilise bases in French North Africa for long; nor could the enemy be prevented from using them. Outside the Mediterranean, the Atlantic communications of Morocco would be under British control, as would those of French West and Equatorial Africa, Madagascar, and possessions in the Americas. British sea power should be able to deny the Germans the use of Dakar and Madagascar, while American co-operation could be counted on in the Caribbean. However, even where sea communications were under British control, the Chiefs of Staff were pessimistic about any action to seize French bases; the most important were garrisoned, and available British forces would not be adequate to capture them in face of resistance. In the case of Syria, mastery of the sea appeared for a few days to be in doubt; it was hoped that the French forces there might be induced to fight on, or that Turkey might take some action. In the event, neither of these hopes was fulfilled, but

169

the Mediterranean Fleet proved strong enough to hold the eastern Mediterranean and isolate the French territories. As for Indo-China and the Pacific islands, the Chiefs of Staff recognised that the best hope was to enlist the assistance of the USA in preserving the *status quo,* while trying to persuade the local French authorities to continue to trade with Britain.

This survey did not indicate much scope for positive action. On 15 June the Chiefs of Staff recommended that, in the event of French capitulation, British representatives in French overseas territories should try to persuade the colonial authorities to continue the war, and offer help in defence against the enemy. At the same time, the Ministry of Economic Warfare should make plans to exert economic pressure on those French colonies which refused to co-operate with the British — a threat which might be held out where necessary to supplement the arts of persuasion. The Minister of Economic Warfare, Dalton, produced a memorandum on 16 June arguing that to stop imports into French colonies would not produce quick results. However, the stopping of exports would be more effective since this would cut off income for traders and producers and lead rapidly to difficulties within the territories. It might also be possible to offer help to French colonies, in the shape of financial support to keep the local administration solvent and enable the banking system to operate, and small supplies of goods which would maintain the prestige, power and comfort of the European populations — Dalton suggested spare parts for cars, clothing, special foods, small arms ammunition and perhaps a few machine guns. For the next few months, some combination of the stick and the carrot, economic pressure and the offer of economic help, was to form the main substance of British policy towards the French colonies, notably in Africa.[3]

Britain's first objective concerning the French empire was therefore to try to persuade individual colonial authorities — governors and service chiefs — to continue the war alongside Britain, even if the French government at home made an armistice. This was an extremely difficult task, since the French empire was by tradition and organisation a centralised body. Its survival in the nineteenth century, despite passing through several changes of regime and innumerable changes of government, had been due to the principle of obedience to whatever regime and whatever government held power in France. For individual governors or colonial generals to pick and choose, to obey one metropolitan government but not another, would have led rapidly to disintegration. In face of this difficulty, the British relied on the extraordinary circumstances of the time, and on the anti-German sentiments of the French services, to outweigh ingrained habits of mind. In fact, the situation produced the natural reaction of rallying round the stricken homeland, which proved in most cases stronger than the contradictory desire to go on fighting the Germans. Moreover, anti-German feeling was at least partly counterbalanced by anti-British feeling, which lingered in the French colonial army and administration as the inevitable result of centuries of colonial rivalry which had only nominally come to an end with the signing of the *entente* in 1904. There was widespread fear that Britain would seize the opportunity afforded by the collapse of France to acquire parts of the French empire for herself. In 1940 French colonial administrators had in their care a large, sprawling and highly vulnerable empire, around which they could see five predators: Germany, Italy, Spain, Japan — and Britain. British greed for French colonies was to become a constant theme for Vichy propaganda, especially after the Anglo-Gaullist expedition to Dakar, and this fear was shared by the Free French.

Given these inherent difficulties, it is not surprising that the British attempt to keep the French empire in the war failed. What is remarkable is that for a few fleeting days it appeared to have some chance of success. Preparation for the British approach began as early as 13 June, when the Chiefs of Staff recommended that if French resistance at home collapsed, efforts should be made to encourage forces overseas to fight on. Instructions were sent to consuls, military attachés and liaison officers in French territories, though these were not to be acted upon without further orders.[4] On 17 June British representatives in French overseas territories were instructed to approach the local French authorities, and tell them that the British government recognised that the French government had been compelled to capitulate under duress; it was appreciated that the French army had laid down its arms against its will, and against the will of the French people. The British intended to continue the struggle, and their forces would do all in their power to help French overseas territories to defend themselves against the enemy. Britain was confident that the co-operation of these

171

territories would be forthcoming, as it already was in the Dutch and Belgian empires which were continuing the war. Later the same day a further circular telegram was sent, acknowledging that continued resistance by French colonies would involve them in financial and economic difficulties; should such questions be raised, British representatives were to say that requests for assistance would be 'very sympathetically considered'.[5]

During the few days between the French request for an armistice on 17 June and the conclusion of an armistice with Italy on 24 June, British policy on the French empire passed through a period of uncertainty. As long as there appeared to be some hope that Pétain's government — or part of it — would go to North Africa, it even seemed doubtful whether the approaches begun on 17 June should be followed up. On 18 June, Charles-Roux protested to Campbell at Bordeaux about these approaches, asking that Britain should not increase the difficulties of those Frenchmen who were working for the same objectives as the British. On 21 June Halifax secured Cabinet consent to the despatch of a telegram to British representatives, warning them of the need for care if they were not to offend French susceptibilities.[6]

On 22 June, when news was received of the signature of the German armistice and of Campbell's complete disillusion with the French government, these warnings no longer applied, but it was still not clear what practical steps should be taken. There was some talk of bribing French governors — a course suggested by a Foreign Office official even before the Bulgarian Minister in London pointed out that the British could buy all the high officials and officers in North Africa for less than the cost of one day's fighting, and they should not be squeamish about it.[7] Another suggestion, made by Dominion High Commissioners on 23 June, was that sending messages through consuls was not sufficient to win over the French colonies, and that missions headed by Cabinet ministers should be sent at once to each colony, accompanied by Frenchmen from London. This grandiose and impracticable scheme was politely turned down by Halifax, although the Cabinet had discussed the possibility of sending Lloyd to North Africa, and were shortly afterwards to send Duff Cooper to Rabat.[8]

There was anxious discussion regarding the possibility of making a specifically French appeal to the French empire. A Foreign Office official observed that the French colonial troops 'will certainly not fight if they think they are doing so for the English'. He thought Britain should promote the formation of a separate French government in the colonies, led by Reynaud or de Gaulle.[9] In Cabinet on 24 June Attlee said that de Gaulle was the most promising head for such a government, but there were doubts as to whether he had the necessary prestige and authority.[10] Attlee's idea was tested by allowing de Gaulle to broadcast on the evening of 23 June, announcing the formation of a French National Committee which it was hoped would lead to the creation of a French government opposed to that of Pétain.[11] However, this broadcast evoked no response in the French empire.

Behind all the uncertainty and advocacy of dubious expedients lay the over-riding fact that the British did not have available what would have been the most persuasive argument of all: force. The ability to send a strong expeditionary force to North Africa might have turned the scale. This was suggested on 20 June by the French military attaché at Tangier, Captain Luizet, later to be a valuable agent for de Gaulle, and also by General Dillon, head of the British military mission in North Africa. These proposals were firmly rejected: too much equipment had been lost in France, and the demands of home defence were too urgent. When Duff Cooper revived the idea on 28 June, a draft report by the Chiefs of Staff on 1 July advised strongly against the release of any British forces for this purpose.[12] The British were therefore unable to approach the French overseas authorities, especially the influential leaders in North Africa, with the offer of an army to help them to resist a German attack. It may be that the prospect of British troops on French colonial soil would not have been wholly welcome to the French governors, but it was quite certain that exhortations to fight on without firm assurances of immediate material aid were futile. There was no escape from this fact of British military weakness. In these circumstances, the same pattern was repeatedly reproduced in most French overseas territories: varying degrees of revulsion against the request for an armistice; British overtures and offers of limited help; then a movement, gradual or rapid, to rally behind Pétain's government, accept the armistice terms, and reject the British approaches. Meanwhile, the British moved correspondingly from hope, through doubt to disappointment.

The key area in deciding the course to be taken by the French empire was North Africa, since in Algeria, Tunisia and Morocco there was the largest concentration of forces outside France. The British Chiefs of Staff put their strength at approximately ten divisions; the Italian Armistice Commission reported a strength of 373,000, of whom 167,000 were French.[13] Moreover, in North Africa there were leaders of reputation and influence, notably General Noguès who combined the post of Commander-in-Chief of the army in North Africa with that of Resident-General in Morocco, and Peyrouton, the recently appointed Resident-General in Tunisia. In the three North African territories, and especially in Algeria, there were significant populations of French settlers who were capable of giving weight to a movement to continue the war. In addition, their self-interest might be engaged in such a movement through their fears of Italian and Spanish designs on North Africa. It was to North Africa, and above all to Noguès, that other parts of the French empire looked for guidance in their perplexity.

Early signs reaching London from North Africa gave some hope of continued resistance. The British Consul-General in Algiers, Lowdon, reported on 19 June that the stupor induced by the first news of the request for an armistice had been replaced by anger, and that the army in Algeria appeared to be violently opposed to laying down its arms without a struggle; it would follow Noguès if he continued the war, and would probably try to overthrow him if he did not. The attitude of the civil administration was different: officials seemed resolved to carry out any orders from France, even if these involved complete surrender, but they faced strong opposition from the population.[14] The British Consul at Tunis, Knight, reported on 18 June that Peyrouton had said that the overture to Germany was distasteful to him, and he was sure that the French government would come to North Africa because the armistice terms would prove to be crushing.[15] On 19 June Knight reported meetings with the local army and air force commanders, whom he found to be generally favourable to continuing the struggle — though General Blanc, the army commander, said he would take no action independently of Noguès.[16] Hurst, the Consul at Rabat in Morocco, telegraphed on 18 June that he found officers there unanimously in favour of going on with the war. On the 19th he reported that the leaders of *anciens combattants* organisations (the old soldiers of the 1914-18 war) in Morocco had told him they had sent telegrams to Pétain and Noguès, urging them to fight on in North Africa. Noguès had assured them that he shared their views.

They also requested that de Gaulle should be told that the great bulk of Frenchmen in Morocco and the rest of North Africa wished to fight on. This reference brought a rapid disclaimer when it became known to the French authorities, who asked that the whole message should be regarded as highly confidential, and de Gaulle told nothing about it.[17]

These reports on local opinion by the British consuls corresponded closely with the sentiments being expressed to the French government by *anciens combattants,* chambers of commerce, mayors, and deputies.[18] Noguès himself telegraphed to Weygand on 17 June to express the consternation of the whole of North Africa at the request for an armistice; and to Pétain on 18 June to say that his soldiers, together with the French and Moslem populations, wanted the French government to cross to North Africa and continue the war. The natives in particular would consider it a betrayal if France were to hand them over to a foreign power without their consent and without a fight.[19] However, though these telegrams demonstrated Noguès' reaction to the request for an armistice, they also showed the limits of that reaction. Noguès wanted to continue fighting under the lawful government of France, transferred to North Africa — not to act against that government. He opposed the tame surrender of North Africa to the enemy — but even this implied that he might feel differently if it were not to be so surrendered. The reasons which later led him to accept the armistice were already apparent.

During the next few days, from 20 to 24 June, the British representatives in North Africa reported the hesitancy of the French authorities and the bewilderment of many of the population. Knight telegraphed from Tunis that numbers of officers and soldiers had called at the consulate to express their determination to fight on. He thought that three-quarters of the reserve officers shared these sentiments, though the regulars were less keen; he also considered that the local forces would in fact obey an order to surrender, which meant that all depended on Noguès.[20] On 23 June the British government called on all French overseas territories to continue fighting, even if the government in France ordered them to surrender, because that government was already under enemy control. Britain would guarantee the integrity and economic stability of territories which agreed to continue the war, and would provide funds to pay the salaries and pensions of French officers

175

and civilian officials — a financial undertaking which went considerably further than those given previously.[21] Nevertheless, when Knight delivered this message to Peyrouton he reported that the Resident-General was proving a man of straw. For his part, Peyrouton told Knight that it was all very well for the British to offer help, but experience showed that British aid came too late.[22] When the British offer was put to Admiral Estéva, who had moved from Oran to Bizerta, it met a stiff response. The admiral was displeased by the offer of funds, saying that if Frenchmen fought on it would be solely in support of their principles, but his main point was that as long as he and his officers remained in the service, they would obey the orders of their government.[23]

From Algiers, Lowdon telegraphed that the Governor-General's reception of the British offer had been very reserved, and that the last word would rest with Noguès.[24] However, Noguès' attitude no longer appeared hopeful; in a broadcast on 20 June he thanked the people of Morocco for their loyalty, but appealed to them not to hamper the government by demonstrations, however well-intentioned, and to remain united, resolute, and disciplined.[25] At Rabat, Hurst was told that Noguès considered the British approaches premature, because the armistices were not yet completed.[26] However, Dillon saw Noguès on 23 June, and thought there was still hope that the French would carry on the war in North Africa. He reported that Noguès had been shocked by the French government's acceptance of the German armistice terms, because only on 22 June he had sent a message to Bordeaux setting out the material he needed to continue fighting. He would not show his hand until the Italian terms were completed, but Dillon thought he might be using this as a device to gain time.[27]

When the Italian terms were completed on 24 June, and Noguès showed his hand, it was to acquiesce in the armistices. That evening he made a broadcast emphasising that there was no question of giving up any part of French North Africa; that there would be no military occupation; and that the government would not agree to any reduction of the forces in North Africa. For the time being, therefore, the integrity of North Africa and its means of defence were assured.[28] Everyone had looked to Noguès, and Noguès had decided, but in a private telegram to Weygand the next day he made it clear that the feeling in favour of fighting on had been strong, and his broadcast assurances had been the minimum necessary to prevent a rising against the government. He had spent much of the night of 24/25 June calming down delegations which had urged him to put himself at the head of the forces of the empire. Anger was still seething under the surface, and there might be an explosion at the slightest provocation if his broadcast promises were not kept. Noguès told Weygand that the government would bitterly regret that — being itself in an atmosphere of rout — it had failed to take proper account of the morale and strength of North Africa.[29] This telegram earned Noguès a sharp reproof from Weygand, and shows that British hopes about North Africa had not been entirely misplaced.

The Italian terms were almost certainly the crucial point for the North African decision. The tradition of discipline and obedience to the central government was very strong, and might have prevailed in any circumstances, but an Italian demand for Tunisia, or for the occupation of ports in Algeria, might well have broken it. When this danger did not materialise there was a general sense of relief, and in Algiers Lowdon noted signs of positive gaiety everywhere when the Italian terms were known and the tension slackened.[30]

So from the evening of 24 June the French North African authorities accepted the armistices. This left the British with only one possible course of action to keep the territories in the war: to unseat the legal authorities and put into power men who would continue the fight. For a time there were hopes that such a course might be possible, especially in Algeria and Morocco. Lowdon at Algiers was in contact with a group which had plans for a *coup d'état,* and the consuls at both Rabat and Marrakesh suggested that de Gaulle should go to Morocco and lead an insurrection there. Others considered that de Gaulle was not sufficiently well known and inspired too little confidence to be able to rally Morocco, or anywhere else in North Africa, merely by his presence; British help would be necessary. Luizet thought that a *coup* in Morocco would need the immediate support of two British divisions.[31]

This brought matters back to the question of force — or rather the lack of it. The British could not send two divisions to Morocco; the best they could manage was to send two men: Duff Cooper and Gort, the former commander of the BEF. The Cabinet decided on this step late in the evening of 24 June, after receiving a report that former ministers of Reynaud's government had arrived in Rabat *en route* for England. (This was the party of deputies and senators which had left Bordeaux on board the *Massilia*; they had in fact arrived at Casablanca, not Rabat.) The Cabinet's instructions to Cooper and Gort were to urge the former ministers to set up a new government in North Africa, Syria, or if necessary in England.[32] The British Consul-General at Rabat tried to stop the mission because Noguès' broadcast on the evening of 24 June had changed the situation in Morocco; but by the time this message reached London Duff Cooper's flying-boat was well on its way, and nothing could be done.[33]

The party landed at Rabat about 7 p.m. on 26 June. Duff Cooper was received by Morize, Noguès' deputy at the French Residency, who told him that the greatest misfortune which could befall France was a split in the ranks; and that as an official he was bound to obey orders, however distasteful they might be. Duff Cooper thus encountered the two main reflex actions of French colonial authorities in face of the armistice, and he gave due weight to these in his report to the Cabinet. Having regard to this attitude, he concluded that any attempt to meet Mandel (the former Minister of the Interior, and the man the British government was most anxious to contact) was bound to fail. He limited his actions to sending a message to Mandel through the consul at Casablanca, hoping he would go to Gibraltar or England, and offering to arrange transport. Meanwhile, Gort had been confined to the hotel where the British party had originally intended to stay the night, and despite a later apology it was clear that the British mission was not to be allowed freedom of movement. After spending the night on board the flying-boat, they left at dawn on 27 June for Gibraltar. From there, Duff Cooper telegraphed the consul at Casablanca, stressing the importance of getting Mandel to England, and instructing him to find a way of doing so with the help of the British destroyer lying off the port. However, he learned that Mandel and the other ex-ministers (Daladier, Campinchi and Delbos) were virtually prisoners on board their ship, whose captain had orders not to leave Casablanca.[34]

The mission thus failed to make contact with the former ministers, or to find any other rallying-point for resistance in North Africa. Duff Cooper told the Cabinet on his return that senior French officials would obey any government provided their personal positions were not in danger, which they did not appear to be under the armistice terms; that the generals in North Africa were reluctant to do anything to provoke the Italian and Spanish forces on their borders; and the admirals too stunned by events to take any action. He had hopes of the junior officers and the civilian population, but these would only be rallied through the landing of a British expeditionary force — an idea which was firmly quashed by the Chiefs of Staff.[35] The British government was again confronted by its own powerlessness, and indeed its problems were worsened by a new uncertainty. When Duff Cooper told the Cabinet on 28 June about the French ex-ministers, and the possibility of bringing them to England, the question was raised as to whether the inclusion of Daladier in an alternative French government might not prejudice its chances of success.[36] Daladier had many enemies, and it was doubtful whether any of the politicians of the old regime, except Mandel, could provide effective leadership for French resistance to Germany. The possibility of getting the *Massilia* away from Casablanca, or of bringing off Daladier himself in a destroyer, was seriously considered, but it was not entirely a disappointment when nothing could be done.[37]

All these events took place before the British attack on the French fleet at Mers-el-Kebir. The die was cast against continuation of the war in North Africa some ten days before that action, but Mers-el-Kebir was the climax of the movement of North African opinion against Britain, and added to it an anger and bitterness which were not previously present. Luizet reported to de Gaulle that the reaction to Mers-el-Kebir was serious, and asked that the British should pay homage to the courage of the French sailors who had been the victims of the British government.[38] Hurst reported hearing from a number of his French acquaintances that the British action had been necessary, but even so their sorrow at the necessity had overcome their former indignation against Pétain's government.[39] Both men repeatedly emphasised the anti-British feeling aroused in the French navy — Hurst described its mood as 'sour and vindictive', while Luizet reported that aircraft in Morocco had been put under a naval commander who was eager to carry out further raids on Gibraltar.[40]

The attitude of Noguès and the French civil administration in North Africa had been determined by 24 June: the armistices were to be accepted. After 3 July, this attitude was reinforced by the bitterness of the French navy and a substantial shift of opinion among the French population. The chances of a *coup* against the

179

French authorities in North Africa were slight at any time, but after 3 July they were non-existent.

Events in North Africa have been traced in detail because they were decisive not only there but in the rest of the empire. With few exceptions, the pattern was similar throughout the French colonies. Everywhere there was an early movement of opinion against an armistice; then a period of hesitation, waiting for news and guidance from France or from North Africa; then acquiescence. At Dakar, the Governor-General of West Africa, Cayla, told the British Consul-General on 23 June that he was convinced that a government would be formed representing the will of the French empire to carry on the war, but on the same day he said he would refuse entry to liaison officers from neighbouring British colonies. On 27 June, Cayla was appointed Governor-General of Madagascar, and turned his attention to his future task.[41] The naval and military commanders obeyed orders and accepted the armistice terms. Dakar's decision was followed by the rest of the colonies of the West African federation. In French Equatorial Africa the Governor-General, Boisson, followed the lead of North Africa; when Cayla was transferred from Dakar, Boisson was appointed to succeed him, with general authority over West and Equatorial Africa. Only in the Cameroons did the situation develop differently for a time, the fact that the territory was a former German colony helping to produce a more belligerent attitude on the part of the French authorities. The High Commissioner, Brunot, received British liaison officers, and was prepared to open economic negotiations with Britain.[42]

In Syria both the High Commissioner, Puaux, and the army commander, General Mittelhauser, at first declared their determination to fight on, but accepted the armistices on 27 June. The other French colonies followed much the same pattern. In French Somaliland the army commander, General Legentilhomme, came over to the British, but without his troops. In Indo-China the Governor-General, General Catroux, was determined to continue fighting, but he accepted his dismissal by the French government and joined de Gaulle purely as an individual.

By the beginning of July, British hopes of keeping all or part of the French empire in the war had been disappointed. There would clearly be no general movement of dissidence, although hope remained alive in certain individual colonies,[43] and the British were left to take stock of the situation.[44] The picture was gloomy, especially after the action at Mers-el-Kebir, when war with France seemed a distinct possibility. Looking at the threats which might be posed from North and West Africa, the dangerous points for Britain were Gibraltar and Freetown. The Chiefs of Staff thought that either French or Axis bomber forces operating from French Morocco might render Gibraltar useless as a naval base, and this would destroy the British position in the western Mediterranean which Sommerville's Force H, operating from Gibraltar, had just re-established. The danger to Freetown was more remote, but even more serious if it should materialise.

Freetown was a vital staging-port and point of assembly for all shipping on the West African route to the Cape of Good Hope. With the Mediterranean virtually closed to convoys, the Cape route had to be used for all British supplies and reinforcements bound for the Middle East and India, all trade with the east, and most of that with Australia and New Zealand. As the only workable convoy assembly port between the Cape and Gibraltar, Freetown had to be safeguarded, but its defences were very weak: a battery of 9.2-inch guns had been planned but not yet provided, and two 4.5-inch AA guns constituted the only anti-aircraft defence. There were no fighters or other aircraft, and the land forces consisted of one battalion of infantry. Yet, as the governor observed, on one day in June there was a quarter of a million tons of shipping in Freetown harbour, including the *Queen Mary*.[45] It was true that the nearest German or Italian forces were a long way from Freetown, but the French had some forty battalions in West and Equatorial Africa, and forty-four aircraft at Dakar; though all the latter were obsolete models and only three were bombers, the absence of any British aircraft made even this feeble force a danger to the Freetown harbour. If German air forces were to reach Dakar, this threat might become very serious. British land forces in West Africa were also extremely weak, though land operations against the British colonies were unlikely because of the distance and the terrain involved.[46] At one point, in a fit of geographical aberration, the War Cabinet instructed the Chiefs of Staff to make a plan for blowing up bridges on the trans-Sahara route in order to prevent the movement of enemy forces from North Africa. The Chiefs of Staff carefully

181

replied that they had 'no information regarding the existence of bridges on the desert route', and thought that in any case only small raiding parties would be able to make such a journey.[47]

The French West African port of Dakar figured repeatedly in British appreciations of the strategic problems posed by the French empire. Possessing an excellent and well-defended harbour, a substantial garrison and an air base, it could be used by aircraft to attack Freetown, or by submarines and surface raiders to attack shipping in the Atlantic. In a detailed report of 16 July on the implications of French hostility, the Chiefs of Staff thought it important to deny the use of this base to the enemy. They held that the garrison was too strong to enable the British to seize Dakar in the face of French opposition, and proposed that any action taken should be limited to the destruction of port facilities by naval bombardment or Fleet Air Arm attack. More important, they recommended the maintenance of a capital ship force at Gibraltar; so long as this could be done, the sea route to West Africa (including Dakar) could be to some degree controlled. A further recommendation was that Freetown should be reinforced when forces were available, and British forces in West Africa increased in the long term by raising new colonial units. Preparations for the worst that might happen — the severance of the West African convoy route — could only be made by planning the diversion of shipping from Australia and New Zealand via the Panama Canal, and from the Cape of Good Hope via Trinidad and the North Atlantic.

These gloomy prospects arose, as the Chiefs of Staff pointed out, from taking the most pessimistic view of what might happen in the French empire in the event of war with France. Even on 16 July they still cherished the faint hope that some parts of the French empire might co-operate with the British, in which case not only might some of these dangers be avoided, but also one specific and important advantage gained: this was a route to send reinforcements of aircraft to the Middle East across Africa. Such a route, which General Giffard (appointed C-in-C West Africa at the end of June) was instructed to try to secure, would cross French Equatorial Africa. Aircraft could be taken by sea to Takoradi, in the Gold Coast, and then flown on the route Lagos-Kano-El Geneina-Khartoum. No landings in French territory would be necessary, although obvious advantages might accrue if Fort Lamy or Fort

Archambault were to become available as staging-posts. Since the previous air reinforcement route to the Middle East through the Mediterranean was closed for all normal purposes, the opening of a route across Central Africa offered great savings of time over the alternative sea route via South Africa. However, the success of such a route depended on at least the acquiescence, and preferably the active assistance, of the French colonies over which it would pass.[48]

Outside Africa, the situation in Syria might in the future offer a threat to the British position in Palestine, Egypt and Iraq. The British sought to maintain the *status quo* by issuing a statement on 29 June that they could not allow Syria to be occupied by any hostile power, nor to be used as a base for attacks on countries which Britain had agreed to defend. However, they very much hoped that no action in support of this declaration would be necessary.[49] They had, as usual, very little strength to spare, and the French had an expeditionary force of three divisions in Syria, plus two weak divisions for local defence. It was thought unlikely that these forces would actually attack Palestine, in view of their own security problems with the Syrian population and the presence of Turkey to the north, but they remained a potential threat which General Wavell in Cairo could not ignore; there remained too the possibility that the Germans or Italians might secure some foothold in Syria.

The British thus reviewed the potential dangers and advantages of the situation in the French empire, but there was little they could do. In Syria, the best they could hope for was the maintenance of the existing French administration.[50] In Africa there was little scope for military action, though recommendations were made for the reinforcement of Freetown by the despatch of an infantry brigade and a fighter squadron by mid-October, or earlier if necessary. The anti-aircraft defences of the port were also to be strengthened as quickly as possible.[51] However, these were only defensive measures, and if anything positive was to be done to win over French colonies to the British side, the most promising instrument seemed to be economic. At the beginning of July, it appeared that there was a good opportunity for the use of economic influence in the French Cameroons. The Colonial Secretary, Lloyd, regarded this as a matter of urgency, and brought it to the attention of the Cabinet on 1, 4 and 7 July. On the 7th the Cabinet agreed to offer (through the Governor of Nigeria) full British collaboration in the administration of the mandate, including the provision of finance for the immediate needs of the administration and for guaranteeing salaries and pensions. The British government was also prepared to buy large quantities of the produce of the Cameroons which could not otherwise be sold.[52] At first, this offer appeared likely to succeed, and on 12 July the Cabinet agreed that similar proposals should be made to other French territories in West and Equatorial Africa. It was to be emphasised that economic assistance would not be extended to territories which adopted an equivocal attitude, balancing between Britain and the Pétain government. Also, the threat was to be conveyed (in a decently veiled form) that the British blockade could prevent the export of colonial produce, and bring about the collapse of the colonial economy.[53]

In the event these approaches came to nothing. Even in the Cameroons, High Commissioner Brunot was brought back into line with the other French colonies by a visit from Admiral Platon, flying from Dakar. Brunot was later replaced by the local army commander, General Husson. HMS *Dragon*, then on a visit to Duala in the Cameroons, was asked to leave, and the policy of the Cameroons changed to one of adherence to the armistice terms.[54] On 1 August the British suspended their plans for economic assistance to the Cameroons and French Equatorial Africa.[55] In any case, there had been no general welcome for the British offers. Boisson, who by the end of July had taken up his new post as Governor-General at Dakar, with control over the whole of West and Equatorial Africa including the Cameroons, appears to have believed that Britain needed French colonial products and therefore he would be able to strike a bargain enabling him to obey the French government while still maintaining commercial relations with the British. However, this was an arrangement in which the British saw no point.[56]

What had once seemed a hopeful prospect for the British failed to materialise. The cohesion of the French empire again asserted itself, proving more powerful than British threats or promises, and the Chiefs of Staff were averse to trying to alter the situation by the threat of force. On 29 July they commented on suggestions which had been made for a show of force at Dakar, and for the despatch of a warship to Libreville (in Gabon), where the Governor had indicated that he might welcome an opportunity to join the British if he could appear to be yielding to *force majeure*. They were sceptical

De Gaulle conferring with Free French Officers at Aldershot. The degree of independence to be allowed to the tiny Free French forces was a constant bone of contention between de Gaulle and the British government.

(Imperial War Museum)

General de Gaulle and General Catroux at Beirut. A British attempt to replace de Gaulle as leader of the Free French by the senior and better-known Catroux was foiled by Catroux's unswerving loyalty to his chosen leader.

(Mansell)

King George VI and General de Gaulle inspecting Free French troops at Aldershot. This was one of the many official photographs taken to promote General de Gaulle to the British people as a leader of consequence.

(Imperial War Museum)

General de Gaulle in London with General Spears, the British Liaison Officer with the Free French.

(Professor M. Llewelyn.)

The Allée Principale in Vichy, as it was in 1940. The charm and elegance of the spa made a bizarre setting for the government of occupied France.
(Popperfoto)

Marshal Pétain, the head of the Vichy government. The aged marshal saw himself as the father of the French people, and his task as that of alleviating their sufferings.
(Radio Times Hulton Picture Library)

Churchill and de Gaulle: a conflict of wills tempered by mutual respect.
(Imperial War Museum)

Members of the Vichy government. Left to right: Unidentified; Admiral Darlan; Paul Baudouin; M. Alibert; Pierre Laval; Adrien Marquet; Yves Bouthillier; Marshal Pétain; M. Caziot; General Weygand; Jean Barnegaray; M. Lemery; General Pujo; General Colson.
(Associated Press)

Map showing occupied and unoccupied France, under the terms of the French armistice.

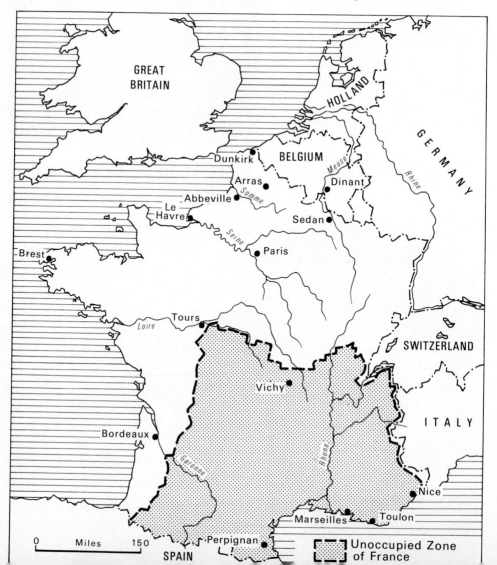

about both ideas, and their views on Dakar are of particular interest in view of later events. They held that a show of force could only be effective if favourable French elements in the town were sufficiently strong and well-organised to seize the opportunity to take control; however, this did not seem to be the case. Otherwise, a show of strength would have to be followed by its actual use. The Chiefs of Staff thought the coastal defences at Dakar were too strong for effective naval bombardment, and the forces available were not adequate to achieve a successful landing in the face of French resistance. Similarly, they held that the delivery of an ultimatum by a warship at Libreville would have to be backed up by the presence of a landing force in case of resistance — and no such force was available.[57] The Chiefs of Staff were clearly opposed to shows of strength which might be revealed as empty threats.

One hopeful sign in late July and early August was the appearance of a dissident movement in the Cameroons. This developed around Mauclère, a colonial official who was willing to attempt a *coup* and rally to de Gaulle. He asked for British assistance, and a guarantee of refuge if his attempt failed, but the British response was limited to expressions of goodwill, with a promise of economic — but not military — assistance if his *coup* succeeded.[58]

There was also hope of dissidence in Chad. Early in July the Governor of Chad, Félix Eboué, had sent his Political Secretary, Laurentie, to Lagos to confer with Bourdillon, the Governor of Nigeria, who was much impressed with Laurentie's grasp of the situation. De Gaulle sent a message to Eboué, who kept in touch with Nigeria and survived a visit from Boisson on 20 July.[59] However, so far no overt move had been made, and Eboué was waiting for a favourable opportunity. By 7 August it appeared that the chance of a *coup* in the Cameroons had vanished, as the French authorities strengthened their control. Bourdillon thought the situation there was dangerous, with German penetration through the Spanish territory of Fernando Po as a likely possibility. He requested in strong terms that the British government should make a definite plan about French Africa — 'even an indifferent plan will be far better than a continuation of the present policy of drift'.[60] The difficulty about this advice was that the British had very few resources with which to back such a scheme. However, early in August such resources as they had were being mobilised to establish

G

de Gaulle at Dakar, and this was a project which met Bourdillon's requirements only too accurately: it was indeed an indifferent plan, adopted as much as anything because it was better than drifting. The Dakar expedition seemed vital if de Gaulle's Free French movement was to be saved from drifting into oblivion, by giving it a new impetus and a firm base, but it was also necessitated by the failure of the British attempts (outlined in this chapter) to rally the French empire to continue the war.

Momentous issues turned on the somewhat feeble and sporadic British activities recorded here, one of which was the whole future of de Gaulle and the Free French movement. If the French empire under Noguès or some other high-ranking leader had fought on, de Gaulle and his handful of followers in London would have been absorbed into the larger body. Another issue was the fate of North Africa, and with it the shape of the war in the Mediterranean and Atlantic. Since 1940 there has been considerable argument as to whether continued French resistance in the empire, and especially in North Africa, was either desirable or possible. On the one hand, it is argued that prolonged resistance would have brought the Axis powers into North Africa, either across the western Mediterranean or through Spain. A weak and disorganised French defence would then have been brushed aside, and the Germans would have been established not only in North Africa but perhaps also in Dakar. The result in this eventuality would have been disastrous for the whole British strategic position in the Mediterranean, West Africa and the South Atlantic. On the other hand, it has been held that there were significant forces available in North Africa; that if the French fleet had joined the British, a German passage across the Mediterranean would have been impossible, while a move through Spain would have been far from easy, especially if Spain was reluctant or hostile. The North African position could then have been successfully held, and this would have brought Britain corresponding strategic advantages both in the Mediterranean and in the Atlantic.[61]

There can be no conclusion to this conflict of hypotheses, but the record of British policy and actions shows that the British government at the time believed their interest to lie in persuading the French empire to prolong the war. It may be that in the rush of events the risks of this policy were not carefully estimated; certainly it was adopted with virtually no strength except the navy (already severely stretched) to give it the backing of force. For some time past, in 1939 as well as in 1940, it had been a habit of the British to encourage others to take up positions in which Britain could offer no military support — only exhortation and goodwill. British policy towards the French empire in late June and July 1940 contained a dangerously high degree of this characteristic. In the event, it was not put to the test of success.

NOTES

1. CAB 80/13, COS(40)466, 14 June 1940.
2. CAB 67/7, WP(G)(40)155, 17 June 1940.
3. In addition to Greenwood's memorandum already cited, this review of the economic and strategic importance of the French empire rests on CAB 66/8, WP(40)207, 15 June 1940, Report by COS Committee on French colonial empire; and CAB 66/7, WP(G)(40)156, 16 June 1940, Memorandum by Dalton.
4. FO 371/24311, C7278/65/17, Hollis to Strang, 14 June 1940, enclosing draft of COS(40)455, 13 June, and telegram to military attachés and others; FO circular telegram, 15 June 1940, to representatives in French territories.
5. *Ibid.,* FO circular telegrams, 17 June 1940.
6. FO 371/24311, C7316/65/17, Campbell to Halifax, 18 June 1940; CAB 65/7, WM(40)178.
7. FO 371/24327, C7343/7327/17, minute by Millard, 22 June 1940; FO 371/24383, C7573/5/18, minute by Lias on conversation with Momtchiloff, Bulgarian Minister in London, 24 June 1940.
8. FO 800/312, H/XIV/457, Massey to Halifax, 23 June 1940; Halifax to Massey, same date.
9. FO 371/24327, C7343/7327/17, minute by Millard, 22 June 1940.
10. *Ibid.,* minute by Ward, 20 June 1940; CAB 65/7, WM(40)178, 180.
11. See above, 103.
12. FO 371/24383, C7366/5/18, Gascoigne (Consul-General at Tangier) to Halifax, 20 June 1940, CIGS to Dillon, 21 June; CAB 21/1432, Dewing to Makins, 24 June 1940; CAB 66/9, WP(40)226, 28 June 1940, memorandum by Duff Cooper; CAB 80/14, COS(40)508 (draft), 1 July 1940.
13. CAB 80/14, COS(40)529(JP), 4 July 1940; Truchet, 375.

14. FO 371/24327, C7343/7327/17, Lowdon to Halifax, 19 June 1940.
15. FO 371/24311, C7316/65/17, Knight to Halifax, 18 June 1940.
16. FO 371/24327, C7343/7327/17, Knight to Halifax, 19 June 1940.
17. *Ibid.,* Hurst to Halifax, 19 June 1940, Nos. 14, 17.
18. Truchet, 36-45.
19. *Ibid.,* 91-2.
20. FO 371/24327, C7343/7327/17, Knight to Halifax, 20 June 1940.
21. FO 371/24327, C7380/7327/17, FO circular telegram to representatives in French territories, 23 June 1940.
22. FO 371/24328, C7394/7327/17, Knight to Halifax, 23 and 24 June 1940.
23. FO 371/24328, C7388/7427/17, Knight to Halifax, 24 June 1940.
24. FO 371/24328, C7392/7327/17, Lowdon to Halifax, 23 June 1940.
25. FO 371/24383, C7366/5/18, Hurst to Halifax, 20 June 1940.
26. FO 371/24328, C7396/7327/17, Hurst to Halifax, 23 June 1940.
27. FO 371/24328, C7478/7327/17, Dillon to S of S for War, 23 June 1940.
28. FO 371/24328, C7392/7327/17, Lowdon to Halifax, 24 June 1940. Cf. Truchet, 55.
29. *Ibid.,* 98-9.
30. FO 371/24311, C9592/7327/17, despatch by Lowdon on the end of his mission at Algiers, 18 July 1940.
31. FO 371/24328, C7392/7327/17, Lowdon to Halifax, 24 June 1940; FO 371/24331, C9592/7327/17, Lowdon's despatch, 18 July; FO 371/24328, C7478/7327/17, Hurst to Halifax, 28 June; C7394/7327/17, Knight to Halifax, 29 June; FO 371/24329, C7490/7327/17, Parr to Halifax, 1 July, Gascoigne to Halifax, 1 July, Lowdon to Halifax, 1 July.
32. CAB 65/7, WM(40)180.
33. FO 371/24328, C7396/7327/17, Hurst to Halifax, Halifax to Hurst, 25 June 1940.
34. CAB 66/9, WP(40)225, 27 June 1940, report by Duff Cooper; cf. Duff Cooper (Lord Norwich), *Old Men Forget* (London 1953), 282-4.

35. CAB 66/9, WP(40)226, 28 June 1940, memorandum by Duff Cooper; CAB 80/14, COS(40)508 (draft), 1 July 1940.
36. CAB 65/7, WM(40)185.
37. FO 371/24321, C7342/839/17, Bond (Casablanca) to Halifax, 2 July 1940, Halifax to Bond, 4 July; Gascoigne to Halifax, 24, 30 July, Halifax to Gascoigne, 25 July; CAB 65/8, WM(40)212.
38. FO 371/24301, C7636/9/17, Gascoigne to Halifax, 5 July 1940.
39. FO 371/24329, C7662/7327/17, Gascoigne to Halifax, 7 July 1940, transmitting message from Hurst.
40. *Ibid.*, Gascoigne to Halifax, 11 and 16 July 1940.
41. FO 371/24327, C7380/7327/17, Cusden (Dakar) to Halifax, 23 June 1940; FO 371/24321, C7808/839/17, report by Admiral Lyon, 4 July 1940.
42. FO 371/24328, C7416/7327/17, Cannel (Duala) to Halifax, 24 June 1940.
43. See below, 185.
44. The main appreciations were: COS(40)480(JP), 22 June 1940, Defence of British interests in West Africa; COS(40)505 (JP), 29 June 1940; Implications of action contemplated in respect of certain French ships; COS(40)529(JP), 4 July 1940, Implications of French hostility; WP(40)256, 16 July 1940, Implications of French hostility.
45. FO 371/24327, C7365/7389/17, Jardine (Sierra Leone) to S of S for Colonies, 28 June 1940.
46. WO 106/2856, Giffard to War Office, 17 July 1940.
47. CAB 65/14, WM(40)196, Confidential Annex, 7 July 1940; CAB 80/14, COS(40)550(JP), 14 July 1940.
48. CAB 80/13, COS(40)480(JP), 22 June 1940, annexed instructions to Giffard; FO 371/24328, C7413/7327/17, Giffard to War Office, 28 June 1940; Halifax to Joint (Leopoldville), 4 July 1940, with attached note on Takoradi air route. See also below, 201.
49. CAB 66/9, WP(40)231, 28 June 1940, memorandum by Halifax; CAB 65/7, WM(40)187.
50. CAB 21/1439, ME(O)(40)22, 1 July 1940; CAB 80/14, COS(40)549(JP), 14 July 1940; CAB 80/15, COS(40)561 (revise) 22 July 1940.
51. CAB 80/15, COS(40)552(JP), 16 July 1940.
52. CAB 65/8, WM(40)189, 193, 196; CAB 66/9, WP(40)252, 7 July 1940, memorandum by Lloyd and attached papers; FO

371/24328, C7416/7, Halifax to Cannel, 6 July 1940.

53. CAB 65/8, WM(40)201; FO 371/24328, C7479/7327/17, S of S for Colonies to Governors of Nigeria, Gold Coast, Sierra Leone, and Gambia, 13 July 1940.

54. FO 371/24329, C7961/7327/17, Joint to Halifax, 25 July 1940; Governor, Nigeria, to S of S for Colonies, 26 July; FO 371/24329, C8032/7327/17, Cannel to Halifax, 28 July 1940.

55. *Ibid.,* Halifax to Joint, 1 August 1940.

56. FO 371/24329, C8215/7327/17, Governor, Nigeria, to S of S for Colonies, 31 July 1940.

57. CAB 80/15, COS(40)569, 24 July 1940; COS(40)577, 27 July 1940; COS(40)585, 29 July 1940.

58. CAB 66/10, WP(40)299, 3 August 1940, memorandum by Lloyd, and attached papers; FO 371/24329, C7961/7327/17, Bourdillon to S of S for Colonies, 26 July 1940.

59. FO 371/24328, C7478/7327/17, Bourdillon to S of S for Colonies, 10 July 1940; FO 371/24329, C8215/7327/17, same to same, 31 July 1940, two telegrams. Brian Weinstein, *Eboué* (New York 1972), 237-44, describes the situation from Eboué's point of view. See below, 199-201.

60. FO 371/24329, C8251/7327/17, Bourdillon to S of S for Colonies, 7 August 1940.

61. A reasoned argument that resistance in North Africa was virtually impossible may be found in E. Bauer, *La Guerre des Blindés,* vol. I (Paris 1962), 134-5; the opposing thesis is the whole subject of Truchet, *L'Armistice de 1940 et l'Afrique du Nord.*

Chapter 9

DE GAULLE:
THE BEGINNINGS & DAKAR

During late June and early July 1940 the British government kept General de Gaulle in the background while themselves adopting different methods in an effort to persuade the French empire to continue the war. Sometimes de Gaulle and his Free French movement appeared to be a possible rallying-point for the furtherance of these endeavours, and at other times they seemed a stumbling-block in the way of their success. In August and September this pattern changed when Gaullist emissaries, in remarkably small numbers, won over the greater part of French Equatorial Africa and established a Free French administration there. An expedition was sent to establish de Gaulle himself at Dakar, where it was hoped that the whole of French West Africa would rally to him. In these two months, de Gaulle and the Free French assumed an importance which they never thereafter lost, despite all the later vicissitudes of their fortunes. The British government and de Gaulle were launched on a strange partnership, the consequences of which were to be felt for at least a quarter of a century.

The beginnings of the partnership were hesitant and uncertain. On 23 June the British Cabinet agreed in principle to recognise a Council of Liberation, or French National Committee, and de Gaulle was allowed to broadcast an announcement of its formation.[1] In the British press it was emphasised that the membership of this committee would depend on the arrival of important personalities who were on their way to Britain — Reynaud was specifically mentioned.[2] However, nobody arrived, and the prominent leaders in the French empire maintained their allegiance to the existing French government. As this became apparent, the National Committee scheme was quietly dropped, and the British government was left with de Gaulle alone. He was not dropped, because Churchill was determined that as many French servicemen as possible should continue the war, and de Gaulle was the best available leader for them, but British policy now went no further. On 28 June the Cabinet published a statement: 'His Majesty's Government recognise General de Gaulle as the leader of all free Frenchmen, wherever they may be, who rally to him in support of the Allied cause'.[3] This was a vague and limited form of recognition, which the Foreign Office held firmly to mean that de Gaulle was merely a military leader and was not recognised in any governmental capacity.[4]

The first attempt to regulate the relations arising from this recognition took the limited form of a memorandum on the organisation, employment and conditions of service of the volunteer forces which de Gaulle was to lead. While this document was mainly practical in nature, its preparation, and in particular the drafting of covering letters to be exchanged by Churchill and de Gaulle, raised questions of principle.[5] In the draft agreement proposed by de Gaulle, there appeared a claim that the volunteer force should be distinctively French, not only in its personnel, discipline and language, but also in its equipment, including warships. The British Admiralty and Foreign Office were anxious that most French ships, and all the larger vessels, should be manned by mixed crews, fly both flags, and be under British command. They were afraid that wholly French crews might go home with their ships — though this was not a fear which they cared to admit openly to de Gaulle. The proposed wording was omitted from the final version, and the British thus reduced the degree of independence of de Gaulle's force, and blocked this early attempt to enhance his status. De Gaulle also tried to secure a statement of British determination to restore 'the territorial integrity and independence of France and of the French Empire as they existed upon the outbreak of war'. This was also whittled away, finally emerging in Churchill's public letter to de Gaulle of 7 August as determination 'to secure the full restoration of the independence and greatness of France'. In a secret covering letter, Churchill explained that this phrase 'had no precise relation to territorial frontiers. We have not been able to guarantee such frontiers in respect of any nation now acting with us, but, of course, we shall do our best'. De Gaulle acknowledged this, with the hope that the time would come when Britain could consider these matters with less reserve. At all stages of these brief but significant negotiations, de Gaulle pressed skilfully for the widest measure of recognition while the British, with equal skill, resisted his efforts.

The result was a situation full of uncertainty. Little clarification was provided by another letter from Churchill to de Gaulle on 5 August, conveying British approval (in principle) of the formation (at a suitable time) of a Council of Defence to organise such French colonies as might in the future join de Gaulle.[6] This was tenuous stuff. Churchill recognised the psychological importance of the Free French, as of the other Allied forces in exile. 'It is most necessary', he admonished Ismay on 12 July, 'to give to the war which Great Britain is waging single-handed the broad international character which will add greatly to our strength and prestige'.[7] Nevertheless, this did not lead him to seek to extend the scope of British relations with de Gaulle. It was possible that in the future the Free French movement might gather strength and secure control over part of the French empire, in which case it might assume more of the character of a government.[8] Meanwhile, its precise status was left in abeyance, and British contacts with de Gaulle were maintained through a mission (carefully called a military mission) headed by General Spears. Relations with the Free French were also handled by the Committee on Foreign (Allied) Resistance, under the chairmanship of Major Desmond Morton, Churchill's friend and personal assistant. This was a British body to consider French affairs, and not — even in the slightest degree — an Anglo-French committee. A suggestion from de Gaulle's headquarters in mid-September that a Free French representative should attend meetings of the Economic Sub-Committee of the Morton Committee was refused.[9]

Despite these hesitations and uncertainties, a brave front on British relations with the Free French was presented to the public, and an intensive effort was made by the British to display de Gaulle as a leader worth following and an ally worth having. At the outset he was not well known in Britain. The press had noted his appointment as Under-Secretary for War by Reynaud, and on 7 June he was described thus in *The Times:* 'Rather aggressively "right wing", intensely theoretical, an almost fanatical apostle of the mass employment of armoured vehicles, he is also clear-minded, lucid,

193

and a man of action as well as a man of dreams and abstract ideas'.[10] This was an interesting thumb-nail sketch of a French junior minister, but would these qualities suffice for the leader of a movement and a national cause? In particular, to be aggressively right-wing was a dubious passport to the goodwill of British left-wing or even middle-of-the-road opinion.

It was clear that de Gaulle would have to be presented to the British public both energetically and tactfully, and on 18 July a publicity agent, Mr Richmond Temple, was appointed to undertake this task. Temple made it his objective to establish de Gaulle quickly as a recognisable figure, and to stop people asking 'Who is de Gaulle?' Maintaining that this must be done 'scientifically — naturally and unnoticeably', he and his staff translated items from Free French headquarters for the press, and ensured that they were distributed and explained; some were actually written in Temple's office, and then sent out as from de Gaulle's headquarters. Public visits by de Gaulle to Free French units were arranged, and photographs taken. Temple's staff also prepared a short book, *De Gaulle's France and the Key to the Coming Invasion of Germany*, which was published in September and given wide attention by the British press.[11] This book struck a careful balance. De Gaulle was presented as 'the Man of Destiny', a national saviour — but his 'sincere modesty . . . would prevent him from claiming such a historic role for himself . . .' He was quoted as saying that he was 'a free Frenchman, believing in God and the destiny of my country, owing allegiance to no man'; that he was concerned with only one thing — to fight for the freedom of France; and that he was not connected with any political party or politician of Right, Centre or Left. He was shown primarily as a soldier, both a military thinker before the war and a successful commander of armoured forces at the battles of Laon and Abbeville in the campaign of 1940. But he was more than a soldier. 'There is in de Gaulle a spiritual quality which influences other men to think and act as nobly as himself. He is destined to be a leader of armies and a leader of men'.[12] Not all these claims would be accepted in retrospect, yet much of this little book now reads like prophecy of a remarkably accurate kind. In the autumn of 1940, copies were sent to British colonies and diplomatic missions; an American edition was produced, and also a French version, which was distributed to French colonial territories whenever possible.[13]

This was a substantial essay in public relations which was of real value to de Gaulle and his movement, but it could not still the doubts within the British government about his suitability as leader of the Free French. As early as 24 June the French Ambassador in London, Corbin, told Halifax that to give British support to the proposed French National Committee was a mistake. There would be no representative Frenchmen on the committee, and since it was formed on British soil it would be treated as no more independent than the Bordeaux government. Corbin described the committee as 'nothing more than a construction of the imagination',[14] which view found some echo within the British government. Dalton was disappointed that no prominent Frenchmen had arrived to join de Gaulle: 'Still no Frenchmen blowing any trumpets anywhere except de G. in London, and his trumpet blasts are becoming a bit monotonous'.[15] It is clear from Duff Cooper's flight to Rabat that the Cabinet would have very much liked Mandel to come to London to lead French resistance to Germany.

A number of reports showed that the response to de Gaulle within the French empire was unenthusiastic. The British Consul in Tahiti reported that the governor and the commander of a warship stationed there both asked 'Who is this General?'[16] From Pondicherry, in French India, came a similar report: 'Representative Frenchmen say with truth that this officer is not a government, that he is a soldier unrecognised as anything by any-. one . . . .'[17] The Governor of Nigeria telegraphed on 26 July that: 'It must now be realised that the name de Gaulle cuts no ice. whatever locally. He is regarded as "one of those political generals" '.[18] Even among de Gaulle's supporters there arose doubts and criticism. From 'François' (Luizet), working clandestinely for de Gaulle in Morocco and Tangier, came a despairing cry on 14 August: 'Do you receive my telegrams? You know my friends and I are only remaining alive for the sake of your cause'. De Gaulle replied twelve days later with a somewhat staccato telegram which may have appeased the feeling of neglect which inspired this appeal, but it was clear to Gascoigne, the British Consul-General in Tangier, that criticism of de Gaulle was growing even among his ardent followers.[19]

What could the British government do? De Gaulle appeared to be the best available leader for the Free French movement. Some hopes were entertained of General Catroux, who was considerably senior to de Gaulle, had served with distinction in North Africa, and held the post of Governor-General of Indo-China. The government took considerable trouble in bringing Catroux to London and ensuring his welcome along the way,[20] and there was clearly some hope that he might take over the leadership. The Foreign Office told the Consul-General at Saigon on 21 July: 'We are satisfied that de Gaulle would make no difficulty about deferring to Catroux'.[21] On his arrival in London on 17 September, Catroux had immediate interviews with Churchill and Lloyd; he later wrote that at both meetings he was offered the leadership of the Free French, but declined, saying that he had already placed himself at the disposal of de Gaulle.[22] Catroux adhered firmly to this position, and went out of his way to greet de Gaulle as his superior officer when they met at Fort Lamy airfield in October 1940.[23] It was indeed fortunate for de Gaulle that his first high-ranking collaborator was a man who adopted such an attitude.

The British therefore had no alternative to de Gaulle, despite the fact that in the light of pure reason his movement amounted to little during the first two months of its existence. He collected a scratch headquarters of men who were unknown and often untried in administrative work, the most senior service officer to join the movement before the arrival of Catroux being Admiral Muselier, who took command of the Free French naval and air forces. However, Muselier was a stormy petrel whom Catroux described as tending to act over-hastily; a Foreign Office official thought he had 'more energy and drive than tact'. In late July and early August he offended officers in the Admiralty by saying that French sailors who joined the Royal Navy instead of the Free French navy were deserters. De Gaulle came to think he would be better out of the country; and the British did not want to find him — as senior officer in London — in charge of the Free French headquarters while de Gaulle was abroad. Twice in August the Morton Committee discussed means of tactfully removing him from the scene, either by sending him to Alexandria, or to visit the West Indies and New Caledonia (in the Pacific) on a slow merchant ship. However, Muselier stayed in London. Rightly or wrongly, he was to take much of the blame for the inefficiency and wrangling of the Free French headquarters in London, though he later established good relations with the British Admiralty.[24]

The forces commanded by de Gaulle's headquarters were small:

on 12 August 1940 the strength of the Free French army stood at 140 officers and 2,109 men; on 19 September the Free French navy comprised 120 officers and 1,746 ratings.[25] British reports on discipline and morale tended to be poor, especially when contrasted with similar reports on the Polish forces in exile whose morale was excellent.[26] The behaviour of the British authorities was partly responsible for the small size of the Free French forces. Although Churchill was insistent on the importance of securing strong French contingents, the Service departments were less enthusiastic. The CIGS, Dill, told the Chiefs of Staff that he would like to get rid of the French troops in England as soon as possible, and they did not demur. Spears reported Dill as saying that he would tell French servicemen in Britain: ' "any man that wants to stay and fight here can do so": and then I hope they will all go back'.[27] The chief sources of recruits consisted of the French units withdrawn from Narvik and not yet returned to France, some men evacuated from Dunkirk and the naval forces which had taken refuge in British ports on 17 and 18 June. The British officers who visited these men were hardly zealous recruiting agents for the Free French forces; they emphasised that everyone was free to choose, and that those who joined de Gaulle were in danger of being regarded as rebels against their government — this was perfectly true, but not encouraging. De Gaulle complained that while this was going on his own representatives were not allowed to put their case freely.[28] On top of all these difficulties came the British action at Mers-el-Kebir, which certainly deterred many potential recruits, especially among sailors.

However, other important influences were also at work. Apart from the natural anxiety of men to return home, where wives and families were bound to be in difficulties if not actually in danger, there was the more ominous possibility that reprisals might be taken, either by the Germans or by the French government, against the relatives of volunteers for de Gaulle's forces. Life in camps for French servicemen in Britain tended to be idle and aimless, and even those who joined the Free French had no strong claim on sparse British equipment and training resources. Moreover, some of the men who wanted to fight on preferred to do so outside the Free French movement, by joining the British services, or sometimes a French-Canadian regiment, rather than 'get mixed up with politics' by joining de Gaulle. It is highly likely that many Frenchmen in

Britain shared the feelings of three petty-officers who were described by a correspondent of the *Spectator* in September. Bored by inactivity, without news of their families, still oppressed by the shadow of Mers-el-Kebir, with no deep love for England and no sure vision of their duty — these men found it by no means obvious that they should join the Free French.[29]

Another potential, though limited, source of recruits for de Gaulle's forces was the French population in foreign countries, and occasional refugees from France or the empire. Offers of service came in a constant stream during the summer and autumn of 1940, from Latin America, Japan, India, Afghanistan, Turkey and many other places.[20] A Corsican captain, breathing fire in every line of his letter, wrote personally to Churchill requesting to be picked up by flying-boat or submarine, so that he could put himself at de Gaulle's disposal.[31] This was an extreme request which the British could scarcely meet, but they showed little eagerness to assist volunteers even in minor ways. The Treasury ruled that British representatives abroad might assist French volunteers by meeting travelling and subsistence costs, but must offer no remuneration. 'Any sums advanced by His Majesty's Representatives under this authority should be recorded under a separate head of charge and should be taken to a Suspense Account in the Foreign Office books pending further instructions. A quarterly report of the totals so expended should be sent to the Treasury, in order that the expenditure may be included in the bill of assistance rendered to the de Gaulle organisation which we hope to be in a position ultimately to present to someone'.[32] In the circumstances of 1940, the customary parsimony of the Treasury was supported by the fact that untrained manpower was of little use. Specialists of various kinds were welcome, but ordinary men of goodwill could not be trained or equipped.[33]

The problem of equipment was a serious one if the Free French forces, however limited in numbers, were to become efficient. If they were to be equipped with French weapons, ammunition and transport, some means would have to be found of manufacturing this material; the process would be slow, expensive and (if the Free French numbers remained small) wasteful. Alternatively, they could be armed with British, or perhaps American, weapons. Although this was in many ways the simpler course, it would not only involve some re-training, but would also mean that the Free French would be in direct competition with the British forces for equipment. For example, modest Free French requests for lorries and armoured cars for use in Chad in late 1940 were met by War Office objections that these could only be supplied at the expense of British units.[34] There was no way round such difficulties until supplies could be greatly increased, and meanwhile the Free French were bound to be poor relations.

A further problem was the legal status of the Free French forces. Under the terms of the French armistices with Germany and Italy, any French nationals continuing to fight were to be treated as *francs-tireurs:* one of the implications of this was that they had no claim, if captured, to be treated as prisoners of war. Legal authorities within the Foreign Office agreed that de Gaulle's volunteers were not the forces of a belligerent state, and therefore not covered by the Hague Convention of 1907. General Wavell's headquarters in the Middle East, which commanded one of the first Free French land units to go into action against the enemy, sought to meet the problem by issuing the troops with documents stating that they were members of the British armed forces. However, these had no legal value, and in any case ran counter to de Gaulle's determination that his troops must preserve their national identity. For the British, this was a minor problem, but it tended to increase British doubts as to the status and usefulness of the Free French recruits. For individual French volunteers, of course, it was by no means a small matter.[35]

Towards the end of August 1940, when de Gaulle's Free French movement had been under way for some two months, its future appeared doubtful. The British government had carefully refrained from recognising de Gaulle except as a military leader — and even in this capacity it appears that they would have preferred Catroux. No significant political figure had joined the movement, which as a rallying-point for the French empire had so far been a failure. Its forces were small, difficult to equip and of doubtful status, while the British administration — despite some direct intervention by Churchill — was less than enthusiastic in offering assistance. Then, at the end of August, this position was dramatically improved when the French colonies in Equatorial Africa came over to de Gaulle, giving his movement a new impetus, a new base and a new importance.

The Free French successes in Equatorial Africa were achieved within the space of four days, from 26 to 29 August. The rallying of Chad to de Gaulle's movement had been planned for some time, and the Governor, Eboué, had been in touch with de Gaulle and the British authorities in Nigeria.[36] The situation in the other territories was much less favourable to Free French action, because the authorities had all chosen to accept the existing government in France. However, in Lagos a plan was worked out by three representatives sent by de Gaulle to West Africa — Pleven, Leclerc and Boislambert. Working with de Larminat, former chief of staff in Syria, who was in Lagos *en route* for London to join de Gaulle, and consulting by telegraph with de Gaulle himself, they decided to make virtually simultaneous moves in Chad, the Cameroons, and the French Congo. This operation was executed with great daring and not a little luck, despite the fact that a battalion of Senegalese troops which was to have been used at Duala in the Cameroons was not available at the crucial time. Chad declared its adherence to de Gaulle on 26 August. In the Cameroons, Leclerc and Boislambert landed with some twenty men in three canoes during the night of the 26th/27th, and by the morning held Duala. De Larminat went to Leopoldville (in the Belgian Congo) in order to encourage dissidence in Brazzaville, across the river in the French Congo. By 28 and 29 August he was able to establish his authority in the city, and declare himself head of government in Free French Africa.[37]

These operations received strong support from the British government. On 29 July the Committee on French Resistance approved de Gaulle's proposal to send representatives to West Africa.[38] Before these representatives set out, they were provided with copies of the letter sent from Churchill to de Gaulle on 5 August 1940, approving the latter's proposal to form a Council of Defence and agreeing to discuss with this body economic matters and questions of defence.[39] The Chiefs of Staff, urged by the Prime Minister, instructed Giffard (C-in-C, West Africa) to give every assistance to the operation at Duala — and this order was repeated even when they learned that the Senegalese battalion could not take part.[40] Moreover, the Free French operations could not have taken place without the use of British territory, communications and transport.

However, the support given to the operations in West Africa itself was more reluctant. The Governor of the Gold Coast believed that, with a few exceptions, the French were unreliable, decadent and without loyalties — 'whether they belong to de Gaulle or to Vichy'. He therefore advocated limiting action against French colonies to the stopping of trade.[41] The Governor of Sierra Leone also advised against an operation in the Cameroons, arguing that even if it were successful the reactions in French West Africa might be disastrous.[42] On 26 August, when the Senegalese battalion was no longer available, Giffard advised very strongly against the Cameroons expedition.[43] However, support for the venture came from Bourdillon, the Governor of Nigeria, who had been particularly impressed by the bearing and grasp of Pleven and de Larminat.[44] Since Nigeria was not only the largest of the West African colonies but also the actual base for the Cameroons expedition, Bourdillon's favourable attitude — albeit with some reservations — was fortunate for the Free French.

In the face of these doubts and hesitations among the British in West Africa, it was the initiative of the Free French which carried the day. De Gaulle telegraphed from London on 26 August, stating that he knew there were differences of opinion between his representatives and the British command, and expressing his own firm convictions that the venture should go ahead.[45] In Africa, de Larminat and his colleagues pressed the matter to a successful conclusion. The British role, though vital, was mainly passive; the Free French were the active partners, but the benefits of the success accrued to both. The British secured the route for aircraft reinforcements to the Middle East, via Takoradi, Fort Lamy and Khartoum, which was to be of crucial importance in the future. The Free French won a territorial base, and above all they gained prestige and self-confidence. The territories themselves were poor and thinly populated, but their psychological value was enormous.

Following these successes in Equatorial Africa came the Anglo-Free French expedition to Dakar. There were powerful reasons for the mounting of this expedition, in that Dakar was a valuable base and if it fell into German hands the whole West African convoy system could be disrupted. In fact, on 19-21 September the Vichy government agreed that a German mission should be sent to Dakar to supervise merchant shipping. When the attack on Dakar began, this mission had reached Casablanca and the French secured its recall on the grounds that arrival at Dakar would justify the claims of British propaganda.[46] The presence of the battleship *Richelieu* and a considerable quantity of gold were added attractions for the operation. Moreover, there was the hope that success at Dakar would be followed by the rallying of Morocco to de Gaulle, which might in turn lead to similar action on the part of Algeria and Tunisia. De Gaulle anticipated this possibility in the instructions he left for Catroux, who was due to arrive in Britain after the Dakar expedition sailed.[47] Churchill was thinking on similar lines, and on 1 September asked the Chiefs of Staff to consider following up a success at Dakar by a similar operation in Morocco.[48] Hopeful reports were received on the likelihood of a *coup* within Morocco with the aid of an expedition from outside.[49] The question of meeting Spanish objections to such a *coup* was seriously considered — Churchill hoped that de Gaulle might be willing to spare some French Moroccan territory in order to purchase Spanish acquiescence.[50]

Such were the advantages to be expected from a successful expedition to Dakar, but the difficulties in preparing and executing such an expedition were great. On no less than three occasions during July 1940 the Chiefs of Staff had declared their disapproval of any attempt to capture the port in the face of opposition, or even to make a naval demonstration against it.[51] In the process of detailed planning the difficulties became steadily more apparent, and postponements and changes of plan resulted. Moreover, there was grave uncertainty as to the very nature of the expedition: whether it was to be an exercise in psychological warfare — a blowing of Free French trumpets before Dakar/Jericho, after which de Gaulle/Joshua would enter the city unopposed; or a military operation, in which resistance would be crushed and the objective seized. The planning of the expedition was thus plagued by problems of both detail and principle, which were only partially resolved.[52]

The first proposal put to the Chiefs of Staff on 4 August was vague. They were asked to consider a possible operation (to be called SCIPIO), evolved by de Gaulle, Spears and Morton, aimed at establishing the Free French in Dakar, West Africa, and Equatorial Africa.[53] On the 5th the Chiefs of Staff produced a plan which was again vague, since the precise destination of the expedition was unknown — though they pointed out that only three ports would be suitable: Dakar, Konakri in French Guinea and Duala in the Cameroons. The project assumed that the troops for the operation would be entirely Free French (2,260 soldiers), while the British would provide transport ships and a naval escort which would withdraw before the expedition reached its destination; it was also assumed that the force would land without meeting any opposition. Provided the Cabinet gave a decision on 5 August, the Chiefs of Staff estimated that the expedition could reach Dakar by 28 August, and the other ports — if they were selected — at later dates.[54]

This sketchy plan was approved in principle by the Cabinet on 5 August; a decision on details was to await further information.[55] However, the principle of the operation itself was called into question that very afternoon at a meeting between the First Sea Lord (Pound) and de Gaulle. The suggestion was made that Vichy warships might interfere with the expedition, in which case British warships might have to escort it right to the landing-place, and if need be sink Vichy vessels. De Gaulle felt that such a situation should not be allowed to develop, and said that if air reconnaissance showed the presence of warships at the selected landing point the expedition should not attempt to land but should sail to the nearest British colony and carry out an invasion of French territory overland.[56] He also stipulated that the British should prevent Vichy reinforcements from arriving after he had taken over the chosen territory. The Chiefs of Staff thought that in these circumstances the British part in the expedition might prove to be both larger and more long-lasting than at first proposed, and they advised Churchill that the operation should be reconsidered in the light of these points.[57]

Churchill met de Gaulle on 6 August, and a changed plan was proposed, which was considered that day by the Inter-Service Planning Staff, and the next day by the Chiefs of Staff. It was now definitely decided that the object of the expedition was to be Dakar and that two Polish battalions were to be added to the Free French forces involved. Three possible landing-places were listed: a beach near Dakar, where infantry might be disembarked if the political conditions in the port were favourable; Konakri, where the whole force could go ashore and undertake an overland approach to Dakar; or Freetown, whence an overland advance into French Guinea could be made. The Planning Staff and Chiefs of Staff were unhappy about all these possibilities, holding that the Atlantic swell might rule out a beach landing near Dakar; that heavy surf might similarly prevent disembarkation at Konakri; and that an overland operation from Freetown would be very difficult in view of the distances and terrain involved. In the course of these discussions, de Gaulle insisted that the operation would not be possible if there were opposition from French forces; his object was to take possession of friendly territory.[58]

The Chiefs of Staff also pointed out that the expedition would raise a serious political problem, involving the general question of British relations with Pétain's government at Vichy and including the risk of war with that government. Their general conclusions were very cautious, expressing fear of embarking on an unlimited liability in a theatre which was not vital to the prosecution of the war, and recommending that the operations against Dakar should go forward only if there was a reasonable prospect of success without a considerable military commitment.[59] Some of these doubts were dispelled and others set aside at a meeting of the Chiefs of Staff, with Churchill in the chair, in the late evening of 7 August. Here it was decided that the only place where a landing by de Gaulle's force could be effective was Dakar, and Churchill argued that sufficient support should be given from British forces if this was essential to secure the success of the expedition.[60] This view was embodied in a directive by Churchill to the Chiefs of Staff on 8 August, which laid down that it was important for British interests that de Gaulle should take Dakar as soon as possible. If the Gaullist emissaries recently sent to West Africa (i.e., Pleven, Leclerc, and Boislambert) reported that Dakar could be taken peaceably, so much the better, but if not, an adequate Polish and British force should be provided together with full naval protection. 'The operation, once begun, must be carried through. De Gaulle should be used to impart a French character to it, and of course, once successful, his administration will rule. But we must drive him on and provide the needful balance of force'. Churchill directed that a plan be prepared forthwith, and emphasised that time was vital. The political question of risking war with Vichy was reserved for the Cabinet.[61]

This meant that the nature of the operation had been drastically changed from that proposed only four days earlier. From being a Free French expedition with British transport and naval escort, not to be pressed against opposition, it had become a British expedition with a Free French character imparted to it, to be carried through once begun. A plan on this new basis was drawn up by 9 August. The Poles, only recently introduced into the operation, were excluded on the grounds that their presence would be politically undesirable, and that the units concerned could not be trained in time. Two Royal Marine brigades were to make up the British landing force, and the Free French forces were to keep in the background except for accompanying parties from the Foreign Legion. Dawn landings were to be made at six separate points. This plan was accepted by the Cabinet on 13 August.[62] It survived for six days.

When the British commanders for the expedition (General Irwin and Admiral J. H. D. Cunningham, appointed on 12 August) came to examine the details, they found that of the six proposed landing beaches, four were ruled out by swell and surf, while the other two were covered by guns and searchlights. Moreover, the installation of hydrophones at Dakar meant that to avoid detection the transports would have to stand some eleven miles off-shore, and there transfer the troops to boats and landing-craft. In view of all these factors, the Chiefs of Staff concluded that surprise would be almost impossible, and that all idea of a bloodless landing would have to be abandoned. The alternative appeared to be the delivery of an ultimatum, supported by an overwhelming show of force; if this were rejected, to attack the port by 'a full-blown combined operation'.[63]

These problems were considered at a meeting of the Chiefs of Staff on 20 August, with Churchill in the chair and de Gaulle also present. Churchill took up the new alternative plan, but discarded the idea of an ultimatum in favour of an emissary bearing a letter from de Gaulle in an attempt to win over the governor. If this failed, and the shore defences opened fire, the British warships would bombard the defences, but with restraint. Should the resistance be determined, British forces would use all means to break it down. It was essential that the operation be concluded before nightfall.[64] This plan was adopted, but still had to be worked out in detail. The Vice-Chiefs of Staff, the two British commanders and de Gaulle met on 21 August, when the latter stressed the need to proceed without undue haste after arriving at Dakar, in the hope that the garrison might be split by internal dissension and indecision. It was agreed that it might not be possible to complete the operation by nightfall on the first day — and thus what was declared essential on 20 August became optional on the 21st.[65]

At this point, further delay occurred. With the adoption of the most recent plan, it had been assumed that the transport ships taking part from Liverpool would leave that port on 23 August and reach Dakar in sixteen days, steaming at twelve knots. This set the date of the operation at 8 September. However, it was discovered that the vessels concerned could in fact only make eight or nine knots. The delay involved in re-loading onto faster ships would have exceeded the time saved, so it was therefore necessary to add five days to the duration of the passage to Dakar — the date now became 13 September. In addition errors in the loading of the ships at Liverpool meant that three days had to be spent in re-stowing cargo. Furthermore, at the meeting on 21 August the British commanders explained that the expedition could not proceed direct to Dakar, but would first have to put in to refuel at Freetown, well to the south. This added another two days to the total voyage. The cumulative effect of all these delays — which might have been foreseen and largely averted by more systematic planning — was to postpone the date of the operation from 8 to 18 September.[66]

On 27 August the Cabinet approved the operation in its final form. The danger of the Vichy government declaring war was recognised, but not considered to be grave.[67] The next day, the Chiefs of Staff took note of a memorandum by General Irwin, explaining that his forces would not be sufficient to deal with full-scale opposition by the Dakar garrison, and that they were short of assault landing-craft.[68] The Chiefs of Staff took no action, but by this stage it is hard to see what they could have done. However, they did not dispute Irwin's assessment, and it was clear that considerable risks were being accepted.

The expedition finally sailed on 30 August. The landing force comprised four Royal Marine battalions, plus one independent company, and two Free French battalions. The naval force consisted of two battleships (the *Barham* and *Resolution*), the aircraft-carrier *Ark Royal,* three cruisers, ten destroyers and three Free French sloops. The warships, assembled from different stations, represented a very large diversion of force from other tasks, including defence against invasion and convoy protection. This diversion, at a time when invasion was thought to be imminent, is a measure of the importance attached to the Dakar operation. The naval force was strong numerically, but not necessarily powerful enough to deal with shore batteries in serious battle. The landing force was inadequate in numbers, equipment and training to undertake an

206

assault landing against determined opposition.

Much therefore depended on whether there would in fact be serious opposition, or whether Dakar would yield to a show of force and the appeal of de Gaulle's emissaries. On this question, most of the available information tended to be hopeful. On 8 August, Pleven and Leclerc reported from Bathurst (capital of Gambia, the nearest British colony to Dakar) that opinion in Dakar was moving towards Britain, though some elements remained extremely hostile — they noted the continuing adverse effects of the action at Mers-el-Kebir. The economic situation was reported to be bad, with reserves of flour running down.[69] A later report, from a Gaullist sympathiser who made his way from Dakar to Bathurst early in September, stated that favourable elements in the town would be prepared to deliver it to de Gaulle, and if the units used in a landing were Free French rather than British, there would be no shooting.[70] (This report came after the expedition had sailed from Britain, but in ample time to affect the later decision as to whether it should proceed after reaching Freetown.) British intelligence at the beginning of September was that the colonial administration at Dakar was hostile to Britain, and the naval commander bitterly so; but the sympathies of the army were divided, and with a strong lead the junior officers — together with air force personnel — would declare support for de Gaulle. The great majority of the Senegalese population was reported to favour the Allies.[71]

This optimistic intelligence appears to have been accepted, though in retrospect some of it looks distinctly dubious, and even at the time there was some information to the contrary. On 28 August the two former British liaison officers in Dakar, Captain Poulter and Commander Rushbrooke, arrived in London. They had been expelled from Dakar after the armistice, and although the Chiefs of Staff had wanted to bring them home from Lagos as early as 10 August, no long-range flying-boat was available at that time. These officers reported that the shore defences were strong, and that the garrison (7,000 Senegalese troops, with a high proportion of French non-commissioned officers) was loyal to its commander and the governor; they took the view that strong resistance would be offered to any Gaullist attempt to take the city.[72] This report, given to Cunningham and Irwin on 29 August, had to be set against other information, all of which had been received since the two liaison officers left Dakar and might therefore be considered more important.

Another problem which beset the British authorities during the planning of the operation was that of security and the leakage of information. The code-name was changed from SCIPIO to MENACE lest some member of German intelligence should know enough ancient history to grasp the connection between Scipio and Africa.[73] Then the Chiefs of Staff Committee itself was reproved for endangering the security of the new code-name by mentioning both it and the destination of the expedition in one document.[74] However, the main concern arose in other ways. On 22 August the Inter-Services Security Board reported to the Chiefs of Staff that about 7 August a French officer had said openly to a friend that Free French forces were bound for Dakar. This officer was said to be vain, indiscreet, and 'very fond of the opposite sex'. It was also reported that a French civilian had spoken in public of a Free French force going to West Africa at the end of the month, and other messages showed that the operation was being discussed openly among other French ranks. The Board held that there was a diminishing chance of the operation achieving surprise, and placed the blame for leakages firmly on the French.[75]

On 29 August the same question was raised in a letter to the Chiefs of Staff stating that the assault landing-craft for the operation had been trundled across England 'like the Durham ox to the wonder and consternation of the countryside'. They had then been hoisted on davits aboard the transports in Liverpool, in full view of everyone, over a period of six days. The writer had been told the destination of the expedition by a man on Liverpool docks, and although he had at first thought this was a rumour being used as cover, he later found enough clues to show that it was accurate. This report, which was accepted by the Security Board as correct, showed that British security arrangements for the Dakar operation were far from perfect, although a further report from the Board to the Chiefs of Staff on 19 September again put the blame on the Free French. De Gaulle himself, while buying his tropical kit at Simpson's in Piccadilly, had apparently remarked that his destination was West Africa. French officers had drunk a toast to 'Dakar' at a restaurant in Liverpool, while Dakar had been a common subject of conversation among the rank and file. However, there were current reports of other destinations, including the Mediterranean.[76]

After all these difficulties in the planning and preparation of the expedition, there followed further problems in its execution. One of these arose from the appearance off West Africa of a squadron of Vichy warships, comprising three cruisers and three *contre-torpilleurs*. This force was bound for Equatorial Africa to reassert the authority of the metropolitan government over the colonies lost to the Free French, not for Dakar as the result of a leakage about the expedition. (Indeed, the French Admiralty gave the British naval attaché at Madrid advance notice that the squadron was to pass Gibraltar, though without revealing its destination.) The Vichy government knew de Gaulle had put to sea, and sent warning telegrams to North Africa and Senegal on 8 and 10 September, but these mentioned no specific destination other than Africa or North Africa.[77] Nonetheless, the movements of the Vichy squadron greatly affected the Anglo-Free French expedition.

The Vichy warships passed the straits of Gibraltar in the early morning of 11 September, and put into Casablanca that afternoon. They reached Dakar on 14 September. On the 19th, the three cruisers (the *Georges-Leygues, Gloire* and *Montcalm*) sailed south from Dakar heading for Libreville, their original destination, but were intercepted *en route* by two British cruisers. The *Gloire* developed engine trouble and was persuaded to go under escort to Casablanca, but the other two French cruisers, while not persisting in their southward course, could not be prevented from returning to Dakar. In the meantime, the cruiser *Primauguet,* which had originally been at Dakar, put to sea on 18 September and was eventually escorted into Casablanca by two British cruisers. The net result of these movements was to strengthen the French naval force at Dakar by one cruiser and three *contre-torpilleurs*, bringing it to a total of one battleship, the *Richelieu* (partly disabled, but able to fire), two cruisers, three *contre-torpilleurs* and three submarines.[78]

Considering the naval power being used by the British in support of the Dakar expedition, this was not in itself a large accession of strength. However, it was assumed at the time that the French squadron from Toulon must have been carrying reinforcements for Dakar (which was not the case), and moreover that the very arrival of the warships was bound to raise the morale of the garrison, remove any sense of isolation, and stiffen determination to resist attack. Such an effect on morale, while impossible to measure precisely, seems likely to have been the most important result of the squadron's arrival at Dakar. It was also significant that, after much shadowing and contact between Vichy and British warships, the French authorities at Dakar were now well aware — whatever their previous intelligence had been — that a British naval force was off West Africa.

The responsibility for allowing the Vichy squadron to reach West Africa became a thorny question within the British government, and especially the Admiralty, but details of this controversy did not affect relations between the British and the Free French. The fact was that the warships were at Dakar, and the immediate question was whether the operation should continue. In Cabinet on 16 September, Churchill stated categorically that the expedition should be abandoned. The Cabinet agreed, and accepted a recommendation from the Chiefs of Staff that de Gaulle and his Free French force should go to Duala and thence to Chad. Orders were sent accordingly to the Dakar expedition.[79] Cunningham, Irwin, de Gaulle and Spears all protested, and requested urgently that they be allowed to proceed. They argued that until it was known how much the arrival of the cruisers had affected morale, their presence did not materially influence the naval situation; that risks had already been accepted, and while these had now increased they were still worth accepting in view of the potential gains; and that it was vital to press on for the sake of the morale of the French population all over West Africa, who were bound to learn of the expedition's arrival at Freetown. Churchill and the Cabinet allowed themselves to be swayed by these representations. The question was considered at three Cabinet meetings, two on 17 September and one on the 18th, and authority was finally given to the commanders of the expedition to proceed and act as they thought best to secure the original aim of the undertaking.[80]

So the operation went on, though further delay meant that the expedition actually arrived off Dakar at dawn on 23 September. While the force was at Freetown, there was also yet another change of plan proposed by de Gaulle. If his emissaries failed in their attempt to secure an unopposed landing, a Free French force should attempt a landing at Rufisque (a beach about ten miles from Dakar), with British troops following only after a bridgehead had been secured. The British commanders accepted this amendment on 17 September.[81]

The first day's operations at Dakar proved that hopes that de Gaulle would be welcomed, or that opposition from the garrison would be negligible, were ill-founded. Gaullist emissaries who landed by plane never returned; others who landed in the harbour from the sloop *Savorgnan de Brazza* had to flee to avoid arrest, and were fired on as they escaped. A thick mist prevented the garrison from being over-awed by the sight of the British warships — if this was ever likely — and appeared to hamper the British shooting more than the French. Free French troops tried to land at Rufisque, but abandoned the attempt in the fog. That evening, Churchill signalled to the commanders: 'Having begun, we must go on to the end. Stop at nothing'. On the other hand, at 4 a.m. the next morning (24 September) the governor of Dakar, Boisson, replied to an ultimatum by saying that he would defend the town to the end. Of these two positions, Boisson's proved the stronger. All the doubts expressed during the planning stage about the difficulty of taking Dakar in face of serious opposition were proved well-founded. An attempt at systematic bombardment from the sea during 24 September proved ineffectual, while the French fire from the forts and the *Richelieu* was accurate and effective. On the morning of the 25th, the battleship *Resolution* was hit by a torpedo from a French submarine, and the British force withdrew out to sea.[82]

At 11.30 on 25 September the Cabinet met in London. They were considerably influenced by the damage to the *Resolution* and by the danger that further persistence, and even a successful landing, would mean a long-term commitment of forces. They therefore decided to call off the attack, and this was done in the afternoon of the 25th.[83]

In assessing the reasons for the failure at Dakar, the most important was probably the simplest: the defending forces fought hard and fired accurately. In the face of such resistance, a landing from the sea and the bombardment of strong shore batteries by warships were extremely difficult operations. Other explanations arise clearly from the story of the expedition. The repeated changes of plan caused confusion and delay, which were exacerbated by the problems over transport and the packing of stores. The planning and preparations were at once too slow for a rapid *coup de main* and too hasty for a properly organised, combined operation. Available intelligence about Dakar proved to be inadequate, and was probably interpreted too optimistically. In the actual execution of the operation, too much went wrong, from the arrival of the Vichy warships to the state of the weather.

If the failure of the expedition is examined with a view to apportioning responsibility between the British and the Free French, most of the weight must fall on the British. The delays and changes of plan were primarily the work of the British planning staffs — for whom, of course, Dakar was not the first priority in the desperate month of August 1940. Free French intelligence about opinion in Dakar was over-optimistic, but so was some of the British, and it was the duty of the British authorities to assess the value of the various reports. On the question of security, the Free French were widely condemned, and doubtless they were indiscreet, but there is evidence of equal slackness on the British side. In any case, the consequences of indiscretion do not appear to have been serious. With regard to the affair of the Vichy cruiser squadron the responsibilities, wherever precisely they might lie, were all British — no-one could have expected the Free French to stop the ships. In the decision to proceed with the operation after the arrival of the cruisers at Dakar, the British commanders and Spears were as insistent as de Gaulle, and carried more weight with the Cabinet. The unsuccessful battle itself was waged by British commanders with British forces, de Gaulle and the Free French playing only a minor part. Dakar was mainly a British failure; if the Free French were sometimes made to bear a disproportionate share of the blame, this was doubtless because they were the weaker partner.

Fortunately for de Gaulle and the Free French, the failure at Dakar was accompanied by a notable if incidental success. The destination of the Vichy cruiser squadron had been Libreville, in Gabon, and its mission was to recover control of the territories of Equatorial Africa. The British fleet covering the Dakar expedition prevented the squadron from carrying out this mission, and the Free French base in Equatorial Africa was preserved. It was the possession of this territory, and the loyalty of those who administered it — de Larminat, Eboué, Pleven — which saved de Gaulle in his period of trial after Dakar.

NOTES

1. See above, 103.
2. See e.g. *The Times, Daily Telegraph, Scotsman,* 25 June 1940.
3. CAB 65/7, WM(40)186; CAB 85/23, CFR(40)4, 13 August 1940, note by secretary of Committee on French Resistance.

4. FO 371/24360, C8172/8172/17, FO circular telegram, 1 July 1940; FO 371/24339, C7693/7328/17, minute by Strang, 7 July 1940.

5. The drafting may be followed in: CAB 67/7, WP(G)(40)181, 10 July 1940, draft of proposed agreement with General de Gaulle; CAB 65/8, WM(40)202, 204, 219; FO 371/24339, C7693/7328/17, minutes by Strang, Cadogan and Halifax, 7 July 1940; FO 371/24339, C7831/7328/17, Dickens to Strang, 9 July 1940, minutes by Roberts and Ward, 8 and 9 July, Strang to Spears, 16 July, minutes by Halifax, 3 August, Churchill, 3 and 4 August, and Strang, 7 August. The agreement was published as France No. 2 (1940), Cmd. 6220.

6. CAB 65/8, WM(40)219; FO 371/24360, C8172/8172/17.

7. CAB 85/23, CFR(40)4, 13 August 1940.

8. CAB 85/22, CFR(40)46th Meeting, 22 August 1940, Item 10.

9. *Ibid.,* CFR(40)53rd Meeting, 16 September 1940, Item 11.

10. This note was by Cyril Falls, military correspondent of *The Times*.

11. The author was given as 'James Marlow'. See the press, 16 September 1940.

12. CAB 21/1454, Committee on French Resistance, 28th Meeting, 15 July 1940; FO 371/24340, C8391/7328/17, memorandum by Temple, 24 September 1940, endorsed by Morton: 'I think that this account of Mr. Temple's work on behalf of de Gaulle is a fair statement and that the expenditure has been justified by results'. The quotations from *De Gaulle's France* are from 22-3, 27-8, 58.

13. CAB 85/23, CFR(40)52, 2 October 1940; FO 371/24342, C10277/7328/17, circular of 24 October 1940.

14. FO 800/312, H/XIV/460, record of conversation between Halifax and Corbin, 24 June 1940.

15. Dalton diary, 25 and 26 June 1940.

16. FO 371/24335, C11403/7327/17, despatch by Edmonds (Tahiti) 24 July 1940.

17. FO 371/24344, C11800/7328/17, Consul-General, Pondicherry, to Government of India, 9 September 1940.

18. FO 371/24329, C7961/7327/17, Bourdillon to S of S for Colonies, 26 July 1940.

19. FO 371/24329, C8567/7327/17, Gascoigne to Halifax, 14 August 1940, transmitting message from 'François' to de

Gaulle; Halifax to Gascoigne, 26 August, with de Gaulle's reply; FO 371/24330, C8722/7327/17, Gascoigne to Halifax, 17 August 1940.

20. FO 371/24339, C7917/7328/17, Halifax to Henderson (Saigon), 7 August 1940; FO 371/24340, C8280/7328/17, S of S for Dominions to High Commissioner, South Africa, 20 August 1940.

21. FO 371/24339, C7917/7328/17, Halifax to Henderson, 21 July 1940.

22. G. Catroux, *Dans la Bataille de la Méditerranée* (Paris 1949), 18-22.

23. *Ibid.,* 50-3.

24. On Muselier, FO 371/24340, C8184/7328/17, Dickens to Barclay, 1 August 1940, minute by Hankey, 5 August; FO 371/24339, C7946/7328/17, minute by Marjoribanks, 20 July 1940 (a favourable view); CAB 85/23, CFR(40)42nd Meeting, 12 August 1940, Item 7, and 47th Meeting, 26 August, Item 3. Cf. Catroux, 23-4, and Muselier's own account of his activities in E. H. Muselier, *De Gaulle contre le Gaullisme* (Paris 1946).

25. CAB 66/11, 12, WP(40)314, 377, 12 August and 19 September 1940; weekly reports by COS Committee on Allied Naval, Army, and Air Contingents.

26. This may be seen in almost any of the reports on the Allied contingents: e.g. CAB 66/10, WP(40)281, 22 July 1940; CAB 66/12, WP(40)377, 19 September.

27. CAB 79/5, COS Committee Minutes, 25 June 1940; Dalton diary, 28 June 1940.

28. CAB 21/1454, Committee on French Resistance, 17th Meeting, 2 July 1940; FO 892/15, note by Spears, 3 July 1940; Passy (A. E. V. Dewavrin), *Souvenirs,* vol. I, *2e. Bureau, Londres* (Monte Carlo 1947), 24-5; de Gaulle, vol. I, 74-6.

29. *Spectator,* 13 September 1940, 265-6; for a group of cadets from St Cyr who applied to join a French-Canadian regiment rather than take what they saw as the political step of joining de Gaulle, see FO 371/24321, C75/839/1117, FO minute, 28 June 1940.

30. FO 371/24342 is filled with correspondence concerning these volunteers; cf. FO 371/24339, C7776/7328/17.

31. FO 371/24340, C8165/7328/17, Antoine Feracci to Churchill, 10 July 1940.

32. FO 371/24339, C7735/7328/17, minute from Treasury to Speaight, Foreign Office, 10 July 1940.

33. *Ibid.,* minutes by Speaight, 18 July 1940; circular telegram to all missions, 20 July 1940.

34. On the general question of equipment for the Free French, CAB 80/18, COS(40)710, 4 September 1940; CAB 85/23, CFR(40)23, 3 September 1940; correspondence in FO 892/1. On equipment for Chad, CAB 85/22, CFR(40)49th Meeting, Item 1, 2 September 1940; CAB 21/1464, Spears to Ismay, 14 December 1940, Ismay to Spears, 15 December.

35. FO 371/24340, C8311/7328/17, memorandum from US Ambassador, 12 August 1940, minute by Malkin, 14 August; FO 371/24342, C9908/7328/17, minutes by Ward and Malkin, 19 September 1940; FO 371/24344, C12114/7328/17, minutes by Malkin and Ward, 18 and 25 November 1940, on correspondence from War Office and C-in-C, Middle East Land Forces.

36. See above 185, and Weinstein, *Eboué,* for an account of Eboué's extremely interesting career.

37. E. de Larminat, *Chroniques irrévérencieuses* (Paris 1962), 121-61; Weinstein, 226-48; de Gaulle, vol. I, 94-5, 289-90.

38. CAB 21/1454, Committee on French Resistance, 36th Meeting, 29 July 1940, 37th Meeting, 31 July.

39. CAB 21/1432, Bridges to Colville, 5 August 1940, enclosing Churchill to de Gaulle, same date. See above, 193.

40. CAB 79/6, COS Committee Minutes, 16, 20, 26 August 1940.

41. FO 371/24330, C8883/7327/17, Governor, Gold Coast, to S of S for Colonies, 17 August 1940.

42. *Ibid.,* Governor, Sierra Leone, to S of S for Colonies, 21 August 1940.

43. *Ibid.,* S of S for Colonies to Governors, Nigeria and Gold Coast, 26 August 1940; WO 106/2856, Giffard to Governor, Nigeria, same date. Cf. de Larminat, 130.

44. FO 371/24330, C8883/7327/17, Governor, Nigeria, to S of S for Colonies, 18 and 20 August 1940.

45. *Ibid.,* S of S for Colonies to Governor, Nigeria, 26 August 1940, transmitting message from de Gaulle to his representatives. Cf. de Gaulle, vol. I, 289.

46. *Délégation française,* vol. I, 261-2, 319, 418, 423, 432-5; Charles-Roux, 333-6.

47. De Gaulle to Catroux, 29 August 1940, de Gaulle, vol. I, 290-92; Catroux, 23-4.

48. CAB 80/17, COS(40)696, 2 September 1940, circulating minute by Churchill, 1 September 1940.

49. FO 371/24330, C8722/7327/17, especially memorandum by 'Jacques', 6 September 1940; CAB 85/23, CFR(40)39, 13 September 1940, report by Palewski.

50. CAB 85/22, CFR(40)52nd and 53rd Meetings, 12 and 16 September 1940; FO 371/24332, C10236/7327/17, Halifax to Hoare, 23 September 1940, transmitting message from Churchill; cf. FO 800/323, H/XXXIV/69, Churchill to Halifax, 29 September 1940, indicating that Churchill held to the same view even after the failure at Dakar.

51. CAB 79/5, COS Committee Minutes, 8 July 1940; CAB 66/9, WP(40)256, 16 July 1940, COS Report on implications of French hostility, para. 35; CAB 79/5, COS Committee Minutes, 25 July 1940.

52. In the whole section on Dakar, in addition to documents cited individually, an important source is the account prepared for the Cabinet after the failure of the expedition. Two successive versions are in CAB 21/1465: HIST(A)1, 20 November 1940, and HIST(A)1 (revise), 5 February 1941, written by Captain Nicholls, RN, and Colonel Yule. See also WO 106/2858 for General Irwin's Report on the expedition, 7 October 1940.

53. CAB 66/10, WP(40)301, 4 August 1940, note by Bridges for COS.

54. *Ibid.,* WP(40)304, 5 August 1940.

55. CAB 65/14, WM(40)219th Conclusions, Confidential Annex.

56. CAB 79/5, COS Committee Minutes, 5 August 1940, 3.30 p.m., and note of conversation between Pound and de Gaulle, same date.

57. *Ibid.,* and minute by COS for Prime Minister, same date.

58. CAB 21/1463, minute by Churchill for Joint Planning Committee, enclosing revised plan, 6 August 1940; minutes of meeting of Inter-Service Planning Staff with de Gaulle, same date. CAB 79/6, COS Committee Minutes, 7 August 1940, 10.30 a.m.

59. *Ibid.,* COS Committee Minutes, 7 August 1940, 3.30 p.m., Annex II, minute by COS for Prime Minister, 7 August.

60. *Ibid.,* COS Committee Minutes, 7 August 1940, 11 p.m.

De Gaulle's ships arriving at Duala, to an enthusiastic welcome. After the disaster at Dakar, this did much to revive de Gaulle's morale.

(Associated Press)

Paul Reynaud who resigned as French Prime Minister on 16 June 1940 and was replaced by Pétain. He was later interned by the Vichy government and deported to Germany in 1942.

(Keystone Press)

Pierre Laval as he appeared, described as a 'Cushion for the Führer's backside', on the cover of the American magazine, Newsweek.

(Imperial War Museum)

British Spitfire seen from a German fighter plane during the Battle of Britain. The British government's reluctance to send fighter reinforcements to France in May and June 1940 was vindicated in British eyes during this battle.

(Keystone Press)

Admiral Gensoul, Commander of the French fleet bombarded by the British at Mers-el-Kebir.
(Musée de la Marine, Paris)

British destroyers including the HMS Rodney lying off Mers-el-Kebir.
(Imperial War Museum)

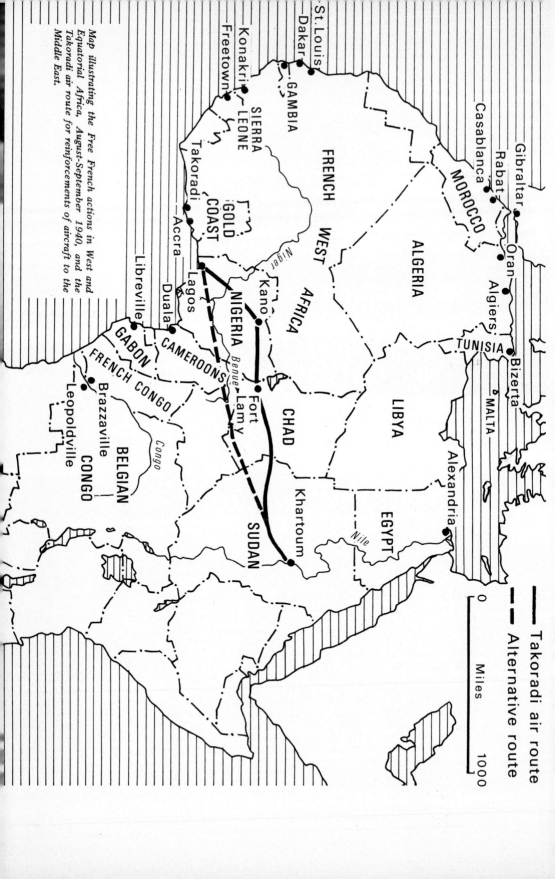

Map illustrating the Free French actions in West and Equatorial Africa, August–September 1940, and the Takoradi air route for reinforcements of aircraft to the Middle East.

Legend:
— Takoradi air route
– – Alternative route

Miles 0 ————— 1000

Labels on map: St. Louis, Dakar, GAMBIA, Konakri, Freetown, SIERRA LEONE, Takoradi, GOLD COAST, Accra, Libreville, Duala, Lagos, NIGERIA, Kano, Niger, FRENCH WEST AFRICA, MOROCCO, Casablanca, Rabat, Oran, Algiers, ALGERIA, Gibraltar, TUNISIA, Bizerta, MALTA, LIBYA, Alexandria, EGYPT, Nile, Khartoum, SUDAN, CHAD, Fort Lamy, Benue, CAMEROONS, GABON, FRENCH CONGO, Brazzaville, Leopoldville, BELGIAN CONGO, Congo

61. *Ibid.,* 8 August 1940; cf. CAB 21/1465, The Dakar Operation, Annex 1.
62. CAB 79/6, COS Committee Minutes, 9 August 1940, 4.30 p.m., and 13 August, 10.30 a.m. CAB 65/14, WM(40)225th Conclusions, Confidential Annex.
63. CAB 80/16, COS(40)643, 19 August 1940, report by Vice-Chiefs of Staff; CAB 21/1463, Hollis to Irwin and Cunningham, 19 August.
64. CAB 79/6, COS Committee Minutes, 20 August 1940, 10.30 p.m.
65. *Ibid.,* 21 August 1940, 10 a.m.; CAB 80/16, COS(40)648 (draft), outline plan of Operation MENACE.
66. CAB 21/1465, The Dakar Operation, paras. 15-16.
67. CAB 65/14, WM(40)235th Conclusions, Confidential Annex.
68. CAB 80/17, COS(40)672, 27 August 1940; CAB 21/1463, minute by Hollis for COS, 29 August; CAB 79/6, COS Committee Minutes, 30 August.
69. FO 371/24329, C8342/7327/17, OAG, Gambia, to S of S for Colonies, 8 August 1940, transmitting message from Pleven and Leclerc.
70. FO 371/24332, C9935/7327/17, same to same, 5 September 1940; C9982/7328/17, same to same, 7 September.
71. FO 371/24331, C9591/7327/17, minute by Mack, 31 August 1940, OAG, Gambia, to S of S for Colonies, 30 August; C9760/7327/17, FO circular telegram, 6 September, intelligence summary on French African colonies.
72. CAB 21/1465, The Dakar Operation, paras. 10, 19.
73. CAB 21/1463, minute from Inter-Services Security Board, 7 August 1940.
74. *Ibid.,* Ferguson to Hollis, 20 August 1940; Hollis to Ferguson, 21 August 1940.
75. *Ibid.,* Ferguson to Hollis, 22 August 1940, with attached report on leakage of information about MENACE.
76. CAB 80/19, COS(40)771(JP), 25 September 1940, with attached report by ISSB, 19 September; this report was reproduced as COS(40)792, 30 September 1940, with as an Annex the text of the letter of 29 August, without a signature.
77. Kammerer, 250-52; Charles-Roux, 323; Jacques Mordal, *La bataille de Dakar* (Paris 1956), 118-21. Cf. FO 371/24332, C10038/7327/17, OAG, Gambia, to S of S for Colonies, 14

September 1940, with report of telegram sent to Senegal.

78. CAB 65/9; WM(40)248, 12 September 1940; CAB 65/15, WM(40)247th,253rd, 254th, 255th Conclusions, Confidential Annexes, 11, 18, 19, 20 September; Roskill, vol. I, 309-16, for a very clear account of the movements; Kammerer, 252-5.

79. CAB 65/15, WM(40)250th Conclusions, Confidential Annex.

80. *Ibid.,* WM(40)251st, 252nd, 253rd Conclusions, Confidential Annexes.

81. CAB 21/1465, The Dakar Operation, para. 31, and Annex V, No. 11; also revised version, Annex VI.

82. For the action at Dakar, see CAB 21/1465, The Dakar Operation, paras. 35-42, and Annex V, Nos. 14-21; Roskill, vol. I, 316-19; Churchill, 427-9; de Gaulle, vol. I, 103-8; Kammerer, 255-62, 517-23; Mordal, *Dakar*.

83. CAB 65/15, WM(40)258th Conclusions, Confidential Annex.

Chapter 10

DE GAULLE:
DOUBTS & DIFFICULTIES

The attack on Dakar was a failure of a particularly public and humiliating kind. On 16 September, after the Vichy cruisers had reached the port and when the Cabinet thought it would be best to abandon the operation, Churchill said that 'a fiasco had undoubtedly occurred, and it was to be hoped that it would not too much engage public attention.'[1] Had the plan been called off there and then this result might have been secured, because no overt action had been undertaken against Dakar. Once the attempt had been made and so manifestly failed, however, popular attention was inevitably engaged and public comment was severe. The *communiqués* issued by the Ministry of Information and Free French headquarters tried to show matters in the best light. The expedition was justified by emphasising the danger that Dakar might come under German control, and stressing that considerable sections of the population there were favourable to de Gaulle. Its abandonment was explained by the chivalrous reluctance of de Gaulle to shed French blood.[2] Nevertheless such explanations failed to carry conviction, and there was some recrimination behind the scenes about the handling of the publicity regarding the operation. The Ministry of Information was reproved for letting the Vichy version of events be put out first, while the Ministry in turn complained that the Service departments had failed to provide up-to-date information, so that rapid and effective publicity had been impossible.[3]

However, the anxieties raised by Dakar were beyond the capacity of even the most skilful publicity to allay. The questions were too obvious: Why were the Vichy cruisers allowed to pass Gibraltar and reach Dakar? Why was the operation, once started, not carried through? If de Gaulle's forces did not wish to shed French blood, why were they sent where this was bound to happen if any fighting occurred? Why was the intelligence concerning support for de Gaulle in Dakar misleading? Clumsy publicity only made matters worse. One phrase in a Ministry of Information *communiqué* attracted particular scorn: that 'serious warlike operations' against the Vichy French had never been intended. As one writer commented: 'Warlike operations are always "serious". If they are not serious, don't start them'.[4] Cassandra, in the *Daily Mirror* of 28 September, wrote: 'The Dakar *débâcle* is worse than appeasement. It has the unmistakable imprint of weak and frightened men. It's going to be hard to convince us that Mr Churchill has feet of clay. But we can't stand a great deal more of this'.

Critical comment, though not all as sharply worded as this, was widespread.[5] Attacks were levelled more at the British government than at the Free French, though the *Daily Telegraph* on 27 September noted that it might be pleaded that the initiative had come from de Gaulle rather than Britain. Ministry of Information reports on public opinion showed that there was general disquiet about both the British and Free French sides of the affair. People were asking whether British intelligence was any good; why the Vichy ships had been allowed to pass Gibraltar; and whether the Free French were full of fifth columnists.[6] A great public outcry arose over the Dakar operation, and there appears to have been a widespread fear of slipping back to the standards of the time before Churchill took control. Some of the agitation about Dakar was linked to the movement to get rid of Chamberlain and other representatives of the appeasement policy. Criticism about Dakar rumbled on in a debate in the House of Commons on 8 October, when Churchill's government was given its first rough passage since its formation.[7]

The public outcry was accompanied by private criticism. Vansittart wrote that de Gaulle was for the time being discredited: 'We had pushed him half way up the hill, but he has now slid back to the bottom . . . .'[8] Menzies, the Prime Minister of Australia, sent a telegram criticising the expedition which Churchill described even three months later, and after emollient messages, as hectoring.[9] Moreover, press reaction in the USA was unfavourable, not towards the attempt, but towards its failure and what was seen as British lack of nerve.[10] In these circumstances, there was a considerable temptation for the British government to take the easy way out of its difficulties, and cast the blame for failure at Dakar on de Gaulle and the Free French. This could easily have been done, and would have responded to at least one of the themes of public criticism. In fact, however, Churchill went out of his way, in public and in private, to express his sympathy and support for de Gaulle. It is true that in the House of Commons he described the Dakar operation as primarily French, which was of dubious truth, but he excluded de Gaulle from blame for the failure and confessed to accidents and errors on the British side, notably concerning the passage of the Vichy cruisers. He went further, and praised de Gaulle in such a way as to emphasise his continued support for the Free French leader. If Churchill looked for a public scapegoat it was in some sections of the press, where he said there had been vicious and malignant comment on Dakar and other matters. (This challenge was taken up with vigour by the *Mirror, Herald,* and *News Chronicle,* and for the *Mirror* signified the beginning of considerable conflict with Churchill's government.)[11] In private, Churchill was sympathetic towards de Gaulle's first proposal following Dakar to go to Konakri, and pointed out to the Cabinet that this would be better for de Gaulle's prestige than merely going to Duala which the Free French already held.[12] Shortly afterwards, on 28 September, he agreed that it would be best for de Gaulle to sail to Duala and consolidate his hold in Equatorial Africa, but he wrote firmly: 'we must first of all allow him to disembark at Freetown, and we must await the fuller expression of his views and wishes. Nothing is to be done meanwhile which would prevent us from giving effect to his reasonable requests'.[13] Even if Churchill had contemplated persuading Catroux to supplant de Gaulle earlier in September, after Dakar he proved himself a foul-weather friend when he might well have disowned him.

De Gaulle for his part observed a strict reticence. Whatever his private thoughts, he stayed silent about the question of responsibility for Dakar. Parr, the recently-appointed British Consul-General at Brazzaville, wrote on 1 November that de Gaulle's attitude had been exemplary; he had not even indirectly suggested that the British were to blame for the failure (as Parr had gathered was largely true), but had himself shouldered responsibility for the decisions taken.[14] When de Gaulle returned to London from Africa at the end of November, he was suitably diplomatic about Dakar in conversation with Halifax, saying that the failure had been due to an unfortunate combination of circumstances.[15] In fact he behaved on this occasion with a tact which has sometimes been thought alien either to his nature or to the part which he had cast himself to play. His restraint, coupled with that of Churchill, did much to diminish the effects of the crisis in Anglo-Free French relations which was brought about by the Dakar expedition.

Nonetheless, these effects were serious, and some of them were prolonged — as, for example, with regard to British distrust of Free French security. The crisis was particularly severe for de Gaulle and the Free French. De Gaulle himself passed through the depths of despair, and later wrote in his memoirs that the days after Dakar were cruel — it was as though an earthquake was rocking his house and the roof was falling in.[16] De Larminat records that de Gaulle's first words when they met after Dakar were: 'Well, do we go on?'[17] De Lariminat's reply was confident — Equatorial Africa was behind de Gaulle, and the Free French should certainly go on. These territories, and the demonstrations of welcome which greeted de Gaulle when he arrived there, played a crucial part in restoring his confidence and sense of mission. When he reached Duala on 8 October, there were crowds and Free French flags; in the next two months he toured his dominions — Fort Lamy and the deserts of Chad, Brazzaville and the forests of the Congo. The experience was for him, in the words of de Larminat, a veritable cleansing of the soul.[18] Spears, still acting as liaison officer with de Gaulle, observed the same effect, though he put it more cynically: 'De Gaulle back from Fort Lamy. Enchanted with all he has seen and by high morale of troops . . . . only disadvantage of trip is previous tendency to assume role of absolute monarch increased but will be dealt with'.[19]

De Gaulle's self-confidence was thus restored, but he still had to revitalise and consolidate his movement which had been shaken by the failure at Dakar. In certain respects, this could only be done in co-operation with the British, since the Free French colonies were entirely dependent on Britain for economic assistance and military supplies. Economic assistance to colonies which rallied to de Gaulle was promised in a letter by Churchill of 27 August, made public on the 29th.[20] The problems faced by the colonies were twofold. First, there were immediate financial necessities. Currency had to be found for the payment of soldiers and administrators, and for all the purposes of daily life and commerce, in territories with only a rudimentary banking service which was now cut off from its head office in Dakar.[21] The men on the spot, both French and British, were keenly conscious of their difficulties, and felt they were not being dealt with sufficiently quickly in London. De Larminat set out his needs at the end of August, but found he had to do so again at the end of September.[22] On 17 September Lord Hailey, then head of an economic mission to the Belgian Congo but taking an active interest in the affairs of the Free French colonies, gave his own personal guarantee that the United Africa Company would be reimbursed if it would advance a million francs to de Larminat to meet his most urgent requirements.[23] De Larminat and the British economic liaison official in Brazzaville, Rodd, showed an enterprising capacity for self-help by printing new bank-notes of large denominations and, incidentally, unusual design, one of which depicted a naked lady in a boat. In order to satisfy local banking regulations these notes could be kept in the vaults, thus allowing smaller notes and change to be released for circulation.[24] Improvisation was, at least in the early stages, the key to success in handling the immediate financial problems.

The second problem was that of the general economic life of the Free French colonies, which depended on the export of their products — palm oil and palm kernels, cocoa, coffee and timber, together with some cotton, rubber, zinc and lead ore. The sale of these items, in particular the crops, was vital to business firms in the colonies and the growers who depended on them. The ideal solution for the Free French, proposed by de Larminat at the end of August, was simply that Britain should buy all surplus products whether they could be used or not. It was pointed out in London that such a policy would mean that French colonies would be treated better than neighbouring British colonies in West Africa producing much the same commodities.[25] The view of the Morton Committee, and its Economic Sub-Committee under Campbell, was that Britain should purchase at once what were known as 'blockade stocks', which had accumulated through the British blockade cutting off trade after the armistice. A commitment to purchase all stocks in the future was another matter, raising not only the question of comparisons with the treatment of British colonies, but the possibility of setting a precedent which would be followed by the Belgian Congo, and by other French colonies which might join de

Gaulle in the future.[26] There were other problems — for example, whether or not the system of imperial preference should be extended to trade with the Free French colonies, which raised the prospect that other Allied colonies would claim the same privilege and thus the whole system would be undermined.[27]

These problems were considerable, and their resolution was made more difficult by the number of ministries which were concerned — Foreign Office, Ministry of Shipping, Ministry of Food, Board of Trade, Colonial Office, Dominions Office, the Treasury. Almost inevitably, the deliberations of the Morton Committee and the preparation of schemes for individual French colonies appeared too slow to the men on the spot in Africa. By the middle of October, there was a note of alarm in messages from the Nigerian government, the Spears Mission and the British economic mission in Leopoldville.

However, the difficulties were not all in London. In the Free French colonies, the change from a well-known pattern of trade to a new one was not easy. Another problem was that in many cases the more experienced colonial officials had remained loyal to the Vichy government, and the Gaullist administration needed time to settle down.[28] The various British agencies involved in dealings with the Free French did not always work smoothly together — one strong telegram from Nigeria declared that the interference of the Spears Mission in economic matters could only result in chaos, and pointed out that Pleven (the principal Free French economic agent in Africa) would prefer in future to deal with a single qualified person on such questions.[29] It was not until December that the general economic situation began to be clarified, with the preparation of lists of purchases from the Free French colonies, and the drafting of a long-term commercial agreement with the Cameroons.[30] Definitive arrangements with the different colonies were finally reached early in 1941.

Only the British could deal with these economic problems, by providing credits, buying produce and finding shipping. Equally, only the British could supply equipment for the Free French forces in Africa. Immediately the rallying of Chad to the Free French cause was announced, de Gaulle asked the Chiefs of Staff for six Blenheim aircraft with British ground crews, and for motor transport. After his return to London from Brazzaville in November, he presented a request for 110 lorries, a battery of Bofors anti-aircraft guns and forty aircraft to be sent to the French forces in Equatorial Africa. The British were reluctant to send war material which was needed in other areas, and reinforcements of aircraft were refused.[31] The Free French colonies were also entirely dependent on the British for naval protection. The Free French navy was very small, and in any case was mainly stationed in British home waters; without the Royal Navy, the Cameroons would have been vulnerable to a sea-borne expedition sent by Vichy — as very nearly happened at the time of Dakar. The British government undertook to defend the Free French colonies from the sea on 29 August, and it was specified that this included defence against Vichy as well as Axis attack.[32]

In theory, the economic, military and naval dependence of the Free French colonies on Britain should have led to a similar dependence in policy and attitude. In fact, this was not so. Even as de Gaulle established his position in Equatorial Africa with the indispensable aid of Britain, so at the same time he asserted his independence of her by his own highly individual methods and qualities of leadership. This was partly accomplished by military action — launching an attack on the Vichy-controlled colony of Gabon, in spite of British disapproval and discouragement. More important, however, he worked through political action, repeatedly seeking to establish the position of the Free French movement as a sovereign entity, the true government of the true France.

Free French military operations overland against Gabon were begun during October 1940, the strategic reasons for pressing the attack being set out by de Gaulle for Churchill on 28 October. The existing Free French colonies in Equatorial Africa and the Cameroons formed a compact block of territory, difficult of access for an enemy. Attacks could come only from the north, across the desert to Chad, or from Gabon, whence the Vichy government might send aircraft to attack Brazzaville, Duala or Pointe Noire. He anticipated that Vichy would make a serious effort to fight the Free French movement in Africa, and would receive assistance from Germany and Italy;[33] it was therefore important to anticipate such developments by capturing Gabon, even at the cost of fighting the Vichy garrison there. The land operations were entirely a matter for the Free French, but the capital of Gabon, Libreville, was difficult to capture overland and an attack from the sea would be necessary. The Free French plans, which were drawn up by Leclerc and approved by de Gaulle, included the direct participation of British warships as a necessary part of the seaward attack. The cruiser *Delhi* was to enter the harbour at Libreville with the landing force, while the cruiser *Devonshire* was to bombard a coastal defence battery. The local British naval commander, Cunningham, accepted these French requests, and signalled a detailed plan to London on 24 October. At this stage, the Free French considered British participation to be vital to the success of the operation, in view of the weakness of their own naval forces and the presence at Libreville of a Vichy sloop and a submarine.[34]

The British naval commanders on the spot were willing to accept their part in the plan — though the commander of the *Delhi* was worried about having to deal with 'amateur seamen' among the Free French — but in London other counsels prevailed. On the one hand, there was a fear of failure. A Foreign Office official wrote: 'I doubt if de Gaulle cd. survive a second Dakar'; and Halifax agreed: 'Certainly we can't risk more failures'.[35] On the other hand, the British government had to consider not only the position in Africa, but also its relations with the Vichy government which were then being developed through the embassies in Madrid. Behind this again lay what was believed to be the delicate internal balance in the Vichy government at a crucial point in its relations with Germany. Laval met Hitler at Montoire on 22 October; Pétain, Laval and Hitler met on the 24th. This did not seem to be the time to risk a conflict with the Vichy government, or to play into the hands of Laval, with his policy of collaboration with Germany.[36] These considerations caused Churchill to intervene, and instruct Cunningham to postpone action at Libreville until he received further orders from London — 'do not act without our signal'. Meanwhile, any Vichy reinforcements for Libreville were to be turned back at sea, if possible without fighting.[37] In London it was believed that without British co-operation the attack would not take place.[38]

The British government thus sought to impose a postponement of the operation against Libreville, but the Free French decided to take matters into their own hands; they began bombing attacks on the Vichy sloop *Bougainville* and launched a frontal attack by sea even without the *Delhi*.[39] This attack commenced during the night of 8/9 November, and the garrison surrendered on the 10th. British participation was confined to maintaining a patrol to ensure that no reinforcements arrived from Dakar, and to an engagement with the

Vichy submarine *Poncelet* when the latter put to sea and ineffectually fired a torpedo at a British sloop.[40] Thus the Free French success at Libreville was accomplished despite British attempts to postpone the operation, and without the British naval assistance which only a few days before had been thought vital. It was a victory for Free French will-power and independence.

This successful assertion of military independence was accompanied by a whole series of moves designed to establish the political independence of the Free French movement. De Gaulle believed in the power of gestures. The day after his arrival at Duala, and only a fortnight after the fiasco at Dakar, he telegraphed to Churchill, 'from French soil free from enemy control', to convey the confidence and friendship of Frenchmen and French subjects. He asked that this telegram and Churchill's reply should be published.[41] The point was made — the *Spectator,* for example, noting that de Gaulle was now in 'the position of one Allied leader speaking to another from his own territory'.[42]

De Gaulle worked towards the same objective in private by a war of attrition of small moves, all intended to advance Free French independence if only by a step. Even his proposal for a united Anglo-French command in West and Central Africa, which appeared to accept subordination, would in effect have advanced the standing of the French. De Gaulle made this suggestion to the British Chiefs of Staff on 27 August, and they agreed in principle. However, they consulted Giffard in West Africa about the form which the unified command might take, and he pointed out that to have a British C-in-C with a French second-in-command could result in a French general commanding all the military forces in West Africa if for some reason the C-in-C should be out of action. To avoid this, a proposal was devised whereby a British C-in-C would have under him a French C-in-C who would command only French forces. De Gaulle agreed to this arrangement, but only on condition that it did not apply to operations against Vichy colonies or forces — he had specifically in mind actions against Gabon where, as has been seen, his reservations were well justified.[43]

Another move, superficially of a military character but involving significant political implications, was de Gaulle's proposal to send a Free French detachment to Greece after Italy invaded that country at the end of October 1940. He pressed the British Chiefs of Staff to send a French force from Egypt, arguing that it would be both politically and morally effective. It would certainly have shown the Free French flag and established a status for the movement as an ally of Greece. Catroux, then commanding the two Free French battalions in Egypt, disliked the idea of splitting up his small force, and also made the prosaic point that infantry serving on the Greek front would need mules. Wavell also thought the move undesirable, especially since the Free French troops were doing well in the Western Desert. Finally, the Greek Prime Minister discreetly expressed his strong opposition to the whole idea, and the Morton Committee decided on 13 December that the proposal should be shelved.[44]

Continuing his attempts to enhance the status of the Free French, and himself as their leader, de Gaulle sought to establish direct relations with the South African government by sending a personal telegram to General Smuts. The British Consul-General at Brazzaville, Parr, advised that Smuts should be consulted in advance to ensure that he was willing to receive such a telegram, but in fact the matter was not referred to Smuts. The Morton Committee considered it on 1 November, thought that de Gaulle's request would not be favourably received, and brought the matter to a halt by the simple expedient of recommending that Parr's telegram to the Foreign Office should be 'lost', and the item be not recorded in the committee minutes, which were communicated to Free French headquarters in London.[45]

De Gaulle also sought to advance the diplomatic standing of his movement by endeavouring to appoint a Free French consul at Leopoldville, capital of the Belgian Congo. He considered persuading the British government to confirm in their posts certain French consuls in British colonies who had joined the Free French movement, but his telegram to Pleven about these questions passed through the Foreign Office where an official minuted: 'I think we shall want to go rather slow on this'. The feeling was that if de Gaulle secured regular consular representatives he would go on to seek diplomatic representation with foreign governments — that is, to be treated as a government. It was thought best to continue the existing system of unofficial Free French representatives, who when necessary could do some consular work; and to advise the Belgian government in London to take a similar line about the post at Leopoldville.[46]

Apart from Britain, the most important government from which de Gaulle could hope to secure some measure of recognition was that of the USA — which continued to recognise the existing French government under Pétain. At the end of September de Gaulle's headquarters in London tried to send a telegram to the Free French representative in New York, Siéyès, instructing him to seek participation in the defence talks about the Pacific which were being held between the USA, Britain and Australia. The argument used was that since all the French possessions in the Pacific had joined the Free French, they should therefore take part in discussions relating to the area. Somerville-Smith, the British liaison officer with the Free French in London, sent the draft of this message to the Foreign Office, commenting that the French 'were trying to run before they could toddle'. A Foreign Office official noted that the telegram could not possibly be sent to New York without first consulting the British Embassy and the State Department. Siéyès had no qualifications to participate in technical discussions — 'nor has General de Gaulle yet achieved such a status as would entitle him to take part in international discussions as if he were already the head of an independent French Government'.[47] However, de Gaulle was not easily put in his place, and on 23 November the same official wrote once more: 'We must . . . make the General realise that his representative in the U.S. cannot behave as the Ambassador of a sovereign state'.[48]

While de Gaulle was on a visit to Leopoldville at the end of October, he was able to circumvent the tiresome and obstructive British intermediaries, and hand the American Consul a communication for his government — the British Consul was given a copy the next day. The message referred to broadcasts in American news services, to the effect that the states of the Western hemisphere had agreed that the USA was to take all necessary measures in the event of the Vichy government developing closer relations with the Axis. De Gaulle pointed out that the French colonies in the Americas — the French West Indies, French Guiana, the islands of St. Pierre and Miquelon — were among the oldest of French overseas possessions, and their occupation, even by a friendly power like the United States, would cause profound grief among Frenchmen. He therefore proposed that, if Vichy collaboration with Germany should compel the USA to take measures for the security of the western hemisphere, the Free French Council of Defence (which had just been formed) should be associated with the administration of the French colonies; the Council would be willing to negotiate agreements with the USA for American use of bases in these areas. The Foreign Office complained that de Gaulle should have consulted them before making such a rash move; but of course it was precisely by avoiding such consultation that he was able to make his point and take up his stance as the defender of French interests.[49]

In December 1940 de Gaulle raised a similar question, though on this occasion — being in London — he first asked whether the British government had any observations. The point at issue was the position of French Indo-China, which was falling increasingly under Japanese control. De Gaulle wished to make a public statement, which would also be conveyed to the Japanese and American governments, that the momentary disaster which had befallen France in no way justified any infringement of the integrity of the French empire, and that the Free French regarded any concessions made by the Vichy government as null and void. This declaration applied particularly to Indo-China. The Foreign Office was unwilling to communicate such a message to either the Japanese or the US government, and the Morton Committee thought it would be unwise for de Gaulle to make any such statement about Indo-China, where he could do nothing practical to influence events. Despite this discouragement, he issued his declaration on 22 February 1941.[50]

In all these dealings with the British, de Gaulle was hampered at almost every turn by British control over his communications. His telegrams had to go through the Foreign Office, the Spears Mission, or Nigeria. Thus the British were forewarned of Free French intentions, and were able to take whatever action they thought appropriate — usually evasion, postponement or obstruction. The only occasion on which he managed to escape this net — a constant reminder of his lack of independence — was when he was able to deliver his message directly to the US Consul at Leopoldville. It was indeed in Africa that de Gaulle was able to exert the greatest degree of independence. The British could control telegrams he sent from Brazzaville, but not his speeches and actions there. It was at this capital of Free French Africa that, on 27 October 1940, he issued a manifesto and two ordinances, followed on 16 November by an 'organic declaration'.

The Brazzaville manifesto proclaimed that there no longer existed a true French government: the body at Vichy which claimed that name was unconstitutional and subject to the invader. 'It is therefore necessary that a new authority should assume the task of directing the French effort in the war. Events impose this sacred duty upon me. I shall not fail to carry it out'. De Gaulle continued that he would undertake to· render an account of his actions to representatives of the French people as soon as these could be freely chosen, and then announced the creation of a Council of Defence of the Empire. The two ordinances set up this body, sketched out its powers, and named its members. It was further stated that these and any future ordinances were to be published in the *Journal Officiel* of the French empire.[51]

The Brazzaville ordinances contained two other points of significance. First, they opened with the words: 'We, General de Gaulle, Leader of the Free French . . .'; secondly, it was made clear that decisions would be taken by de Gaulle himself, after consultation if need be with the Council of Defence. Finally, the organic declaration set out a legal case, based on various laws of the Third Republic, for regarding the Vichy government as unconstitutional and justifying de Gaulle's position.[52]

These documents combined a proud claim to sovereignty and legitimacy with humdrum provision for the working of everyday affairs — which was the point of publishing decrees in the *Journal Officiel*. The British were not only baffled by them but pained by de Gaulle's style and methods. One Foreign Office official found it strange that he should hark back so elaborately to legislation enacted during the Third Republic, and could not see the point of 'all these constitutional niceties'. Another took exception to the royal 'We' used by de Gaulle, and wrote flatly: 'This is quite Fascist'. Halifax found it tiresome that de Gaulle should have acted without prior consultation with Britain, but pointed out that earlier correspondence between them had provided for the establishment of a Council of Defence at some future time. The policy adopted by the British government was not to quarrel openly with de Gaulle's actions, but to explain officially that he was merely setting up an administration for the Free French colonies, not an alternative French government. Moreover, the press was asked to soft-pedal the whole affair. The Morton Committee also decided to request Spears to maintain closer contact with de Gaulle, 'in order to guide his steps and to prevent any further embarrassing declarations'.[53]

Britain's embarrassment was the greater because the Brazzaville manifesto came only four days after Pétain's meeting with Hitler at Montoire, at a time when the British aim was to sway public opinion at Vichy against the policy of collaboration with Germany, rather than to give offence by conniving at attacks on the legality of the Vichy government. The fact was that de Gaulle had slipped under the British guard. On his own territory, he had not only avoided British surveillance of his communications, but had also proclaimed his independence and asserted his freedom of action. This lack of consultation and disregard for British embarrassment were essential parts of his policy. The failure at Dakar was put firmly behind him. Faith would triumph. Meanwhile, the British would have to get used to the new situation, and they began to show some signs of doing so. De Gaulle's next *coup* after the Brazzaville manifesto was the creation of the Order of Liberation, with the Cross of Liberation as its decoration. On receiving this news, a Foreign Office official minuted: '. . . I fear that this is de Gaulle's own business and we can hardly interfere'. To which Cadogan added: 'I am afraid not. I don't think it will really make much difference'.[54]

However, this note of quiet if reluctant resignation was not characteristic of the British attitude to de Gaulle in the autumn of 1940. In British eyes his cure for the crisis brought about by Dakar was almost as bad as the disease itself. His self-assertion and constant attempts to behave as though he was a government caused as much heart-searching among the British as did the doubts raised by the Dakar fiasco. There were other issues which also involved de Gaulle's status and future, one being the question of whether he should set up his permanent headquarters in Africa or return to London; another point was the possible effect of British relations with Vichy on his position. Consequently, between October and December 1940 there was a great deal of discussion within the British government concerning de Gaulle and the Free French movement.

The divergence of opinion revealed in this discussion was considerable. Broadly speaking, the greatest difference was between officials in London, who showed varying degrees of scepticism and even hostility towards de Gaulle, and the two British representatives who saw most of him in Africa, who spoke most strongly in his support.

Among officials in London, there was some doubt and

disapproval of de Gaulle even before he failed at Dakar. At a meeting in the Foreign Office on 6 September to discuss relations with the Free French, the Colonial Office representative said that de Gaulle showed 'an undesirable tendency to be carried away by his ambitions' — with which Somerville-Smith agreed.[55] This kind of assessment later gained further ground. Roger Cambon, formerly of the French Embassy in London, told a Foreign Office official on 1 October that the weakness of de Gaulle's position lay largely in 'his attempt to command rather than to persuade'; this view was echoed by British officials, one of whom noted that a number of de Gaulle's telegrams had 'a somewhat imperious tone', while another found his ideas 'out of proportion and his pronouncements extremely heavy-handed'.[56] Such reactions to de Gaulle's style of speaking and writing were almost inevitable, but all the more significant since they were combined with serious doubts about his political competence. Cadogan minuted on 16 October: 'I hardly know Gen. de Gaulle, but from what I know of him, I should say that, while he may be a good soldier, he may not be much else, and if we are to build up an Administration of Free France we shd. have to look for other helpers'.[57]

There was a general feeling that de Gaulle was really a good soldier who was getting out of his depth by launching into politics. Strang commented on a telegram about the strategic situation in Equatorial Africa: 'De Gaulle is at his best as a soldier',[58] while Morton, in a memorandum of 4 November, wrote that he 'has so far shown little aptitude for political art, whatever his merits as a soldier'.[59] Campbell thought that it would be fatal for de Gaulle's prestige if he returned to London from Africa, and gave the impression of being 'merely a political general'; it would be better for him to lead his troops against the enemy, perhaps in Egypt.[60] Palewski, Reynaud's former *chef de cabinet* who came to London to join the Free French movement, and whose views commanded respect in the Foreign Office, also held that de Gaulle's political approach was mistaken. He thought that the general's African schemes were pointless: 'He would have to get away from the idea of a nigger kingdom and repair his damaged military prestige, for example by a successful action against the Italians. The capture of Gabon would be no good. He would have to get around, be seen in French territory and above all be military'.[61]

The gist of all these comments was that de Gaulle should stop

233

trying to play politics, stick to being a soldier, and get into action against the enemy. Though straightforward advice, it was based on a complete misconception of what de Gaulle was and what he was trying to accomplish. He was not a plain soldier: he had moved in political circles, and his army career had had political aspects. Moreover, his aspirations for the Free French movement were essentially political, and any military contribution by Free French forces would be subordinate to political considerations. His aims were the establishment of a true French government, and through that the restoration of France itself — in the image conceived by de Gaulle.

There were of course some people who saw de Gaulle's movement in political terms, but even they tended to get it in the wrong perspective. One view was that de Gaulle was surrounded by fascists, or that he himself tended towards fascist ideas. A Foreign Office reaction to the organic declaration from Brazzaville has already been quoted — 'This is quite Fascist'.[62] Again, in the House of Commons on 5 November Colonel Josiah Wedgwood (a Labour member of individual views, sternly dedicated to waging the war) asked what proportion of British funds was being spent on de Gaulle's forces. When refused an answer, Wedgwood further asked the Financial Secretary to the Treasury whether he was aware that considerable sums were being wasted on a force whose officers were 'largely Fascists'.[63] Shortly before this Attlee, writing privately to Halifax, had said he was disturbed by de Gaulle's entourage: 'There are people serving him who are of poor character and many of them have Fascist tendencies'.[64]

Another, and opposite viewpoint was to see de Gaulle as being surrounded by supporters of the Third Republic, and by devotees of socialism and the Popular Front. These ideas appear to have arisen partly from British press reports of the adherence of left-wing journalists, such as Geneviève Tabouis, Elie-J. Bois and Henri de Kérillis to the Free French. One of de Larminat's first acts after escaping from Syria was to warn de Gaulle of the danger of consorting with such people, and urge him to restrict membership of his National Committee to those who were unassailably free from political ideology. Later, he urged de Gaulle to make his sole motto *'Honneur et Patrie'* — anything else would leave him open to political reproach.[65] Campbell wrote in October that de Gaulle's entourage included 'a number of Jews and others who might be supposed to have Leftward tendencies', and that this had counted against him in France.[66]

In fact, neither line of criticism was justified. As far as it was in de Gaulle's power to control events, there were to be no politics of this kind in the Free French movement. Muselier too, knowing that his officers included men who had fought on opposite sides in the Spanish Civil War, ordered that there should be no talk of politics (or religion) in the officers' mess. In practice however, despite this lead from the top, such an ideal could not be wholly fulfilled. The few Frenchmen who gathered round de Gaulle in the early months constituted a miniature France, and therefore unavoidably contained all that country's divisions.[67] Since the sources of these early recruits included the army, the colonial service and the overseas communities, there tended to be more from the Right than from the Left, even if left-wing journalists more frequently caught the eye of Frenchmen overseas. Such divisions were suppressed as much as possible, however, and any political bias was the result of accident rather than policy. It was symbolic, though this could scarcely be publicised, that two of the first secret emissaries sent to France by the Free French movement in August 1940 were a former Cagoulard and a socialist militant.[68] De Gaulle tried to make the point in public at a press conference in London on 3 December, and endeavoured to show that he was not tied to the Third Republic: 'France will not consent to return to the political, moral and social position she was in before. This is true for the whole world, but above all for France, which has suffered a defeat: this war is a revolution'. He also went out of his way to answer a question which the journalists present did not ask: 'I do not want to be a dictator; I want to be a leader . . .' (He actually used the English word — 'Je veux être un leader . . .')[69] Doubtless he did not convince everyone, but his course was set and remained steady.

In contrast to observers in London, the two British representatives who saw most of de Gaulle in Africa, Parr and Spears, adopted a more favourable and — as events turned out — a more far-sighted view of the general and his movement. Robert Parr took up the newly created post of Consul-General at Brazzaville at the end of October 1940. On 14 November he wrote to an official in the Foreign Office, Mack, conveying what he considered to be the most important observations of his first fortnight there, concerning the personality of de Gaulle. Parr believed that de Gaulle had deliberately set out to make an impression on him because he needed a sympathetic interpreter to London. 'He is, I think, convinced that he needs an interpreter to present him to H.M.G. as he feels himself to be, the focusing point and symbol of the resurrection of France. He realizes that, on the scales of the war considered as a whole, his present forces are negligible, but he regards them as the "little leaven" '. De Gaulle was anxious that the British government should recognise this. 'Until his mind — indeed I shld. say, until his soul is reassured on this score he will never be really at ease and never able to pull his full weight'. Parr expressed his own agreement with de Gaulle's position: 'General de Gaulle is the leader of a people and we must sooner or later recognize him as the head of a state unless his work is [to] fail of its real achievement. Moments and occasions must be chosen, but the principle can be established at once . . . '[70] This was a remarkable piece of interpretation and prophecy, though the letter in which it was contained appears to have gone no further than Mack and Strang in the Foreign Office.

However, one of Parr's telegrams attracted serious attention, being passed on by Halifax to Churchill with the note that its final section was probably an accurate representation of de Gaulle's attitude and that of his chief supporters in Equatorial Africa. In this telegram of 21 November, Parr pointed out that enemy and Vichy propaganda alleged the Free French movement to be no more than a British device, and colour would be lent to this assertion so long as opinion in Britain and elsewhere continued to estimate the movement solely in terms of its fighting contribution. 'When once, however, public opinion recognises General de Gaulle as servant and prophet of a great ideal . . . all the rest will be added to him'. Parr accepted that it was difficult to define de Gaulle's position so long as a government, recognised by the USA and for some purposes by Britain existed in France. But he reverted to the point made in his letter to Mack: de Gaulle was at present head of the Free French. 'Ultimately, unless some *coup d'état* should enable certain statesmen to escape from France, he will be for a period the head of a state. In the interval he may well become head of the French Empire'. Meanwhile, de Gaulle was 'profoundly convinced that he represents the people and spirit of France and that it is not only his right but his bounden duty to speak in their name'. He saw this as the most important part of his mission, and it was necessary for the

British government to assure him that they accepted it. Parr argued that this was a major and far-reaching issue of policy: '. . . it is essential that our attitude should be patent to the world, that it should be endorsed by public opinion in England and that it should be confirmed by all our dealings with the Free French movement . . . any suggestion, however unintentional and from whatever quarter, that opinion in England tends to regard the movement in the light of a colonial adventure, to be controlled by us as subsidiary to the main issue of the struggle between Western democracies and barbarian, must result in bitter discouragement that can only weaken the movement and prejudice our relations with France after the war'. Remembering de Gaulle's long post-war feud with 'the Anglo-Saxons', it would be hard to envisage a more perceptive piece of analysis.[71]

The head of the British mission with de Gaulle was General Spears, who thus continued his earlier work as liaison officer in France. By October 1940 his relations with de Gaulle were not altogether easy, as was recognised in London.[72] Some of Spears' reports were sceptical or admonitory in tone: he wrote of de Gaulle's tendency to assume the role of absolute monarch; expressed himself horrified by the Brazzaville manifesto; and reminded London that the high-sounding Council of Defence consisted in effect of de Gaulle and de Larminat.[73]

In spite of this occasional sniping, when Spears prepared a long appreciation of British policy towards the Free French movement, which he circulated in December 1940 after he and de Gaulle had returned to London, his analysis and recommendations were favourable. In the French empire, he argued, there was an ineradicable distrust of Britain, and fear that she intended to seize French territory. In these circumstances, any purely British attempt to win support for themselves was a waste of time. If the British wanted help from the French colonies, they must support de Gaulle and demonstrate that he was not just a cover for British policy. In France itself, Spears believed that the Free French movement must look primarily to the industrial workers, because the middle classes had succumbed to fear of communism, and the peasants were too scattered and ill-organised to be effective. He thought de Gaulle's chances of being accepted as a leader by the workers were good, despite his being a general and therefore likely to be type-cast as a reactionary; this was because he was the one

237

figure to stand out in resistance to Nazi rule, and because there was 'something pure and disinterested about him which emerges in his speeches'.

For these reasons the Free French movement was important for Britain, but it was a delicate plant, depending for its life not only on the faith which de Gaulle could inspire by his own integrity, but also on the sustenance which Britain alone could provide. This support was crucial: '. . . if we do not support him, if we blow hot and cold on him or act as if any one else would do as well, if, inspired by fear of momentary danger or for the sake of a momentary advantage we are tempted either to set up rival figures or to pursue a course suggesting diminished faith in him, then he and his movement will be extinguished'. Spears had no doubt that this should not be allowed to happen, and expressed his own confidence in de Gaulle: 'The obscure personality of last June, whom so many considered a hopeless figure to back because he was so little known, is a world figure today. That position he could not have obtained without British support, but it has been achieved principally by his own efforts. He has made his mistakes and I for one have deplored them, but he is nevertheless a very great man'. Spears was therefore disturbed to learn that the British government still had some hopes of Weygand, who was not a great man and whose speeches all urged loyalty to Pétain. To give any support to Weygand was to undermine de Gaulle's position, and the British must therefore choose between them; if they chose de Gaulle, they must give him unfailing support.[74]

This appreciation received a mixed reception in London. Foreign Office opinion held that, while Spears was correct to emphasise the importance of de Gaulle's movement, the general was at the same time a stumbling-block for many Frenchmen who were otherwise well-disposed to Britain. Strang had minuted on an earlier telegram from Spears: 'It is unfortunately true that in the French mind resistance to the Axis and support for de Gaulle are not synonymous'. Herein lay the importance of Weygand, who was believed to command wide support in North Africa (where he was Vichy's Delegate-General) and in the army. It therefore appeared worth while to avoid choosing between Weygand and de Gaulle, and even to hope they might be brought together.[75]

The main tenor of the views put forward by Parr and Spears was that Britain should commit herself firmly to de Gaulle. Parr went so far as to argue that Britain would at some point have to recognise de Gaulle as head of a state, which in retrospect appears to have been sound advice, at any rate in the context of Anglo-French relations. Certainly Parr and Spears made an accurate assessment of de Gaulle's personality and aspirations, but their advice was not taken. When considering policy in its wider context, especially in relation to the USA which was firmly committed to recognition of Vichy and very dubious about de Gaulle, it was impossible for the British government to act in the clear-cut manner advised by Parr and Spears. Also, in the last three months of 1940 there were a number of other factors which militated against any increased and more definite commitment to de Gaulle. Firstly, there was the problem posed by the Free French headquarters in London, which in de Gaulle's absence looked less and less like an organisation which Britain could trust. Secondly, there was the fact that relations with de Gaulle proved distinctly difficult when he returned to London from Africa at the end of November, especially over questions of propaganda. Lastly, there was the whole complicated matter of Britain's relations with Vichy, necessitating a tentative rather than a clear-cut policy towards de Gaulle.

De Gaulle's headquarters in London had always appeared to the British as somewhat ramshackle. Of necessity its beginnings had to be improvised, and its organisation was sketchy, but after de Gaulle's departure on the Dakar expedition the Free French staff remaining in London reached new depths of inefficiency and internal quarrelling. Passy, head of Free French Intelligence, described it in retrospect as a period of his life which was worse than being sent to the galleys. At least part of the difficulty had been created by de Gaulle himself before going to Africa, when he left Muselier in command of the Free French forces in Britain, Fontaine as head of the civilian service and Passy as chief of staff.[76] One of the reasons for this division of responsibility was his distrust of Muselier, who as senior officer was the obvious man to be left in charge; it may be too that de Gaulle was chary of leaving behind anyone whose authority might be sufficient to rival his own. The result was confusion, with repeated conflicts between Muselier and Fontaine. Some ·of the British officials concerned with the Free French movement in London tended to side with Fontaine, and accept his criticism that Muselier was meddling with matters outside his sphere of responsibility. Schemes for getting rid of Muselier

239

were discussed in the Morton Committee, one of which involved sending him to Equatorial Africa with some Free French warships. However, by October his relations with his British naval colleagues had vastly improved and the Admiralty supported him, both against schemes to send him away and against instructions from de Gaulle himself to send warships to Pointe Noire.[77]

Under such divided leadership the Free French officers in London quarrelled and intrigued, part of the trouble being that they did not have enough to do. Among the Free French volunteers there were officers with no troops to command; they had little training or taste for the administrative work which had to be done, especially in the financial and economic affairs of the Free French colonies. These men had not taken the bold step of joining de Gaulle in order to sit behind a desk and write memoranda about palm-oil.

The atmosphere of boredom and intrigue which reigned at Free French headquarters in London had a bad effect on recruits for the movement. One Frenchman escaped from a German prison camp and made his way to London to join de Gaulle, only to find the depot where volunteers were received 'ill-organised, dirty and generally unattractive'; he thought the inefficiency, intrigue and lack of discipline at the Gaullist headquarters were the very same defects which had destroyed the French army in the battle of France.[78] The wife of another volunteer (whose husband was at Duala) wrote of her painful encounter with Free French headquarters: 'Utter disorder. An indescribable muddle. Intrigues, pettiness, no organisation'.[79]

The British were well aware of all this. Morton wrote on 11 October that Lord Bessborough (the chairman of one of his sub-committees) was 'nearly suffering from a nervous breakdown owing to the appalling time he is having with these Frenchmen. I don't wonder'.[80] He thought the strictures of the Frenchman who had escaped from prison camp to join de Gaulle were fully justified. Mack considered the conditions at Carlton Gardens were 'quite appalling', and had discouraged a number of potential recruits.[81] However, it was difficult for the British to intervene. It was easy enough to say that there should be one sound man in sole charge of the Free French headquarters; the Morton Committee thought that Palewski was a good candidate.[82] On the other hand, Morton made it clear that Churchill had 'rightly adopted the attitude that the Free French Movement must be French, and strict limits are set to the extent to which we can interfere with its private internal affairs'.[83] The best solution anyone could think of was to have de Gaulle himself return from Africa and reorganise his own headquarters.[84]

Meanwhile, it appeared to the Foreign Office that the Free French headquarters in its existing state of disorganisation and unreliability was a security hazard. Somerville-Smith was reproved for giving Fontaine a copy of a telegram from Berne, and a new system of distribution was devised which removed Somerville-Smith from the list of those who automatically received copies of telegrams on French affairs.[85] Officials were dismayed when the wife of a Free French volunteer wrote to 'François' at Tangier through the ordinary post, via the British Consulate.[86] With memories of Dakar in the background, there seemed good reason to distrust Free French security. Such distrust was probably at least partly responsible for Muselier's arrest by the British authorities on 2 January 1941, on charges that he had betrayed the Dakar expedition and was conspiring to hand over a submarine to Vichy. Held prisoner for eight days before being released on the grounds that the evidence against him had been forged by a member of Passy's staff, he resumed his duties and received handsome apologies from the British.[87] From Britain's viewpoint, even the settlement of this affair reflected badly on Free French headquarters; while de Gaulle was reminded once again of the precariousness of his movement's position in London, at the mercy of the British authorities.

De Gaulle never wavered in his determination to escape from this situation and establish his independence, while the British for their part still strove to blunt his resolution. At the end of October and during November 1940, there was a good deal of discussion in London concerning his future movements — whether he should stay in Africa, go to Cairo and take command of the Free French force in the Western Desert, or return to London. One of the arguments widely used in favour of his return to London was that it would be easier to control him there — as one official put it, 'he has of late got rather out of hand'.[88] In the event it proved only slightly less difficult to control the general even when he was in London; he returned to argue his own case and make his own demands, which were set out in nine points he submitted to Churchill on 27 November. These included fresh demands for equipment and aircraft (de Gaulle claimed that there were American planes in Britain which rightly belonged to France); requests for further and

241

more rapid help for the Free French colonies; and a proposal to send a Free French warship to St Pierre and Miquelon, off Newfoundland, to bring them over to the Free French cause. He also disputed the extent of British control over propaganda to France.[89]

Even in London de Gaulle was far from amenable to British control, and relations with him were difficult. Matters were further complicated by the British contacts with Vichy which were being pursued in the autumn of 1940.[90] De Gaulle was kept informed of the substance of these exchanges, his reactions being at best sceptical and at worst hostile. He believed that even if the Vichy government were actually to resume the war against Germany, this would be merely an act of despair rather than an admission of past error; in any case Vichy had forfeited all prestige and authority to wage war again.[91] Should Weygand or Noguès seek an arrangement with Britain rather than accepting the terms which Germany seemed likely to impose at the end of October, de Gaulle insisted that Britain should meet any such approach by a declaration of support for himself and the Free French. Further, the Vichy representatives should be asked to get in touch with de Gaulle in order to collaborate with him in forming a war government.[92]

On 3 November de Gaulle set out his position even more explicitly. He explained that he understood the reasons impelling the British government to treat Vichy with care, and even to hope for a change of heart by Vichy leaders. However, speaking in the name of the Council of Defence, he pointed out that the Free French attitude, 'arising from motives essentially French', must be different from the British. The whole principle underlying Vichy's dealings with Germany and Italy was a crime, and the very acceptance of collaboration with France's enemies was an intolerable degradation. Moreover, from a practical point of view, no policy of conciliation towards Vichy could produce favourable results because Vichy was not a free agent. De Gaulle thus made a firm statement of his objections to negotiations with Vichy. He did not object to Britain encouraging leaders who might break away from Vichy, though he doubted whether they would actually do so, but if such leaders approached the British government, no agreement should be concluded with them without the direct participation and formal consent of the Free French Council of Defence. When Parr passed on de Gaulle's memorandum, he commented that he was impressed by the depth of anxiety felt by the Free French about the British attitude to Vichy. This opinion arose not from mere prejudice, but from the considered conclusion that the British were reasoning from disproved premises about the Vichy government, and there was therefore no chance that their approaches to Vichy could meet any dependable response.[93]

The most important element in de Gaulle's attitude was a point of principle: if the Vichy government was legitimate, then de Gaulle must be a rebel. However, de Gaulle knew that, so far from being a rebel, he represented the true France: therefore Vichy was a sham, and could never be anything else. The British for their part had to deal with a situation in which Vichy was a reality to be reckoned with, and in which they might well wish to deal with Weygand directly without the presence of Gaullist representatives.

When de Gaulle returned to London, he discussed these matters directly with Churchill and Halifax. He was firmly of the opinion that Weygand was too old and too timid for any bold move. Noguès was the same — nothing could be expected from that generation. De Gaulle considered that the real force at Vichy was Darlan, who was unalterably anti-British and who believed France's defeat to be irreversible. When Halifax asked de Gaulle outright whether he thought Britain was wrong in trying to find some *modus vivendi* with the Vichy government, de Gaulle replied guardedly that they might not be wrong in the short run, because small concessions could prevent Vichy from taking irrevocable action against Britain; but in the long run, small concessions could only have a delaying effect, at the risk of offending the vast majority of the French people who were coming to realise that the Vichy government was wholly bad, and under the orders of Berlin. It was plain that de Gaulle preferred to take the long view.[94]

In all his differences with the British government, de Gaulle was fortunate to have a firm supporter in Churchill. On 1 October, when the Cabinet were discussing relations with Vichy, Churchill reminded them of British engagements to de Gaulle, and insisted that de Gaulle 'had not behaved badly at or after Dakar, and had fallen in with our plans'.[95] Again, Churchill minuted on 26 October: 'Surely something should be said to Genral de Gaulle apprising him of the course we have taken, and of the fact that we have communicated with General Weygand, or tried to. In view of our relations with de Gaulle, and engagements signed, he has a right to feel assured we are not throwing him over'.[96] During the discussions on de Gaulle's movements at the end of October and early November, Churchill insisted that a severely worded draft telegram to de Gaulle should be held back: 'I should certainly not be ready to telegraph in my own name these dictatorial instructions to de Gaulle'.[97]

This did not mean that Churchill approved of all de Gaulle's ideas, or preferred to deal with him to the exclusion of other Frenchmen. He did not wish him to go to Cairo, where he thought his presence likely to bring to a head 'the collision between Weygand France — of which I still have some hopes — and Free France'. He was afraid that de Gaulle and his movement might become 'an obstacle to a very considerable hiving off of the French Empire to our side', because Weygand and Noguès resented him. Churchill wanted to have de Gaulle back in London, where he would be more amenable to control, rather than 'skirmishing around as an independent potentate in West Africa'. But he also thought that differences with de Gaulle were best dealt with tactfully and in person: 'It will be much easier to point all these things out to de Gaulle at close quarters than when he is a distant potentate'. So de Gaulle was invited to return to London for consultations, in telegrams much warmer and more tactful in wording than originally proposed.[98]

Despite the various difficulties and divergences of opinion between himself and de Gaulle, Churchill wrote him a formal letter at the end of the year noting the Brazzaville manifesto and organic declaration. The letter stated that the British government would be 'happy to treat with you, in the capacity of Leader of Free Frenchmen in which they have recognised you, and with the Council of Defence established by the decrees of 27 October 1940', on all questions involving collaboration with French overseas possessions under de Gaulle's authority. It was further carefully stated that the British government expressed no view on the constitutional and juridical considerations contained in the manifesto and organic declaration. This disclaimer was retained when the letter was published on 6 January 1941, although de Gaulle had sought to have it omitted.[99]

This was not the kind of recognition which de Gaulle would have preferred, but it was for him a step in the right direction; after a long silence, the British had formally noted the Brazzaville declarations. De Gaulle was able to go into the New Year with his equivocal position marginally improved, and with his own claims for himself and his movement undiminished. The British for their part remained uneasy and uncertain about their relations with him, and unwilling to take the clear stand recommended, in their different ways, by both Parr and Spears.

NOTES

1. CAB 65/15, WM(40)250th Conclusions, Confidential Annex.
2. *The Times,* 24, 26 September 1940, giving statements by Ministry of Information and Free French headquarters.
3. CAB 85/22, CFR(40)56th and 57th Meetings, 25 and 27 September 1940, Items 3 and 5 respectively; CAB 21/1463, Morton to Hood, 25 September 1940.
4. Tom Wintringham, *Daily Mirror,* 28 September 1940.
5. E.g. *Daily Mirror,* 27, 28 September 1940; *Daily Herald,* 25, 27 September; *News Chronicle,* 26, 27 September; *Daily Telegraph,* 27 September; *Daily Express,* 27 September; *Spectator,* 27 September.
6. INF 1/264, 26 September 1940.
7. *H.C. Deb.,* vol. 365, cols. 289-352.
8. FO 371/24302, C10490/9/17, minute by Vansittart, 27 September 1940.
9. Churchill, Appendix D; CAB 21/1324, Churchill to Salisbury, 3 January 1941.
10. *The Times,* 28 September 1940, despatch from New York correspondent.
11. *Daily Mirror,* 9, 10 October 1940; *Daily Herald, News Chronicle,* 9 October.
12. CAB 65/15, WM(40)259th Conclusions, Confidential Annex, 26 September 1940.

13. CAB 80/19, COS(40)788, minute by Churchill for COS, 28 September 1940.

14. FO 371/24332, C10236/7327/17, Parr to Mack, 1 November 1940. M. Henri Laurentie, in a letter to the author of 19 June 1973, has written that when de Gaulle visited Fort Lamy he showed no rancour against the British over Dakar.

15. FO 800/312, H/XIV/478, minute by Halifax, 28 November 1940.

16. De Gaulle, vol. I, 112.

17. De Larminat, 171.

18. *Ibid.*, 173.

19. FO 371/24334, C11367/7327/17, Spears to Ismay, 20 October 1940.

20. CAB 65/8, WM(40)235; *The Times,* 29 August 1940.

21. In an interview on 27 May 1973, Lord Rennell of Rodd gave the author valuable information on the economic and financial problems of the Free French colonies, and on British measures of assistance. Lord Rennell acted as liaison official on economic matters with the Free French colonies, and in the autumn of 1940 worked closely with de Larminat.

22. FO 371/24330, C9134/7327/17, Joint to Halifax, 25 August 1940; FO 371/24332, C10183/7327/17, same to same, 22 September.

23. *Ibid.*, C10089/7327/17, Joint to Halifax, 18 September 1940.

24. De Larminat, 168-71; information from Lord Rennell.

25. FO 371/24330, C9134/7327/17, Joint to Halifax, 25 August 1940; Halifax to Joint, 29 August.

26. CAB 85/27, CFR(EP)(40)28th Meeting, 4 September 1940, Item 1.

27. FO 371/24334, C11091/7327/17, Halifax to Joint, 22 October 1940; CAB 85/28, CFR(EP)(40)67, 25 October 1940, note by Fontaine.

28. CAB 85/27, CFR(EP)(40)46th Meeting, 14 October 1940, Item 1; CAB 85/22, CFR(40)64th Meeting, 14 October, Item 6.

29. FO 371/24334, C11147/7327/17, Governor, Nigeria, to S of S for Colonies, 19 October 1940.

30. CAB 85/28, CFR(EP)(40)85, 91, 17 and 26 December 1940.

31. CAB 79/6, COS Committee Minutes, 27 August 1940; CAB 80/23, COS(40)987, de Gaulle to Ismay, 26 November 1940; CAB 80/24, COS(40)1071, 30 December 1940. Cf. above, 198-9.

32. CAB 21/1433, minute by Hollis for Chiefs of Staff, 29 August 1940. The assurance was given at a meeting that afternoon between Churchill, de Gaulle, Spears and Morton.

33. FO 371/24334, C11228/7327/17, Spears to Ismay, 29 October 1940, transmitting message from de Gaulle to Churchill.

34. *Ibid.,* signals from FOC First Cruiser Squadron, 0145/19 October, 1547/24 October, 1825/23 October; signals from HMS *Delhi,* 0136, 0138, 1330/22 October, 0134/23 October.

35. *Ibid.,* minutes by Speaight, Cadogan and Halifax, 23 October 1940.

36. CAB 65/15, WM(40)276th Conclusions, Confidential Annex.

37. FO 371/24334, C11228/7327/17, Churchill to FOC First Cruiser Squadron, 1641/25 October.

38. *Ibid.,* minute by Strang, 24 October 1940.

39. FO 371/24335, C11905/7327/17, FOC First Cruiser Squadron to Admiralty, 2333/2 November.

40. *Ibid.,* minute by Mack, 10 November 1940, and attached telegrams.

41. FO 371/24343, C10986/7328/17, de Gaulle to Churchill, 9 October 1940, with minute by Colville, 10 October.

42. *Spectator,* 18 October 1940, 378.

43. CAB 79/6, COS Committee Minutes, 27 August 1940; CAB 80/18, COS(40)747, 15 September 1940; FO 371/24331, C9443/7327/17, War Office to Giffard, 31 August 1940, Giffard to War Office, 1 September; de Gaulle to COS, 5 October 1940.

44. FO 892/32, de Gaulle to Free French Committee, Athens, 16 November 1940 (this telegram simply said that a Free French detachment would shortly be sent to Greece); CAB 79/8, COS Committee Minutes, 29 November 1940; FO 371/24346, C13086/7328/17, Halifax to Palairet (Athens), 5 December 1940, Palairet to Halifax, 6 and 12 December; Catroux to de Gaulle, 9 December; minute by Mack, 13 December.

45. FO 371/24334, C11673/7328/17, Parr to Halifax, 31 October 1940; minute by Mack, 2 November 1940.

46. FO 371/24346, C12879/7328/17, de Gaulle to Pleven, 27 November 1940; minute by Barclay, 30 November, agreed to by Mack and Strang.

47. FO 371/24343, C10826/7328/17, Somerville-Smith to Speaight, 1 October 1940, enclosing draft telegram dated 25 September; minute by Speaight, 1 October.

48. FO 371/24344, C11773/7328/17, minute by Speaight, 23 November 1940.

49. FO 371/24335, C11514/7327/17, Joint to Halifax, 27 October 1940; minute by Barclay, 29 October.

50. CAB 85/23, CFR(40)120, 8 December 1940, draft declaration by de Gaulle; CAB 85/22, CFR(40)87th Meeting, 9 December 1940, Item 6; de Gaulle, vol. I, 356.

51. The *Journal Officiel* was for France what a combination of *Hansard, Statutes of the Realm,* and the *London Gazette* were for Britain.

52. Texts of the documents are in de Gaulle, vol. I, 303-5, 313-17. The organic declaration was drafted in London by Cassin, and amended slightly by de Gaulle before its issue: FO 371/24345, C12412/7328/17, minute by Morton for Churchill, 23 November 1940.

53. CAB 85/22, CFR(40)70th Meeting, 28 October 1940, Item 4; CAB 65/9, WM(40)278, 28 October 1940; FO 371/24344, C11512/7328/17, Halifax to Lampson and Butler, 30 October, C11498/7328/17, minute by Mack, 21 November; FO 371/24345, C12412/7328/17, minutes by Speaight and Mack, 20 and 21 November.

54. FO 371/24345, C12572/7328/17, minutes by Strang and Cadogan, 18 November 1940.

55. CAB 85/23, CFR(40)38, 12 September 1940: record of meeting, 6 September 1940.

56. FO 371/24313, C10629/65/17, minute by Tower of conversation with Cambon, 2 October 1940; minute by Hankey, 9 October; FO 371/24344, C12109/7328/17, minute by Strang, 14 November 1940.

57. *Ibid.,* C11290/7327/17, minute by Cadogan, 16 October 1940.

58. *Ibid.,* C11228/7327/17, minute by Strang, 30 October 1940.

59. CAB 85/22, CFR(40)73rd Meeting, 4 November 1940, memorandum by Morton, approved by the committee.

60. *Ibid.*, CFR(40)72nd Meeting, 1 November 1940, Item 1.
61. FO 371/24344, C12110/7328/17, minute by Mack on conversation with Palewski, 5 November 1940.
62. See above, 231.
63. *H.C. Deb.*, vol. 365, col. 1203.
64. FO 800/323, H/XXXIV/88, Attlee to Halifax, 30 October 1940.
65. FO 892/23, de Larminat to de Gaulle, 12 July 1940; FO 371/24350, C9180/7389/17, de Larminat to de Gaulle, 26 August.
66. FO 371/24303, C11003/9/17, minute by Campbell, undated but appended to other minutes of 16-18 October 1940.
67. Henri Michel, *Les Courants de Pensée de la Résistance* (Paris 1962), 15-16, 23-7.
68. Henri Noguères, *Histoire de la Résistance en France de 1940 à 1945,* vol. I (Paris, 1967), 47-9.
69. The fullest account of de Gaulle's press conference is in the newspaper *France,* 4 December 1940. Cf. FO 371/24346, C13297/7328/17, minutes by Mack, 5 December, Strang, 6 December, and Halifax, 8 December; Mack to Peake, 9 December.
70. FO 371/24346, C13072/7328/17, Parr to Mack, 14 November 1940.
71. FO 371/24335, C12865/7328/17, Parr to Halifax, 21 November 1940; minute by Halifax for Churchill, 25 November. The author acknowledges with gratitude two most valuable and interesting interviews with Sir Robert Parr in September and October 1972.
72. FO 371/24334, C11367/7327/17, minute by Strang, 22 October 1940.
73. *Ibid.,* Spears to Ismay, 20 October 1940; FO 892/32, Spears to Ismay, 2 and 9 November 1940.
74. FO 371/24346, C13242/7328/17, memorandum by Spears, undated. A minute by Mack, 20 December 1940, notes that Spears prepared this memorandum while he was in Africa — that is, before the end of November.
75. *Ibid.,* minutes by Barclay, 17 December 1940, and Mack, 20 December; FO 371/24344, C12109/7328/17, minute by Strang, 14 November 1940; FO 892/16, minutes by Morton and Ismay, 12 December 1940.

76. Passy, 81, 86; Muselier, 93-4.
77. CAB 85/22, CFR(40)63rd, 67th, 68th, 69th Meetings, 11, 21, 23, 25 October 1940; FO 892/18, Dickens to Spears, 30 October 1940; FO 892/25, record of meeting between Dickens and Muselier, 18 October 1940; FO 371/24334, C11228/7327/17, Halifax to Joint, 28 October 1940; Muselier, 103-4.
78. FO 371/24344, C11509/7328/17, minute by Codrington, 24 October 1940.
79. FO 371/24345, C12367/7328/17, extract from letter intercepted by the postal control.
80. FO 892/15, Morton to Somerville-Smith, 11 October 1940.
81. FO 371/24344, C11509/7328/17, minutes by Morton and Mack, 1 November 1940.
82. CAB 85/22, CFR(40)63rd Meeting, 11 October 1940, Item 3.
83. FO 371/24344, C11509/7328/17, minute by Morton, 1 November 1940.
84. CAB 85/22, CFR(40)72nd Meeting, 1 November 1940, Item 1.
85. FO 371/24344, C11150/7327/17, Mack to Somerville-Smith, 19 October 1940; Somerville-Smith to Mack, 20 October; minutes by Speaight and Mack, 27 and 31 October; Strang to Loxley, 2 November.
86. FO 371/24345, C12367/7328/17, minute by Speaight, 13 November 1940; Speaight to Somerville-Smith, 15 November; Somerville-Smith to Speaight, 16 November.
87. Muselier, 138-57; de Gaulle, vol. I, 124-6.
88. FO 371/24314, C12069/65/17, minutes by Cadogan, 5 November 1940, and Strang, 8 November; CAB 85/22, CFR(40)73rd Meeting, 4 November 1940, Item 5.
89. CAB 85/23, CFR(40)108, 29 November 1940, Free French Requirements; cf. CFR(40)113, 3 December. See below, 296-7.
90. See below, chapter 11.
91. FO 371/24331, C9443/7327/17, Governor, Nigeria, to S of S for Colonies, 3 October 1940.
92. FO 371/24335, C11596/7327/17, de Gaulle to Churchill, 25 October 1940.
93. FO 371/24303, C11852/9/17, Parr to Halifax, 3 November 1940.
94. FO 800/312, H/XIV/477, 478, minutes by Halifax, 27 and 28 November 1940.

95. CAB 65/15, WM(40)263rd Conclusions, Confidential Annex.

96. FO 371/24335, C11596/7327/17, minute by Churchill, 26 October 1940.

97. *Ibid.,* minute by Churchill, 5 November 1940.

98. *Ibid.,* minutes by Churchill, 5 and 8 November 1940; Churchill to de Gaulle, 9 and 10 November.

99. CAB 85/23, CFR(40)140, Churchill to de Gaulle, 24 December 1940; CAB 85/22, CFR(40)95th Meeting, 30 December 1940; *The Times,* 6 January 1941.

Chapter 11

BRITAIN AND THE VICHY GOVERNMENT

For de Gaulle the government of Marshal Pétain, established at Vichy from the beginning of July 1940, was unconstitutional and merely an instrument of German policy. For the British the situation was not so simple, although there were times when British public statements about Pétain's government were closely aligned to de Gaulle's position. On 25 June Churchill said in the House of Commons: 'What our relations with the Bordeaux Government will be I cannot tell. They have delivered themselves over to the enemy and lie wholly in his power'. On 20 August he referred to the fact that all the other Allied governments were continuing the fight, and said: 'That France alone should lie prostrate at this moment is the crime, not of a great and noble nation, but of what are called "the men of Vichy" '.[1] Despite such remarks, the facts were that the Vichy government existed; it exercised authority in the unoccupied zone of France and in the greater part of the French empire; and it controlled a fleet which was still considerable even after the British attacks of 3-8 July. Moreover, this government was recognised by the USA, on whose help and goodwill Britain was heavily dependent, and also by His Majesty's Governments in Canada and South Africa. In these circumstances, it was scarcely possible for the British government to treat Pétain's administration with the grand disdain adopted by de Gaulle. They had instead to develop a rather more complicated policy towards it.

In the course of formulating such a policy, Britain was handicapped by the lack of reliable knowledge concerning the nature and aims of the Vichy government. Its public appearance was discouraging. During July 1940, Pétain's actions were transforming France into an authoritarian state with fascist trappings, apparently ready to fit into the Nazi New Order for Europe. The former motto of *'Liberté, Egalité, Fraternité'* was replaced by *'Travail, Famille, Patrie'*. A special court was set up at Riom to try those who were held responsible for leading France into war and for her defeat: Reynaud, Daladier, Blum and Gamelin were to be brought before it. A 'National Revolution' was proclaimed, trade unions dissolved, and the outline of a corporative state sketched out. In October Jews were excluded from a number of professions including public service and teaching, and there was also considerable evidence of Vichy's subservience to Germany. German economic pressure was made clear, for example through the imposition of occupation costs totalling four hundred million francs per day, and through German control of the demarcation line between the occupied and unoccupied zones of France, which they could close at will. The likelihood of political, and perhaps military, collaboration between France and Germany was broadcast to the world by the meetings at Montoire: the first on 22 October between Hitler and Laval, the second on the 24th between Hitler and Pétain. In the French official *communiqué* of 26 October, and in a broadcast by Pétain on the 30th, it was announced that the principle of collaboration had been agreed, and that the details would subsequently be worked out.[2] All this boded ill for relations between Britain and the Vichy government.

However, it was possible to question whether the whole truth about Vichy policy was conveyed in public appearances and pronouncements, and to look for more hopeful signs beneath the surface. One might argue that the new system of government in France was of no more concern to Britain than the authoritarian regime of Salazar in Portugal, a country with which Britain maintained friendly relations.[3] Equally, it could be asked whether Franco-German collaboration in principle would turn out to mean something fairly innocuous in practice. Nevertheless, it was difficult to get beneath the surface in order to test the truth of such views: France, Britain's nearest continental neighbour, had virtually become an unknown land. French newspapers were scanned for hints; the *Petit Dauphinois,* for example, reached nearby Switzerland reasonably quickly, and extracts were telegraphed to London from Berne. From Tangier, the British Consulate regularly sent titbits from the *Dépêche Marocaine*. Paris newspapers filtered through to London after some delay, and were studied with something akin to the art of the crystal-gazer. British representatives in neutral countries, notably Spain and Switzerland, reported diplomatic gossip and the travellers' tales of visitors from France, as well as the studied conversation of their French colleagues. Sometimes information was passed on even at fourth hand, as when the British Minister at Berne reported that the Norwegian Minister had told him that a colleague had heard from a colleague at Vichy a story about the arrest of Laval on 13 December 1940 — this proved, incidentally, to be a story containing a fair element of truth.[4] American diplomats and the State Department passed on a good deal of information, and there were valuable reports from newspaper correspondents, whether neutrals working in unoccupied France itself or British citizens hovering on the Spanish border.

Even the rather random intelligence provided by such sources as these was sufficient to cast doubt on any simple interpretation of Vichy policy. One French newspaper might say that the book of relations with England was closed, and France was ready to join a continental bloc; but another stated that France's failure to declare war on England, coupled with continued relations with British Dominions, indicated that her policy was to preserve liberty of action.[5] The latter possibility was also advanced by a German informant, highly recommended by Vansittart, whose report went to both Halifax and Churchill. This source maintained that the success of the British forces would ultimately decide the direction of French foreign policy, because France, conscious of her own weakness, would seek an alliance with the strongest power.[6] In 1940, of course, this was not entirely comforting when one considered Germany's strength at that time, but it might offer hope for the future.

Another frequent report was that opinion at Vichy was divided. While some were willing to go to any lengths to collaborate with Germany — Laval was usually mentioned in this context — there were others who set limits to this process; Pétain, Weygand and sometimes Baudouin were put in the latter camp. Massigli, a French diplomat well regarded in London, reported in September that Pétain disapproved of Laval; another French diplomat hoped that Weygand would come over to the Free French. At the end of August an American representative passed on a message that Baudouin was privately better disposed towards Britain than his public statements indicated, these having been decidedly anti-British.[7] Reports of this nature encouraged a hope that the Vichy faction tending to be less anti-British and pro-German might develop its so far tentative resistance to German demands. Other reports, including one from Murphy, the American *chargé d'affaires* at Vichy, hinted that Doriot — the most prominent French fascist — might emerge as a French dictator in place of Pétain.[8] Conversely there were repeated reports, both in the press and from private sources, that Pétain himself intended to move his government to Paris, thus placing himself physically within the grasp of the Germans.[9]

Among the leading personalities at Vichy, information and comment concentrated on Laval and Pétain. Laval was seen as the advocate of collaboration with Germany, even to the point of participation in the war against Britain. Mack minuted on one occasion that Laval was 'quite capable of giving anything to the Germans', though he did not think that either the French people or other Vichy ministers would follow him into war with Britain.[10] On the other hand, after the Montoire discussions a former French official at the League of Nations reported that Laval had manoeuvred Pétain into the meeting with Hitler. This time Mack commented: 'Laval seems able to trick the poor old Marshal and we should always bear this in mind.'[11] The French Ambassador in Berne told the British Minister there that Laval believed collaboration with Germany to be inevitable, because Germany was certain to win the war.[12] The same picture emerged from a report of a conversation with Laval by an American journalist, in which Laval said: 'Germany is going to win this war. That I know and can assure you'. He hoped for the defeat of England, which would serve French interests, because if Germany won there would be peace and unity in Europe whereas if England triumphed Europe would again be divided. By collaborating with Germany, France would gain rewards in the final peace settlement.

In the Foreign Office, this report was judged to be an accurate statement of Laval's position.[13] On 13 December, shortly after it reached London, Laval was dismissed from his post as Foreign Minister and briefly placed under arrest, as a result of a palace *coup* at Vichy. The British were glad to see him go — Halifax told the Cabinet that his dismissal could only be in British interests, even though he had little confidence in Flandin, Laval's successor as Foreign Minister.[14] A Foreign Office official thought that Pétain had been influenced by the state of French opinion, which had shifted in favour of Britain; and that the *coup* showed that Laval's policy of complete subservience to Germany lacked the approval not only of the Marshal, but also of Darlan and Huntziger (Minister of War).[15]

There was a curious episode in early December, when a member of the House of Lords suggested that Laval might be bribed to adopt a more favourable policy. The proposition came to Halifax, who minuted to Cadogan: 'I don't suppose we want to consider bribing Laval, do we? (a) unprofitable. (b) unpleasant'. Cadogan replied: 'I shouldn't bother about (b)', but argued that since Laval's attitude was dictated by his belief that Germany would win the war, it would require a very large sum to persuade him to abandon his German friends. Moreover, it would be unwise to hand over much money before Laval 'delivered the goods' — and Cadogan was unsure what goods he was expected to deliver. Even if the manoeuvre succeeded, the British would only have handicapped themselves for the future, when Laval's unpopularity would come home to roost. In short, Cadogan concluded, 'There is not enough market value in him'. The matter was referred to Churchill on 13 December, the day of Laval's dismissal, so that the correspondence ended with a brief minute by the Prime Minister: 'He is no longer worth buying'.[16]

British opinion on Laval was virtually unanimous. On the other hand, opinions about Pétain were diverse and often contradictory. Some reports depicted him as an insignificant figure, and Cambon told the British at the beginning of October that, while Pétain was opposed to the Anglophobe attitude of Baudouin, no reliance could be placed on him; he was bound to disappear within a short time, although he might linger as a figure-head without influence.[17] Other reports held that, on the contrary, Pétain wielded the real power at Vichy. Murphy told a British official in Washington that Pétain and Baudouin were the important pair and that Pétain used Laval to do his dirty work for him.[18] Frankowski, a Polish diplomat who remained at Vichy until October 1940, told Campbell that Pétain was still the master there, and as long as this was so his government was unlikely to hand over the fleet or empire to the Germans.[19] Again, at the end of December there was a report from Washington to the effect that Pétain had dismissed Laval for going too far in his

257

negotiations with the Germans and encroaching on Pétain's prerogative.[20] In this assessment, Pétain was regarded as the ultimate wielder of power, stepping in to dismiss his underling, Laval.

On the crucial issue of collaboration with Germany, several reports indicated that Pétain was determined to limit his commitments. Even after the meeting at Montoire on 24 October, the British government found reason to hope that he had not irrevocably committed himself to the German side, and this view was pressed on de Gaulle on 1 November.[21] Early in December a message sent by Darlan through the French naval attaché at Madrid was regarded as demonstrating that neither Pétain nor Darlan wished to break with Britain. Pétain personally assured the French naval attaché that he would never allow French forces or bases to be used against Britain, even though he had to collaborate with the Germans in civilian matters for the good of France. The memorandum from Madrid reporting this conversation was considered of great importance in London.[22]

When Pétain's motives were discussed, considerable emphasis was placed on his overwhelming preoccupation with particular French interests: to find some means by which the French people could survive under German domination, and to protect and bring home the French prisoners of war who would father the next generation of Frenchmen.[23] Generally speaking, British observers gave Pétain credit for a patriotism and concern for France which tended to be denied to Laval. These distinctions, and the view that there was a significant difference in policy between Pétain and Laval, were not accepted by everyone, however. Churchill sometimes tended to lump the Vichy leaders together and in a trenchant memorandum of 14 November he wrote: ' . . . these men have committed acts of baseness on a scale which has earned them the lasting contempt of the world . . . Laval is certainly filled by the bitterest hatred of England, and is reported to have said that he would like to see us "crabouillés", which means squashed so as to leave only a grease-spot . . . Darlan is mortally envenomed by the injury we have done to his fleet. Pétain has always been an anti-British defeatist and is now a dotard'.[24] This did not mean that Churchill ruled out contacts with these men, but he was averse to drawing fine distinctions of character and attitude.

Such questions of personality were important to Britain because of the effect it was assumed they would have on relations between

France and Germany. The Montoire meetings appeared to bring this vital issue to a head, and the British government was keenly aware of its position as a distant spectator of events which were of such close concern. Churchill said in Cabinet on 28 October, four days after Pétain met Hitler, that it was extraordinary that they had received no information about what had happened in the negotiations.[25] In fact, there was no lack of information: what was lacking was proof of its reliability. On 24 October the *Daily Telegraph* published a Swiss newspaper report setting out the terms which the Germans were said to have presented to France. The substance of this statement, with some minor variations, reached the Foreign Office from several sources, one in Madrid being described as 'absolutely sure'. The information was also summarised in an intelligence report of 31 October. Germany was to receive Alsace and Lorraine, and for the duration of hostilities was to have the use of air and naval bases in France and the Mediterranean. Italy was to receive the *Alpes Maritimes,* half Algeria, and Tunisia — also Corsica according to some reports. Spain was to receive all or part of Morocco (some reports said Germany was also to have a share). Indo-China was to go to Japan and the remainder of the French empire was to be administered jointly by France, Germany and Italy. The French fleet and air force were to be surrendered to the Axis powers.[26] Such terms were sweeping, and if the reports had proved correct the British position would have been seriously endangered. Nevertheless, it was clear on 28 October that Churchill did not believe them to be necessarily accurate, and still thought it possible that Vichy might have agreed to join the German bloc without in practice becoming more hostile to Britain than before.[27] Indeed, hot on the heels of these reports came the denials. On 29 October news came from Berne concerning a statement by Baudouin that every word so far published about the Franco-German negotiations was false, especially the reports about the cession of colonies, the use of bases, and the surrender of the navy and air force.[28] Other reports came in saying that the German terms had been greatly modified, and that a battle over acceptance or rejection was going on at Vichy.[29] The British were left in a state of acute anxiety, but with some grounds for thinking that nothing irrevocable had occurred.

In this state of uncertainty, with a dearth of information about personalities and policies at Vichy, general attitudes and prejudices (which always affect policy) had an unusual importance in London. These attitudes varied widely, from instinctive mildness towards Vichy to instinctive toughness and belligerence. Mildness tended to be preached from Madrid where Sir Samuel Hoare, the former Foreign Secretary, was Ambassador. Broadly Hoare's arguments were that it was to Britain's advantage for Pétain's government to continue, lest worse befall; also that Spanish non-belligerence might be prejudiced if the Vichy government fell or declared war. His political opponents recalled his support of an appeasement policy in the 1930s and his sympathy with Right-wing dictatorships, and believed these considerations to be influencing his arguments. Certainly Hoare urged extreme caution and mildness in dealing with Vichy, both in his official telegrams and in unofficial letters to Halifax. Halifax was sympathetic to this approach: 'I agree in the main with your advice that we should treat Vichy tenderly', he wrote to Hoare on 29 November.[30] He also dissented from Churchill's wish to threaten to bomb Vichy if the French again bombed Gibraltar, on the grounds that it would turn French feeling against Britain, and that to bomb an open town would damage Britain's reputation.[31]

At the opposite end of the spectrum were those whose instinct was to be rough with Vichy. Dalton, for example, was belligerent by nature and much opposed to Hoare, both because he believed Hoare's policies would be ruinous to the blockade, and on more personal grounds. (In his diary, Dalton referred to 'the finicking, flickering figure of Sir S.H.')[32] Dalton was in favour of toughness towards Vichy, and strongly against any avoidable relaxation of the blockade of unoccupied France. Among officials, Vansittart held similar views. He wrote on 8 July: 'I should no longer be punctilious about the Vichy Govt. It is Fascist and will become more so'.[33] Morton, in a memorandum at the end of November, argued that British policy towards Vichy should be bold, straightforward and uncompromising — Vichy responded to toughness.[34] More important, both Attlee and Churchill were in this camp. Attlee's view was put succinctly in Cabinet on 3 October: 'He had little faith in the Vichy Government as at present constituted, which, he thought, was in the grip of the Germans and had no will of its own'.[35] Churchill's forthright views on the leading personalities at Vichy have already been quoted, and his general attitude matched these views. He laid down early in August that 'no excessive scruples with regard to the Vichy Government' should be allowed to interfere with the war effort. He was in favour of using threats when appropriate, including the threat to bomb Vichy itself.[36] He thought that Vichy, under pressure from Germany, would like to feel they had 'a nice, soft, cosy, forgiving England on their other side'. Rather than adopt such an attitude, Britain should confront them with 'difficult and rough situations, and make them feel that we have teeth as well as Hitler'. He was in favour of contacts with Vichy, and trying to promote useful tendencies there; but the best way to do this was to 'make sure the Vichy folk are kept well ground between the upper and nether millstones of Germany and Britain. In this way they are most likely to be brought into a more serviceable mood during the short run which remains to them.'[37] This was a far cry from Halifax's view that 'we should treat Vichy tenderly' — which the Foreign Secretary wrote fifteen days after receiving the Prime Minister's stern memorandum.

Corresponding to such attitudes as these, British policy towards Vichy had a dual character. On the one hand, it had a number of hostile aspects, as in the support given to de Gaulle and the Free French which was an act of hostility towards Vichy which could scarcely be disguised. Further, the British were engaged through propaganda in a form of subversion against Vichy. It is true that, for reasons which will be discussed later, attacks on Pétain himself were discouraged, but Laval was treated as a first-class target for abuse and defamation, and British propaganda sought to emphasise the degree of German control over the whole of France (including the unoccupied zone), and to bring home the weakness of the Vichy position. Moreover, the British decided on 25 June to apply the blockade to the whole of metropolitan France, and on 13 July to extend it to Algeria, Tunisia and French Morocco.[38] If enforced, these decisions would be a grave blow to the economy of unoccupied France, which in normal times did not produce all its own food and depended heavily on imports of coal and petroleum products.

During August 1940 the British government came under pressure from a section of American opinion, led by Herbert Hoover, to permit food to be sent to occupied countries in Europe under certain safeguards. The British resisted this pressure, which did not at that point have the support of the US government. A memorandum for the Cabinet by Dalton on 7 August argued that the blockade should be maintained in full, and that there should only be starvation in 'the enslaved area' during the next winter if the Germans deliberately created it.[39] The government stated its position in the House of Commons on 20 August. First, Dalton arranged questions for himself, designed to emphasise the case for the blockade. 'Would it not be true to say that any food suplies from the unoccupied part of France could be taken by Germany into the occupied part, if anybody were silly enough to supply them with the opportunity?' To which Dalton replied: 'Yes, Sir. My Hon. Friend has very accurately stated the position'.[40] Then Churchill made a formal statement that requests for the passage of relief supplies of food must be refused, and that Germany must bear the responsibility of feeding the peoples she had conquered.[41] Thus no relief was offered to Vichy on humanitarian grounds. Indeed, in September the Prime Minister instructed that economic pressure should be extended as far as possible to those parts of the French empire outside North Africa which did not rally to the Free French. 'Join de Gaulle or starve' was the approach which he recommended. The system of compulsory navicerts to control contraband was extended to French West Africa in October, though the difficulties proved to be too great for Churchill's simple alternatives to be made effective.[42]

Support for de Gaulle, propaganda and blockade made up the hostile aspects of British policy towards the Vichy government. Gradually, however, there developed another aspect, which if not friendly was at least hopeful. The commonly used phrase for what the British Government hoped for from the contacts which developed with Vichy during the autumn of 1940 was a *modus vivendi* — a means by which the two governments might live together at a certain modest level of agreement.

Among the reasons which prompted the British government to seek a *modus vivendi* was their desire to keep the French empire out of German control. Since the greater part of that empire maintained its allegiance to the Vichy government, the British wanted some assurance that bases there would not be handed over to the Germans. The Chiefs of Staff argued on 4 September that, while Britain should ultimately direct her efforts towards detaching French colonies from Vichy and securing their co-operation in the war, 'for the present our aim should be to maintain the stability of any Government not actively hostile to us, particularly in West Africa, where an upheaval might endanger our interests, while we ourselves are so weak in that area'.[43] The Dakar operation, while running counter to this recommendation, gave an extra impulse to this line of thought. Halifax argued that Dakar might have stimulated the self-confidence of the French government and colonial authorities. 'If it were possible to transform any such growth of French self-confidence . . . into growing resistance to German or Italian designs on the French empire, the results of Dakar might not prove to be so completely to our disadvantage'. His conclusion was that Britain's main purpose was 'to secure that the French Colonial Empire should be healthily anti-German and anti-Italian and be got to act accordingly. Provided it will so act, it is immaterial to us whether it be under leaders that will not break with Vichy, or under de Gaulle'. Putting this case to the Cabinet on 1 October, Halifax added that the British might find it easier to persuade the French colonies to adopt a desirable attitude *with* the assent of Vichy rather than without it.[44]

It was also important for Britain to persuade Vichy to refrain from attacking colonies which had joined de Gaulle. An attack by sea would bring into play the British pledge to defend them by naval action; an attack by land, while not covered by the pledge, could scarcely be ignored if it became serious. A significant Vichy offensive would compel Britain to choose between resistance and leaving de Gaulle to the mercy of Vichy. 'We must do our best', Halifax telegraphed to Hoare on 7 November, 'to avoid being placed before this choice'.[45] It would therefore be advantageous to Britain if Vichy would undertake to maintain the colonial *status quo* by leaving the Gaullist colonies alone. This need not be a matter of principle, as Halifax explained. The British were not asking Vichy to abandon the *right* to recover their colonies, only to refrain from exercising it.[46]

A further reason for seeking some understanding with Vichy was the continuing British anxiety about the French fleet. This was heightened at the end of October and the beginning of November by the Montoire meetings and various reports that the French intended to move the *Jean Bart* from Casablanca into the Mediterranean. Churchill told the Cabinet on 1 November that neither the *Jean Bart* nor the *Richelieu* could be allowed to enter the

Mediterranean. Pound argued that the long-term risk of the battleships being added to the German navy was balanced by the immediate risk of a battle with the French fleet if they were intercepted at sea. Halifax hoped to avoid both risks by informing the Vichy government that the warships would not be allowed to pass Gibraltar.[47] It would also be useful if, as part of an understanding with Vichy, an assurance could be received about safeguarding the French fleet.

All these arguments were given extra urgency by the Montoire meetings and Pétain's acceptance of the principle of collaboration with Germany, although the British government hoped that Vichy might yet be weaned away from such a course. At the time of Montoire, attempts were made to do this by a personal message from the King to Pétain, and by asking Roosevelt to use his powerful good offices.[48] Ultimately the weaning process would have to be achieved by offering some substantial concession to Vichy, and there was no doubt as to the form the Vichy government wished this to take: a relaxation of the blockade, and an undertaking that there would be no further British or Gaullist attacks on French colonies. When these questions were put, however, serious problems arose.

The British blockade of unoccupied France was only partially effective since French traffic across the western Mediterranean, from North Africa to southern France, was outside British control. Geographically, the straits of Gibraltar offered an excellent opportunity for intercepting trade between unoccupied France and the outside world, but in practice the shortage of warships and fear of French reprisals prevented this opportunity from being exploited. As early as 11 July 1940, Admiralty instructions laid down that escorted French merchant ships bound for ports in unoccupied France should not be interfered with; only unescorted vessels were to be brought into Gibraltar for contraband control. On 12 August this order was confirmed by the Cabinet, and it held good for some months, while the Vichy authorities gradually increased the passage of escorted ships.[49]

It was thus scarcely accurate to speak of offering Vichy a 'relaxation' of the blockade: what was not being enforced could not be relaxed. The real question was whether the British government should try to enforce the blockade, or should seek some agreement with Vichy giving formal sanction to the existing leak. On this there were two strongly held and evenly balanced opinions.

One view, held by the Ministry of Economic Warfare with support from the Foreign Office, was that the leak in the blockade was sufficiently important to endanger the whole system of economic warfare, and should therefore be stopped. The most important trade was that with West Africa in groundnuts, palm kernels and palm oil, which could make a considerable difference to the supplies of vegetable fats in Europe. There was ample evidence of the steady movement of French shipping through the straits of Gibraltar in the autumn of 1940. Between 15 September and 5 October, twenty French ships were escorted eastwards through the straits, and three westwards. The escorts were often merely symbolic — sloops, armed trawlers, or survey ships. Figures for October showed twenty-nine ships passing eastwards and two westwards; in November, twenty-five and nine vessels respectively. In addition to the West African trade, ships were reaching France from Madagascar and Martinique, and there was evidence that sailings between New York and Casablanca were being planned. It was obvious that neutral states would begin to ask why they should trouble to observe the British blockade regulations against trading with the Axis territories when the Vichy French did not; it was also possible that neutral ships would join the French convoys. The trade thus carried on was ostensibly with unoccupied France, but there were reports that of the total foodstuffs imported into Marseilles, the Germans took 60 per cent and the Italians 20 per cent. In this way a powerful case was built up for checking the leak in the blockade; this would be achieved not by stopping every French ship at the straits, but by occasional interceptions which would act as a deterrent.[50]

To the Admiralty this presentation of the situation was over-simplified and incomplete. Their prime concern was the naval strength available for the tasks which had to be performed, and an Admiralty memorandum of 30 September 1940 stated that: 'Our naval strength is already inadequate for fighting Germany and Italy, and the Admiralty consider that our policy towards the Vichy government should be largely governed by the need to keep the calls upon our naval forces (other than for operations against Germany and Italy) down to a minimum'.[51] Alexander, the First Lord of the Admiralty, put it to Dalton, the Minister of Economic Warfare, on 3 January 1941 that the margin of naval strength in relation to commitments was 'smaller than at any time in modern naval history.

We have in fact no margin at all, and we are taking risks all over the world'.[52] It followed from this that the Admiralty wanted to avoid the risk of a serious clash with Vichy warships such as would arise from the interception of escorted convoys. They were also seriously worried about Gibraltar. In reprisal for the attack on Dakar, the French bombed Gibraltar, dropping some 150 bombs and damaging the dockyard.[53] The Admiralty held that this showed how easily Gibraltar could be made untenable as a naval base, and they argued that to check French trade through the straits at the expense of losing the use of Gibraltar would not be worth while. They therefore preferred to avoid having to enforce the blockade, and instead to negotiate some form of agreement with Vichy whereby imports to unoccupied France would be limited. This would include voluntary contraband control at Gibraltar and an undertaking that cargoes would not be passed on to the Axis powers. A substantial weakness in the Admiralty case at this point was the lack of means to ensure that such undertakings would be kept; there were also considerable grounds for thinking that the Germans were most unlikely to accept being deprived of West African produce in a mood of tame acquiescence.[54]

The Cabinet discussed these conflicting views at intervals during October and November, but found the arguments so finely balanced that a decision was difficult to reach. Churchill was uneasy about the leak, and anxious to adopt a firmer line, being particularly concerned that acceptance of the Admiralty argument about the risk to Gibraltar would mean giving way to Vichy whenever the threat of bombing was used. On the other hand, a tentative exchange of views with Vichy on economic matters was begun, and the Montoire meetings gave added impetus to the desire to reach an accommodation with Pétain's government. The Cabinet therefore decided in principle on 18 October that escorted French convoys should no longer be immune from contraband control at Gibraltar; but in practice matters remained in suspense until 18 November when Dalton again raised the question in Cabinet. At this meeting, Churchill held that the time had come to be prepared to take risks in order to intercept French traffic through the straits. The naval situation had been improved by the crippling of the Italian fleet at Taranto, and he did not think that a serious clash with Vichy warships would in fact arise. Despite the Admiralty's reluctance, therefore, the Cabinet ruled that contraband control should be applied to escorted French shipping — though the possibility of economic conversations with Vichy was kept open. Orders were issued on 19 November for the interception of convoys during the next two days, after which the warships concerned would be needed elsewhere.[55] The first successful operation took place on 1 January 1941, when four French ships were taken into Gibraltar. Between 1 January and 18 May 1941, a total of thirty-three French vessels were intercepted in various waters, mostly at the straits.[56] At a meeting between Dalton and Alexander on 11 February, the Ministry of Economic Warfare and the Admiralty went far towards overcoming their differences, and agreed on a policy of occasional interceptions based on advance warning about important cargoes.[57]

Thus, despite all the difficulties, Cabinet opinion moved in favour of trying to impose the blockade, and in fact it was occasionally enforced although a good deal of trade continued. It was not easy therefore to find any concession on the blockade which would be of substantial value to Vichy. On another issue, Vichy sought an assurance that the British and de Gaulle would refrain from attacking or subverting further French colonies. This raised additional problems, though less complicated than those concerning the blockade. The very existence of British contacts with Vichy aroused de Gaulle's suspicions, though Britain had insisted to Vichy from the start that de Gaulle could on no account be abandoned or repudiated.[58] Even from the viewpoint of British interests alone, it was not clear whether it would be best to leave the Vichy colonies undisturbed. Morton and the Foreign Office maintained that, while it would be unwise to try to seize colonies for de Gaulle by force, internal *coups* to bring them over might be encouraged.[59] Moreover, it was by no means easy to prevent de Gaulle from taking action, whatever the British thought; in November 1940 the Free French attacked Libreville despite British discouragement. After this, de Gaulle was contemplating attacks on Dahomey or Niger, and while the British could deny him facilities in Nigeria, he might well find ways round such obstacles.[60]

De Gaulle took the view that the Vichy government was too deeply compromised with the Germans to be trustworthy, and this attitude was shared by many British ministers and officials. Behind all the problems raised by contacts with Vichy there loomed the fundamental question of whether, even if some agreement could be reached, it would be kept. In all these circumstances, it is remarkable that exchanges between Britain and Vichy took place at all, and hardly surprising that they were slow, difficult and inconclusive. The bases of the discussions have already been analysed, and the course of events may be briefly summarised.[61] During September 1940 various messages were passed from Vichy to London through the embassies at Madrid, asking for non-enforcement of the blockade and for a colonial *modus vivendi* which would safeguard Vichy colonies against further Gaullist *coups*. The British replied cautiously that the movements in Equatorial Africa had been spontaneous — a statement of dubious accuracy — and that they had given undertakings to de Gaulle from which they would not withdraw. They refrained from commenting on the blockade. However, they were willing to maintain contact with Vichy through Madrid.[62]

The attack on Dakar brought a threatening message from Darlan, but also a further request from Baudouin that supplies be allowed to reach France so that the government should not be entirely driven over to the German side. The British answered on 3 October, expressing willingness to discuss means of ensuring that Vichy colonies did not fall under Axis control, nor Vichy warships pass into Axis hands. For their part, the British would be prepared to study French proposals on trade between the colonies and unoccupied France. The French reply on 14 October was very stiff in tone, especially on the subject of de Gaulle, but affirmed that the Vichy government would keep control of its fleet and empire, and again requested an economic agreement. On 19 October the British repeated their own points about the fleet and empire, but said they were willing to discuss trade between French North Africa (including the Moroccan ports on the Atlantic) and unoccupied France.[63] At this point the Montoire meetings intervened, and on 1 November Hoare was instructed to ask where the Vichy government stood, and to threaten the bombing of Vichy itself if France declared war on Britain. However, the British followed this on 7 November with a definite proposal on the colonial situation. If the Vichy government could satisfy the British that they were 'resolved and able' to defend their colonies against the Axis, no conflict need arise between them. Provided Vichy would refrain from attacking the Gaullist colonies, Britain would refrain from further action against Dakar. This suggestion made no headway: the French *chargé d'affaires* at Madrid objected that his government could not surrender its right to recover the mutinous colonies. A French note on 11 November protested against the support given by Britain to French rebels, and said the French government would safeguard the unity of their empire by all means in their powers; this sounded threatening, but the note also stated that the French had never initiated any attack against Britain, and would not do so.[64]

Hoare suggested on 10 November that it would be best to commence economic negotiations. After much discussion in London about the blockade and relations with Vichy, instructions were sent to him on 23 November. The British asked that Vichy should tacitly refrain from attacking the Free French colonies, and should resist Axis attack or infiltration in their own colonies. Britain did not covet any French territory, but emphasised that any colony which declared for de Gaulle would be protected from the sea in accordance with the undertaking given to the general. Acceptance of these conditions would constitute a provisional arrangement to hold the situation while means of reaching a *modus vivendi* were sought. On this understanding, the British were willing to begin economic discussions, starting with the question of trade between North Africa and unoccupied France.[65] On 10 January 1941, after a long silence, the Vichy government presented a memorandum on its economic requirements: navicerts for the import of 600,000 tons of wheat and 200,000 tons of maize, with an undertaking that they would be consumed in unoccupied France and not used to release other foodstuffs for the Germans. The memorandum also asked for discussions on other imports.

The British not only considered these requests excessive, but were also perturbed that Vichy had informed the Germans of the negotiations. On 24 January, therefore, the requests were refused. Talks on a possible economic agreement should be limited to Morocco.[66] In fact an agreement had been signed on 29 November 1940 between French Morocco, Spain and Britain, by which Britain provided credits for Spain to buy green tea; she would exchange this for Moroccan phosphates, and the whole of this traffic would be exempted from the blockade. In February 1941 a further agreement was reached by which Britain agreed to supply some goods to Morocco direct, while French Morocco provided Spain with foodstuffs. In making these arrangements, however, the British were more concerned with their effects on Spain than with Vichy.[67]

The Vichy government protested that the British, after opening economic discussions, were being wholly obstructive; but the British were adamant.[68] The only concessions made in February and March 1941 were to allow certain supplies of preserved milk and vitamins to enter unoccupied France, there to be distributed to children by the American Red Cross; also to allow two shiploads of flour to be sent from the USA to the unoccupied zone. These concessions were only made at the insistence of the US government.[69]

In the end, very little came of these lengthy and somewhat confused exchanges via Madrid. Neither did anything definite emerge from various other contacts which were made between the British and Vichy governments. In November and December a Canadian diplomat, Dupuy, went to Vichy as his government's *chargé d'affaires,* and had conversations with Pétain and Darlan. The Cabinet paid close attention to the information which he sent back; this was at first disturbing when Pétain said that he might have to cede bases in the Mediterranean; later more hopeful when Pétain and Darlan both stated that this was out of the question, and that they would resist German pressure to attack Gaullist colonies at least until February 1941.[70] Similar assurances were received from Pétain through Professor Rougier, an unofficial agent of the Marshal, in mid-December. According to Rougier, Pétain would not cede either bases or the fleet, and was prepared to accept the secession of Equatorial Africa as a *fait accompli* so long as no attacks were made on other colonies. Cadogan thought that the combined assurances through Dupuy and Rougier amounted to rather more than the British had expected. On 19 December Halifax summed up the recent exchanges by noting that the main assurances sought from Vichy had been received, though no progress had been made in economic discussions.[71] How far this result was significant depended on whether the assurances were reliable, and on this Halifax made no comment.

In the autumn and winter of 1940 there was another and different aspect to British relations with Vichy. A slender hope persisted that some of the French leaders might be persuaded to re-enter the war on the British side, and Churchill wrote to Hoare on 19 October: 'It passes my comprehension why no French leaders secede to Africa where they would have an Empire, the command of the seas and all the frozen French gold in the United States . . . surely the opportunity is the most splendid ever offered to daring men'.[72] It was chiefly to Weygand that the British looked for the fulfilment of such hopes, and in September 1940 he was appointed Delegate-General of the French Government in North Africa, a position of at least potential independence. When his appointment was announced, there was some doubt in London as to whether he was going to North Africa to impose obedience to the armistice or to prepare for resistance against Germany, either with or without Pétain's consent.[73] Gaullists in Morocco were not hopeful — André thought Weygand was honest, but too timid and old to take any great initiative.[74] However, the British thought it well worth while to make contact with Weygand and sound out his views. At the end of October they examined a plan to send General Heywood (a former military attaché at Paris) to Tangier to get in touch with Weygand, though eventually this idea was dropped.[75]

A number of approaches were made to Weygand by other channels. For example, a message was sent on 31 October through a French officer, emphasising British confidence in victory, trusting that the French government would refuse any arrangement with Germany likely to delay that victory, and affirming British determination to preserve the French empire if it would act with Britain in opposing the Axis.[76] When Professor Rougier (acting in an ill-defined capacity on behalf of Pétain) visited London, the opportunity was taken to send a message to Weygand. Rougier was in London from 23 to 29 October, and saw Cadogan, Halifax and Churchill; his information about the situation at Vichy was thought valuable, especially since his visit happened to coincide with the meetings at Montoire. He repeated the French appeals for relaxation of the blockade, and said that Weygand had told him he would defend French overseas territory against attack from any quarter — including de Gaulle. However, Rougier thought that Weygand's mission of reorganisation in North Africa might reach the stage where the territory could become a rallying-point against the Axis. As press reports came in concerning the agreement which Pétain was alleged to have made with Hitler, Rougier expressed the view that Weygand would react sharply against such terms. It was agreed that Rougier should go to see Weygand and Noguès, with a note — seen by Halifax — setting out the basis for conversations with them. This note emphasised the high morale of the people in London, and Britain's capacity to carry on the war. Assurances were given about the future of France, on condition that she did nothing

271

to help the Axis, or better still assisted Britain to victory. In the latter case, the possibility of a relaxation of the blockade was held out. However, no assurances about the future of France could be given if she were to help the Axis by ceding bases. Rougier went to North Africa and saw Weygand, but reported at the end of November that the British could hope for little from him in existing circumstances. Weygand would obey instructions from Vichy, and would fight against anybody who attacked Morocco, whether it was Spain, Germany or Britain.[77]

During November overtures were also made to Weygand by Catroux, in consultation with Eden while the latter was on a visit to Cairo. Catroux tried to persuade Weygand, first by letter and then through an emissary, that the strategic situation in the Mediterranean was already favourable to the Allies, and could be decisively swung to their advantage if Weygand brought North Africa into the war.[78] Then at the end of December Churchill sent a further message to Weygand (with a copy to Pétain) through Dupuy, offering the support of six British divisions if Weygand would resume the war in North Africa, or if the French government itself would do so.[79]

Nothing came of these approaches. Weygand opposed any cession of bases to Germany, but would not contemplate resuming the war in North Africa until, in his own judgement, the situation warranted it. This was not the case in the autumn and winter of 1940, and Weygand limited his objectives to preserving his freedom of action and safeguarding the future by developing relations with the USA. If the approaches had borne fruit, relations between the British government and de Gaulle would have been significantly altered, to de Gaulle's detriment. A Foreign Office official wrote on 27 October that, in the event of a hint from Weygand and Noguès that North Africa was prepared to resist the Germans, the British government would be wise to deal with them directly, at any rate in the preliminary stages, without bringing in de Gaulle. It was well known that Weygand regarded de Gaulle as an upstart and a rebel, but despite this the Foreign Office view in November was that the British should seek in the long term to bring the two together in 'a *modus vivendi* between soldiers'.[80] This was only the rough sketch of a possibility, but if Weygand and de Gaulle could somehow have been brought together, the likelihood was that the former, by reason of his rank, experience, and surviving prestige, would have been the senior partner. Spears attacked such ideas in a paper of 10 February 1941. 'What a pitiful figure he [de Gaulle] will cut if we drive him onto the world stage between Pétain and Weygand, while we applaud the trio with equal impartiality, asking if Noguès and Darlan can be induced to join the party and respond to a call for an encore'. (Something like this was indeed attempted in January 1943, when de Gaulle was urged onto the world stage for a brief handshake with General Giraud.)[81]

Spears was much disturbed by what he regarded as a tendency to appease Vichy. He held that this was a waste of time, because the Vichy government was not its own master. 'If you are bent on appeasing, don't waste time on the dog, appease the man who holds the lead'. He argued that the British should take a bold, positive line, making it plain that they would not fight Vichy unless attacked, but proclaiming loudly and clearly that 'Free France is our ally and has our full and unstinted support'.[82] In February 1941, the same month as Spears' notes were circulated, Churchill wrote firmly: 'We have received nothing but ill-treatment from Vichy'. It was necessary 'to be stiff with these people', and assert the blockade whenever ships were available. An end should be put to what Churchill called the 'cold-shouldering' of de Gaulle and the Free French, 'who are the only people who have done anything for us, and to whom we have made very solemn engagements'.[83]

Attempts to reach some useful arrangement with the Vichy government had been made, and had produced little result. Approaches had been made to Weygand to persuade him to resume the war, and had likewise come to nothing. If the choice had been for Britain alone to make at the beginning of 1941, it is possible that they would have opted firmly for de Gaulle. But the situation was not so simple. The United States government had recently sent a new ambassador to Vichy, and were opening an active diplomatic campaign in North Africa. The British could not afford to repudiate or damage such policies, and instead they handed over the initiative in dealings with both Vichy and North Africa to the Americans.[84]

NOTES

1. *H.C. Deb.,* vol. 362, col. 304; vol. 364, col. 1168.
2. On the Montoire meetings and Franco-German collaboration, see Warner, chapter 7; Michel, *Vichy Année 40*; and Jäckel, chapters 6-8.

3. FO 371/24303, C11451/9/17, Eccles to Makins, 15 October 1940.

4. FO 371/24348, C13594/7362/17, Kelly (Berne) to Halifax, 16 December 1940.

5. FO 371/24312, C7855/65/17, Kelly to Halifax, 18 and 19 July 1940.

6. FO 371/24312, C9036/65/17, minute by Vansittart, 9 August 1940; minutes by Halifax, 11 August, and Morton, 23 August.

7. FO 371/24303, C11135/9/17, Rendel (Sofia) to Nichols, 28 August 1940; FO 371/24312, C9420/65/17, Livingstone (Geneva) to Halifax, 31 August; C9704/65/17, Kelly to Halifax, 19 September; FO 371/24313, C10248/65/17, minute by Mack, 21 September; C10221/65/17, Gascoigne to Halifax, 22, 23, 25 September; C10511/65/17, Knatchbull-Hugessen to Halifax, 27 September.

8. FO 371/24311, C7822/65/17, memoranda by Tower, 16, 27 July 1940; Kelly to Halifax, 28 July 1940. FO 371/24312, C9469/65/17, Selby to Halifax, 2 September, reporting conversation with Murphy; minute by Barclay, 3 September.

9. FO 371/24312, C8003/65/17, memorandum by Tower, 23 July 1940; C8830/65/17, minute by Mack, 15 August; C8976/65/17, Kelly to Halifax, 21 August; *The Times,* 25 July 1940.

10. FO 371/24303, C10863/9/17, Kelly to Halifax, 10 October 1940; minute by Mack, 13 October.

11. FO 371/24314, C11778/65/17, Livingstone to Halifax, 1 November 1940; minute by Mack, 6 November.

12. FO 371/24304, C12949/9/17, Kelly to Halifax, 29 November 1940.

13. FO 371/24348, C13186/7362/17, Kelly to Halifax, 6 December 1940; Kelly to Makins, same date, with verbatim text of interview; minutes by Barclay, 10 December, Strang, 11 December, Speaight, 25 December.

14. CAB 65/10, WM(40)306, 16 December 1940.

15. FO 371/24315, C13610/65/17, minute by Mack, 15 December 1940.

16. FO 800/312, H/XIV/479, Anderson to Halifax, 12 December 1940; minutes by Halifax and Cadogan, 12 December; minute by Halifax for Churchill, 13 December; minute by Churchill, 15 December.

17. FO 371/24313, C10629/65/17, minute by Tower, 2 October 1940.
18. *Ibid.,* C11106/65/17, Butler to Mack, 3 October 1940.
19. FO 371/24314, C12248/65/17, minute by Campbell, 6 November 1940.
20. FO 371/24348, C13913/7362/17, Butler to Halifax, 27 December 1940.
21. FO 371/24303, C11713/9/17, Churchill to de Gaulle, 1 November 1940.
22. FO 371/24304, C13500/9/17, memorandum by Hillgarth (naval attaché, Madrid), 6 December 1940; minutes by Barclay and Mack, 17 and 18 December. This memorandum was given special circulation to Prime Minister, members of the War Cabinet, and the King.
23. FO 800/323, H/XXXIV/90, Hoare to Halifax, 1 November 1940; FO 371/24304, C13677/9/17, Thomson to Stirling, 13 December.
24. CAB 67/13, WP(40)448, 14 November 1940.
25. CAB 65/9, WM(40)278.
26. FO 371/24312, C8913/65/17, French Department, Summary of events in France, 22-28 October 1940, 31 October 1940; FO 371/24335, C11416/7327/17, Hoare to Halifax, 25 October.
27. CAB 65/9, WM(40)278, 28 October 1940.
28. FO 371/24348, C11459/7362/17, Kelly to Halifax, 29 October 1940.
29. *Ibid.,* Campbell (Belgrade) to Halifax, 29 October 1940; FO 371/24348, C11545/7362/17, Hoare to Halifax, 28 October.
30. FO 800/323, H/XXXIV/97, Halifax to Hoare, 29 November 1940; Hoare's letters to Halifax are also in this file.
31. CAB 65/9, WM(40)273, 18 October 1940.
32. Dalton diary, 1 December 1940.
33. FO 371/24311, C7341/65/17, minute by Vansittart, 8 July 1940.
34. CAB 85/23, CFR(40)102, 26 November 1940.
35. CAB 65/15, WM(40)265th Conclusions, Confidential Annex; cf. Attlee's similar remark, WM(40)263rd Conclusions, Confidential Annex.
36. CAB 21/1454, Committee on French Resistance, 40th Meeting, 7 August 1940, Item 1; FO 371/24303, C11713/9/17, Ismay to Strang, 31 October 1940.

37. CAB 67/13, WP(40)448, 14 November 1940, memorandum on relations with Vichy.

38. CAB 65/7, WM(40)181; CAB 65/8, WM(40)202. On all blockade matters, see W. N. Medlicott, *The Economic Blockade,* vol. I (London 1952), especially chapter XVI.

39. CAB 67/8, WP(G)(40)208, 7 August 1940.

40. *H.C. Deb.,* vol. 264, col. 1118; Dalton diary, 19 August 1940.

41. *H.C. Deb.,* vol. 264, cols. 112 et seq.

42. CAB 85/22, CFR(40)55th Meeting, 23 September 1940, Item 4(b); CAB 85/23, CFR(40)48, 26 September 1940; Medlicott, 436, 440.

43. CAB 66/11, WP(40)362, 4 September 1940.

44. CAB 66/12, WP(40)392, 27 September 1940; CAB 65/15, WM(40)263rd Conclusions, Confidential Annex. Halifax repeated his arguments on 3 October: WM(40)265th Conclusions, Confidential Annex.

45. FO 371/24303, C11713/9/17, Halifax to Hoare, 7 November 1940.

46. *Ibid.,* Halifax to Hoare, 12 November 1940.

47. CAB 65/16, WM(40)281st and 285th Conclusions, Confidential Annexes, 1 and 8 November 1940.

48. FO 371/24334, C11099/7327/17; see the account in Woodward, vol. I, 414-16.

49. FO 371/24321, C8262/839/17, Gascoigne to Halifax, 6 and 10 August 1940; C8276/839/17, Gascoigne to Halifax, 11 August; CAB 65/8, WM(40)224.

50. These arguments were set out in: CAB 66/12, WP(40)410, 9 October 1940; CAB 66/13, WP(40)446, 15 November; CAB 80/22, COS(40)945(JP), 16 November; ADM 1/10861, Dalton to Alexander, 26 November; FO 371/24304, C13094/9/17, Stirling to Mack, 4 December and enclosed memorandum; CAB 85/23, CFR(40)127, 13 December.

51. CAB 66/12, WP(40)396, 30 September 1940.

52. ADM 116/4414, Alexander to Dalton, 3 January 1941.

53. CAB 100/5, Cabinet War Room Record, No. 388, 0700 hrs, 24 September — 0700 hrs, 25 September 1940.

54. CAB 66/12, WP(40)396, 30 September 1940, and 418, 13 October; CAB 79/7, COS Committee Minutes, 18 November 1940.

55. CAB 65/15, WM(40)263rd and 265th Conclusions, Confidential Annexes; CAB 65/9, WM(40)267, 273; CAB 65/10, WM(40)290, 292, 301; ADM/116/4650, Admiralty to FOC, North Atlantic, 0150/19, 2110/19, 19 November 1940.

56. CAB 65/17, WM(41)14; ADM 111/4650, Alexander to Churchill, 21 May 1941.

57. ADM 116/4414, minutes of meeting, 11 February 1941; CAB 66/15, WP(41)67, 26 March 1941.

58. FO 371/24332, C9825/17, Hoare to Halifax, 3 September 1940; minute by Mack, 6 September; CAB 65/15, WM(40)263rd Conclusions, Confidential Annex.

59. CAB 85/23, CFR(40)56, 4 October 1940; FO 371/24303, C12183/9/17, FO minute, 18 November 1940.

60. CAB 85/23, CFR(40)92, November 1940.

61. See the full account in Woodward, vol. I, 409-32.

62. FO 371/24332, C9825/7327/7327/17, Hoare to Halifax, 3, 11 September 1940, Halifax to Hoare, 6, 10 September; C9849/9849/28, Hoare to Halifax, 13 September, Halifax to Hoare, 15 September.

63. FO 371/24303, C11868/9/17, FO minute, 6 November 1940; FO 371/24334, C11099/7327/17, Hoare to Halifax, 14 October 1940, Halifax to Hoare, 19 October.

64. FO 371/24303, C11713/9/17, Halifax to Hoare, 1, 7 November 1940, Hoare to Halifax, 10 November; C12183/9/17, Hoare to Halifax, 11 November.

65. *Ibid.,* Halifax to Hoare, 23 November 1940.

66. FO 371/28342, Z87/87/17, Cadogan to Dupuy, 11 January 1941; Z252/87/17, Hoare to Eden, 10 January, minute by Eden, 23 January, Eden to Hoare, 24 January; CAB 65/17, WM(41)11, 29 January.

67. Medlicott, col. I, 567, 569-70.

68. FO 371/28343, Z971/87/17, French *aide-mémoire,* 5 February 1941, minute by Barclay, 18 February.

69. CAB 66/15, WP(41)67, 26 March 1941, memorandum by Dalton.

70. CAB 65/10, WM(40)287, 289, 304, 308; CAB 66/14, WP(40)486, 19 December 1940, memorandum by Halifax.

71. FO 371/24361, C13251/11442/17, Charles (Lisbon) to Mack, 6 December 1940, enclosing Rougier to Churchill and Halifax, 5 December; minutes by Strang, Cadogan, and Churchill, 12

and 15 December. CAB 66/14, WP(40)486, 19 December 1940, memorandum by Halifax. For Rougier, see below, 271.

72. FO 371/24334, C11099/7327/17, Churchill to Halifax, 19 October 1940, with draft telegram to Hoare, despatched 20 October.

73. FO 371/24332, C10076/7327/17, minute by Campbell, 7 September 1940.

74. FO 371/24331, C9730/7327/17, Gascoigne to Halifax, 9, 13 September 1940; FO 371/24332, C10076/7327/17, same to same, 18 October.

75. FO 371/24335, C11432/7327/17, note by Heywood, 25 August 1940; minutes by Strang, 17, 23 October, and Cadogan, 18 and 23 October; Beaumont-Nesbitt to Strang, 6 November. FO 371/24335, C11416/7327/17, Gascoigne to Halifax, 25 October; minutes by Strang, 23, 30 October, and Cadogan, 30 October. CAB 65/9, WM(40)276, 24 October.

76. FO 371/24335, C11613/7327/17, Gascoigne to Halifax, 30 October 1940, Halifax to Gascoigne, 31 October.

77. CAB 65/9, WM(40)276, 278, 279; CAB 65/10, WM(40)285. FO 371/24361, C11442/7327/17, note by Strang, 25 October 1940, on conversation between Rougier, Churchill and Halifax; memorandum by Rougier, undated, for his conversation with Weygand, copies sent to Hoare and Gascoigne, 1 November; Halifax to Hoare, 1 November, with a summary of the memorandum. FO 371/24314, C11418/65/17, minute by Halifax, 25 October. FO 371/24335, C11513/7327/17. Gascoigne to Halifax, 2 November. FO 371/24303, C12904/9/17, Gascoigne to Halifax, 30 November. See L. Rougier, *Mission sécrète à Londres (les accords Pétain-Churchill)* (Geneva 1946) for his claim after the war that his mission resulted in a secret agreement between Pétain and Churchill, and that the memorandum for his conversation with Weygand was in reality a protocol embodying this agreement. This claim is not confirmed by the contemporary British documents. See also G. Schmitt, *Les accords sécrets franco-britanniques de novembre-décembre 1940* (Paris 1947), which dissects Rougier's account.

78. Catroux, 70-4; de Gaulle, vol. I, 369.

79. CAB 65/16, WM(40)311th Conclusions, Confidential Annex, 30 December 1940; CAB 79/8, COS Committee Minutes, 24 December; Churchill, 550-1.

80. FO 371/24335, C11596/7327/17, minutes by Strang and Halifax, 27 October 1940, Churchill, 26 October; FO 371/24303, C12183/9/17, two FO minutes, 18 November 1940.
81. FO 892/65, memorandum by Spears, 10 February 1941.
82. *Ibid.,* and a second memorandum of 21 February. These papers were circulated to the Morton Committee on 12 and 23 February: CAB 85/25, CFR(41)47, 63.
83. *Ibid.,* CFR(41)54, 18 February 1941, circulating minute by Churchill, 16 February.
84. The American side of this story may be followed in W. L. Langer, *Our Vichy Gamble* (New York 1947), and Robert Murphy, *Diplomat among Warriors* (New York 1964).

Chapter 12

PROBLEMS OF OPINION AND PROPAGANDA

After the British press and public opinion had absorbed the swift and disastrous events surrounding the collapse of France, they had to adjust to the new state of French affairs. France — whether Vichy France or Free France — became much less prominent in British minds once the excitement of the armistice had died away. The press suffered from the same dearth of information as did the government, but this changed as correspondents went to the Spanish border, journalists returned from France, and reports of various kinds filtered through. Gradually a picture of the new French situation emerged.

The first events in France to make a significant impact on British public opinion were the constitutional changes at the beginning of July, which ended the Third Republic and began a new authoritarian régime. The *Economist* recognised that what had happened in France was more than a simple military defeat, but rather 'the extinction of the spiritual force we knew as France and the appearance in its place of an unknown entity whose mind and language we find it difficult to understand.' It was likely that Pétain's régime would be a pale imitation of the German, Italian and Spanish dictatorships — 'strong wine watered down with Vichy'.[1] The certainty that it would be fundamentally hostile to Britain was a view which was widely shared. On 8 July the *Daily Herald* declared that the French people faced fascism. 'Behind the senile, pathetic relic Pétain stands the real organiser of treachery — the mean-spirited, perfidious trickster Laval'. Similarly, on 11 July the *Daily Telegraph* wrote that a fascist régime was being imposed on France.

281

The main objective of Pétain and Weygand, and the politicians with whom they worked in the betrayal of their country, was to abolish freedom and establish a slave state. It was widely believed that the new régime, under the influence of Laval, would follow Italian fascism more closely than German nazism. In any case it was the rule of reaction, a police state, which was being instituted.[2]

Of the leaders at Vichy, both Pétain and Laval had a bad press. On 8 July Cassandra wrote in the *Daily Mirror* of 'the traitors of Bordeaux, led by Marshal Pétain, the world's oldest disciple of Judas Iscariot'. At the time of Dakar, the *News Chronicle* denounced 'Marshal Pétain and his little clique of fellow-traitors . . . The antique Marshal pours out upon these deluded "defenders" of Dakar the froth of his senile praise . . .'[3] Pétain's speech after Montoire provoked the *Mirror* again: 'we have had this week the latest lamentable whimper from the French Fuehrer, poor doddering Pétain. It is indeed a piece of unintelligible dither, with its craven claim that France has obligations to her victor . . .'[4] The *Daily Herald* dissented from this view, holding that there was a distinction between Pétain and Laval; Pétain was an honourable man who had to be persuaded that his actions were for the good of France, whereas Hitler's real business was with Laval.[5] The *Telegraph* was sceptical of such attempts to exonerate Pétain; it might be that the Marshal was too feeble to discern the treachery of his entourage, but even so he himself was playing into the Germans' hands. 'He aspires to be a dictator of regeneration, but the only power which he puts forth is directed to introduce the brutality of Nazism and place the territories of France overseas at its mercy'.[6]

Laval, however, was the more common target. The *Telegraph* was sure he was ready to be the French Quisling, even to the extent of bringing France into the war against Britain.[7] The *Daily Mirror* lumped him in with Baudouin: 'the intriguers of Vichy, the Lavals and Baudouins and feeble-minded generals'; and 'the Laval-Baudouin policy of "collaboration" with Germany . . . ' The *Mirror* also published a striking cartoon captioned 'A Frog he would A-wooing Go', showing Laval as a frog knocking on the German door.[8] Weygand on the other hand tended to be spared, even by the press of the Left. Alexander Werth, writing in the *New Statesman* of 14 September, wondered whether Weygand would merely carry out instructions from Vichy and Berlin in his North African post, or whether he would act more independently — Werth thought he would probably sit on the fence until the Battle of Britain was decided.[9] At the close of the year, the *Mirror* published a cartoon of Weygand, in a noble and pensive attitude, gazing at a sword: the caption read 'Now, Weygand?'[10]

The British press were much less definite in their views about de Gaulle and the Free French than they were about Vichy, and de Gaulle remained under something of a cloud despite the public relations work of Richmond Temple. The rallying of Equatorial Africa was greeted with modified enthusiasm, but events at Dakar raised doubts and resentment. Under the surface there lurked a suspicion that de Gaulle might be a fascist, and even some of the favourable comments on Free France seem likely to have been ineffective. Charles Morgan wrote a long article in the *Spectator* which was largely based on his view of the French character. 'The paradox of the French', he wrote, 'is that though, in certain material respects they are intensely self-regarding and close-fisted, they are also givers-out, not of money, but of ideas.' The French Revolution had 'proceeded by the method of flinging an idea to heaven', and then taking wings to bring it to earth — not a British method. 'The first and most urgent need is that the Free French should fling to heaven a new idea, an alternative to both the Pétain regime and to the Third Republic'.[11] This was in many ways a highly perceptive analysis, but even the readers of the *Spectator* may have found its mode of expression a little obscure.

From these various attitudes, it appears that the press reflected and perhaps helped to form opinion about France in the country. In January 1941 the Ministry of Information conducted an opinion survey on France. The results showed 75 per cent of those interviewed to be hostile to the Vichy government, on the grounds that it was in the hands of Hitler and unrepresentative of the French people. When asked about de Gaulle, 40 per cent were favourable, 30 per cent unfavourable, and 30 per cent uninterested. Those who were unfavourable to de Gaulle regarded the Free French movement as ineffectual, and some thought it was potentially reactionary. In reply to a question on Anglo-French friendship in the future, opinion was virtually unanimous that this was either unlikely or undesirable. The Morton Committee, to which these findings were transmitted, was dismayed, but the representative from the Ministry of Information said that while his ministry was trying to counteract the general anti-French feeling in the country, it was essential to move very discreetly; he thought there were signs that public opinion was slowly becoming less hostile to France.[12]

Attempts to influence opinion in Britain about France were much less important than similar efforts to influence opinion in France about Britain. In late 1940, after the fall of France, propaganda appeared to be an important arm of policy because it was believed to have been a major factor in German successes, especially in France. It was often said that French morale had been rotted by German propaganda.[13] It may well be that the role of propaganda in the German victories was exaggerated; even so, the British were bound to think it important because it was one of the few weapons they could bring into immediate use against the enemy. In 1940 there could be no hope of invading Europe in the foreseeable future; a bombing offensive on a large scale would take a long time to mount; economic blockade was a long-term weapon. Propaganda, even if it was not as potent a weapon as some claimed, was better than inaction.

For propaganda to be used as an effective means of influencing French opinion, a whole series of problems had to be grappled with. Some were administrative in nature: the need for an organisation to disseminate propaganda to a defeated and occupied France had not been foreseen, and improvisation was necessary. There were inter-departmental disputes, notably between the Ministry of Information which controlled overt propaganda, and the Ministry of Economic Warfare which controlled covert (or 'black') propaganda. In addition there was some friction between the Foreign Office and the Ministry of Information.

There were also wider questions, the most fundamental of which concerned the object of propaganda and its place in British policy and strategy. This raised the whole issue of the nature of the conflict the country was engaged in, and the manner in which it should be fought. One school of thought held that the war was essentially ideological, and must be fought as a revolutionary struggle, offering a rival 'new order' to the Nazi 'new order' being established in Europe. In public, this school was represented for example in a pamphlet, *100,000,000 Allies — If We Choose,* which was published in September 1940 by Gollancz. This argued that Britain must combine blockade and bombing with revolutionary activities inside Europe. There were a hundred million people suffering under Nazi tyranny, and Britain could make the bravest of them her allies if she pledged herself to the cause of European revolution. The *New Statesman* held the same view, and a leading article on 6 July proclaimed: 'Either we turn this war into a war of European revolution or we shall be defeated. There is no half-way house. Against the brute force of Hitler, no mere material forces or military power will prevail. But against the idea for which Hitler stands — the European peoples more terribly enslaved than they ever were to the forces of capitalism — the revolutionary idea can prevail.' Harold Laski, broadcasting in August, took up the same theme: 'victory, on sober analysis, means the organization of a European revolt against Hitlerism. And that revolt can only come from the workers'.[14] The *News Chronicle* often took the same line, as when a leading article of 30 September, mostly dealing with Spain, concluded: 'It is a great misfortune for Britain that the British Government still fails to realise the essentially revolutionary nature of the present struggle'.

Similar arguments were put forward within the government, and not only by Labour members. A memorandum by Duff Cooper dated 20 July argued that for millions of people in Europe Nazism and Fascism were a genuine faith, made more powerful by victory. The immediate defence of Britain was in the short term an equally powerful incentive to the British people; but when the danger grew less imminent it would be necessary to offer a wider vision — a freely federated Europe, and at home greater equality of opportunity and a more even distribution of wealth.[15] This idea met with a wide response. At a meeting on 30 July between Halifax and those ministers not in the War Cabinet, there was much talk — led by Bevin, the Minister of Labour and a lifelong trade unionist — about the need to offer some attractive economic prospect to the people of Europe. It was pointed out that in Britain the government was willing to spend nine million pounds a day in wartime, yet in peacetime was not prepared to find ten million pounds for economic help in County Durham without being certain of a return on the money. Halifax himself said that the British people would no longer tolerate a system which permitted large numbers of men to be unemployed, and that people abroad would also be influenced if Britain could put up an economic counter-plan to Hitler's 'new order'.[16] The Overseas Intelligence Department of the BBC also argued strongly that it was vital for Britain to offer an alternative to

285

the Nazi 'new order', and to show that she was determined to improve her own social system and lead the reconstruction of Europe after the war.[17]

There was, however, considerable opposition to this line of thought, the most powerful coming from Churchill himself who was determined to concentrate every effort on the war; he did not want to risk the dissipation of energy and unproductive conflicts of opinion which would arise from any attempt to formulate war aims in the shape of a new order for Europe. On 15 October, for example, he replied to a Parliamentary question asking for a statement of war aims: 'We are, among other things, fighting it [the war]in order to survive' — and when Britain's capacity to do this was demonstrated she would be in a better position to see what to do after victory.[18] Survival itself posed sufficient problems in 1940.

The danger of conflicts of opinion was indeed serious. The point was effectively put by Clive Bell in a letter to the *New Statesman* on 27 July: 'You, yourself [the editor] have described this war — correctly, in my opinion — as a war for Socialism; you cannot be surprised if those who happen not to be Socialists (three-quarters of the population, say) feel their ardour cool appreciably as they read your words'. The *Economist* made a similar comment on the argument of *100,000,000 Allies — If We Choose,* remarking that a programme of European revolution was more likely to provide Hitler with millions of recruits rather than Britain. The best weapon was still national feeling — the *Economist* pointed to de Gaulle, who was fighting 'quite simply that France as a national community may be free'.[19] The point was reinforced by J. H. Huizinga, the Dutch historian then serving with the Netherlands government press service, who wrote to the *New Statesman* to say that the Dutch people did not need the promise of a golden future or a new order: 'In countries like Holland there is more rejoicing over one well-aimed bomb than over a thousand wordy pamphlets. In their agony these countries feel no inclination towards new orders of any kind. They desire only one thing: return of the old order, that is, of freedom and independence . . .'[20]

If the concept of preaching a revolutionary war and a new vision of Europe were to be applied to France, objections immediately became apparent. This would involve attacking the Vichy government, including Pétain, which in view of information about French opinion seemed likely to be a self-defeating exercise.

Support would also have to be offered to ideas associated with the Popular Front government in 1936, and this would only appeal to one particular section of French opinion. A revolutionary appeal would certainly be unpopular with the conservative elements in French colonial society and the armed forces, which Britain wished to win over. Moreover, revolutionary propaganda might involve risking a complete breach with Vichy, which the Admiralty in particular wished to avoid. Such arguments as these were responsible for an approach to propaganda far removed from that of a revolutionary war, and based instead on the calculation of short-term advantage, compromise and caution. So far as France was concerned, the object of propaganda should be confined to winning the French people over to a more favourable view of Britain, and encouraging a revulsion against Germany which would itself spring from patriotism.

Whichever approach was adopted, it was of crucial importance to know the actual state of opinion in France. An immense amount of effort was devoted to this task, and the Ministry of Information, the Foreign Office and the BBC all prepared regular reports on the subject. As the fragments of information built up, one point was constantly repeated: the popularity of Pétain throughout France, though especially in the unoccupied zone. There was a general feeling that in the immediate aftermath of the armistice the vast majority of Frenchmen had been stunned by defeat.[21] In their stupor they had turned gratefully to the well-known figure of the Marshal, believing him to be honest, patriotic and above the political intrigues of the Third Republic. One British official at Madrid reported early in November that all recent visitors from France were agreed that Pétain was untouchable. He went on: 'Think of Mistinguett: how those legs, which once twinkled so divinely, never lost their enchantment for the French public. No matter if the revue, in which this bygone creature appeared, was a hotch-potch of ill-assorted flops. The theatre was crowded, and her lower limbs adored. So it is with the Marshal, the male Mistinguett of beaten France. It makes no difference that the vehicle, in which he is presented, is the most villainous contraption. He is, and will be, cheered till he dies'.[22] This expressed with style and wit the almost unanimous view of the position in France. Information reaching the Foreign Office indicated that Pétain's meeting with Hitler did not change this attitude; instead, Frenchmen saw in it some hope that the difficulties of the country might be alleviated before winter set in.[23] There were occasional reservations: a young corporal who escaped from Brittany in November said that the young people in France had never known Pétain as a hero, only in his decadence.[24] Such views were rare, however, and the general picture of Pétain's massive popularity remained untouched.

The reverse side of this was a series of reports indicating a revulsion of feeling against the régime of the Third Republic which Pétain's government had replaced. The same official at Madrid again summed up the common view: 'The French . . . have lost confidence in their social and political structure. They cannot be expected to revive a system that accompanied their defeat, even if it were not responsible for it'.[25] There were frequent reports indicating that everything to do with the former party system was discredited — though one intelligence summary held that the whole of France was agreed, not only on the rottenness of the former 'Republic of Pals', but also on the futility of Vichy's attempt to replace it.[26]

There were wide variations in reports concerning the impression made by de Gaulle and the Free French movement on French public opinion. The British Consul-General at Barcelona, passing on information from the Dordogne and Perpignan early in September, wrote that support for de Gaulle was increasing there. A Foreign Office official found this encouraging, but only on the rather gloomy grounds that there were few such indications.[27] A Swedish newspaper reported in September that de Gaulle's voice on the radio was known to hundreds of thousands of Frenchmen; but another Baltic journalist believed that de Gaulle was not yet seen as the Messiah he believed himself to be, and simply did not have the prestige to confront Pétain.[28] In November the British postal censorship reported that there was little praise for de Gaulle in intercepted letters from France, though this might be the result of previous Vichy censorship activities. There were even fewer signs of ill-feeling against him, if that was any comfort.[29] On the other hand, further intelligence from Barcelona in October claimed that de Gaulle's supporters were in a majority in France.[30] The Dakar episode was variously reported as being disastrous, and as having done de Gaulle less harm than might have been expected.[31]

The development of French opinion about Britain was watched with particular interest. In July and August the general impression was of widespread anti-British feeling, and an Englishwoman wrote from south-west France on 13 July that there was much talk about the 'dirty English'. A Foreign Office official commented that 'The tale of the unpopularity of the English rings grimly true in this letter',[32] and other sources also reported strong feeling against Britain after the action at Mers-el-Kebir. Yet there were exceptions, and two officers in the Seaforth Highlanders travelled from the north of France to Marseilles without once being refused a night's shelter, even though they always explained who they were.[33] At the end of September the general trend of the information began to change, and pro-British sentiment was reported to be increasing. This movement appeared markedly stronger in the occupied than in the unoccupied zone, though even there it was not uniform and there was some indication that the bourgeoisie and shopkeepers preferred a German victory. One remark recurred repeatedly from different sources: Frenchmen who were pro-British said 'We hope the British win'; those who were anti-British said 'We hope those British swine win'.[34]

This movement corresponded with a growth of anti-German feeling. Early reports indicated that the German occupation forces were behaving correctly; in August and September there was evidence of a change in their attitude, partly in reaction to minor acts of sabotage. During the autumn the German incorporation of Alsace and Lorraine into the Reich, the requisitioning of foodstuffs, and acts against the Catholic Church combined to produce growing hostility towards the occupying power. This showed itself publicly in demonstrations on the Champs-Elysées on 11 November, and in the circulation of the first clandestine news-sheets, some of which were known in London. On 1 January 1941 the British and de Gaulle were bold enough to appeal over the radio for French people to stay indoors from 3 p.m. to 4 p.m., and secured a widespread response in the occupied — though not the unoccupied — zone. There were signs that the urban working classes tended to be the most anti-German section of the population, if only because unemployment in towns was high; while the peasants tended to pursue their own work when they were left alone to do so.[35]

Such information, often contradictory, and dealing so much in generalisations that it was bound to be misleading on details, made an uncertain basis for a propaganda campaign in France. The most tangible feature appeared to be the popularity of Pétain, and the

K

British were repeatedly advised that to attack the Marshal would alienate almost all Frenchmen. Yet the strongest pro-British feeling was found in the occupied zone, where Pétain did not rule and the most active anti-German feeling among urban workers, who might be susceptible to a revolutionary style of propaganda. There was insufficient guidance here to resolve the problem of the general objective to be pursued by British propaganda in France. Nor was there enough to deal with the closely related question of the tone or manner to be adopted. On the one hand was the argument that France was sick and should be nursed; the French people, suffering from shock, should be told smooth and even flattering things in order to restore their confidence and self-esteem, rather than harsh things to bring home the humiliation of defeat and occupation. On the other hand, a much tougher line might be adopted. Leeper, a former Foreign Office official serving in the Ministry of Information, wrote at the beginning of December that British tactics so far had been too hesitant; they should declare firmly that they were going to win because they would stop at nothing. 'The French will have to realise that the Germans are not the only tough people & that another equally tough people mean to win this war'.[36]

In these circumstances, there was much doubt and dispute relating to the British propaganda policy towards France, although on certain specific issues the line was clear. From early July onwards, the Vichy government sought to lay the blame for the defeat of France on the British. It was alleged that Britain had abandoned the French at Arras and Dunkirk, and then refused help in the battle on the Somme; in general, it was claimed that they had not provided the forces they had promised. The British government were anxious about the likely effect of these accusations on French opinion, and also on opinion in the USA where there was evidence that nearly 40 per cent of the population believed that Britain had — at least to some extent — let the French down. A deliberate attempt was therefore made to counter the Vichy allegations, and detailed statements were produced to show that all undertakings given to the French had been fulfilled. A French officer broadcast on the BBC on 'the facts of Dunkirk'. Catroux said in an interview with the *Daily Mail* that Britain had sent more divisions than France had asked for, and the RAF had done most of the aerial fighting for both armies.[37]

Another charge which the British felt had to be rebutted was that of starving France by a hunger blockade. In fact the British blockade, of unoccupied France at least, was too ineffective to achieve anything of the sort, but this was obviously not an argument which Britain wished to use. They tried to get their blow in first, with a broadcast by Harold Nicolson at the end of July warning that the Germans would reduce the occupied countries to starvation rations, take the food for themselves, and then blame the British blockade. Later, the standard British defence was that there was adequate food in France, and that any shortages were due either to maldistribution by the French government or German requisitions. In the event, reports from France indicated little resentment about the blockade — though it is hard to say whether this was due to its ineffectiveness or to an appreciation of its true purpose.[38]

These issues were fairly simple to deal with, but on wider issues of propaganda policy doubt prevailed. Disputes over two particular broadcasts illustrate the difficulties which might arise. One was a talk which was to have been given on the BBC French service at 6.15 a.m. on 23 November by Henry Hauck, labour adviser to de Gaulle. (Five-minute talks for French workers were regularly broadcast at that time.) The theme was that the French ruling classes had a tradition of cowardice and treason, while the ordinary people on the contrary had constantly shown courage and patriotism. This thesis was illustrated by historical examples including Joan of Arc, the Revolutionary wars, the war of 1870 and the Commune. Similarly, the argument ran, the soldiers of 1940 had fought heroically when they found leaders worthy of them; but the French leaders had stabbed the people in the back, and made an alliance with Hitler and Mussolini against their own countrymen. The speaker then appealed to his audience to remain faithful to the democratic and revolutionary traditions of their ancestors: when the time came, they would rid France of the gangsters who had sold the people to the enemy to protect their own riches. The text was approved by the Ministry of Information, but the BBC decided not to broadcast it, and passed it to the Foreign Office with a covering note asking: 'Are we to address other countries as though we were a revolutionary government ourselves, and if we do, will the countries we so address give us credit for anything but hypocrisy?' Foreign Office officials approved of the BBC decision to hold up the talk — 'it is not often that we can compliment them on their political sagacity', one wrote. It was held that the talk would cut across Britain's current diplomatic activity, which was directed to reaching

291

some form of accommodation with the 'better elements' of the Vichy government. There were also doubts as to the accuracy of Hauck's analysis — 'The people of France are as a whole responsible for the fall of France, and the workers were as defeatist and pacifist and ca'canny as anybody else', wrote one official. All this was conveyed to the Ministry of Information in suitably tactful terms.[39]

Hauck erred in one direction, but at the same time another broadcaster was accused of erring in the other direction, and being too favourable to Vichy. On 22 November Colin Coote, an eminent journalist of conservative views, gave a broadcast on the British Home Service at the popular listening time of 9.20 p.m.; his subject was 'Why France collapsed'. He said that Frenchmen who had opposed the war were of very different types, and some, like Pétain, were honest and upright men. What they all had in common was the conviction that France was certain to lose; and that even if by a miracle she won, the British would only insist on a soft peace, and Germany would have to be fought again in another twenty years. There was no simple division in France between honest and dishonest men, between brave men and cowards. In particular, Frenchmen would not believe that Pétain and Weygand were either dishonest or cowardly. They had seriously believed that the collapse of France would be followed by that of Britain, and that Britain could not defend herself, never mind the French empire — it would therefore have been impossible in June 1940 to carry on the war in the empire where there were no industries to provide equipment. Coote went on to sketch the chaos of the fighting in France, saying that he did not think there had been any alternative to capitulation on the mainland. His final words were to emphasise that there was nothing in the collapse to preclude a French recovery; and that the British should do special honour to those who had stood firm in the collapse, and undergone trials which the British people were now only beginning to understand.

This talk differed from Hauck's in that it was for British listeners; but it could of course be picked up in France, and would in any case reach Frenchmen in Britain. One Foreign Office official thought it a model of its kind, and suggested it should be used in direct broadcasts to France: 'This is what is wanted, and not M. Hauck's revolutionary outbursts'. Another official, however, argued strongly that the British were trying to instil a spirit of resistance into the

French empire, and 'this pro-Vichy surrender stuff only hinders'. The British view was that the surrender had *not* been inevitable, and that the war could have been continued from the empire — 'Mr. Coote helps the defeatists'. The broadcast was twice discussed by the Morton Committee, where it was again pointed out that the statement about the empire was diametrically opposed to the opinion of the British government. 'The way of broadcasters is hard', commented Strang.[40]

It was dangerous for propaganda to be too revolutionary, since it might interfere with British negotiations with Vichy. Equally, it was dangerous to show too much understanding of the Vichy position, for that might discourage resistance to the Germans. What course, then, should be steered? One negative commandment for broadcasting to France was firm: Thou shalt not attack Pétain. Even after the Montoire meetings, it was agreed that references to the Marshal should be limited to saying that it was hard for a man of such courage and integrity to be compelled to obey German orders. Moreover, remarks in the British press, which could not be made subject to the same directive, were sometimes rebuked if they were thought to go too far — as they frequently did.[41] While Pétain was spared, Laval was singled out for attack. The French Section of the Ministry of Information noted on 23 October that during the past week there had been no references in broadcasts to Pétain, but various items about 'the unspeakable Laval'. One broadcast, for example, on 11 October, marvelled that Laval had changed sides so often in his life, and yet had never been on the side of France — there was much more in the same vein.[42]

It was difficult to draw the demarcation line between attacks on the régime in a general way and on Pétain in person. The half-hour French programme on the BBC, *'Les Français parlent aux Français'*, made great play with slogans. One of their best was on the Vichy motto: *Travail, Famille, Patrie* — *'Travail* — *introuvable; Famille* — *dispersée; Patrie* — *humiliée'*.[43] Although this motto was closely associated with Pétain personally, the broadcasters were permitted constant repetition of their barbed comment upon it. On the other hand there was a perpetual dilemma over whether the BBC should use the phrase 'Vichy government' or 'Pétain government', or even whether these were not both slighting references, for which 'French government' should be substituted in broadcasts.[44]

On the positive side a number of useful themes for propaganda emerged, of which the strongest was an appeal to patriotism and to distinctive characteristics of French life. Martial music was often played, and — from fragments of evidence which reached London — was apparently much appreciated. Anniversaries were frequently employed to invoke the spirit of France. French history, unhappily, was just as likely to divide Frenchmen as to unite them, but a good balance was maintained. The anniversary of the death of Robespierre on 28 July was followed closely by that of Lyautey on the 31st; this not only meant that Left and Right factions could both be satisfied, but it was possible to present both men as being, above all, great and patriotic Frenchmen. The same balance was struck between appeals to French workers, generally socialist in tone, and appeals to French Catholics, (with special broadcasts for the feasts of St Anne and St Michael for example) which were particularly directed at the people of Brittany.[45]

Another side of the appeal to patriotism was the encouragement of anti-German feeling. This began tentatively, but in October and November the German annexation of Alsace and Lorraine, and the consequent expulsion of many of the inhabitants, provided an excellent theme. Even before then, the occupation costs had been a good target. A broadcast by Churchill, delivered in French on 21 October, combined both appeals with great force. Hitler, he said, was set on wiping out the French nation, with its characteristic culture and inspiration to the world. 'All Europe, if he has his way, will be reduced to one uniform Boche-land, to be exploited, pillaged and bullied by his Nazi gangsters'.[46] All the time, the broadcasters were working hard to reawaken hopes of victory. Their best ammunition was provided by the success of the RAF in the Battle of Britain, and by the re-election of Roosevelt which presaged a further increase of American help for Britain.[47]

In February and March 1941 an attempt was made by the Foreign Office and the Ministry of Information to combine the themes of propaganda to France in a systematic way. There was much common ground, but marked differences in emphasis and approach. The Foreign Office wished to emphasise the theme of hatred for the Germans, stressing the extent of German control in France, and at the same time proclaim the certainty of British victory and the gallantry of the Free French (though without embarrassing Pétain). They thought it foolish for Britain to become identified with any particular group or parties: the appeal should be to all Frenchmen to hate the Boche. The Ministry of Information considered that the positive aim of propaganda should be to stimulate French resistance to the enemy; the negative side should be to expose German lies and defend British policies. In particular, the positive side should foster an attitude which impeded co-operation with either Pétain's government or Germany, and would pave the way for an 'eventual revolt by the French people. Propaganda should be directed to particular groups, for example peasants and workers, who seemed best disposed to receive it. A constructive statement of British ideals was needed in order to show that Britain was fighting for a new and progressive civilisation, based on equal liberties for all, and not for the system which had disappointed the French people before the war and helped to cause France's defeat. These ideas should be developed without regard for the susceptibilities of the Vichy government.[48]

The existing differences on the ultimate aim of propaganda to France were not resolved, though in the meantime a great deal had been achieved in an improvised and empirical way. By October and November 1940, the BBC had considerable evidence to show that it had a large audience in both zones of France, and that an invaluable habit of listening to the British radio was being fostered. The standard of broadcasting in French was recognised to be remarkably high, and drew a genuine if oddly phrased tribute from the Ministry of Information staff: 'The highly individual intelligence of the French, which has so many disadvantages, must be held responsible for this gratifying result'.[49]

In propaganda, as in other subjects, there were difficulties between the British authorities and de Gaulle. These hinged, as always, on the issue of British control as against Free French independence. The French broadcasters of *'Les Français parlent aux Français'* were highly competent and patriotic, and gave their support to de Gaulle; however they were not in his service, but that of the BBC and the Ministry of Information. The Gaullist movement itself received only five minutes of radio time each day, and Gaullist statements and news items were subject to Ministry of Information censorship before being broadcast. For example, in a speech at Leopoldville on 27 October 1940, de Gaulle announced the creation of the Council of Defence and stated that 'the government of Vichy has definitively passed over to the enemy'.

When re-broadcast on the French news from London the same day, this passage was struck out.[50] Again, on 30 October, de Gaulle's headquarters in London proposed to broadcast (during the period allocated to the movement) a categorical statement that the Vichy government was unconstitutional. The Morton Committee ruled that no broadcast could be permitted which implied that Britain did not recognise the Vichy government as the *de jure* government of France, and the proposed broadcast was stopped.[51]

The position of the daily French-language newspaper *France* was similar. *France* was founded and financed by the Ministry of Information, and remained under its authority although the editorial staff was French. It was intended that the paper should be in close touch with de Gaulle, and it gave him general support but was not under his control. Indeed, its *directeur,* Pierre Comert, was a man of left-wing views, who suspected de Gaulle of authoritarian tendencies and was in conflict with some of his staff. The newspaper bore on its front page the motto *'Liberté — Egalité — Fraternité'*, not the Gaullist device of *'Honneur et Patrie'*.[52] In October and November 1940, the Free French protested to the British authorities about alleged left-wing tendencies in *France,* which were said to be disturbing the morale of French servicemen. However, the real issue was that of control. In a memorandum of 4 October Fontaine argued that serious problems arose from a situation in which the line taken by *France* was not always that of the Free French, and in which the Free French were associated in peoples' minds with *France* without in fact being responsible for it. It was therefore vital that *France* should be placed under Free French control.[53] The reply from the Ministry of Information was categorical: *France* was founded and paid for by the Ministry to pursue the policy of the British government, which might differ from that of the Free French. They entirely rejected the idea of putting the paper under de Gaulle's direction.[54]

From the British point of view this was eminently sensible; but for de Gaulle the whole situation of *France* and of broadcasting in general was most unsatisfactory. When he returned to London from Africa at the end of November, he set out to change matters. In a note to Churchill, he argued that broadcasts and publications in French put out from London were naturally considered by their listeners and readers to represent the views of de Gaulle and the Free French. This was not always the case, and some difficulties were caused when there were differences of opinion. It was therefore necessary to make the position clear, either by placing these broadcasts and publications under de Gaulle's control, or by stating categorically that they had nothing to do with the Free French, who had no responsibility for them.

The Ministry of Information refused to accept this proposal. They held that practically all French-language propaganda, whether broadcast or in print, was recognised by its recipients as coming from the British government and representing its views. Therefore it was not necessary to take either of the courses set out by de Gaulle, both of which were in any case objectionable in themselves. To give de Gaulle control of all propaganda to France would be to give him effective influence over policy towards Vichy, and also over certain aspects of policy towards other states, such as the USA and Japan. Yet these other states would not necessarily believe that control of propaganda had been handed over, and would continue to attribute the opinions expressed to the British Government, which might be extremely embarrassing. To take the second course would mean stating in every broadcast and publication that the views affirmed were not necessarily those of de Gaulle. This would cause listeners and readers to think that they were *contrary* to de Gaulle's views, and it would be easy for Vichy and the Axis to exploit divisions so openly advertised.[35]

De Gaulle in his turn rejected these counter-arguments. At the end of December he returned to the attack, claiming control both of the Gaullist broadcasts and the French half-hours, and asserting that the British did not impose censorship on other exiles such as the Dutch, Belgians, Poles, Czechs and Norwegians. The Ministry of Information again stood firm, pointing out that broadcasts, even by members of allied governments, were in fact subject to censorship, and their texts were submitted to the Ministry in advance; it would be impossible to give de Gaulle more favourable treatment than that given to others. Moreover, it was vital that propaganda should be treated as a whole, and planned by one authority. This was particularly important for France, where the position was delicate and British policy required great care in presentation. De Gaulle's policies were not always approved by the British government, and some of his past remarks attacking Pétain and Weygand had unfortunate effects.[56] In February 1941 de Gaulle again took up the matter with Churchill, who side-stepped by passing it back to the

Ministry of Information; and so the dispute rumbled on. The Free French were able to use the radio station at Brazzaville for their own broadcasts, and the Ministry of Information complained that this station attacked Pétain in ways which were not in accord with the British line of propaganda; however it was not possible for the British to censor broadcasts from Free French territory.[57] So neither side was satisfied, and relations between the British and Free French continued in their normal state of friction.

At the beginning of 1940, relations with France constituted the most important single element in British foreign policy. The alliance between the two countries was confidently expected to provide a sure foundation for wartime strategy and for the ultimate peace settlement. By the end of the year all this had changed, and relations with the United States had taken top priority. Relationships with both Free and Vichy France were uncertain and difficult and appeared unlikely to provide a sure foundation for the future. As events turned out, the future in France was to lie with de Gaulle, but British relations with him were never easy. Churchill was to say later that the hardest cross he had to bear was the cross of Lorraine, but it was already evident in 1940 that de Gaulle too had his difficulties with the British, who repeatedly obstructed his wishes and refused to recognise his movement as a government. Had the British been able to follow the advice of Parr and Spears in late 1940, and commit themselves wholeheartedly to de Gaulle, the later course of Anglo-French relations might well have been different. Unfortunately the balance of sea-power, the influence of the USA, the prestige of Pétain, and a desire to keep open options rather than make a definitive choice all combined to prevent this commitment. The result was a grievous friction in relations between Britain and de Gaulle which persisted from the fall of France in 1940 to her resurgence in 1944-45, and beyond that for nearly a quarter of a century.

NOTES

1. *Economist,* 6 July 1940, 7.
2. See e.g. *The Times,* 9 July 1940; *Daily Telegraph,* 11 July; *Spectator,* 12 July; *Economist, New Statesman,* 13 July.

3. *News Chronicle,* 25 September 1940.
4. *Daily Mirror,* 2 November 1940.
5. *Daily Herald,* 28 October 1940.
6. *Daily Telegraph,* 19 October 1940.
7. *Ibid.,* 25 October 1940.
8. *Daily Mirror,* 24, 25, 30 October 1940.
9. *New Statesman,* 14 September 1940, 250.
10. *Daily Mirror,* 31 December 1940.
11. *Spectator,* 19 July 1940, 60.
12. CAB 85/24, CFR(41)10th Meeting, 30 January 1941; CAB 21/1451, memorandum, undated and unsigned, but clearly by Morton.
13. For an influential statement of this view, see BBC Overseas Intelligence Department, Monthly Intelligence Report, Europe, 8 July 1940.
14. *Listener,* 15 August 1940, 236.
15. CAB 66/10, WP(40)275, 20 July 1940.
16. FO 800/325, H/XXXIX/69, Halifax to Duff Cooper, 30 July 1940, Duff Cooper to Halifax, 2 August.
17. BBC Overseas Intelligence Department, Monthly Intelligence Reports, 5 August and 2 September 1940.
18. *H.C. Deb.,* vol. 365, col. 596.
19. *Economist,* 14 September 1940, 330-1.
20. *New Statesman,* 7 December 1940, 566.
21. FO 371/24313, C10629/65/17, Political Intelligence Department (PID), French Section, Opinion in France, 15-18 September 1940.
22. FO 371/24314, C11239/65/17, Eccles to Makins, 5 November 1940.
23. *Ibid.,* C11253/65/17, PID, French Section, Opinion in France, 20 October-4 November 1940.
24. FO 371/24304, C13537/9/17, memorandum from French Section, MOI, to Mack, 29 November 1940.
25. FO 800/325, H/XXXIX/75, Eccles to Halifax, 17 August 1940.
26. FO 371/24313, C11072/65/17, MOI Intelligence Report, 16 October 1940.
27. FO 371/24312, C9659/65/17, Hoare to Halifax, 3 September 1940.
28. FO 371/24313, C10631/65/17, Law to Mack, 25 September 1940; A. Arenstam, *Tapestry of a Débâcle* (London 1942), 74.

29. FO 371/24314, C11691/65/17, Postal Censorship Report, France, 15 November 1940.
30. FO 371/24313, C10842/65/17, Patron (Barcelona) to Halifax, 15 October 1940.
31. *Ibid.,* C11072/65/17, MOI Intelligence Report, 16 October 1940.
32. FO 371/24312, C8003/65/17, minute, 29 July 1940, with extracts from the letter.
33. *Ibid.,* C7918/65/17, memorandum by Mack, 6 August 1940.
34. FO 371/24313, C10540/65/17, MOI Intelligence Report, 18 September 1940; C10629/65/17, 2 October; C11072/65/17, 16, 30 October; FO 371/24314, C11691/65/17, Postal Censorship Report, France, 25 October 1940; C11253/65/17, PID, French Section, Opinion in France, 4-17 November 1940.
35. See sources quoted in the previous footnote. Also: FO 371/24312, C8003/65/17, minute of 29 July 1940; FO 800/312, H/XIV/473, Monckton to Halifax, 29 September, and first enclosure; FO 371/24313, C10976/65/17, British Embassy, Washington, to Foreign Office, 27 September, and enclosures; FO 371/24314, C12811/65/17, MOI Intelligence Report, 20 November. Cf. M. Baudot, *L'opinion publique sous l'occupation. L'exemple d'un département français* (Paris 1960), 15; Noguères, vol. I, 117-18, 255, 261.
36. FO 371/24311, C7519/65/17, minutes by Roberts and Strang, 27 and 30 June 1940; FO 371/24304, C13606/9/17, memorandum by Leeper, 3 December, with minutes by Vansittart (agreeing) and Mack and Strang (dissenting).
37. FO 371/24301, C8016/65/17, Lothian to Halifax, 28 July 1940, minutes by Whitehead and Perowne, 2 and 3 August; Halifax to Lothian, 6 August. CAB 21/974 is a file on the rebuttal of the French allegations. *Daily Mail,* 26 September 1940. CAB 85/23, CFR(40)74, report by French section, MOI, week ending 30 October 1940.
38. Nicolson in *Listener,* 27 June 1940, 1188. CAB 85/22, CFR(40)44th Meeting, Item 6; FO 371/24313, C11072/65/17, MOI Intelligence Report, 16 October 1940.
39. FO 371/24304, C13009/9/17, Cummings (BBC) to Randall, 23 November 1940, enclosing text of Hauck's proposed talk; minutes by Randall and Speaight, 23 November, Mack and Strang, 25 November; Strang to Harvey, 4 December.

40. FO 371/24304, C13001/9/17, text of Coote's broadcast (published in *Listener,* 5 December 1940, 799, 817 — despite the fuss); minutes by Speaight, Mack, Strang and Cadogan, 25, 26, 27 November. CAB 85/22, CFR(40)82nd and 84th Meetings, 25 and 29 November.

41. CAB 85/22, CFR(40)67th Meeting, 21 October 1940; CAB 85/23, CFR(40)45, 20 September 1940; CAB 85/24, CFR(40)8th Meeting, 23 January 1941. FO 371/24313, C11072/65/17, French Section, MOI, Advisory Committee, 30 October 1940; FO 371/24303, C12084/9/17, note by Brogan, 14 November. BBC European Intelligence Department, Monthly Intelligence Report, 30 September, 28 October, November, 23 December 1940, 21 January 1941.

42. CAB 85/23, CFR(40)72, 23 October 1940, CFR(40)78, 6 November; BBC Written Archives, French Scripts, 1940, 11 October, 2, 9, 12 November.

43. BBC Written Archives, French Scripts, 1940, *passim.*

44. CAB 85/22, CFR(40)57th and 94th Meetings, 27 September and 27 December 1940. FO 371/24304, C13820/9/17, Hoare to Halifax, 21 December 1940, and attached minutes; eventually Eden (30 December) ruled that 'the government of Marshal Pétain' would be best.

45. BBC Written Archives, French Scripts, 1940. Cf. FO 371/24313, C11072/65/17, French Section, MOI, Advisory Committee, 16 October 1940, for a good example of holding the balance.

46. BBC Written Archives, French Scripts, 1940. For Churchill's speech, see 21 October; cf. Churchill, 575-6.

47. BBC Written Archives, French Scripts, 1940: September for the Battle of Britain, 6 November for Roosevelt.

48. CAB 85/25, CFR(41)71 and 75, memoranda by PID, Foreign Office, 28 February 1941, and MOI, 6 March.

49. BBC European Department, Monthly Intelligence Report, 28 October, November 1940; CAB 85/23, CFR(40)118, 5 December 1940.

50. FO 371/24344, C11512/7328/17, texts of news agency report of de Gaulle's speech, and typescript of French news talk, 27 October 1940.

51. CAB 85/22, CFR(40)71st Meeting, 30 October 1940.

52. CAB 85/22, CFR(40)41st, 44th Meetings, 9, 16 August 1940;

CAB 85/23, CFR(40)19, 29 August. On Comert, see P-L. Bret, *Au feu des événements* (Paris 1959), 196-8; Passy, 43-4.

53. FO 371/24303, C11056/65/17, minutes by Strang, Mack and Sargent, 4, 10, and 11 October 1940, and correspondence between Mack and Wharton; FO 371/24345, C12846/7328/17, Cowell to Speaight, 14 November, and enclosed memorandum; FO 892/24, memorandum by Fontaine, 4 October; CAB 85/22, CFR(40)61st Meeting, 7 October.

54. FO 892/24, Law to Somerville-Smith, 11 October 1940.

55. CAB 85/23, CFR(40)108, 113, 29 November, 3 December 1940.

56. CAB 85/25, CFR(41)8, 4 January 1941; CAB 85/24, CFR(41)2nd Meeting, 6 January 1941.

57. *Ibid.,* CFR(41)14th and 15th Meetings, 13 and 17 February 1941.

APPENDIX

THE PROJECT FOR FRANCO-BRITISH UNION

I. Draft Declaration of Union considered by the British Cabinet on
16 June 1940.

At the most fateful moment in the history of the modern world, the Governments of the United Kingdom and of the French Republic desire to make this declaration of indissoluble union and unyielding resolution in defence of liberty and freedom against subjection to a system which reduces mankind to a life of robots and slaves.

The two Governments declare that France and Great Britain shall no longer be two nations but one.

There will thus be created a Franco-British Union.

Every citizen of France will enjoy immediately citizenship of Great Britain; every British subject will become a citizen of France.

The devastation of war, wherever it occurs, shall be the common responsibility of both countries and the resources of both shall be equally, and as one, applied to its restoration.

All customs are abolished between Britain and France.

There shall not be two currencies, but one.

During the war there shall be one single War Cabinet. It will govern from wherever it best can. The two Parliaments will unite. A constitution of the Union will be written providing for joint organs of defence and economic policies.

Britain is raising at once a new army of several million men, and the Union appeals to the United States to mobilise their industrial power to assist the prompt equipment of this new army.

All the forces of Britain and France, whether on land, sea, or in the air, are placed under a supreme command.

This unity, this union, will concentrate the whole of its strength against the concentrated strength of the enemy, no matter where the battle may be.

And thus we shall conquer.

II. Final draft Declaration of Union, as amended by the British Cabinet on 16 June 1940.

At this most fateful moment in the history of the modern world, the Governments of the United Kingdom and the French Republic make this declaration of indissoluble union and unyielding resolution in their common defence of justice and freedom against subjection to a system which reduces mankind to a life of robots and slaves.

The two Governments declare that France and Great Britain shall no longer be two nations, but one Franco-British Union.

The constitution of the Union will provide for joint organs of defence, financial and economic policies.

Every citizen of France will enjoy immediate citizenship of Great Britain; every British subject will become a citizen of France.

Both countries will share responsibility for the repair of the devastation of war, wherever it occurs in their territories, and the resources of both shall be equally, and as one, applied to that purpose.

During the war there shall be a single War Cabinet, and all the forces of Britain and France, whether on land, sea or in the air, will be placed under its direction. It will govern from wherever it best can. The two Parliaments will be formally associated.

The Nations of the British Empire are already forming new armies. France will keep her available forces in the field, on the sea, and in the air. The Union appeals to the United States to fortify the economic resources of the Allies, and to bring her powerful material aid to the common cause.

The Union will concentrate its whole energy against the power of the enemy, no matter where the battle may be.

And thus we shall conquer.

Source: CAB 65/7, WM(40)169, Annexes I and II.

SELECT LIST
OF SOURCES

The principal sources used for this study are listed below, the list being confined to sources referred to in the footnotes. Extensive guides to literature on the subject may be found in the books by Guy Chapman, Henri Michel, and Geoffrey Warner, noted in Section 5. A full coverage of the available printed material may be found in the bibliographical sections of the *Revue d'Histoire de la deuxième Guerre mondiale* (Paris, quarterly).

1.   UNPUBLISHED SOURCES
Public Record Office
War Cabinet Papers (CAB)
Foreign Office Papers (FO)
Admiralty Papers (ADM)
War Office Papers (WO)
Ministry of Information Papers (INF)

BBC Written Archives[1]
French Scripts, 1940
Overseas Intelligence Department, Monthly Intelligence Reports

British Museum
Cunningham of Hyndhope Papers

London School of Economics
Hugh Dalton Papers

1.   I owe much to the help of Miss Ruth Hodgson, the BBC Written Archives Officer, who guided me in the use of these papers.

2. PUBLISHED DOCUMENTS

La Délégation française auprès de la Commission allemande d'Armistice, vol. I, (Paris 1947).

Discours et Messages du Général de Gaulle, 18 juin 1940 — 31 décembre 1941, (London 1942).

Documents on German Foreign Policy, series D, vol. IX, (London 1956).

Hansard, *Parliamentary Debates,* fifth series.

Journal Officiel de la République Française.

Rapport fait au nom de la Commission chargée d'enquêter sur les événements survenus en France de 1933 á 1945, (Paris, n.d.), *Rapport, Témoignages.*

3. MEMOIRS AND DIARIES

Arenstam, A., *Tapestry of a Débâcle,* (London 1942).

Baudouin, P., *Neuf Mois au Gouvernement,* (Paris 1948).

Bouthillier, Y., *Le Drame de Vichy,* vol. I, *Face à l'ennemi; face à l'allié,* Paris (1950).

Bret, P-L., *Au Feu des Evénements,* (Paris 1959).

Bryant, A. (ed.), *The Turn of the Tide: the Alanbrooke Diaries,* vol. I, (London, 1957).

Catroux, G., *Dans la Bataille de la Méditerranée,* (Paris 1949).

Charles-Roux, F., *Cinq Mois tragiques aux Affaires Étrangères,* (Paris 1949).

Chautemps, C., *Cahiers secrets de l'Armistice,* (Paris 1963).

Churchill, W. S, *The Second World War,* vol. II, *Their Finest Hour,* (London 1949).

Cooper, Duff (Lord Norwich), *Old Men Forget,* (London 1953).

Cunningham of Hyndhope, Lord, *A Sailor's Odyssey,* (London 1951).

Dilks, D. (ed.), *The Diaries of Sir Alexander Cadogan, 1938-1945,* (London 1971).

Freeman, C. D., and Cooper, D., *The Road to Bordeaux,* (London 1940).

Gaulle, C. de, *Mémoires de Guerre,* vol. I, *L'Appel, 1940-1942,* (Paris 1954).

Godfroy, R. E., *L'Aventure de la Force X,* (Paris 1953).

Harvey, J. (ed.), *The Diplomatic Diaries of Oliver Harvey, 1937-1940,* (London 1970).

Larminat, E. de, *Chroniques irréverencieuses,* (Paris 1962).

Macleod, R. and Kelly, D. (ed.), *The Ironside Diaries, 1936-1940,* (London 1962).

Murphy, R., *Diplomat among Warriors,* (New York 1964).

Muselier, E. H., *De Gaulle contre le Gaullisme,* (Paris 1946).

Passy (Dewavrin, A. E. V.), *Souvenirs,* vol. I, *2e. Bureau, Londres, Monte Carlo* (1947).

Reynaud, P., *La France a sauvé l'Europe,* two vols., (Paris 1947).

——————— *Au Coeur de la Mêlée,* (Paris 1951).

Robert, G., *La France aux Antilles de 1939 à 1943,* (Paris 1950).

Rougier, L., *Mission secrète à Londres (les accords Pétain-Churchill),* (Geneva 1946).

Spears, E. L., *Assignment to Catastrophe,* vol. I, *Prelude to Dunkirk,* vol. II, *The Fall of France,* (London 1954).

Weygand, M., *Rappelé au Service,* (Paris 1947).

4. BRITISH OFFICIAL HISTORIES

Butler, J. R. M., *Grand Strategy,* vol. II, (London 1957).

Ellis, L. F., *The War in France and Flanders, 1939-1940,* (London 1953).

Medlicott, W. N., *The Economic Blockade,* vol. I, (London 1952).

Playfair, I. S. O., *The Mediterranean and Middle East,* vol. 1, (London 1954).

Roskill, S. W., *The War at Sea,* vol. I, *The Defensive,* (London 1954).

Woodward, E. L., *British Foreign Policy in the Second World War,* vol. I, (London 1970).

5. SECONDARY WORKS

Adam, C. F., *Life of Lord Lloyd,* (London 1948).

Amouroux, H., *Le 18 juin 1940,* (Paris 1964).

Arnoult, P. *et al., La France sous l'Occupation,* (Paris 1959).

Baudot, M., *L'Opinion publique sous l'Occupation. L'exemple d'un département français* (Paris 1960).

Bauer, E., *La Guerre des Blindés,* vol. I, (Paris 1962).

Birkenhead, Lord, *Halifax,* (London 1965).

Chapman, G., *Why France Collapsed,* (London 1969).

Collier, B., *Leader of the Few,* (London 1957).

Colville, J. R., *Man of Valour: the life of Field Marshal the Viscount Gort,* (London 1972).

Haight, J. McV., *American Aid to France,* (New York 1970).

Horne, A., *To Lose a Battle,* (London 1969).

Hytier, A. D., *Two Years of French Foreign Policy: Vichy, 1940-1942,* (Paris, Geneva 1958).

Jäckel, E., *La France dans l'Europe d'Hitler,* (Paris 1968).

Kammerer, A., *La Passion de la Flotte française: de Mers-el-Kébir à Toulon,* (Paris 1951).

Langer, W. L., *Our Vichy Gamble,* (New York 1947).

McCallum, R. B., *England and France, 1939-1943,* (London 1944).

Marlow, J. (pseudonym), *De Gaulle's France and the Key to the coming Invasion of Europe,* (London 1940).

Maugham, W. Somerset, *France at War,* (London 1940).

Maurois, A., *The Battle of France,* (London 1940).

Michel, H., *Les Courants de Pensée de la Résistance,* (Paris 1962).

——————— *Vichy Année 40* (Paris 1966).

Mordal, J. (Cras, H.), *La Bataille de Dunkerque,* (Paris 1948).

——————— ——————— *Dunkerque,* (Paris 1960).

——————— ——————— *La Bataille de Dakar,* (Paris 1956).

Noguères, H., *Histoire de la Résistance en France de 1940 à 1945,* vol. I (Paris 1967).

Schmitt, G., *Les Accords secrets franco-britanniques de novembre-décembre 1940,* (Paris 1957).

Truchet, A., *L'Armistice de 1940 et l'Afrique du Nord,* (Paris 1955).

Tute, W., *The Deadly Stroke,* (London 1973).

Varillon, P., *Mers-el-Kébir,* (Paris 1949).

Warner, G., *Pierre Laval and the Eclipse of France,* (London 1968).

Weinstein, B., *Eboué,* (New York 1972).

6. ARTICLES

Bell, P. M. H., 'Prologue de Mers-el-Kébir', *Revue d'Histoire de la deuxième Guerre mondiale* (January 1959).

Beloff, M., 'The Anglo-French Union Project of June 1940', in *The Intellectual in Politics,* (London 1970).

Cairns, John C., 'Great Britain and the Fall of France', *Journal of Modern History,* (December 1955).

Dhers, P., 'Le Comité de Guerre du 25 mai 1940', *Revue d'Histoire de la deuxième Guerre mondiale,* (July 1953).

Marin, L., 'Contributions à l'Histoire des Prodromes de l'Armistice', *ibid.,* (July 1951).

D'Hoop, J. M., 'Les projets d'Intervention des Alliés en Méditerranée orientale, 1939-1940', in Comité d'Histoire de la deuxième Guerre mondiale, *La Guerre en Méditerranée, 1939-1945* (Paris 1971).

Johnson, D. W. J., 'Britain and France in 1940', *Transactions of the Royal Historical Society,* fifth series, vol. 22.

Noel, L., 'Le Projet d'Union franco-britannique de juin 1940', *Revue d'Histoire de la deuxième Guerre mondiale,* (January 1956).

Thomson, D., "The Proposal for Anglo-French Union in 1940," Zaharoff Lecture, 1966.

INDEX

08202

D
750
B44

Bell, Philip Michael Hitt.
    A certain eventuality : Britain and
the fall of France / [by] P. M. H. Bell.
[Farnborough, Hants.] : Saxon House,
1974.
    viii, 320 p., [16] p. of plates : ill.,
maps, ports. ;

    Bibliography: p. 307-311. Includes in-
dex.

    1.World War, 1939-1945—Diplomatic his-
tory. 2.World War, 1939-1945—Great Britain. 3.World War, 1939-1945—France. 4.
Great Britain—History—George VI, 1936-
1952. 5.France   —History—German occupation, 1940-1   945. I.Title